HOPE & FOLLY

MEDIA & SOCIETY
Richard Bolton, Series Editor

Simon Watney *Policing Desire:*
Pornography, AIDS, and the Media

Constance Penley *The Future of an Illusion:*
Film, Feminism, and Psychoanalysis

MEDIA &

SOCIETY

HOPE & FOLLY

THE UNITED STATES
AND UNESCO
1945-1985

WILLIAM PRESTON JR.,
EDWARD S. HERMAN, AND HERBERT I. SCHILLER

PREFACE BY SEÁN MACBRIDE
INTRODUCTION BY ELLEN RAY AND WILLIAM H. SCHAAP

MANUSCRIPT PRODUCED BY THE
INSTITUTE FOR MEDIA ANALYSIS, INC.
NEW YORK, NEW YORK

UNIVERSITY OF MINNESOTA PRESS • MINNEAPOLIS

UNESCO DISCLAIMER

The United Nations Educational, Scientific and Cultural Organization
(UNESCO) has declined to approve, authorize or sponsor this book
and has refused to participate in its publication. The conclusions,
viewpoints and opinions expressed in this book are wholly those of
the Institute for Media Analysis, Inc. and the individual authors and
do not reflect those of UNESCO. UNESCO has not participated in the
writing of this book and disclaims responsibility for its contents.
UNESCO will not receive any royalties or other payment from the sale
of this book.

Copyright © 1989 by the Institute for Media Analysis, Inc.,
145 West 4th Street, New York, NY 10012.
All rights reserved. No part of this publication may be reproduced, stored
in a retrieval system, or transmitted, in any form or by any means,
electronic, mechanical, photocopying, recording, or otherwise, without the
prior written permission of the publisher.

Published by the University of Minnesota Press
2037 University Avenue Southeast, Minneapolis MN 55414.
Printed in the United States of America.
Book and cover design by Lois Stanfield.

Library of Congress Cataloging-in-Publication Data

Preston, William, 1924–
   Hope and folly : the United States and Unesco, 1945–1985 / William
  Preston, Jr., Edward S. Herman, and Herbert I. Schiller ; preface by
  Seán MacBride ; introduction by Ellen Ray and William H. Schaap ;
  prepared by the Institute for Media Analysis, Inc., New York, New
  York.
     p.   cm—(Media & society)
  Bibliography: p.
  Includes index.
  ISBN 0-8166-1788-0—ISBN 0-8166-1789-9 (pbk.)
    1. Unesco—United States. 2. United States—Foreign policy—1981—
  3. Unesco in the press—United States—History—20th century.
  4. Press—United States—Influence. I. Herman, Edward S., 1925–
  II. Schiller, Herbert I., 1919– . III. Institute for Media
  Analysis. IV. Title. V. Series.
  AS4.U83P74 1989
  341.7'67—dc20   89-33643
                                           CIP

The University of Minnesota
is an equal-opportunity
educator and employer.

This book is dedicated, with great respect, to the memory of Seán Mac-Bride (1904–1988), a giant of a man, who eschewed a life of privilege to work tirelessly for the disadvantaged of the world, for peace and disarmament, and for greater understanding and compassion among all the people of this earth. He was the only human being ever to be awarded both the Nobel Peace Prize and the Lenin Peace Prize, a tribute both to the universality of his life and to his consummate diplomacy.

He was the driving force behind the expression of the New World Information and Communication Order. It was our honor that he served as the founding Chairman of the Board of the Institute for Media Analysis. His preface to this book was one of his last writings.

CONTENTS

PREFACE, by Seán MacBride   ix

INTRODUCTION, by Ellen Ray and William H. Schaap   xiii

THE HISTORY OF U.S.-UNESCO RELATIONS,
by William Preston, Jr.   3

   I. Introduction: An Overview   5

  II. The Indictment in Context   9

 III. Patterns and Problems in the American Past   14

 IV. The Nazi Challenge and Two World Wars:
    The Hostile Imagination Unleashed   24

  V. UNESCO's Origins:
    Liberal Hopes and Liberal Assumptions   32

 VI. Politicizing UNESCO in the U.S. and Abroad:
    Cold War Intrusions, 1946-1960   48

    A. Information and Mass Communications   48

    B. Anticommunism   60

    C. Culture   70

 VII. Challenge and Change Confront Cold War Concepts:
    The 1960s   87

VIII. Backlash and Reaction:
    The Road to Withdrawal, 1968–1981   120

  IX. The United States Exits: 1981–1985   148

   X. Epilogue: A Post-Mortem Interpretation   188

U.S. MASS MEDIA COVERAGE OF THE U.S. WITHDRAWAL
FROM UNESCO, by Edward S. Herman   203

  Introduction   205

    A. Objective Coverage Versus Propaganda   205

    B. *The Record of Earlier Studies of Mass-Media Treatment of UNESCO*   207

  II. An Analysis of U.S. Mass-Media Treatment of the U.S. Withdrawal From UNESCO   213

    A. *Sourcing*   214

    B. *Premises, Frames of Reference, and Agendas*   228

    C. *Ideological Language and Tone*   244

    D. *Rewriting History*   253

    E. *Programmatic and Management Deficiencies: Misrepresentations and Suppressions*   258

    F. *Misrepresentation of the NWICO Threat to a "Free Press"*   267

    G. *The Non-Correctability of Error*   273

    H. *Non-Disclosure of Corporate Interest*   277

  III. Summary and Conclusions   281

IS THERE A UNITED STATES INFORMATION POLICY? by Herbert I. Schiller   285

    I. Introduction   287

    II. U.S. Dominance in the Early Postwar Period   289

  III. The Hutchins Commission on Freedom of the Press: The Cooperative Option   290

  IV. The Western Doctrines of Free Flow and Free Press   292

    V. Hey-Day of Free Flow and the Emergence of the New Nations   294

  VI. The Call for a New International Information Order   296

  VII. The Western Counter-Attack against the NIIO   298

  VIII. The Technology Gambit   299

  IX. The United States Attack on UNESCO   303

    X. U.S. Information Policy in the 1980s: The Reagan Era   306

  XI. Conclusion   308

APPENDIXES   313

    I. Constitution of UNESCO   315

    II. The Directors-General of UNESCO   327

  III. Anatomy of a Smear: Ed Bradley and "60 Minutes" on UNESCO, by Edward S. Herman   328

  IV. Speech of E. Gough Whitlam, April 13, 1985   338

    V. Interviews Conducted by William Preston, Jr.   350

BIBLIOGRAPHY   351

INDEX   359

PREFACE

Seán MacBride

Through the ages, mankind has been dominated by an aggressive desire to exercise power over other human beings. This compulsion to dominate and conquer is what has always led to wars.

Until the advent and development of explosives, railways, and internal combustion engines, wars were relatively limited and even often regarded as sporting events. But in the wake of the Industrial Revolution, the need to control war began to be recognized universally.

In 1868 the major nations adopted the Declaration of St. Petersburg, which proclaimed that the rights of belligerents in a war were not unlimited. On the initiative of Tzar Nicholas, a conference was convened at The Hague in 1899 to consider the "reduction of international armaments and the substitution of pacific methods to replace force and violence in the sphere of foreign relations." This conference resulted in the adoption of a convention for the pacific settlement of disputes which was adopted by 24 major states. It was the first acknowledgment that the modern development of warfare and weapons was endangering civilization and that, therefore, an effort had to be made to curb the warlike propensities of humanity.

The trend toward the outlawing of wars was heightened by World War I, in which some ten million people were killed. It was the unprecedented destructive nature of that conflict which prompted the formulation of the Kellogg-Briand Pact of 1928, which in turn led to the General Treaty for the Renunciation of Wars, which was signed on August 27, 1928. This treaty, in effect, for the first time outlawed war and the use of force in international affairs. However, it was not accompanied by any measures aimed at disarmament and proved, therefore, to be ineffective.

Then there was World War II, in which some 60 million human beings were killed, more than half of them civilians. And on August 6, 1945, the atom bomb was dropped on Hiroshima, killing some 140,000 people; three days later, another, dropped on Nagasaki, killed a further 70,000 people.

The failure of the League of Nations to prevent World War II, and the advent of nuclear weapons, posed to the leaders of the world problems of a magnitude never before envisioned. It was no longer merely a question of preventing an ordinary war, but it was the very survival of the human race which was at stake. As Arthur Koestler put it:

> From the dawn of consciousness until 6 August 1945, man had to live with the prospect of his death as an individual. But since the day when the first atomic bomb outshone the sun over Hiroshima mankind as a whole has had to live with the prospect of extinction as a species.

The world leaders at that time had a much better sense of moral responsibility and of the dangers which faced the human race than do our present-day leaders, and they realized that oblivion was now the only alternative to world disarmament. After prolonged discussions they finally came to the conclusion in 1962 that the only way of saving humanity from nuclear destruction was to proceed to general and complete disarmament. This decision was followed through by the adoption unanimously of the proposal by the Soviet Union and the United States of the Eight Principles upon which the Treaty for General and Complete Disarmament would be based. Very briefly, this agreement provided for the destruction of all existing nuclear weapons and a prohibition against the manufacture of such weapons, and the reduction of all other armaments and of armies to the maximum numbers and capacities that would be reasonably required to maintain peace and order within the boundaries of each State.

These decisions would sound the death knell for arms manufacturers and would call for a very considerable reduction of the size of existing armies. The agreement also provided for the elimination of all foreign bases throughout the world. But the forces in favor of armament—not only the arms manufacturers but also the military establishments and the financial and industrial structures that profit from arms races and wars—are much more extensive and powerful than is usually appreciated. To them, disarmament spelled disaster. When they realized, in 1962, that the governments of the world were agreeing on General and Complete Disarmament, all the forces of the military-industrial complex were mobilized to oppose and disrupt the disarmament agreement between the governments of the world and the United Nations.

These forces extend their influence in most countries to the parliaments and the governments themselves. They work as well through the secret services and other secret organs of government, influencing parliamentarians and other officials, and particularly concentrating on journalists and other media people.

Control of the media, written and electronic, is of vital importance to those who wish to destabilize a government or to create tensions in different parts of the world. We have had many examples of this in the Congo, Vietnam, Chile, Angola, and the Middle East. Secret services and news agencies were used to distort events in order to justify military intervention. In some cases the military intervention would be operated by proxy or by bogus liberation movements that were financed and armed by the major power involved, which, more often than not, was the United States.

In some situations, the only protection available to the country under attack was the United Nations; not by direct intervention but by providing a forum in which the facts could be exposed. Indeed, this was one of the objectives that the founders of the United Nations had in mind when the charter was adopted. And be it said in their favor, the American leaders of that period were motivated by the high principles which were reflected in the Universal Declaration of Human Rights.

However, since then, the United States has not hesitated to ignore the provisions of the charter and other United Nations decisions and to resort to actions not far removed from those of non-governmental terrorists. By behaving in such a manner, the United States has certainly created a very bad impression for its views of international relations. By the continual use of force, or the threat of the use of force, in countries such as Cuba, Panama, Nicaragua, El Salvador, Lebanon, and Grenada, the United States has lost credibility and the confidence of most states that respect the Rule of Law and Human Rights.

The misbehavior of governments and of persons occupying high positions of trust has also been very damaging to the credibility of governments. The payment of bribes to people in high positions has eroded the modicum of respect and trust which is so necessary. Watergate, Muldergate, Irangate, the Lockheed bribery case, and the Mafia cases in Italy have all combined to destroy the confidence of the ordinary people in governments and their establishments.

Since the days of President John F. Kennedy, the U.S. has been resentful of the United Nations and of its agencies. It resented any criticism of its policies or actions. Threats of withholding payment of its contribution were not infrequent, and, in recent years, carried out. Finally, the U.S. withdrew completely from the International Labor Organization. It was also critical of the other U.N. agencies, in particular of UNESCO, and with the help of a section of the U.S. media, the U.S. mounted a full campaign against UNESCO and finally resigned its membership. Under the Reagan administration the campaign against the U.N. and UNESCO was stepped up very considerably. It came to the point where U.S. officials stated that the departure of the U.N. from New York would not be unwelcome. The U.S.-influenced press joined in the campaign of denigration of UNESCO and of its director-general. In this way, American public opinion was conditioned for the decision of the U.S. government to leave UNESCO.

The campaign against UNESCO and its Director General was reminiscent of McCarthyism. Of course, the Western powers were not really so committed to UNESCO's objectives regarding its educational and scientific program for Third World countries; the betterment of education, the elimination of illiteracy, and the development of scientific expertise in the underdeveloped areas of the world were not regarded as top priorities for the United States. Hence UNESCO was to be brushed aside.

The fact that the then director-general, Amadou-Mahtar M'Bow, was a black African, and a French-speaking African at that, did not endear him to the American establishment. And here I would pay tribute to Mr. M'Bow for his courageous leadership of UNESCO over two terms of office.

One of the great dangers facing democratic countries arises from the operations of the secret services. In many cases they have formed separate squads to carry out secretly illegal and criminal acts. In some cases they act on their own initiative; in others, they act with the sanction of their governments and carry out terrorist activities; they have unlimited financial resources and do not hesitate to blackmail or assassinate people who get in their way. The activities of secret services are damaging to democracy and are destructive of the proper application of the Rule of Law.

This book is about such matters. The only way of dealing with the problems to which I have referred is by informing public opinion, which is not conscious of the gravity of the present situation.

INTRODUCTION
Ellen Ray and William Schaap

"What really bothers me about the MacBride Report[1] is the way it calls for the licensing of journalists." We were lunching with a senior editor of one of the most prestigious newspapers in the United States.

"What are you talking about?" we said. "It specifically does *not* call for the licensing of journalists."

"Don't be ridiculous. Of course it does."

"Have you *read* the MacBride Report?" we asked.

"No, but I don't have to."

"What do you mean by that?"

"I've read dozens of news articles and feature stories about the Mac-Bride Report, and they *all* say that it calls for the licensing of journalists. Don't try to tell me they all are wrong and you are right."

THE MACBRIDE REPORT

This conversation, which took place not long after the United States had withdrawn from the United Nations Educational, Scientific, and Cultural Organization, is a tribute to the strength of the campaign of disinformation against UNESCO which developed over the 1980s.

Our friend[2] was not alone in criticizing a book he had never read; this practice was encouraged by its foes before the report was published. On May 17, 1980, after it had been presented to the UNESCO director-general, but before it had been officially released, *Editor and Publisher* had this to say about the MacBride Report:

> Whether you have read it or not, the IPI [International Press Institute], ANPA [American Newspaper Publishers Association], ASNE [American Society of Newspaper Editors], IAPA [Inter-American Press Association], the World Press Freedom Committee believe there is enough wrong with it to constitute a threat to the existence of a free press everywhere.[3]

When Seán MacBride was asked what it was about his report that upset the United States government and establishment so much, he replied:

> That is a difficult question to answer, because the criticism of the United States was obviously made by people who had never read the Report. It criticized things that the Report never said. It invented recommendations which the Commission never made . . . recommendations which were made in the opposite sense to the recommendations that were made.[4]

Indeed, the criticisms of the report, and of UNESCO in general, deviated so sharply from reality that the notion of a hidden agenda was hard to avoid. This held true for general as well as specific criticisms. As one commentator noted, "The high moral tone in which the U.S. decision to withdraw from UNESCO has been couched presents a sharp contrast with the political realities that lead to that decision."[5] "Most obviously," another observer noted, the crisis at UNESCO is "part of a challenge to U.S. hegemony by most of the rest of the world."[6]

The purpose of this book is to put the anti-UNESCO campaign in historical perspective, to elaborate the *entire* history of U.S.-UNESCO relations, without which it is impossible to understand fully the events of the last few, stormy years of what was once a staunch alliance. Indeed, it is only in light of this history that the intensity and significance of the campaign against UNESCO can be appreciated. It is also necessary in order to understand the gulf that separated the realities of U.S. policy from the general, often greatly distorted, perceptions of that policy.

In fact, there *were* some material threats to vested American interests in some of the positions advocated by UNESCO, although they were greatly exaggerated by media which, at the same time, would not tolerate any discussion of this exaggeration.[7] Indeed, they warped the public's perception of the entire issue by converting these relatively minor threats to private, material interests into dangerous and evil threats to fundamental principles. (This manipulation is discussed at length in Section II of Part II of this book, Edward S. Herman's detailed analysis of the media coverage of UNESCO; see especially Subsection H, on the real corporate interests, and Section IV of Part III, Herbert I. Schiller's analysis of U.S. media policy.)

Another, albeit implicit, purpose of this book is to raise one more voice in defense of international cooperation and the United Nations system. The virulence of the irrational attack against that system has intensified of late. In a time when we can destroy our planet not only by nuclear holocaust, but also, it seems, by the senseless rape of the world's environment, universal, international cooperation is more important than ever.

UNESCO—indeed the United Nations system itself—has been subjected to harsh criticism from the most conservative elements of the

Western establishment since its creation. But the tenor and the scope of the dispute rose to a crescendo in the middle and late 1970s and the early 1980s. To some extent this heightening of the debate was a function of the change in membership—and the outlook of members— wrought by the decline of colonialism through the 1960s, and the concomitant loss of Western power and influence in the United Nations, where each nation has one vote. (This phenomenon is discussed in detail below in Sections VI and VII of Part I, William Preston, Jr.'s historical overview, and by Schiller in Part III, Section V.)

The U.S. backlash was a natural complement to what became known as the Reagan Doctrine, an attempt to reverse any decline in U.S. influence wherever and whenever possible. Since 1980, when the Heritage Foundation published *Mandate for Leadership*, a vast collection of conservative proposals—adopted nearly in its entirety by the Reagan administration[8]—minimization of the role of the U.N., indeed its elimination, has been the chilling plan on the Heritage agenda and a right-wing priority. (The role of the Heritage Foundation is discussed below and in Preston: Part I, Sections VIII and IX; Herman: Part II, Section II, especially Subsections A, D, and F; and Schiller: Part III, Section X.)

Among the several controversies that brought UNESCO into the line of fire was a series of battles focusing on Israel's role in the territories it occupied after the 1967 war. (See Preston: Part I, Section VIII.) In 1970, then Director-General René Maheu complained that Israel was preventing the distribution of school books in the occupied territories; he was vilified in the U.S. press.[9] UNESCO criticized Israel's archaeological policies in Jerusalem (see Preston: Part I, Section VIII), for which it was also bitterly attacked; and for two years, from 1974 to 1976, the UNESCO General Conference (not the director-general, but the actual executive body) refused to include Israel in any of its regional groupings. (It was, in fact, the newly elected Amadou-Mahtar M'Bow who defused this conflict and saw that Israel was admitted;[10] ironically, M'Bow, as noted below, was continually baited by UNESCO critics as being anti-Israel.) But there was one particular issue that overshadowed all the others in the UNESCO embroglio: Communications.

COMMUNICATIONS

In reality, sweeping world changes were making communications and the flow of information a new and critical area. Among them was the development of satellites and other high technology methods of instantaneous communication (see Schiller: Part III, Section VIII); also significant was the growth in influence—outside the West—of the Non-Aligned

Movement. But several symbolic events combined to propel UNESCO into the forefront of the communications battle.

In 1974 a new director-general was elected, Amadou-Mahtar M'Bow of Senegal, first seen as a "moderate," but soon recognized as an outspoken critic of the Western media's insensitivity to the Third World.[11] In 1978 UNESCO issued the Mass Media Declaration, which calls, rather blandly, for the "wider and better balanced dissemination of information."[12] And in 1980 UNESCO published the MacBride Report, after nearly three years of painstaking research, analysis, debate, and compromise.

Despite the fact that M'Bow's election, and the passage of both the Media Declaration and the MacBride Report, were unanimous decisions, approved by *all* the Member States, including the United States and the United Kingdom; despite the fact that the Declaration of 1978 "unequivocally supports government-free news media and omits press-control proposals";[13] despite the fact that the MacBride Report *nowhere* calls for licensing of journalists; despite all the *facts* apparent to anyone who took the trouble to read the documents or had the minimal sophistication to distinguish between UNESCO debates and UNESCO final reports and declarations, the organization was depicted as the greatest threat ever to freedom of the press and the "free flow of information." The reality—objective challenges to Western commercial oligopoly and control, however limited—was not discussed. (See Herman: Part II, Section II, Subsection F.)

This transformation was accomplished by distortion, misrepresentation, selective quotation, and all the other methods of disinformation, including outright lies and fabrications in the Western media. (For the historical development of this campaign, see Preston: Part I, Sections VIII and IX; and see Herman: Part II, generally; and see in particular Appendix III, in which Herman dissects one particularly vicious television "documentary" on UNESCO. For a good sense of the anti-UNESCO campaign in the United Kingdom, see the speech by Gough Whitlam, set forth in Appendix IV.[14])

THE HERITAGE ATTACKS

One of the most significant movers and shakers in the entire campaign against UNESCO has been the Heritage Foundation. It has spewed forth a plethora of publications criticizing the United Nations and virtually every branch of it. Dozens of books, pamphlets, background papers, and memorandums have attacked the U.N., the General Assembly, the FAO, UNCTAD, the ILO, UNICEF, and, of course, UNESCO.[15] A brief description of some of the anti-UNESCO material will give the flavor of the Heritage Foundation line.

Backgrounder Number 221 appeared in October 1982, entitled "For UNESCO, A Failing Grade in Education." It criticized UNESCO for advocating the New International Economic Order, which it described as "a simplistic scheme to redistribute the world's wealth and resources to more than 100 underdeveloped nations, creating a global welfare state financed mainly by the U.S. and the western industrial nations." It calls the NIEO "Fabian socialism," a secret plan to create a "world government." It accused UNESCO of trying to "take NIEO into the classroom," by advocating such nefarious doctrines as "teaching international human rights," "disarmament education," and "moral education." It sniped at Director-General M'Bow for shifting UNESCO's focus away from "its original goal of creating world 'intellectual cooperation' towards emphasis on Third World 'development.'"

In December 1982 Heritage published *Backgrounder* Number 233, "UNESCO, Where Culture Becomes Propaganda." This paper attacked the World Conference on Cultural Policies sponsored by UNESCO in Mexico City. M'Bow was faulted for "leading the charge against western media and cultural projects." The concept of "cultural imperialism" was ridiculed as a "game played at Mexico City." The notion that Western television exerts an undue and improper influence on the Third World was dismissed as so much Soviet propaganda—because one of the authors of one of the studies cited by advocates of this position is an official of an organization "closely aligned with the editorial policies of Moscow [*sic*]," the International Organization of Journalists (IOJ).[16]

Another typical Heritage *Backgrounder* was Number 253 in March 1983, entitled, "The IPDC: UNESCO vs. the Free Press." UNESCO, it said, "has declared war against the western free press." It described the New World Information and Communication Order as the logical result of UNESCO's approval of the New International Economic Order— which is called "a formula for a global socialist state"—and the presence at its meetings of personnel from the IOJ. The NWICO, Heritage says, "preaches redistribution of the wealth of ultramodern and global mass communication infrastructures created by the western world." This, to say the least, is an astonishing reading of the MacBride Report, which, as noted earlier, was approved unanimously. (See Herman: Part II, Section II, Subsection C, for a discussion of this use of the terminology of socialism in the media campaign against UNESCO.)

This particular *Backgrounder* also demonstrates how Heritage, and other critics of UNESCO, deliberately confuse subjects that are *discussed* with policy positions that are *adopted*. It says, "Out of this meeting [at UNESCO Headquarters in Paris, on the protection of journalists] came suggestions for regulating the reporting and the movement of journalists. Devices like international I.D. cards and a code of ethics for the press administered by an 'International Commission for the Protection of Journalists' were proposed." Nothing whatsoever along those lines, of course, was ever *passed*. This same paper describes Seán MacBride as a "Moscow-aligned radical." M'Bow is criticized for having been a "student radical" at the Sorbonne in the late 1940s and early 1950s!

On October 19, 1983, Heritage published *Backgrounder* Number 298, "The U.S. and UNESCO at a Crossroads," by Owen Harries, a former Australian ambassador to UNESCO. Harries was a John M. Olin Fellow at Heritage, its pointman in the fight against UNESCO.[17] This paper, a ten-page diatribe, described UNESCO as "a worst case model of the U.N. system." It rehashed all the standard complaints, but went further. It proposed a specific U.S. policy: "The United States should announce formally that it will withdraw from UNESCO in one year unless there are substantial changes in the organization." Harries also called for substantial reductions in U.S. contributions to the budget, even while remaining a member. Ironically, given the history of U.S. domination of UNESCO's early years (see Preston: Part I, Sections V and VI), Harries demanded that UNESCO have "a proper respect for the interests and view of minorities."

Harries made a final push for U.S. withdrawal in Heritage Executive Memorandum Number 68 of December 5, 1983, "The U.N. and UNESCO: Time for Decision." "The only effective political leverage available to the U.S.," he insisted, was the withdrawal announcement. Shortly thereafter, President Reagan took his advice.

In a fund-raising letter sent out October 8, 1984, as the time approached for the United States' announced withdrawal, December 31, 1984, Heritage president, Edwin J. Feulner, Jr., bragged that President Reagan's decision to withdraw was a "direct result" of the Heritage campaign in general and the Harries *Backgrounder* in particular. But he bewailed the fact that UNESCO's supporters were urging Congress to stop the withdrawal. "I need your help," he wrote, "to stop a corrupt third-world despot from undoing one of the Heritage Foundation's most significant achievements." He urged recipients to "send the enclosed postcard to U.N. Ambassador Jeane Kirkpatrick to let her know whether you think the United States should get out of UNESCO."[18]

Finally, on December 10, 1984, Heritage sent out Executive Memorandum Number 68, also by Owen Harries, "UNESCO—Time to Leave." It argued that no significant reform had taken place and that, despite efforts by the U.S. National Commission for UNESCO to persuade the administration to reverse itself, the withdrawal should be allowed to take place as planned.

Harries outdid himself in hypocrisy. His original paper had suggested that the withdrawal announcement might prompt changes during the ensuing year which would enable the U.S. to remain. Now he stated that "apart from the merits of the case, the fact that the U.S. has taken the decision to withdraw, after due deliberation, in itself is a compelling reason for not retreating from it or delaying its implementation. A great country which values its reputation should carry out what it has solemnly announced it will do. To do otherwise is to invite derision and contempt, not only in UNESCO but generally."

The administration, despite objections from some quarters of the State Department, was not about to reverse itself.

The administration's actual intentions were significantly different from its public pronouncements during the year preceding withdrawal. Indeed, Assistant Secretary of State Gregory Newell prepared an "action memo" in January 1984 that discussed the degree to which the media would be manipulated during the ensuing year. (This plan is discussed in Herman: Part II, Section II, Subsection A, and in Preston: Part I, Section IX.)

THE CRITICS OF HERITAGE

The Heritage Foundation's campaign was not without its critics, although they had little influence and received almost no coverage in the mainstream media. The United Nations Association of the United States published numerous line-by-line, statement-by-statement rebuttals of the Heritage *Backgrounders* and Memorandums. They demonstrated that most short Heritage papers contained dozens of lies, distortions, and omissions.

A detailed analysis by the UNAUS, "Lies, Distortions, and Nonsense from the Heritage Foundation,"[19] debunks the Heritage insistence that the UNAUS "fails to note the grave threat posed to press freedom by NWIO under the shibboleth of 'protection of journalists' (i.e., licensing of Western newsmen in the Third World)." The analysis points out that UNAUS had stressed that the MacBride Report explicitly warns that "to propose a licensing system for journalists was dangerous since it would require someone to stipulate who would be entitled to claim such protection."

The U.N. Department of Public Information also issued a detailed report[20] exposing some two dozen errors of fact and misrepresentations in one Heritage report. And the Southern California Division of the UNAUS published a series of analyses and rebuttals to the Heritage Foundation *Backgrounders*.[21]

The American scientific establishment was also dismayed by the U.S. pullout. The president of the National Academy of Engineering, the foreign secretary of the National Academy of Sciences, and many prestigious members of the American Association for the Advancement of Science all objected to the withdrawal.[22] All, unfortunately, to no avail.

Finally, although it was far too late to be closing the barn door, on April 29, 1985, Canada's United Nations Ambassador Stephen Lewis gave a rousing speech to the UNAUS national convention in New York City. He lambasted the Heritage Foundation, in the most undiplomatic language. He said:

> And then there are other critics . . . there are others still who are quite simply malevolent and they do great damage. They pretend to be dispassionate, analytic, concerned. Poppy-cock. Folderol. They are, by and large, neo-isolationists in their views of the world, and they are made up of the Heritage Foundation and others of their ilk.

Heritage, he insisted, specialized "not in insightful analysis, but in inspired sophistry," and engaged in "philistinism." The right-wing press, led by *The Washington Times*, attacked Lewis; the U.S. mission dismissed his remarks as "the same kind of intemperate rhetoric everyone in the U.N. grows used to."[23] Heritage, with its unique logic, deplored Lewis's "interference in American internal affairs," and promptly called upon the Canadian government to fire him. But the Canadian prime minister, Brian Mulroney, who refused to withdraw from UNESCO, supported him: "When he speaks," Mulroney said, "he speaks for the government of Canada and I thought he spoke well."[24]

THE ATTACKS AGAINST M'BOW

Amadou-Mahtar M'Bow was under attack virtually from the time he took office as director-general in November 1974 until the day he left office in November 1987. One of the first widely read attacks appeared in the March/April 1976 issue of *Columbia Journalism Review*, written by Joel Blocker, who had recently resigned after two years as director of UNESCO's public information office. Blocker's hatchet job, "The Bad News From UNESCO," dealt primarily with Israel's isolation at the United Nations. The article was blatantly anti-Arab and at the same time accused M'Bow, ever so subtly, of anti-Semitism.[25]

Blocker complained that "in 1975, the U.N.'s Food and Agriculture Organization and Environment Program were taken over, respectively, by a Lebanese and an Egyptian." He described M'Bow as "a handsome, personable Senegalese Moslem." He deplored M'Bow's defense of two UNESCO resolutions on Israel, one denying it membership in UNESCO's European regional group, "the only member to be so deprived," the other "sanctioning it for alleged continuing abuses in Jerusalem." The very phraseology belies any objectivity on Blocker's part. (Shortly thereafter, in fact, Israel was admitted to the European regional group.)

The author demeaned M'Bow's "tendency to respond to western criticism by associating it with the color of his own skin." For M'Bow to suggest that there was any racism in the Western media was, to Blocker, ridiculous. But most outrageous was the way in which the author imputed to M'Bow anti-Semitism: "A high U.N. official," he writes, absolving himself of responsibility for what follows, "puts it this way: 'For him, the press is immoral, sensationalistic, decadent, without ethics. He believes that it is in the nature of the press to sell itself, that it is open to manipulation by monied interests. He never quite says "Jewish" money and would be shocked if told there was anything anti-Semitic about his views.' "

It is, in fact, not M'Bow but the anonymous "official" who is being stereotypically anti-Semitic, assuming — quite incorrectly — that most of the Western press is owned by Jews and assuming — equally erroneously — that most representatives of the "monied interests" are Jews. M'Bow is being accused of not *quite* saying anything anti-Semitic and not *quite* thinking any such thing, but *being* so nevertheless.

The attacks on M'Bow escalated during the campaign to get a U.S. withdrawal announcement and during the one-year waiting period that followed. They are described in the main text of both Preston's and Herman's sections. Indeed, the campaign became so personalized, replete with canned newspaper editorials captioned "M'Bow Must Go," that many commentators viewed the issue as, in fact, one of personalities. (See Herman: Part II, Section II, Subsection B.)

After the British announcement of withdrawal, *South* magazine[26] published an analysis which quoted Jean Gerard, the last U.S. ambassador to UNESCO,[27] as pointing out that the accomplishment of all the requested reforms "still would not by itself be enough." And Representative James Scheuer notes: "If UNESCO were to appoint a responsible person tomorrow, the U.S. government might change its mind." From this, *South* concludes: "There: it is not politics or polemics, not mismanagement, or poor accounting, it is M'Bow, and Reagan wants him out."

In fact, as this book attempts to demonstrate, this is a simplistic and false analysis. The campaign against him profoundly misrepresented what M'Bow stood for; he was not guilty of what he was accused of; but he was simply a symbol, an excuse. What the United States wanted was a UNESCO that followed its orders, as it had in the 1940s and 1950s and 1960s. (See Preston: Part I, Sections VI and VII.) Now M'Bow, in fact, is out, and the U.S. has not rushed to rejoin UNESCO. Perhaps the new administration will reconsider, but the problem is not one of personalities.

ABOUT THIS BOOK

A word about the history of this book is in order. When critics of UNESCO learned that the Institute for Media Analysis had been commissioned by UNESCO to prepare a study of U.S.-UNESCO relations, the book was attacked before it even existed. The Heritage Foundation, the World Press Freedom Committee, and *presstime* (the journal of the American Newspaper Publishers Association) all referred to the work in progress. *Presstime* carried an article suggesting that "a cheap shot against the press is in the making that will add no luster to UNESCO's image."

This prompted UNESCO's public information chief in New York, Joseph A. Mehan, to respond, pointing out that every study of American media treatment of UNESCO ever conducted concluded that the press had been unfair, to say the least, to UNESCO. He cited A. H. Raskin's study of the 1981 UNESCO General Conference in Belgrade conducted for the National News Council; two State Department Reports to Congress, in February 1982 and February 1983; an August 1983 report by the Annenberg School of Communications on the 1982 General Conference in Paris; an August 1984 University of Oregon study on press coverage of UNESCO; and a University of Washington study published in May 1986. All of these, Mehan noted, determined that American reporting on UNESCO was decidedly biased against the organization and totally unbalanced.[28]

CONCLUSION

Ironically, in its desire to bring back the United States and the United Kingdom, the current leadership of UNESCO is playing down all of the issues about which the Reagan administration has complained. UNESCO has begun a campaign to eradicate the memory of the Mac-Bride Report and no longer itself distributes either the abridged or the unabridged version, although it says the problem is merely one of funds.[29]

If, as some supporters of UNESCO fear, the organization bows to U.S. pressures, there could be a reversion to the old days; if, on the other hand, UNESCO continues to uphold the principles it has supported throughout its history, regardless of the political philosophies of whatever bloc of nations might be dominant at a given time, it may continue to aspire to the goals of its founders. And, one can hope, the U.S. and the U.K. will rejoin, in time, because, in remaining on the outside, they—and all of us—are the losers.

NOTES

1. UNESCO, *Many Voices, One World: Towards a New More Just and More Efficient World Information and Communication Order* (the report of the International Commission for the Study of Communication Problems) (New York: UNESCO, 1980), 332 pages. The members of the Commission were: Seán MacBride of Ireland, President; and Elie Abel of the U.S., Hubert Beuve-Méry of France, Elebe Ma Ekonzo of Zaire, Gabriel García Márquez of Colombia, Sergei Losev of the U.S.S.R., Mochtar Lubis of Indonesia, Mustapha Masmoudi of Tunisia, Michio Nagain of Japan, Fred Isaac Akporuaro Omu of Nigeria, Bogdan Osolnik of Yugoslavia, Gamal El Oteifi of Egypt, Johannes Pieter Pronk of the Netherlands, Juan Somavia of Chile, Boobli George Verghese of India, and Betty Zimmerman of Canada.

2. We do not name our friend, to spare him the embarrassment; he is an otherwise sophisticated author, journalist, and very senior editor.

3. "The MacBride Report," *Editor and Publisher*, May 17, 1980, p. 8; cited in "The U.S., Its Press, and the New World Information Order," Report No. 488 of the Freedom of Information Center of the School of Journalism of the University of Missouri at Columbia, February 1984, p. 4.

In point of fact, the report nowhere calls for the licensing of journalists. In one section, Chapter 5, "Rights and Responsibilities of Journalists," Part 3, "Professional Regulations" (pp. 236–38), the report summarizes the arguments for and against the official licensing of journalists, and concludes that the "advisability of adopting legal rules defining a juridical status for the journalistic profession is viewed differently from country to country." In the recommendations that apply to journalists, Section III, "Professional Integrity and Standards" (pp. 261–65) there is *absolutely nothing* that resembles a call for licensing. In one brief recommendation — which has itself been frequently described incorrectly — the report says that the adoption of codes of professional ethics for journalists "is desirable, provided that such codes are prepared and adopted by the profession itself — without governmental interference" (p. 262). That is it. Anyone who wanted to could have read these eight pages and seen that the report does not advocate licensing journalists or call for the imposition of codes of conduct.

4. "ORTK Talks to Seán MacBride," *Our Right to Know*, Fall/Winter 1984–85, p. 4, interview by Ellen Ray in Athens, Greece, October 1984.

5. Ian Reinecke, in one of a series of responses to the U.S. decision to withdraw, published in a special issue of the *Journal of Communication*, Vol. 34, No. 4 (Autumn 1984), p. 97. The changing world makeup and its impact at the United Nations is discussed in Preston: Part I, Sections VI and VII.

6. Alexander Wilson, "UNESCO: Decolonization and the Public Sphere," *Borderlines* (Canada), Spring 1985, p. 5.

7. One telling example is the attack on Inter Press Service, a Rome-based international wire service specializing in news from and about the Third World. IPS was scheduled to be awarded a role in a proposed U.N. Development Program plan for a subscription network "to circulate information among Third World scientists, bureaucrats, businessmen, and trade unionists." The State Department intervened, saying that IPS "has consistently opposed U.S. interests in economic, political, and information matters." Unnamed American media organizations, the State Department said, in a cable to its U.N. mission, objected that the proposed network would "be providing U.N. money to build the IPS into a world-class competitor of the commercial news agencies." The plan was derailed, and State Department officials later admitted, not for attribution, that their objections had been raised only at the insistence of the commercial interests. They even admitted that, after reading IPS copy, the political charges were unfounded. See Peter Hall, "What's All the Fuss About Inter Press?" *Columbia Journalism Review*, January-February 1983. Inter Press's U.S. affiliate, Interlink Press Service, was subsequently forced to fold.

8. Indeed, Edwin Feulner, Jr., the president of Heritage, was appointed by President Reagan to chair the U.S. Advisory Commission on Public Diplomacy, which evaluates USIA programs, Fulbright scholarships, and the National Endowment for Democracy programs. See Arthur Gavshon, et al., "The Heritage Foundation Goes Abroad," *The Nation*, June 6, 1987.

9. See the discussion in Siradiou Diallo, "L'acharnement de Washington," *Jeune Afrique*, December 26, 1984.

10. *Ibid.*

11. When M'Bow first spoke out against the international media oligopoly, in 1977, he was castigated by many, including Gerald Long, the managing director of Reuters, who insisted he knew of no manipulation of the news whatsoever. The criticism coming from Reuters was rather ironic, as it had worked clandestinely for the British government since at least World War I. In fact, a 30-year-long media network operated by British intelligence, which included some Reuters agents, "overshadow[ed] any comparable CIA propaganda activities so far revealed." Richard Fletcher, "How the Secret Service Shaped the News," *The Guardian* (London), December 18, 1981. And see, David Leigh, "U.K. Propaganda Machine Worked On In Peacetime," *The Observer* (London), December 20, 1981, and Richard Fletcher and Tony Smart, "The News Manipulators," *Africa Now*, March 1982. The role of the CIA in U.S. media manipulation is discussed in Preston: Part I, Section VI, notes 93–97.

12. Quoted in Leonard R. Sussman and David W. Sussman, "Mass News Media and International Law," *International Political Science Review*, Vol. 7, No. 3 (July 1986), p. 344, at p. 349.

13. *Ibid.*

14. And see Gavshon, *The Heritage Foundation*, n. 8.

15. Some 37 publications are listed on the inside back cover of Heritage's bestseller, *A World Without a U.N.* (1984); the list is incomplete.

16. The role of television and motion pictures in the dynamics of international cultural policies is a serious one. See, for example, David P. Forsythe, "Reagan and UNESCO: Freedom and Culture," *Cultural Democracy* (Baltimore), No. 25 (October-November 1982), p. 11; and Don Adams and Arlene Goldbard, "Gentlemen's Agreements: The U.S. and World Cultural Policy," *ibid.*, No. 17 (November-December 1981), p. 8. Adams and Goldbard argue that some of President Reagan's hostility to UNESCO can be traced directly to the long-time opposition of Hollywood trade organizations to any foreign interference with media product importation.

17. More information on Owen Harries's anti-UNESCO activities can be found in Appendix IV, Gough Whitlam's speech on the campaign against UNESCO in the United Kingdom. See also, Arthur Gavshon, "Why Britain Should Keep Faith with the UNESCO Dream," *The Guardian* (London), October 4, 1985; Gavshon, "The Power and Influence Behind America's Right," *The Guardian*, November 24, 1985; and Gavshon, "A Star Turns on the U.N.," *The Guardian*, February 21, 1986.

18. Kirkpatrick, in fact, "wholly supported" the U.S. withdrawal. U.S. Senate Committee on Governmental Affairs Hearing, "U.S. Financial and Political Involvement in the United Nations," May 7, 1985, p. 13.

19. Dated September 16, 1983, and submitted by UNAUS Chairman Elliot L. Richardson to Heritage Chairman Frank Shakespeare by letter of September 27, 1983.

20. "Comments on Heritage Foundations Paper," February 24, 1984.

21. See, for example, "The Heritage Foundation and the United Nations: 'Whatever It Is—I'm Against It,' " January 1983.

22. See Walter Sullivan, "Politics Hasn't Hampered UNESCO's Scientific Method," *New York Times*, May 29, 1984.

23. Ralph Z. Hallow, "Attack on Heritage Foundation Ignites Furor," *Washington Times*, May 8, 1985.

24. William Frye, "I Won't Stop Attacking UN's Foes: Lewis," *Montreal Gazette*, May 9, 1985.

25. This article presages a debate that raged more intensely in the 1980s, the suggestion urged by supporters of Israel that to be opposed to policies of the State of Israel is to be an anti-Semite.

26. *South*, January 1985.

27. And a former legal associate of the maniacally anti-Communist New York City attorney (later disbarred), Roy Cohn.

28. Letter from Joseph A. Mehan to the Editor, *presstime*, February 11, 1987. These studies are discussed in Herman: Part II, Section I, Subsection B.

29. This action was condemned by resolutions of the Union of Democratic Communications and of the International Communications Association. As a result, UNESCO allowed the World Association for Christian Communication in London to publish, in association with it, an edition of the MacBride Report.

HOPE &
FOLLY

William Preston, Jr.

THE HISTORY OF U.S.-UNESCO RELATIONS

I. INTRODUCTION: AN OVERVIEW

In the immediate aftermath of World War II, in a burst of idealism, the victorious allies created the United Nations Educational, Scientific, and Cultural Organization (UNESCO). "Since wars begin in the minds of men," UNESCO'S preamble began,* "it is in the minds of men that the defenses of peace must be constructed."[1] Goaded by the examples of Nazi tyranny, propaganda, and racism, and inspired by the optimism of victory and the belief in human solidarity, brotherhood, and understanding as the only sure basis of international peace, the founders hoped UNESCO would be the genie of global amity and cooperation.

This small beachhead of mutual trust created to modify the behavior of the still unredeemed world would slowly instill those necessary habits of civilized interaction. In time, as UNESCO'S programs in education, science, and culture took effect, the organization would push back suspicion, intolerance, and hatred, to help attain the peace and security for which so many millions had sacrificed their lives. Never had so much been promised to so many by so few.

However, almost before the ink had dried on UNESCO'S constitution, some of its founding members threatened the organization with their discordant national interests and political ideologies. The utopian launching of this magnificent venture sent it forward, not fatally flawed, but tainted by the very human weaknesses it was designed to forestall and correct. The world, as always, would have to lift itself up by its own bootstraps, yet UNESCO could and would provide an essential leverage for that effort, when and if the world was willing to let it.

It was thus clear from the start that UNESCO would always live in "the best of times and the worst of times," poised between the impossible expectations of its charter and the abysmal realities it had to confront daily, an elusive hope bouncing in the wake of bipolar and multilateral conflict and confrontation, where poverty, hunger, disease, ignorance, and underdevelopment had first claims on the minds of men in most parts of the world.

Neither UNESCO nor the world gave up on each other during the succeeding decades of ominous turmoil, with minor exceptions. Such was the immense attraction of the ideals that the organization promoted as the conscience of mankind. Yet that moral claim itself had a frustrating mission: It imposed standards of responsible behavior and raised questions about equality and justice that disturbed the attitudes and assumptions of many members. It is not a given that men enjoy having the defenses of peace constructed in their minds.

*For the full text of the UNESCO Constitution, see Appendix I.

As in so many other unions, therefore, the early romantic illusions gave way to a more querulous, nagging relationship. It became easy for the world (or some of it) to criticize its UNESCO partner, since it often did not deliver the mutual understanding expected of it. It also meddled in all sorts of affairs the world (or some of it) considered off-limits. The world, one might say from UNESCO's perspective, was impossible to please, making endless, often contradictory, demands and never providing money enough to do half of them. Nevertheless, if there were mutual recriminations, there was also a mutual regard for the common tie and its importance. The two achieved much together over the years.

UNESCO itself changed and matured. Not only did it grow into institutional middle age with a certain hardening of the bureaucratic arteries, but it also developed the ecstatic capacity to be born again, revived and redefined by the newly independent nations of Africa and Asia that enriched the dialogue of international cooperation after 1960. Suffering from postcolonial stress, they added a dimension of immediate necessity to UNESCO's often abstract long-range goals and challenged the superpower agenda with independent norms of their own. By 1983, 161 countries formed a UNESCO membership that Nobel Peace Prize laureate Seán MacBride somewhat prematurely labeled "Many Voices, One World."

As UNESCO survived and prospered during these decades of cold war, hot war, national liberation, terrorism, and covert operations, a token of good works and intellectual cooperation in a cacophony of political anarchy and ideological propaganda, one of its senior supporters was also treading its way warily through the same pervasive quicksand. As co-founder and benefactor, the United States had committed itself to the liberal internationalism that Woodrow Wilson had earlier projected as its destined future. In 1945 the country simply assumed the congruence of that structure of collaboration and the achievement of the "American Century." History's beneficence would secure both in a remarkable compatibility of opposites. The U.S. and UNESCO would go forward together.

Since reality turned out to be more complex, obdurate, and surprising, as UNESCO also learned, the United States often found itself improvising policies and pursuing ends that challenged or subverted the aims of the international educational, scientific, and cultural community. Nor had it accurately assessed those strains of ideology and isolation in its own tradition that might endanger the very tenets of global cooperation. It might be argued, in fact, that the United States was also poised precariously between the expectations of its high-minded international aims and the abysmal realities it had to confront within itself.

The Challenge of History

History, however, had the upper hand over both the United States and UNESCO. It challenged each of them to accord to their ideals a decent respect, to adjust to a changing world, to contain their rebellious internal elements, to manage their respective policies, and to maintain that mutual commitment to peace and well-being to which they had each dedicated themselves at the end of the war.

If History not only wrote the exams but also graded the results, what kind of report card would these two participants receive? Of one thing we can be certain. No student ever takes over the teacher's role. History would look askance at the United States' evaluating and judging UNESCO while itself dropping out of the course.

It is time, then, to give History its due; time to evaluate, as History might, these two international contestants and the roles each of them has played over the 40 years of their troubled, yet often successful collaboration. Only then will it be possible to assess with some accuracy the United States withdrawal from UNESCO that took effect at the end of 1984. History may judge the United States in error, may even suggest that UNESCO should have expelled the United States for truancy and conduct unbecoming a world power. But whatever the judgmental outcome may be, beyond that immediate sorting out of rights and wrongs there lies in this saga the larger tragedy of international cooperation. For it may help us understand whether the world is once again in the "twilight of internationalism."[2]

However, acceding to History's demands in this instance will not be easy since UNESCO has already been indicted, tried, and convicted in the court of American public opinion whereas the United States as the prosecutor and hanging judge has largely escaped the scrutiny of that same audience. And in the aftermath of the U.S. withdrawal, the UNESCO case, unlike other famous political trials such as that of Sacco and Vanzetti, has not attained the status of a never-ending wrong. Quite the opposite. UNESCO is at present a nonissue in the United States, scorned and forgotten, a minor remnant in the dust bin of American foreign-policy history. If the public responds at all, it is to the memory of a virulent and successful defamation campaign in which UNESCO was paraded as the purveyor of "moral carbon monoxide," the epitome of a "corrupt, anti-western organization," threatening to extinguish the light of liberty around the world.[3]

The historical challenge then is that of discovering context and perspective in a relationship that consumed 40 years of recent U.S. history, one-fifth of its entire lifetime as a nation. In doing so, the recovery of meaning will be similar to the rescue efforts that have restored to significance other lost and unnoted members of the human panorama, Blacks, women, and the poor. It is not a coincidence that UNESCO's newly enfranchised majority represents the two-thirds of the world's population that live on the margins of Western recognition. This majority desperately needs a historical affirmative-action program. At the same time, the United States needs to remember its own past. Its self-inflicted amnesia has for too long encouraged a fateful righteousness — an inflexible, unsympathetic response to those same realities it too experienced as a member of an earlier Third World.

The retrial of *United States v. UNESCO*, on appeal to the higher court of History, will not be bound by the original evidence, which was both too limited and too misleading. New facts must be introduced, different questions must be asked, and alternative interpretations must be explored. Only then can the true significance of this notable event attain the recognition it deserves in the annals of world affairs.

The Real Questions

What is it about this case that cries out for explanation and redress, and why should it not be left to rest in peace in the graveyard where international ideals lie? To begin with, why was UNESCO selected by the Reagan administration for summary punishment? Did the complaint objectively establish its case or was UNESCO a scapegoat satisfying some domestic ideological agenda? Why did the specter of UNESCO become acute when it did and why did the campaign sweep to victory with such ease? What had happened to both the United States and UNESCO over 40 years to bring this separation to pass, and how should the responsibility for it be apportioned between them?

What benchmarks are there along the way to measure the onset of estrangement and disillusion? Was it fated for disaster from the start by some intrinsic incompatibility on one side or the other? Or did each of them fail somehow to adjust to the new realities of international life? Were the issues that delineated the crisis real ones or only rhetorical covers for causes that did not become overt? And were there not alternative courses of action that both the U.S. and UNESCO might have followed to resolve their differences in the spirit of the universalism and idealism that characterized their initial compact of global cooperation?

Beyond these larger questions, there exist other canons of judgment that singularly failed to surface during the final debates. What standards of evaluation should be applied to an international, intergovernmental agency? What are the measurements of its success or failure? What kind of results can rightly be expected in education, science, and culture in the short run when their impact is intended to be slow, indirect, and long-range? What is the relationship between expectations, projects, and resources? How much better or worse did UNESCO manage its far-flung affairs than, say, the U.S. State Department did its own? And how did

UNESCO successfully handle its rapid growth in numbers and goals in an extraordinarily short period of time?

The UNESCO preamble continues to resonate in our ears, calling us back to the declarations of hope of those earlier postwar years. We remember the lofty aspirations and commitments of the founders, architects of a new model of international cooperation. Were they right to make the attempt, or was it but another example of the folly of those who pursue chimerical dreams of mutual understanding and brotherhood?

No, building the defenses of peace in the mind of men is not folly; the folly is to give up trying.

NOTES

All short references are to books and articles cited in full in the bibliography.

1. UNESCO Constitution, in Laves and Thomson, p. 415.
2. Hughes, "Twilight," pp. 25–48.
3. See any Heritage Foundation publication attacking UNESCO. Also "Heritage Foundation Letter raising $75,000 to combat Wagner and Barody," Appendix 5, *Report of a Staff Study Mission to Paris-UNESCO*, House Committee on Foreign Affairs, pp. 55–56.

II. THE INDICTMENT IN CONTEXT

While it is important in criminal detection to recreate or visit the scene of the crime, as we shall do in the narrative body of this account, it is also necessary to have clearly in mind the nature of the supposed criminal act, the charges that have brought the suspect before the bar of historical justice. One need only recall the practices of Rep. Martin Dies of the House Un-American Activities Committee or Sen. Joseph McCarthy of the Senate Government Operations Committee to realize as well that accusation may even precede the commission of an offence, particularly in cases of political excitement. And however extreme or outrageous the indictment, its content and character must be firmly fixed in the public mind so that the people may judge the succeeding discovery of the truth in its proper context. Due process requires no less.

In addition, analysis must clarify exactly what the words may mean. A semantic interpretation is in order. In pursuing an examination of the statements that the U.S. made in building its case against UNESCO, care must be taken to evaluate the terms rigorously. The use of "code" words and expressions that hide ideological assumptions—a crime of which the U.S. finds UNESCO regularly guilty—may also be discovered in the mundane rhetoric of diplomatic discourse.

The U.S. Complaint

The substance of the American complaint first appeared publicly on December 28, 1983 when Secretary of State George P. Shultz delivered his country's notice of intention to withdraw at the end of the following year. Although periodic assessments of the U.S./UNESCO relationship had occurred over the decades in both the Congress and the executive branch of government, none had proposed or even forecast that drastic step. Noting that "trends in the policy, ideological emphasis, budget and management of UNESCO were detracting from the organization's effectiveness . . . [and] led UNESCO away from the original principles of its constitution," Shultz claimed those trends "served the political purposes of member states, rather than the international vocation of UNESCO." Further, he urged the agency "to redirect itself to its founding purposes" and "to rigorously avoid becoming a servant of one or another national policy." Shultz also called for "efficiency" and "fearless program evaluation" and deplored "the injection of political goals" and "the compromise of such goals as individual human rights and the free flow of information."[1]

As Shultz's somewhat terse proclamation was fleshed out in later communications, congressional testimony, and delegate speeches in Paris, the broad themes of U.S. discontent and disillusionment developed their full ideological stature and breadth. Although distorted by echoes of anticommunism, the judgments against UNESCO represented an attack against the Third World majority in the United Nations and its apparently powerful (and to the United States, uncontainable and irresponsible), nationalism. The litany of charges included: (1) politicization: the intrusion of extraneous, controversial, contentious, sensitive, divisive issues into arenas that should remain technical, basic, nonpolitical, and functional; (2) statist or collectivist statist concepts: the intrusion of alternative arrangements for or modifications of current international orders dominated by free-market capitalism and transnational corporations and the tendency to prefer government institutions of development to those of the private sector; (3) group or people's rights: the extension of individual rights to larger entities and into arenas of protection beyond the traditional (reflecting the Four Freedoms,* perhaps, or the example of corporate rights already on the table); (4) majority tyranny in decision-making: the corruption of democracy in UNESCO legislative and executive bodies denying to minority groups veto power over budget allocation and level and program selection.[2] These were the dominant, priority issues that basically accused UNESCO of being a pawn of an adventurous and dangerous non-Western bloc of less developed countries.

---

*The Four Freedoms, announced by President Roosevelt in his State of the Union address to Congress in January 1941 comprised freedom of speech, of worship, from want, and from fear.

Other criticisms focused on UNESCO as a mismanaged, top-heavy, overly centralized, inefficient organization mired in elitism, favoritism, cronyism, and low morale. The usual atrocity stories that circulate in any large bureaucracy, and personal insinuation about the director-general's manic preoccupation with power and bullying tactics, added colorful opportunities for outrage to the overall theme of administrative chaos. Yet these attentions to the internal distress of UNESCO were secondary to the questions of power-sharing and ideological confrontation that remained the real thrust of the indictment. Operational style has often been a red herring for attacks on the substance of program and attitude, the reaction to Franklin D. Roosevelt's New Deal being a good example.[3]

The Ideological Nature of the Attack

Had the ideological mistrust not existed, the purely management defects of UNESCO would probably have been the objects of concerted reform over time. But the issues of ideology and power brought an intensity of feeling and a demand for retribution that could not be resolved within the one-year deadline for change established by the United States. And the best evidence of that obsessive fury was the controversy over the proposed New World Information and Communication Order (NWICO). Perceived as an attack on the free press and the free flow of information, the NWICO became the new subversive phenomenon in international affairs. It aroused the same reactions as cases of seditious libel had in the past. And the U.S. and other Western media gave sensational and distorted accounts of the fearful prospects the NWICO might bring about.

What assumptions can be detected behind the brutal accusations in the indictment? Did the United States really believe this was the first time UNESCO had become "a servant of one or another national policy"? Had it honestly forgotten its own manipulation of UNESCO in line with U.S. national interests or think that an organization of this kind is somehow immune (or could be) from the tawdry and selfish sovereign demands of its membership?

Did the United States assume that the original or true UNESCO operated in the world as a political virgin, solely pursuing an international vocation in an arena devoid of politics and political predators? It seems that the U.S. assumed the existence of conditions that could not come-about until and unless UNESCO had successfully created those defenses of peace in the minds of men, and that was still a distant dream.

"Politicization" is, of course, loaded with negative connotations that verge on the sordid and carry the implications of "playing politics" and political bossdom. It is something "they" do and "we" don't. The neutral, objective, clean alternative, the "grace" from which UNESCO had fallen according to the U.S., appeared under the name of "functionalism," and its most likely practitioners are "experts" with no political axes to grind. An international meteorological union predicting weather comes closest to the "technical self-determination" and autonomy that UNESCO is being called upon to form. It is the pursuit of "realistic, practical, concrete activity." The U.S. must then believe that all there is to "building the defenses of peace" is for UNESCO to engage in some narrow technical work. Saving a monument or teaching an illiterate to read might qualify (if there was an agreement that these projects advanced peace and security and if there was no controversy over which monument or illiterate or in which country and with which values and techniques or from which ideological spectrum of the globe). Even experts have political agendas.[4]

Since UNESCO's statement of purpose provides it with a license to operate as broad as the intellectual vision and cultural diversity of humankind and since it has been asked to play the role of philosopher in the search for peace, an arena bound to generate differences of opinion both as to means and ends, then the accusation of politicization must infer the wrong politics, those to which the United States objects.

Politicization as well as statist concepts and other symbolic forum issues are also charges more accurately aimed at member states, not UNESCO. Since the latter should rightfully air all signals entering its free marketplace of ideas, it is in fact obliged to be a sounding board for the many voices of its constituency. Blaming UNESCO for what its members say is a bit like criticizing Hyde Park for the oratory that blares forth from its many soap-boxes. Would the Reagan administration withdraw from Congress because of the caustic denunciations it regularly receives from its opponents to the left of the Heritage Foundation ?

Once the Pandora's Box of political vilification is open, of course, it may embarrass the accused as well as the accuser. It is a commonplace of international life that the United States has politicized and is still politicizing numerous agencies, including the U.N., that are subservient to its foreign-policy goals and economic objectives. As long as those agencies remain subordinate to the discipline and dictates of the rich and powerful industrial countries, "politicization" of them will not surface as an international issue nor will the virus of disinformation about their affairs undermine their "autonomy" and credibility.[5]

The New Order

Other felonies for which UNESCO is held responsible (statism, group rights, and majority tyranny) encompass the major disagreements about the present and future organization of the world's polity, economy, and culture. What direction should it take and for whose benefit and under whose control? While all three concepts evoke automatic distaste when purveyed as threats to the liberal values and free-market system of the West, their shock value is enhanced by association with the idea of a new international order of one sort or another. This is an act of deliberate semantic gamesmanship to undermine the Third World agenda and give it an obnoxious connotation of over-reaching, absurd change.

There are several ways of looking at the new order phenomenon. One could argue that the real new order is, in fact, the technological and communications revolution, and the resources behind it, propelling the developed, industrialized steamroller across the face of the earth. In opposition to this onslaught, the less developed countries (LDCs) raise cries of objection (and well they might) which translate as peremptory demands for "new orders" of their own rather than as the redress of grievances that they are. The LDCs are thus reported as sponsors of a New International Economic Order (NIEO), NWICO, New World Cultural Order, and even New World Copyright Order. The LDCs resist; decolonization or national liberation has left them politically free but orphans of the economic storm and victims of the pace of technological change. In the international arena their power as a political majority is often circumscribed by the discipline of the capital markets and access to the West's resources, by weighted voting and the veto, by the control of advanced technology and foreign aid, and by the first come, first served allocation of the world's remaining largess. In the face of this power, the "new order" proposals are one chance to influence world opinion and redirect its focus of attention.

Another interpretation of the appearance of new orders is their role as symbols of delayed or incomplete nationalism. One is reminded of the emancipation of southern slaves after the Civil War. Having "been in the storm so long," they envisaged something more than freedom, but did not even receive the promised 40 acres and a mule. And freedom itself was defined by the shackles of segregation and the boundaries of the urban ghetto, the domestic forms of neo-colonialism. The U.S. and the West are still advocating the Booker T. Washington philosophy, hoping to move the Third World into "constructive channels" of collaboration without "abandoning the control of action to them." It is a process that Robert Cox and Harold Jacobson have described as "collective colonialism," wherein international organizations become the proxies for the former imperial powers managing their interests while spreading the costs and shifting the appearances of rule.[6]

In a recent *New Yorker* article, William Pfaff observed that "four of the last five American Presidencies have been damaged or wrecked by attempts to dislodge or dominate radical nationalism in a non-Western country," or by the consequent discovery of illegal operations designed to achieve the same purpose. Although Pfaff did not include UNESCO in his list of examples, the U.S. indictment of UNESCO's character and the extended campaign against its integrity and credibility would seem to represent a similar intervention, another short-term American effort to stop history.[7] In an earlier surge of nationalism, the major powers stared amazed at its power and defused its explosive reality by talking of "the Serbian question" or "the Balkan question" or "the Middle Eastern question." Is it reasonable to think of the West now speaking of "the UNESCO question"?

But to describe U.S. interventions and the nation's apparent innocence of the slow unfolding of its history does not necessarily explain the indictment. What brought it all about in the first place and how did it happen in that particular manner? The long-run historical causes and the acting out of the play must still get us to the final curtain. For that we must turn back to those days when the United States itself assumed an uncertain nationhood and then too quickly became a world power.

NOTES

1. George P. Shultz to Amadou-Mahtar M'Bow, December 28, 1983, MS copy, UNESCO Liaison Office, New York.
2. U.S. National Commission for UNESCO, *What are the Issues*; House Subcommittee on Human Rights and International Organizations, "U.S. Withdrawal from UNESCO," *passim*.
3. *Ibid.*
4. Sewell, *Functionalism*, viii, 3, 5–12, 38, 53–58; Cox and Jacobson, pp. 30–35.
5. Cox and Jacobson, pp. 428–36; Sewell, *Functionalism*, pp. 93–94, 199, 212–15.
6. Cox and Jacobson, pp. 428–36; Litwack, *passim*.
7. Pfaff, pp. 44–56.

III. PATTERNS AND PROBLEMS IN THE AMERICAN PAST

In 1920, after a bitter battle between isolationists and the proponents of collective security, the United States rejected the multilateral option of international cooperation. In 1945 it dove in head first with all its clothes on. This sweeping about face has generally been called the country's coming of age, and *ex post facto* interpretations of isolationism's earlier victory even ascribe the outbreak of World War II in part to American abstinence from its League of Nations responsibilities. Has anyone ever wondered whether the United States made the right decision in 1920 and the wrong one in 1945? Perhaps the country was not ready for internationalism the first time and perhaps it was still not properly prepared for that role when the United Nations system came into being. While that proposition may seem farfetched, it at least raises the question of the maturation that may be necessary for effective committed participation in any system of long-term international collaboration.

The United States is not, of course, the first or only country to run before it learns to crawl; still the question must be asked: How ready was the United States for the immense and complex responsibilities it assumed in UNESCO? What ideological and structural restraints would affect its participation in international cultural cooperation broadly conceived?

Awareness of its own past might be a good place to start, that is a sense of history. The U.S. today seems not to care about the struggle between "memory and forgetting." In fact, the walkout from UNESCO might be considered the end result of a long journey "across the desert of organized forgetting."[1] Had this not occurred, the United States might have understood both itself and its Third World neighbors much better. It then could have engaged in successful cultural relations, listening to and learning from others and perhaps have recognized how it is more culture bound than its supposed antagonists. In other words, being out of touch with its own Third World origins and habits of mind, the U.S.A. has developed a kind of retardation of its ability to function well in organizations dominated by the Third World. What should it remember?

In 1791 Alexander Hamilton, secretary of the treasury of his newly liberated nation, wrote a Report on Manufactures that deplored the inequality and imbalance in his country's trade with Europe. "The lack of reciprocity," he complained, "would render us the victims of a system which would induce us to confine ourselves to agriculture and refrain from manufactures . . . [and] could not but expose us to a state of impoverishment." Hamilton asked the developed world of his day "whether by aiming at too much they do not lose more than they gain."[2] The same issue is alive and well in the less developed world today, as vital and immediate as it was in Hamilton's time. A "system" is still there and it is not radicalism to challenge it.

As a less developed country, the United States also received start-up assistance through foreign aid and greatly benefited from its free ride in the "cultural common market" of the old world, a factor that Philip Coombs believes provided "enormous strength" for development, though it happened in an entirely unplanned manner.[3] And in its own struggle for independence and modernization, the U.S. proclaimed a doctrine of "group rights" in the very expression with which its Constitution opens, "We, the People." It also promoted a variety of economic projects under various forms of "statism," to wit, state-run turnpikes, canals, and railroads and state banks, since it recognized that the free-market private sector lacked the resources to build the essential infrastructure of the market. Even the early press had its financial backing and political outlook determined by linkage with the main political parties of the day whose provision of government printing contracts was not only an essential subsidy but also shaped the flow of news.

Thirty-four years after its constitutional beginnings, this upstart Atlantic coast nation also startled the old world by enunciating a "New World Diplomatic Order" (otherwise known as the Monroe Doctrine) which defined the acceptable terms for European intervention or transfer of colonial property in the Americas. To the established states of Europe, then joined in their own limited United Nations, the Holy Alliance, the brash declaration of such a sweeping re-evaluation of their accustomed rights must have seemed more notorious and outrageous than any of the proposals now emanating from the UNESCO forum in Paris. And for years thereafter American politicians from mayors to presidents pursued the rhetoric of vilification against supposed big-power enemies, in what was then called jingoism, "twisting the British lion's tail" being an especially popular and politically beneficial form of that genre.*

Nor should the United States ever forget the deep-seated anxieties that characterized its own struggle for cultural autonomy and independence or its own fears lest it be the victim of "cultural imperialism." They did not (and do not) differ from the self-protective policy initiatives pursued by Third World countries today. Foreign ideas and "isms" struck a raw nerve as early as 1798 when the Federalists passed the Alien and Sedition Acts. Assuming that "those who corrupt our opinion . . . are the most dangerous of all enemies," the new laws targeted the then most suspect intruder into the internal realm of accepted ideas, the immigrant or French-influenced native dissenter. In today's more sophisticated communication arena, corruption of opinion may emanate from film, radio, television, or direct satellite broadcasting.[4]

The Cult of Subversive Propaganda

The American version of the doctrine of cultural imperialism is, of course, the cult of subversive propaganda that has penetrated deeply into the national psychology. Nativism—that fear of an internal minority because of its supposed foreign connections—flourished throughout the nineteenth century. In the twentieth century nativism joined forces with Americanization programs which were designed to acculturize the outsider to acceptable local norms. Anti-alien and anti-radical repression was imposed by force, by deportation, by immigration and naturalization legislation, and by political trials, all of which served as an earlier substitute for "jamming," the victims being not radio signals but the voices of unwanted diversity in the spectrum of opinion at home.[5]

*As late as the 1930s, the Mayor of Chicago made political capital threatening to punch King George V in the nose were he to visit the windy city.

These traditional phobias, hallmarks of the insecurity of the less developed country the United States once was, did not disappear as it rapidly transformed itself into an industrial giant at the turn of the century. Instead, they seemed to spread and take on institutional shapes, the two most prominent ones being the intelligence services of the FBI, the military, and later the CIA itself, with their covert surveillance functions, and the various congressional committees against subversion or "un-American" activities, investigating all manner of suspect belief and behavior.

The nation's preoccupation with its cultural integrity, a supposedly passing phase of political immaturity, thus became linked to its status as a world power. National security, once designed as protection for the culture within, would now reach out to impose the same demands on the expanded arena of United States involvement without. Both the CIA and the internal security committees were to challenge the U.N. and UNESCO to conduct their operations without violating American definitions of subversive activity anywhere on the earth. And CIA covert cultural operations would not necessarily be building the defenses of peace in men's minds as UNESCO might have imagined.

While anticommunism came to define the limits of dissent, the American liberal center also established standards of acceptable behavior that seem, in hindsight, to have been dress rehearsals for its treatment of unruly Third World proponents of change. The latter, in fact, should themselves have studied the history of popular protest in the United States to avoid having to repeat it. Two examples, both relevant to the UNESCO debate, may illuminate the patterns that still affect the dynamics of power between the United States and those challenging its economic and political dominion. Populism, as the voice of the internal Third World of the time—the less developed regions south of the Mason-Dixon line and west of the Mississippi—mounted a campaign to free itself from economic dependence, political inferiority, and cultural oblivion. The Populists' "unintimidated self-respect," economic cooperation, racial and class unity, and information power represented the most powerful opposition the system had yet experienced. In 1896 Populism went down to a crushing defeat.[6]

Disinformation played a large role in this defeat, as did cultural intimidation and corporate coercion. Aided by the national press and collaborators in the educational and religious hierarchies, the established order revived the animosities and symbolism of the Civil War. They distorted the nature of their opponents' program, instigated racial demagogy, threatened workers, engaged in political fraud, and fomented violence against Populists and their press in a masterpiece of coordinated salesmanship the Heritage Foundation would envy today. The system had once again preempted "the cultural high ground" and stilled the voice of mass insurgency in favor of its own "hierarchical values."[7]

Since this same authority denied American labor effective organizational power for 65 years and drove radicalism out of it, wrecked four radical union movements, isolated and disrupted two major radical political parties, and imposed an impressive self-censorship on the citizen's ability to imagine alternative political programs, its behavior would seem to corroborate two maxims about America's commitment to the free market in ideas. The United States has been excessively hostile to attacks on its basic values and has not been willing to condone free expression that proposes any fundamental transformation in its society. And those points of view have characterized its reactions in the international sphere as well, inhibiting its tolerance for the diversity that universality of organizational membership implies.

If the Populist example might have alerted the Third World to the restraints on popular protest, the American experience with political machines could have instructed them about attitudes toward certain forms of popular government. The Founding Fathers wrote feelingly, of course, on the need to insulate the legislature from the perils of popular passion and the excesses of democracy. And there was considerable elite apprehension about the unrestrained democracy of the frontier as though it were a kind of political hooliganism. George Washington also deplored the "baneful effects of the spirit of party." But it was the urban bosses and their immigrant Third World supporters who most aroused the elite initiative for reform in the late nineteenth and early twentieth century, just as the UNESCO director-general (the "boss") and the Third World majority in the UNESCO General Conference (the machine) are stirring up antagonism today.

Civil Service reformers and Progressives were determined to end the democratic principle of patronage and rotation in office dating back to the early republic. They replaced it with the idea of a career civil service presented as the reward of merit rather than as a privilege of aristocracy. Patronage, in fact, became synonymous with corruption. As Progressives pursued their class interests and power, they also undermined the political cohesion of the masses by other structural innovations; nonpartisan voting, city-wide elections, voter registration, city-manager government, and expert commissions, while a national free market in ideas eroded the local autonomy and class and ethnic roots of popular opinion. U.S. politics shifted from a labor intensive (organized masses) to a capital intensive (financial resources) operation with the consequent impact on its ideology and policies.[8] And this is why the Reagan administration tries to portray Amadou-Mahtar M'Bow as the Boss Tweed of international organizational life today.

Both the defeat of Populism and the attack on political machines represented, of course, battles over the control of opinion and the engineering of consent. Each contest seriously altered and diminished the free flow of information and the free market in ideas. Yet those doctrines have entered the UNESCO debate arena as untarnished and compelling symbols almost totally unburdened by the historical realities of their past. Their mythical power, so obvious in the realm of ideological confrontation, must be juxtaposed against their manipulation and appropriation by interests with other than freedom agendas. There are thus two realms of interpretation, one dealing with flow and market the other with semantic subterfuge or, in its modern format, disinformation.

Free Enterprise and the Media

Individual freedom guaranteed by the U.S. Bill of Rights has, over time, protected not only personal integrity but also property and corporate power, including that of the mass media. "Free enterprise" itself, that shibboleth of the American Way, originally connoted individual enterprise in sharp opposition to its feared nineteenth-century rival, the corporation. The latter took over the value-laden term as it moved to supremacy in the economy and adopted the then current definition of a legal "person" as including corporations (a definition enshrined in the Fourteenth Amendment to the U.S. Constitution), to ensure its freedom from regulation by popular government. It did, however, successfully argue in court that its workers should be entitled to liberty of contract, a freedom that union organization would negate.

As the newspaper business also became corporate and more oligopolistic, free flow and free market became the ideological bulwarks of the producers of information whose immense resources gave them a highly preferred position within the market. They could define the range of realistic alternatives to be considered and control the agenda of discussion. Less influential producers of information succumbed in competitive failure or by governmental attack as the radical, labor, and socialist press did in World War I. Between the effective monopolistic marketing position of the giants and the codes of press behavior imposed for "public safety" and "national security," there was little room for the diversity that free-flowing markets theoretically guarantee. The media universe became the information producers' haven and all the other members of that world simply consumers of their wares, an audience no longer able to market its own opinions and ideas. The free market disseminated information from the top down and on a national basis.[9]

Then, in 1945, the U.S. media recognized the possibilities for power and profit in creating an international forum on the same basis and in shaping the world's perception of reality. UNESCO, they hoped, would be that forum, but, in fact, other voices resisted that blueprint, preferring to remain producers and architects of their own information and destiny.

Alongside the cultural baggage the United States brought from its own liberation, modernization, and rise to imperial power lay the many layers of national interest that defined its traditional outlook on the world. Like the other strata of ideology and structure, these, too, had not yet fossilized and they formed important attitudes conditioning the conduct of a multilateral foreign policy. When the Reagan administration withdrew from UNESCO, in fact, its vocabulary of judgment revived most of the themes that had guided the U.S. since the white man and the Native American concluded their first treaty. The "Big Stick" philosophy of Theodore Roosevelt, the "international police power" he proclaimed that made the U.S. responsible for intervening against "chronic wrongdoing and impotence"; the strange coalition of racism, chauvinism, and moral stewardship with which William McKinley justified the acquisition of the Philippines; Woodrow Wilson's self-righteous missionary diplomacy—shooting Mexicans into an appreciation of self-government; and, it might even be argued, John Foster Dulles's disdain for neutralism and fondness for "massive retaliation," all formed a Greek chorus of echoes out of the U.S. past.

A curious hypocrisy has concealed the contradictory purposes the United States has pursued, most especially from itself. Since the elaboration of its "Manifest Destiny" to expand, its claim of invincibility and omnipotence as Number One has always been framed as a world responsibility, devoid of power-lust and ambition, thrust upon it and reluctantly and unselfishly accepted. However, the public expression of this contradiction, as seen in the perennial conflict between hardliners and liberals, has not emphasized the "Pax Americana" so much as it has delineated the ideology of freedom, equality, opportunity, and justice. Although Grover Cleveland's secretary of state, Richard Olney, might claim that "the United States is sovereign on this continent and its fiat is law,"[10] other doctrinal announcements more typically have suggested Pan-Americanism, the Good Neighbor, free trade, the Open Door, trusteeship, the Peace Corps, the Alliance for Progress, territorial integrity, and equality of treatment in all spheres of influence. At times the United States has even derided its own authority, posing as "Uncle Sucker" during the war debt controversy in the 1920s and as a "pitiful giant" under Richard Nixon.

Yet even while the U.S. defined its empire as "informal," an empire of welfare recipients and client states, it set limits to the choices its beneficiaries might make. It offered them orderly economic growth, stability, technical assistance, and political reform; they in turn had to fit into the world economy on American terms, follow the American model of development regardless of their indigenous culture, and stop short of choosing radical political alternatives. Order took precedence over democracy, and containment against fundamental change in the world system remained a dominant priority. Dollar diplomacy, loan embargoes, and, as UNESCO would learn, financial sanctions against international agencies offending U.S. interests served to enhance the latter's pervasive influence.

This long tradition of unilateral and bilateral foreign policy with its evasive dualism would bring to future multilateral engagements a Herculean uncertainty. Would the U.S. help educate, uplift, and civilize the world as an unselfish partner in the search for mutual understanding and peace? Or would it turn to international nagging, and bully the world into serving its own ends? Would idealism or realism prevail? And would UNESCO become a kind of veiled protectorate, a quasi-colony of American policy or a genuine international partner? At the end of World War II, the United States seemed buoyed by the excitement of world leadership and the allure of altruistic service, but the vita of accomplishment it presented contained an essential ambiguity. Would UNESCO's collaborator be the generous humanitarian peacekeeper or the tough, morally ambiguous adventurer that denied admission to Jewish refugees fleeing the Nazi tyranny but was about to welcome their killers?

A Survey of the History to Come

These patterns of behavior and outlook suggest an overall national character that determines U.S. multilateral responses. They also represent a mosaic of internal domestic interests, all of which play a role in that international relationship. This survey anticipates the history to come, and enhances an understanding of it.

Some dozen major groupings or alignments can be discerned in the broad constituency which will influence UNESCO policy-making. Anticommunist members of the national security establishment see the relationship in East-West terms and view the U.N. system as an instrument of containment against the Soviet challenge throughout the world. Since UNESCO came into being at the onset of the Cold War, it was seen as a potential psychological warrior and propaganda spokesman for Western values in the larger anticommunist struggle.

The grassroots constituency was more diverse, composed of a political spectrum ranging from pro-to anti-U.N. Heirs of the Roosevelt New Deal, and members of the many organizations supporting international collaboration were enthusiastic fans of UNESCO, but some of them were shaken loose from their commitments by the politics of un-Americanism. The snakes in the grassroots from UNESCO's point of view were old America Firsters, American Legionnaires, Daughters of the American Revolution, China-lobbyists, nativists, Congressional investigators of deviance and disloyalty, patriots who distrusted globaloney, and an assortment of neo-isolationists. The F.B.I. would give them intelligence agency support. They came to see UNESCO as an internal security witness being asked, "Are you now or have you ever been anti-American?"

In between extremes, a large, amorphous, almost inert majority slowly fermented, mostly uninformed and inattentive and rarely interested in international news. Since it could not itself shape policies, its role was reactive, created by the impact of the powerful lobbies that interested themselves in world affairs.

Among the most influential and determined of those participants were the media conglomerates, willing and able both to monitor UNESCO and to shape American thinking about it. From the advertisers to the press and broadcasting industries to the wire services to the film and publishing centers, and finally to the technological inventors of the electronic communications future, as exporters of U.S. culture, they were intimately involved in UNESCO's mandate in the same arena. Their hope envisioned the organization as a U.S. communications consortium; if it were not to be, they would be the first to know and to publicize their displeasure.

Other exporting industries were expected to support UNESCO's contributions to international standards facilitating trade, to international scientific advancement, and to the creation of a more stable, educated, and prosperous consumer society. Cognizant of the economic realities and geopolitical nuances of the global marketplace, they were ready to support the multilateral negotiation of technical assistance and foreign aid directed to development.

UNESCO also attracted the attention of single-issue lobbies as its broad mandate intersected with their agendas. Monument restoration and preservation, for example, might entice the tourism following. International training and support of the arts could reach out to that specific community and its patrons. On a more negative note, peace and disarmament projects could upset the Pentagon, banks, and the arms industry. So, too, the programs of education or archaeological reconstruction if focused on refugees or sited in disputed territories might alienate supporters of one or another nation.

On the other hand, UNESCO attracted a significant following of intellectuals, professionals, academics, artists, and free-lance adherents of good works, scattered in the educational, scientific, and cultural nongovernmental organizations linked to UNESCO's goals. It was a large, diverse constituency accustomed to international cooperation and eager to pursue it. Whether it could be united on behalf of this new U.N. alliance was unclear. It lacked practice in pressure-group influence, had notable inexperience in publicity, and thus a traditional, fragmented disciplinary outlook, often consumed by its passion for narrow over-specification in exotic fields. Functionalists and technocrats might not see the big picture or want to; others might simply settle into the grant-supported world of UNESCO as if they had joined yet another university seminar.

All these publics were to be eventual booby traps for UNESCO's presence on the national foreign-policy scene; and none was more dangerous to UNESCO than the formulator and administrator of that policy, the executive branch of the U.S. government and its State Department. Largely freed from accountability because of its abstruse and secret nature and its distance from the focus of public interest, foreign policy in general has always been the prerogative of the president and his advisers. This is true not only of big power diplomacy and bilateral relations; it is even more obvious in the conduct of international multilateral affairs, especially with the numerous lesser members of the United Nations system. A president can, of course, orchestrate significant attention to any international body by the stature of the people he appoints as delegates and by the notoriety and emphasis he directs to the execution of its business. The U.N. itself was often to be the beneficiary of such respect. It was not clear whether UNESCO would attract or sustain a similar concern and status.

However, even if it were out of the orbit of presidential attraction, UNESCO could still retain a significant hold within the State Department. But crucial developments would have to occur first. The department would have to make multilateral diplomacy a priority, invent and foster a bureau devoted to cultural relations and deem this pursuit important, stimulate foreign-service career officers to serve by appropriate patterns of reward and promotion, nominate outsiders of prestige and influence to the UNESCO ambassadorship and mission, and see to it that other policies did not undermine the programs designed to enhance and fulfill UNESCO's goals.

The executive response would surely create much of the setting in which the hopes for UNESCO's future would or would not be fulfilled. Not education, nor science, nor culture is likely to make the front page of the paper. Nor do they provide an attractive and immediate a reward for practitioners of diplomacy. The foreign-service establishment was thus both immune from public pressure with a creative free hand at the UNESCO desk and, at the same time, ambiguous and uncertain about engaging in that creativity. And that tension between opportunity and neglect was a counterpoint to the larger polarity between commitment to national interest on the one hand and to international service and cooperation on the other.

While the United States brought to the UNESCO idea a certain traditional ideology and character, formed during a century and a half of national experience, it also was influenced in its response by its own immediate historical background. Although UNESCO itself was still not even a dream in some philosopher's mind, premonitions of it were beginning to stir in the aftermath of the first great global conflagration.

The 1920s and '30s spawned some of the theories that came together in 1945 and those same years further underlined the issues that were to make UNESCO such an attractive option for the peacemakers. Both the shock of the bloodbath in the trenches and the consequent evil fury of Nazi doctrine and propaganda seemed to bring the same desperate and urgent message: someone had to dam the flow of hatred and intolerance lest the world be submerged forever in the violent manifestations of that bitterness.

NOTES

1. The quotations are from Kundera.
2. Quoted by Seth Spaulding in his "Panel Commentary," in Department of State, *Critical Assessment*, p. 12. Emphasis added.
3. Coombs, pp. 140–42.
4. Preston, *Aliens and Dissenters*, p. 22.
5. *Ibid.*, *passim*; Goldstein, *passim*.
6. Goodwyn, *passim*.
7. *Ibid.*
8. Ginsberg, pp. 118–19, 149–76.
9. *Ibid.*; Rosenberg, pp. 178–233.
10. Quoted in LaFeber, p. 262.

IV. THE NAZI CHALLENGE AND TWO WORLD WARS: THE HOSTILE IMAGINATION UNLEASHED[1]

If war is 13,000 years old, as some experts believe, it has probably engaged the attention of reformers for almost as long.[2] However, its twentieth-century configuration has added new dimensions of analysis to that reform impulse because the same economic and technological advances that have made war more total and more devastating have also made its control more possible. Yet even here humanity faces another double bind; the means of communication and mutual understanding may *cause* as well as *prevent* the outbreak of conflict. As William Randolph Hearst told one of his photographers on his way to Cuba in 1898, "You furnish the pictures and I'll furnish the war."[3] Indeed, education could be a source of chauvinism and unreasoning antagonism toward all neighboring states.

As far back as the Thirty Years War the idea of intellectual cooperation in the cause of peace had surfaced. In the nineteenth century and more frequently still in the twentieth, institutes and scientific associations had taken on international shapes in the hope of solving common problems, sharing knowledge, and instilling the habit of cooperation at least among the educated elite. When mass public education became an adjunct of the modern state and when popular journalism with its vast circulation rose to preeminence in the industrialized West, could modern mass propaganda be far behind? World War I answered that questions.[4]

All the participants quickly exploited the enormous propaganda potential of mass communications and the mass marketing of grotesque poster images to turn public opinion against the enemy. Dehumanizing and demonizing each other with tales of unimaginable brutality and violence, the combatants clearly understood, as George Creel's American Committee on Public Information asserted, that they were in "a fight for the mind of mankind." But the excesses of that information debauchery led some of the survivors to contemplate the communication horror they had created in succeeding years. The advent of radio raised the stakes even higher since access to men's minds could now be instantaneous, world wide, across national borders, and apparently unstoppable. It was beginning to sink in to a few men's minds that "propaganda is an armament" and, if the world were to survive, it better be disarmed in the war of words.[5]

Stunned by the ferocious impact of mass communications, yet trapped by the usual cultural lag in the face of rapidly changing technology, reformers took a few uncertain steps forward to control the propaganda menace in the interwar years, proposals that would anticipate the postwar debates in UNESCO. One route led down the traditional elite road of intellectual cooperation, a trickle-down version for dispensing mutual understanding. Another recognized the mass base of international friction and attacked the abuses of radio. A third position acknowledging the narrow political orientation of the League of Nations stressed that the collective security mandate protecting territorial integrity was not enough. Numerous nations, therefore, fashioned new programs of cultural relations as part of their normal foreign-policy outlook. And a fourth point of view featuring the role of the press evaluated the reasons for its failure to promote better international harmony. Taken together these activities testified to increasing global concern over the underlying economic, social, cultural, and ideological origins of conflict among nations. The technological revolution had now moved them all into potentially malevolent proximity living a broadcast away from the mob mentality.

If human beings were to clean up their act, what innovations and ideas would spur them on? A League Committee formed in 1921 invented the International Institute of Intellectual Cooperation five years later (IIIC), largely a French-influenced approach. In 1925 the International Bureau of Education was founded to promote cooperation at the elementary and secondary levels neglected by the IIIC. The International Council of Scientific Unions stood as the preeminent representative of the unofficial collaboration of the world's scientists. France, Germany, the Soviet Union, and the United Kingdom, meanwhile, led in governmental attention to transnational cultural affairs. While these supposed a positive long-range fallout of beneficial results, the fast track of immediate reform dealt with the press and radio where "menacing, inflammatory, subversive, and war-mongering" incitements could easily undercut whatever positive effects more abstract detached formulas were having on the international mind.[6]

Broadcasting and Interwar Propaganda

While it has become customary to ascribe ulterior motives to Soviet peace and disarmament schemes, in fact they surfaced as a contemporary and Western response to radio broadcasting's more insidious propensities. As early as 1922, corporate spokesman Owen D. Young, president of General Electric, warned the nations of Europe to beware that medium's dangerous side—propaganda—urging them to refrain from "hurl[ing] insults at each other in furious language." Soon thereafter in 1927 some international legal authorities suggested that states had the responsibility to control "propaganda, fake news, or defamation" directed at foreign countries by citizens of their own nation. Twenty-seven states passed such legislation. The 1928 Kellogg-Briand Pact outlawing war implied that incitements to war were equally criminal and should be brought within the rule of law (a notion later pursued at Nuremberg). A number of nations signed bilateral treaties doing just that, and in 1936 at the Geneva Convention on Broadcasting in the Cause of Peace, twenty-two nations agreed "to insure that their transmissions do not constitute an incitement to war, or to acts likely to lead to war." Neither the three Axis powers nor the United States signed, the latter insisting on the private nature of its media from which only "voluntary and patriotic cooperation" could be requested. In 1933 and again in 1940, Latin Americans nurtured agreements to use radio to foster good will among them and to avoid disruptive and defamatory broadcasts.[7]

As the fascist dictatorships got a feel for the "total radio" concept, the quantity of libelous and subversive propaganda in the air increased dramatically. Designed to destroy morale and unity abroad and prepare the minds of their own people for war, these preparatory communication forays behind soon-to-be enemy lines helped create the concept of group libel. As a defense this is, of course, a people's or group's rights policy since it protects from malicious defamation any group, class, or race, and even under some legislation any profession or religion. Defined as unprotected speech in the United States in the 1952 Supreme Court decision, *Beauharnais v. Illinois* (343 U.S. 250), group libel became a recognized rule of international law, even though it had little effect on the circulation thereafter of "false and slanderous charges" among the world's sovereign states.[8]

Although ideological warfare, which could be called the Fifth Column of the air, dominated the nefarious abuse of radio in the 1930s, other broadcasters tried to shape minds in less aggressive ways. The imperial powers used short-wave transmission of information to help maintain control over their colonies scattered around the globe. And the League created "Radio Nations" in an unsuccessful effort to promote mutual understanding and good will. Failure to stem the tide of false news and disinformation in those decades led still others to champion the international right of reply as a legally enforceable self-defense, a sort of equal time to build the ramparts of peace occasionally. The International Juridical Congress favored it in 1929, and the International Federation of Journalists followed suit in 1934. The United States, where the idea was an anomaly, remained opposed, although the right did not contradict the free-flow/free-market traditions of that nation.[9]

Fascination with the power and responsibility of radio as the favored medium of international communications did not impede examination of the press. In successive League-sponsored conferences between 1926 and 1932, experts explored such issues as "property rights in news," identity cards, peacetime censorship, and expulsion of journalists. Supporting free-press principles in general, these same meetings echoed the concerns expressed about the broadcast media and called upon the publishing industry to avoid news "causing international misunderstanding and suspicions detrimental to peace." Participants even promoted a "professional code of honor" with an enforcement instrument to prevent "false information" from attaining wider circulation.[10] Enlarging on ideas of press responsibility dating back to 1893, the League of Nations also passed resolutions in 1927 opposing all news that was "obviously inaccurate, highly exaggerated, or deliberately distorted" and called on the press not "to cause . . . suspicions detrimental to international peace." In 1931 the International Federation of Journalists set up a "tribunal of professional honor with the power to declare unworthy anyone publishing mendacious information capable of arousing the public against a foreign nation." And Czechoslovakia and Switzerland took steps to block the importation and circulation of foreign propaganda literature. The New World Information Order was already struggling to be born.[11]

Although the United States succumbed to the lure of poisonous propaganda during World War I, its official policy during the interwar years upheld the free-flow/free-market doctrines on behalf of a free-enterprise press. It remained, therefore, opposed to or aloof from various reform proposals that attempted to create legal sanctions controlling the explosion of contaminated information, though it supported the international cultural cooperation then just beginning to take important shape. However, several significant challenges to this high-minded liberal neutrality led the U.S. into policy initiatives contradictory to the pure private-sector free-flow philosophy by which it defined its international stand. These challenges included: the European cartel of news agencies, the radio and right-of-reply regulations adopted abroad, the Axis propaganda offensive in Latin America, and its own development of cultural relations as an instrument of national policy.

On its face, U.S. opposition to the world-wide division of wire-service rights among the British, French, and German press associations seemed to strike a blow for the free-market philosophy of competition. Ever since its formation in 1870, the Associated Press had rankled at this monopolistic agreement, and, after its 1907 founding, the United Press objected as well. Still it was consistent with the trust movement then underway in the United States, of which John D. Rockefeller was the imaginative and leading proponent. However, criticisms leveled by the U.S. agencies against the European cartel, not only anticipated later denunciations by the Third World but also raised questions about bias in the free market of news, those innate distortions produced by culture and national origin themselves. To the U.S. the cartel's coverage was "slanted" both in the selection of stories and the rewriting of them. The European wire services negatively misrepresented the U.S. scene and favored news serving the "diplomatic and imperial interests" of their own nations. At the Geneva meetings, the United States felt, however, that "false news" had nothing to do with culture or even monopoly power; it had its origin in government control and the solution was a free press. It would never admit that news was a commodity, even while arguing for property rights in that news.[12]

The broadcast regulations being proposed and adopted in Europe against war-mongering and subversive and defamatory propaganda should have won the support of the U.S. free-market advocates, for they went no further in theory than the Federal Communications Commission did. Radio was, after all, licensed by the U.S. government, operated in the "public interest and convenience,"[*] and had to observe the fairness doctrine. Given the immense harm radio propaganda could inflict, "this broader responsibility [of regulatory collaboration] cannot be disclaimed," one critic asserted, "by merely invoking the phrase 'free speech.' " An international obligation required something more. As already noted, support for an international right of reply did not even involve a violation of the free-market ideology, although it might have been seen in the United States as an invasion of the press owners' property rights.[13]

However, when Axis propaganda took on an international character and began promoting an intellectual imperial intervention into Latin America, this cultural subversion aroused Monroe Doctrine reflexes to the north. The free-enterprise flow of information did not seem to promise that truth would, in fact, defeat lies in the free marketplace of ideas. What the Axis "total radio" *Blitzkrieg* had done was to suggest how inequality of power, resources, and content can undermine the very mean-

[*]By the Federal Communications Act of 1934.

ing of marketplace theory. Radio Berlin was a media giant able to establish a preferred position, drive out less powerful voices, and control the agenda of debate. The United States had to respond, but it was not sure exactly how to do so. If it remained fixated on pure and simple free-flow doctrine, the government might do nothing at all, but then the fascists might win an influential ideological share of the Latin American mind — and market.

The U.S. solution embraced a government initiative with a covertly funded private-sector component aimed partially at the elite leadership but directed also to the public at large and not sure in its self-definition whether it was a national-security project or another Open Door adventure in missionary diplomacy. The U.S. would have preferred the world to convert to its way of life, attracted by the very "exceptionalism" of their values. In that sense, it must have imagined cultural relations as a kind of genetic-engineering experiment to turn the international mind into the American mind. But soft-sell liberalism always had a harder side of national interest that foreigners distrusted. As Margaret Blanchard has argued, the United States knew how to combine "noble intentions" and "nobility of purpose" with "self-interest" and "commercial advantage."[14]

Fighting Axis Propaganda

To turn aside the Axis threat and position itself in the arena where minds are actively shaped, the U.S. government created the State Department's Division of Cultural Relations in 1938 and the office of the Coordinator of Inter-American Affairs in 1940. The United States thus became the last of the big powers to adopt culture as a part of its diplomatic outreach, and it did so for reasons that deformed its cultural-relations program for years to come. Beginning as a negative reaction to an alien ideology, it remained rooted in a defensive stance of bipolar anti-Nazi and later anticommunist extremism without paying sufficient regard to the feelings of the people to whom it was directed. The U.S. lacked the sense of reciprocity, that ear for local culture and its message for the U.S. It tended to be yet another conversion experience. These attitudes were to plague the U.S.-UNESCO relationship as well. In addition to their reactive origins, cultural relations also suffered from the immediacy of the crisis that brought them into being. The U.S. was fighting off the inroads overseas of Nazi propaganda, which demanded instant results and thus led to an emphasis on short-run returns over long-run benefits in cultural contacts.[15]

Initially the Division of Cultural Relations focused on Latin American elites with student exchanges to the U.S., designed to instill pro-U.S. attitudes among the candidates for leadership positions at home. The United States' own intellectual modernization had by then created a superstructure of institutions with which the government could collaborate to keep its own intervention at a distance. The American Council of Learned Societies, the American Library Association, the Institute of International Education, and the American Council on Education would serve this purpose. Quickly abandoning the notion of cultural reciprocity, the office of Inter-American Affairs went into action by covertly funding private organizations to promote State Department cultural policies; those in turn became increasingly oriented to national-security ends. Exclusion of the ideologically suspect foreign-exchange candidate led to war-time visa denials for Pablo Neruda owing to Communist Party membership and Jacques Maritain for his Gaullist connections.[16]

The two programs expanded rapidly. In Latin America by the war's end, 27 cultural centers were operating and 200 American schools were receiving OIAA financial support through the American Council on Education. In 1941 the Division of Cultural Relations had moved into China hoping to induce "intellectual liberalization." By then a second level of covert involvement had developed: The OSS secretly bankrolled a graduate school of journalism at Chungking in 1943. A Near East section began operations in the same year, so that in 1945, the year UNESCO was given constitutional form, the United States had 48 cultural-relations officers and 70 libraries in some 30 countries. The purpose of all this was still to penetrate the minds and control the behavior of others along U.S. lines by "completing the global liberal revolution begun by Great Britain." Americans apparently believed that culture "could wield irresistible political influence" and that they could Americanize the world without manipulating it.[17]

As the United States was improvising its cultural-relations policies, that program itself was overtaken by the impact of World War II, a mobilization of ideology that added new techniques and strategies to the assault on men's minds. Both the Office of War Information (OWI) and the Office of Strategic Services (OSS) had a role in this modernization of propaganda which influenced the nation's opportunity for effective cultural relations and multilateral cultural cooperation in UNESCO. Formed in 1942, the OWI, under leaders like Archibald MacLeish and Elmer Davis, hoped it could deliver the facts and contribute to the "informed and intelligent understanding" necessary to sustain wartime morale and to formulate agreement on and support for the allies' postwar goals. MacLeish and Davis were, perhaps, premature UNESCO utopians already imagining ways to build the defenses of peace. Their point of view was rapidly victimized by the military bureaucracy, chary of sharing information and of truth-talking, and by the political leadership that distrusted the liberal definition of the postwar world. They wanted to suppress the facts about Vichy, China, colonialism, and other embarrassing political realities. Although it had not wanted to manipulate opinion, the OWI became an adjunct of military-sponsored psychological warfare and win-the-war boosterism. By 1945 OWI propaganda could claim that nowhere in the world must the U.S. "renounce its moral and ideological interests . . . as a powerful and righteous nation."[18]

Information as deception and covert dirty tricks symbolized the wartime operations of the OSS under Colonel William Donovan. Totally false (or "black") propaganda, designed to disrupt enemy plans and destroy enemy morale, became ingrained as a legitimate arm of the national-security interest without regard to its impact on the practitioners or the U.S. citizenry and constitutional system. Subverting and transforming facts became an intelligence agency obsession, one that would become a covert companion to the more overt forces of international persuasion. The United States would come to UNESCO with intelligence operations controlled by an elite to shape the minds of men in other ways. Even the ideal of international education, to which UNESCO would devote so much of its resources, may have had a hidden U.S. agenda attached to it. In 1943 Congress set up a Liaison Committee on the subject to promote the plan for a U.N. permanent educational agency to assume for the United States its "habitual and unpopular role of missionary to the world."[19]

By the end of World War II, the nations of the world and their peoples had obviously embraced and fortified the "hostile imagination" to an extent never before believed possible. The technology of hate and deception and the evil undercurrents of slander and defamation had contaminated cultural relations for some three decades. Yet numerous countries and their intellectual and professional elites had also created institutional opportunities for human solidarity and transnational cooperation. Mind changing had been and would remain one of the foremost priorities of the day and possibly the only way out of the slums of violence in which the "hostile imagination" must always dwell. But what form would that mind changing take under whose control and for what ends?

From the U.S. experience a large number of options seemed possible. The United States could adopt the multilateral UNESCO approach to shape the minds of men or it could improve and ensure the full reciprocity of its own cultural-relations activities. It might also turn its cultural relations into a unilateral weapon of an aggressive foreign policy, a kind of cultural pacification program. A combination of overt and covert cultural diplomacy might also be utilized to spread American values and reconstitute the international mind. The United States might even make UNESCO an instrument of its own cultural priorities if it had the political influence to do so.

The choices seemed clearly delineated. Would culture or information as propaganda dominate? Would minds be shaped by the fast media or the slow? Would cultural relations be truly reciprocal or one way? Would the national interest and the American way triumph or would universalism and cultural relativism prevail? It had, unfortunately, been the common experience everywhere for the truth to yield to the propaganda of self-interest and national security. But as the exhausted victors looked out over the smoking ruins of battle in 1945, building the defenses of peace in the minds of men must not have seemed such a bad idea.

NOTES

1. The term "hostile imagination" appears in Keen.
2. *Ibid.*, p. 16.
3. Whitton and Larson, p. 28.
4. Karp, pp. 1–18; Sathyamurthy, pp. 15, 17; Whitton and Larson, pp. 1–3, 249.
5. Keen, pp. 25, 29, 33–40, 44, 49, 52, 61–62; Whitton and Larson, pp. 1–4; Preston and Ray, p. 2.
6. Karp, pp. 6–16; Sathyamurthy, p. 17; Whitton and Larson, pp. 9–10; Laves and Thomson, pp. 10–17.
7. Whitton and Larson, pp. 3–4, 62, 65, 70–76, 124–28, 161.
8. *Ibid.*, 34–38, 105–23.
9. *Ibid.*, 34, 189–90.
10. Blanchard, pp. 11–14.
11. Whitton and Larson, pp. 6, 249–50.
12. Blanchard, pp. 5–15.
13. Whitton and Larson, pp. 160–61, 187–89.
14. Blanchard, pp. 4, 8.
15. Ninkovich, pp. 2–3, 11, 26–52.
16. *Ibid.*; Karp, pp. 16–17.
17. Ninkovich, pp. 55–75; Karp, p. 17.
18. Winkler, pp. 31, 35, 50–51, 156, and *passim.*
19. Preston and Ray, p. 3; Ninkovich, p. 75.

V. UNESCO'S ORIGINS: LIBERAL HOPES AND LIBERAL ASSUMPTIONS

Historians studying the wartime statements that U.S. political leaders made about the significance of and the necessity for international educational and cultural exchange must surely believe they are witnessing an assembly of faith healers selling ideological nostrums to an audience of true believers. The revival atmosphere that characterized this burst of utopian expectations had its inevitable backlash, but at the time no one seemed aware of national and international political realities. Quite the opposite. The deluge of slaughter and the menace of its total and final climax under the atom's bright sun only confirmed the authenticity of everyone's incredible paroxysm of hope.

Secretary of State Cordell Hull, a Tennessee pragmatist, began the exhortation in 1940 when he insisted that "education has a role of the first importance to play in building the foundations of a just and lasting peace." At the 1945 U.N. founding conference in San Francisco, President Harry Truman urged the gathering to "set up an effective agency for consistent and thorough interchange of thought and ideas, for there lies the road to a better and more tolerant understanding among nations and among peoples." His secretary of state, James M. Byrnes, added, "I can conceive of no more important endeavor than to make the mind of man a constructive force for peace. That effort is fundamental . . . men work together most effectively when they have learned to think together and feel together." And alluding to the nuclear menace, Byrnes concluded that "basic security lies in the creation of mutual trust and confidence among the peoples of the world."[1]

In London, Prime Minister Clement Attlee keynoted UNESCO's November 1945 founding conference by raising the basic question, "Do not wars, after all, begin in the minds of men?" Were the "peoples of the world . . . [not] islands shouting at each other over seas of misunderstanding?"[2] And J. B. Priestley called the meeting "the most underrated conference in all history." William Benton, assistant secretary of state and vice-chairman of the American delegation also claimed that UNESCO in its potentialities was "the most underrated organization in history" and could "weigh the balance for peace." Pursuing a "democracy of mind and spirit" where "every culture would be free to live and develop," Benton believed UNESCO might become "a force of the first magnitude" for "peace and prosperity by a moral and intellectual revolution." No piece of the U.N. system was "more intimately related with the day by day life of people and more necessary"; it would be "part of a great plan of worldwide teamwork" and "indispensable."[3]

Certain that UNESCO could reflect the "depth and fervor of the human hope and expectation" that created it, Archibald MacLeish, chairman of the U.S. delegation, confirmed that the organization was of "particular importance" to his countrymen helping them and all their fellow citizens elsewhere "to root out the prejudice and ignorance which have separated them in the past." UNESCO would be, in fact, "a new thing in the history of international undertakings." The U.S. public apparently agreed, for 85 percent of them in a 1945 poll favored an organization "which would marshall the forces for understanding among the peoples of the world."[4]

As Benton defined the project, its very immensity did not seem to daunt him or others. They were going to accomplish the intellectual equivalent of geology's continental drift, moving the people of the earth from their nation-bound assertions of "my country, right or wrong" to a far-reaching "my world, my human race," and in a tiny fraction of geological time.[5] They pictured schools all over the globe that would "teach children how to understand the peoples of other countries." And they acknowledged that UNESCO's responsibilities would be "as wide and intangible as the human mind and spirit."[6]

If this mandate was to be "as vast as it was imprecise" and, as one critic later complained, with "a bannerhead phrase that had all the resounding opacity of such phrases at their most dense," did anyone then wonder whether the joint convulsion of optimism had any dangerous side effects?[7] The French, in their eternal, cynical practicality, did, suggesting that the UNESCO project just might be "a pork barrel riding on a cloud."[8] Yet in just sixteen days of intense consultation in London in November 1945, 44 nations concocted a constitution giving concrete paper reality to their dreams and hopes. Within a year the United States Congress had passed legislation committing their country to this adventurous undertaking by an "overwhelming" vote of approval.[9] It would turn out to be the high point of allied unity and of American political enthusiasm. Other currents of ill-will and misunderstanding were already in circulation, and the great UNESCO gamble still faced the hurdles of self-definition and organizational integrity.

The New Multilateralism

If those explorers of international intellectual and cultural cooperation bravely set sail for a distant shore, what kind of multilateral vessel was to carry them there and did it have a compass? Multilateralism is, of course, a far more complicated operation than the favored two-way diplomatic intercourse. What is more, the nations assembled in London were embarking on a cultural and educational voyage, even though those topics remained subordinate to political, military, and economic interests. Moreover, this was a multilateral experiment at a time when even their bilateral training was still underdeveloped. And the UNESCO founders were imagining a mass experiment in the most novel and untested fields of human endeavor.

It is interesting to compare what was being said at that very time about the U.S. State Department to get a sense of the odds against it. In *A Modern Foreign Policy for the United States*, Joseph M. Jones, a career foreign-service officer, wrote, "The Department is an unbelievably inefficient organization. It is not run, it just jerks along."[10] And Secretary of State Dean Acheson recalled that, "Nobody has been able to run the [State] Department in 150 years." Even if these statements were exaggerated, they represented a lack of planning of clear lines of authority and function, and of coordination. Presidents had often deplored the State Department's "built in inertia, deadened initiative, and tendency toward excessive delay."[11] Some years later Dean Rusk was to say that "the heart of the bureaucratic problem [in State] is the inclination to avoid responsibility."[12] If UNESCO was to surmount the bureaucratic problems endemic to the conduct of foreign affairs and fulfill the goals of its founders, it would also have to be something new under the sun in that quagmire of administration. The miracle in purpose would have to be accompanied by a miracle in management as well.

The planners, of course, were as optimistic in creating the structure of operations as they had been in delineating the goals. They believed they had inoculated UNESCO against the most common infections of international collaboration and armed it against the propensity to self-destruct. In the first place, it was to be independently run by a cadre of international civil servants free from the taint of national self-interest and governmental control. Loyalty to one's country was to be perfectly compatible with loyalty to internationalism, promoting "security and welfare everywhere" being true service to one's own country's highest interests.[13] UNESCO staff members would also have those qualities of "integrity, conviction, courage, imagination, drive, and technical grasp" that would guarantee professional, objective, and successful organizational performance.[14] In his testimony to Congress, Benton said the United States had the obligation "not to seek to exert influence upon the U.S. citizens who may be chosen for that staff."[15]* Their selection, in fact, would largely be guided by the nations' professional and voluntary organizations recommending candidates to their governments, and doing so as members of the UNESCO National Commissions in each country. The director-general and his staff would not "seek or receive instructions from any government or any authority exterior to the organization." Thus insulated and backed by the nongovernmental organizations (NGOs), UNESCO would represent "people speaking to people" through their own representative institution.[16]

Not only would this provide an independent civil service, it would also guarantee an unbiased, objective search for knowledge and its nonpartisan formulation and exchange in the name of mutual understanding. UNESCO's hard currency would be neutral and technical and apparently universally accepted truths as certain as the data discovered by the natural sciences. The founders seemed to have envisioned a World Bank of Knowledge protected against fraud by some pure fact and idea law or fair trade in information legislation. To control the hair-trigger of political outrage by nation states, UNESCO would not publish anything offensive to them or engage in any activity that constituted an "intervention in matters essentially in [their] domestic jurisdiction." The U.S. Congress, for example, excluded atomic energy and any "information or knowledge . . . in which such disclosure is prohibited by any law of the United States."[17] UNESCO certainly was not to possess the authority to tell any government what to do; it was essentially "a service and advising institution," conceiving, planning, and proposing the programs that

*However, the practice was quite the contrary. See below, at Section VI, Subsection B.

its international secretariat believed to be the most essential defenses of peace that could be built in men's minds.[18]

Nor would the world's intellectual leadership in UNESCO follow any narrow partisan definition of its expansive mission, for they would speak in "all the universal languages of science, art and learning."[19] As a partnership of all cultures, UNESCO would preserve and stimulate each of them in a truly reciprocal interchange of traditions, values, and ideas, honoring each for its unique contribution to the total "planetary" civilization in which they all must co-exist.[20] Fundamental to the success of the United Nations, UNESCO would command the respect of the learned communities for its fair-minded objectivity, of governments for its international neutrality, and of peoples for its cultural sensitivity. This may have been the UNESCO of which George Shultz was thinking when he urged it to return to its "original principles" and "founding purposes," but that UNESCO had not, of course, ever existed except, perhaps, in the dreams of its founders.

Several contemporary and timely warnings, however, cautioned its original nation-state members to abide by the rules and allow UNESCO the fair-play latitude to live up to those expectations. William Benton said it would remain "only a piece of paper if starved for leadership or funds or bypassed when governments deal with knotty problems."[21] Jaime Torres-Bodet, who was to become UNESCO's second director-general, reminded the founding conference that if its programs "educated for peace while life itself taught war, we should not be creating men, we should be breeding victims of life."[22] Nor could the search to reduce tensions and misunderstanding avoid "debate on the ultimate issues of life" and simply exchange "meaningless agreement on shallow generalities about the unity of mankind," as Reinhold Niebuhr pointed out.[23] Countries would have to accept some diminution of their sovereignty and find a national interest in UNESCO's work itself; cultural exchange could not become cultural politics or the ideals of 1945 would be vitiated at the start. More important, since communication between peoples could as easily intensify fear as ease their mutual suspicions, its quality would necessarily become one of UNESCO's primary concerns. All in all, the founders had written a menu that allowed no substitutions; the question was whether they would now order à la carte.[24]

"Free Press" and the UNESCO Constitution

Testing of the UNESCO constitution began with its formulation and has continued to the present. As definitions of purpose and organizations of power, constitutions attract politics the way honey lures flies. Since the UNESCO idea blossomed as part of a victor's peace among allies with their own national agendas and was then given flesh and blood by its first leadership, the liberal hopes and assumptions had to be reconciled with both the realities of certain self-serving intentions and the practical adjustments to life of the organization itself. What did the U.S. think the constitution meant, and how did other countries and UNESCO itself perceive it? And what did they all want it to become?

The United States brought a wish list of national political priorities linked to its traditional foreign-policy aims and its current status as the postwar world's dominant power. It still believed in the open-door concept of informal empire, a free-trade/free-market position that regarded international organizations as important elements in reducing barriers to free flow of all kinds and in stabilizing internal order wherever those barriers collapsed. Confident in its ability to disperse its immense resources and know-how effectively and thereby triumph in any competitive contest, the U.S. preached international cooperation while practicing elite control. If imperium once followed the flag, it now might find entry through international standards legitimized by collective agreement. UNESCO might reproduce Western-style economic liberalism and political values in the name of the free-flow concept of mutual understanding. Today UNESCO, tomorrow the world.

However, influencing the minds of men and creating that mutual understanding were the Pandora's box of politics in the history of the United States relationship with UNESCO. It is one of the immense ironies of the postwar era that the world war would be followed by the war of words, as nations realized the limitless opportunities of mass communications in changing values and perspectives. The Information Age was dawning and the UNESCO preamble invited its constituents to "build the defenses of peace" on a global scale and thereby modify behavior everywhere. The United States naturally believed it had the resources, skills, and point of view to achieve this purpose single-handedly. It was a mission waiting to happen.

Realizing that culture now "could wield irresistible political influence," a fact underscored by the prewar and wartime propaganda successes, the U.S. delegation to UNESCO insisted that communications receive an equal emphasis with education, science, and culture as one of UNESCO's main priorities.[25] And the U.S. meant, of course, mass communications, for those were the fast track of immediate impact on minds as opposed to the traditional instruments of the "slow" print media in the other three arenas. "Ideas," Benton insisted, "are weapons" and the mass media obviously were the information equivalent of missile delivery systems. Unleashing the U.S. media by guaranteeing the international freedom of the press, breaking the foreign wire-service cartel's monopoly of world news, and promoting "the free enterprise model of news dissemination" would thus tie the self-interest of U.S. publishers, broadcasters, and wire-service owners to UNESCO's search for the architecture of peace.[26]

U.S. journalistic entrepreneurs purported to be convinced that a free press and the free exchange of news would end international misunderstandings and prevent war. Dismissing their commercial ambitions and profitable investments as irrelevant, the media leaders defined their product as unbiased, impartial, and reliable, in fact, the basis of peace, since their news would not be tainted or falsified by government censorship or control. So intense was this commitment to the free-market ideology that they strenuously opposed at first any United States government information activity at all in the postwar international sphere. William Benton and his State Department allies had to fight hard to overcome this hostility, a sort of dress rehearsal for the controversy aroused by Third World critics of free-market information policies in succeeding decades. Even some of American industry's own practitioners considered the official media position "a sanctimonious, smug attitude" and wondered, "Did God anoint them?"[27]

Although the industry leaders believed in the U.S. media's capacity to free people from dictatorship and propaganda by dispensing the truths that their columns concocted, their government recognized the inadequate dimensions of that free-market approach in winning the battle for men's minds. While also emphasizing the truth of governmental communications, the State Department specialists believed their version of the American Way represented a higher form of truth. This Orwellian insistence that some truths are more equal than others meant that the United States would bring to its participation in UNESCO both the media commitment to free-market ideology and circulation of information and the government's own contention that its information had an even higher priority in promoting peace. UNESCO was thus in double jeopardy, a potential partner of media monopolies and a possible collaborator in the propaganda voice of its foremost and most influential contributor.[28]

The campaign to internationalize the First Amendment* had its immediate origin in the 1944 congressional resolution and the election year platforms of both political parties which committed U.S. policy to international freedom of the press. The free-press theme reappeared at the 1945 Potsdam Conference and in a U.S. proposal to include it in the United Nations Charter, an effort defeated by British and Soviet opposition, though endorsed at the Chapultepec Conference in Mexico City in 1945. Guarantees of press freedom also became part of the peace treaties with Italy, Romania, Hungary, Finland, Germany, and Japan. Congressional advocates unsuccessfully proposed free-press riders to relief legislation for the United Nations Relief and Rehabilitation Agency (UNRRA) and were later to incorporate that theme as a quid pro quo of economic Point 4 assistance: no free press, no relief. But the State De-

---

*The text of the First Amendment to the U.S. Constitution reads in part as follows: "Congress shall make no law . . . abridging the freedom of speech, or of the press."

partment objected that this would look like "cultural imperialism," thereby anticipating its Third World critics of the future.[29]

Anticommunism and Witch Hunts

If commercial advantage masqueraded as an "ethical imperative" in UNESCO's communication sector and helped turn it into "a hotbed for politics" in the upcoming "struggle over the empire of ideas," as William Benton put it, anticommunism was also preparing to politicize the neutrality and integrity of that nascent organization.[30] In the 1938 congressional elections, a domestic conservative reaction had stimulated the House Un-American Activities Committee under Representative Martin Dies to narrow the acceptable range of political discourse by attacks on New Deal liberals and other left-wing "dupes." The Foreign Agents Registration Act of that year and the Smith Act of 1940 tightened up the surveillance and possible punishment of subversives with foreign or un-American ties. A renewed Red Scare temporarily went into limbo when the wartime alliance with the Soviet Union surfaced, but dangerous ideological styles of guilt by association and even inference remained in place. At war's end they would re-emerge and search for new targets of opportunity and not exclude the U.N. and UNESCO.[31]

It seems to be an American habit, after all, to combine internationalism with fits of nativist hysteria, the latter as an anti-subversive antidote to the very notion of global involvement. Attorney-General Palmer's red raids provided the backdrop for the League of Nation's debate. Joe McCarthy helped introduce the United Nations to the American people. Yet others had already anticipated McCarthyism and set the stage for it in 1945 as UNESCO itself saw the light of day, years that came to be called "prelude to repression." At the FBI, J. Edgar Hoover was interviewing Whittaker Chambers and Elizabeth Bentley, and warning President Truman that the State Department should dismiss Alger Hiss, organizer of the Dumbarton Oaks Conference on the U.N. and the San Francisco U.N. Conference that followed. International organizations might be found suspect by association with State Department "reds" if Congress accepted the stories of Communist infiltration therein. And some Congressmen did, while others kept an abiding suspicion of multilateral agencies' political orientation.[32]

However, within the State Department, that soon-to-be target of the congressional witch hunt, an anticommunist security system was already in place checking the minds of men for signs of subversion. Ruth Shipley, in charge of the Passport Office, had already complained that she had had to issue travel documents to "many communists" in various overseas agencies during the war. When members of the OWI, OIAA, and OSS, now closing down, found themselves assigned to State, they also discovered themselves subject to a rigid screening of their political beliefs. As William Benton described it, many "undesirables," i.e., "Communists or Communist sympathizers" had served in the wartime information branches. Since a large reduction in force was necessary in any case, Benton worked out a secret deal in the fall of 1945 with Senator Pat McCarran to amend the department's appropriation act in order to facilitate dismissals of "suspected security risks." The legislation allowed the secretary of state to bypass civil-service procedures and terminate an employee "for the good of the service" without "branding" anyone as a risk. Benton claimed all known or suspected risks had been discharged, although he admitted it was "not perfectly done."[33]

While attacking subversives on the home front, Benton also worried about Communist influence abroad that might endanger UNESCO. Since the organization seemed destined to be located in Paris, and since the Americans were worried lest France go Communist, Benton negotiated with the French to limit the headquarters commitment to five years and won French agreement to hold the general conferences elsewhere and not to insist on a French director-general.[34] These ominous intrusions of anticommunism in 1945 forecast an intense political battle for UNESCO's soul from the very start of its career.

The Politics of Technology

Just as the press and personnel concerns seemed somewhat distant from intellectual cooperation among educational, scientific, and cultural elites — intimating that government would not cede its political interests to independent professionals — some of the same foreign-policy considerations also arose in apparently technical arenas. Illiteracy and poverty were not in the U.S. national interest either. As Walter Laves succinctly summed it up, UNESCO had a major role to play in creating "an educated citizenry" because "the level of education is directly related to the level of international trade [and] education can be a very influential factor in economic progress."[35] Since one-half to two-thirds of the world still remained less developed, the United States had to help them achieve Western-oriented progress. "We need markets overseas and opportunities for investment," Laves argued, and UNESCO could help fulfill those expectations.[36] Culture might be a similar tool of economic influence, for trade was believed to follow and prosper from cultural contacts.[37] It was crucial to U.S. foreign commerce, Averell Harriman said, "to have the world understand America, its life, the quality of its workmanship and the quality of its products."[38] And if UNESCO's science might make possible a "dialogue" with the Soviet Union, it might also support "corporate multi-nationalism" and help replace German scientific and technological pre-eminence with Anglo-American supremacy.[39]

The quality of U.S. participation in UNESCO would also depend on its own definition and management of cultural relations since those were supposed to complement and support similar activities at the international level, a kinship of interests expected of all member states. However, at war's end that prospect was still somewhat uncertain. Foreign-service career officers had not yet had time to internalize this new system of diplomatic contact nor were they convinced it led to the usual opportunities to advance. They regarded the newcomers from the wartime propaganda and information areas as a "dubious and unassimilable group" and nurtured "deep-seated suspicions" about their usefulness to traditional diplomacy, according to Benton. Certain old-line State Department regulars even spread unfriendly rumors about Benton to sabotage the man and his program. In addition, the State Department did not clearly distinguish between the roles both information and cultural relations should play and what results were to be expected from each.[40] And the tendency was already developing to regard both as political instruments, tools of foreign-policy priorities of the moment and projecting American influence outward upon the world in a unilateral one-way movement.[41]

In spite of the strong currents of national interest lurking below the smooth surface of benevolence, the United States maintained a deep-seated conviction that UNESCO would itself avoid politics. Having successfully masked its own ideological agenda from itself and mastered the art of cognitive dissonance, the U.S. expected to join an organization committed to its own liberal definition of the postwar world. It would serve U.S. ends through strictly technical international means devoid of partisan advantage.[42]

Meanwhile, what of the UNESCO idea itself apart from the U.S. conception of it? This international *tabula rasa* of hope needed interpretation to give its abstract nature form and personality. If one assumed there were at least three worlds, the rich industrial West, the socialist East, and the impoverished, underdeveloped South might all perceive different futures for UNESCO. Even within these blocs, varieties of national tradition might spawn an equal number of possible directions for UNESCO to take. Nor would the "separate fiefdoms of specialized professionalism," as James Sewell has described them, necessarily agree on similar programs of action to carry out the idealistic intentions of UNESCO's constitution. From its origin, UNESCO represented "pluralism rampant" and its purpose and nature have been the subject of intense controversy ever since. This was not only because of the ambiguity and breadth of its goals, but also because it had to serve "the common welfare of mankind" by good works and redeem man's mind by ideological indoctrination in the cause of peace. Could any organization devoted to saving the flesh and the spirit of humanity avoid doctrinal dispute, the outbreak of heresy, or finally the call for reformation? Certainly not if this true church of secular salvation became a consort of any national interest no matter how righteous it might claim to be.[43]

The West and the Start of UNESCO

Drawing immediate inspiration from the Atlantic Charter and its social obligations spelled out in the Four Freedoms and from the revulsion against Axis propaganda, the Council of Allied Ministers of Education (CAME) united in 1942 to win the struggle for men's minds and decontaminate the residue of hate the Nazis had instilled. Initially aimed at educational and cultural relief and rehabilitation, CAME developed longer range plans for a permanent presence on the international scene. The Americans joined the movement in 1944. When UNRRA and allied de-Nazification programs in the enemy territories pre-empted the political duties of the occupation phase of recovery, CAME proposed what was to become UNESCO to carry on the work and make it universal.[44]

Since the Soviet Union did not join UNESCO until 1954, preferring the bilateral route in cultural relations, the planning and formulation of the new organization remained a Western project—but not a totally harmonious one. As front-line victims of war-mongering and subversive propaganda, and as proponents during the interwar years of international conventions restraining its dissemination, the Europeans did not express the same enthusiasm for unfettered mass communications. And they suspected the U.S. drive for international press freedom might be aimed at their own entrenched wire-service prerogatives.[45] The London-based *Economist*, for example, in December 1944 recognized that free-flow doctrine would give U.S. resources a dominance and make the world safe for the Associated Press as well as for democracy.[46] The British, in fact, saw the U.S. mania for eliminating all barriers to the flow of information as similar to "a large naval power proclaiming freedom of the seas," and they enlisted Latin Americans and others in opposition "under the banner of cultural self-determination," another premonition of Third World anguish in the 1970s.[47] For their part, the French focused on intellectual elite cooperation as the basis of peace in keeping with their long-standing leadership in that field and combined it with advancing the status of the NGO participation.[48]

Membership representation and the choice of a director-general also occasioned differences among the allied founders. The United States draft, interestingly, given its current denunciation of the concept, proposed a more "statist" scheme of organization with persons elected to the Executive Board as representatives of states, not selected as individuals of rank in their professional community (as finally determined). The U.S. also favored a strong director-general, as Roger Coate argues, "to build the global democratic order."[49] Believing he could swing the election to an American, Benton thought Francis Biddle would become the walk-in candidate, but Biddle could not be persuaded. When Julian Huxley of England won nomination, his left-wing atheistic philosophy distressed the U.S. But they limited Huxley's term to two years and took the deputy director-generalship position with its important oversight of administration and budget. Benton acknowledged the reality of politics in the fight to control UNESCO since that involved power over the ideas UNESCO would circulate and promote.[50]

However grand the design and the sense of its limitless potential and however intense the political maneuvering over the agenda of action, neither seemed capable of generating the funds commensurate with the dreams or the demands for help. Is there some law of funding that budgets must be in inverse proportion to the size of the plans they are intended to support? Given the expectations and the urgent needs, the budget was "minuscule"—about one-half that of the University of Chicago. Huxley's proposed ten million dollar budget itself did not come close to executing a decent program and the United States held it to six million. Forty years later the budget was still an issue, but some of the illusions of accomplishment had adjusted to the penurious realities. One wonders whether nations could tolerate a UNESCO with the funds actually needed to build the defenses of peace.[51]

Getting Started

By the fall of 1946 UNESCO had received the requisite ratifications to set up shop and begin business in its temporary headquarters in Paris. The new director-general and his Secretariat staff might well have wondered what kind of hot potato they had been handed and have walked away from the job right then. Only the "frenzied enthusiasm" of the founders and "the passionate hopes" of their human constituency must have attracted them to the awesome task that was about to commence.[52] The road they would travel was heavily booby-trapped, and it was not at all clear that there was any cure for the hatred and mistrust it was now their duty to alleviate. Any assessment of UNESCO must, therefore, start with the realization that it had been created to accomplish, not the difficult, but the impossible. No wonder Priestley and Benton used the word "underrated"; the U.N.'s collective security, peace-keeping mandate was easy by comparison.

The miracle that UNESCO was instructed to perform involved reshaping the collective attitudes and values of the world's population still living within the as yet undiminished boundaries of national sovereignty and diverse cultural traditions. This massive psychological and therapeutic challenge was to be undertaken both on the couch of intellectual collaboration across a spectrum of disciplines and also in the daily social engineering by mass communications. The habit of international co-operation and the mutual regard for each others' dignity and freedom would develop in the planning and execution of innumerable works of global improvement and projects of transcultural understanding. Both the elite and the popular mind would supposedly respond favorably to the double dose of technical progress relieving physical distress of all kinds and of emotional catharsis easing the mental anxieties that sabotaged human solidarity. UNESCO itself would have to be a jack-of-all trades, initiating, servicing, operating, collecting, preserving, publishing, storing, and analyzing. It would have to be a world educator, librarian, scientist, historian, arts council, archaeologist, social scientist, communicator, diplomat, negotiator, and talent scout.

Though its duties and responsibilities seemed improbably broad, their discharge might be limited by inherent contradictions in its authority to act. UNESCO was a creature of national governments yet in some ways independent of and greater than them. How much independence and autonomy would it attain especially as it reached out to influence minds across and within the territorial limits of its member states? As the invention of the West imbued with Western values, would its purpose be to universalize those standards or provide a forum for their re-examination and amendment by those with different norms? How would it find agreement on aims or methods when its own pluralism enhanced national, regional, cultural, and disciplinary diversity? And what would happen to UNESCO's influence if the world again polarized into hostile camps battling each other for access to the very minds UNESCO was trying to alter?

In the genesis of UNESCO, the founders assumed they were creating an organization that would transform the future. That is, of course, a conceit of all inventors, especially of the utopian variety. No one contemplates how the future will transform the organization; no utopian is that far-sighted. However, before UNESCO could grab hold of the world and change it the world changed and, one might say, took UNESCO by the throat. What had the founders not foreseen? They did not recognize the disruptive force of their own technology on the cultures and minds of people that were the supposed beneficiaries of it. UNESCO would not, therefore, have an opportunity to apply its healing solutions in a stable world economy. Rather it would have to operate in the global equivalent of a massive urban renewal project where it would attempt to get the developers to listen to the human and cultural impact statements of its many clients. This technological revolution and the pace of change were to be forms of culture shock that changed men's minds faster than UNESCO could restore them. This was unexpected and UNESCO became the arena for the hue and cry that followed; a place where the weak could lodge their grievances against the strong. And the more involved UNESCO itself might become in technical assistance, the more time it would have to spend adjusting the local attitudes and values to the consequent cataclysm of change, trying to restore enough balance to build the defenses of peace.

Nor did the founders in their victorious ethnocentrism envision the rapid decolonization of the world in the immediate postwar years. UNESCO had been established as a kind of club of the rich and powerful West intent on institutionalizing traditions and practices that had been a part of their own modernization. Unlike the Wilsonian concept of the League of Nations, the U.N. system had been conceded the right to universality of membership. The explosion of national liberation would become a culture shock for the West, a forced and sudden affirmative-action program that would challenge Western ascendancy in that once exclusive fellowship of the elite. And UNESCO once again would have to pursue its own agenda of work while containing and moderating the ideological aftershocks of this earthquake of independence. In addition, the organization would have to adjust rapidly to the influx of new members with their many importunate demands for assistance and equality of treatment, straining UNESCO's resources and management skills. One is reminded of the continental expansion of the United States with the strains and divisions of the territories' admission to equal membership it occasioned. If Lincoln could argue that the union could not exist half slave and half free, then UNESCO might plead with equal urgency that the world could no longer survive one-third rich and two-thirds poor.

Inequality of resources had not, in fact, been given its due as a potential virus of discord for UNESCO's future health. This imbalance would have an impact in several ways. In the arena of mass communications and free flow, the sudden release of superior information power upon the world would increase rather than diminish the tensions and misunderstandings UNESCO had been called upon to relieve. Intense intrusions of messages, like the technology itself, would challenge the indigenous cultures on the receiving end, tending to cast them as dependents in a process of cultural recolonization. As T. V. Sathyamurthy has noted, "It is impossible to sustain a healthy international community by means of a one-way transfusion of skills of a moral and political character from one culture to another." UNESCO's voice for a dynamic and reciprocal interchange with "a mutual assimilation" would have to struggle against the unexpected magnitude of alien voices imposing by propaganda the values of their own culture on others. And much of that one-way intervention of norms would be conducted by covert and deceptive forms of disinformation.[53]

Financial power would also express its authority in UNESCO's own internal governance, since the assessments of member states represented their overall economic status. While originally viewed as the moral equivalent of a progressive income tax, the scaling of dues without any right to enforce their collection left those making significant contributions with the prerogative of a veto should UNESCO somehow offend their national interests. It was the self-same privilege of financial extortion among the newly independent United States that crippled their own union during the decade under the Articles of Confederation. UNESCO could not have known how its own autonomy would be assailed by similar sanctions or the threat of them during future controversies over sensitive political issues.

Although the disparity of wealth was to play its role in complicating UNESCO's work, none of the actors at the London founding conference could have imagined how quickly and completely the organization's environment would be contaminated by cold-war rivalries. Once the allied unity had dissipated, UNESCO would find itself one of the endangered international species, likely to have its neutrality and program objectives exposed to the devastating emanations of ideology from one or the other center of imperial power. Even at the regional level continuing episodes of international violence would overwhelm UNESCO's search for mutual understanding. These unresolved instances of internecine struggle were destined to explode like delayed-action bombs in UNESCO's midst, as the Palestinian problem and the Namibia issue would do, mini-cold wars of mutual animosity as heated as the larger division between East and West.

As the high tide of allied enthusiasm receded in the late 1940s, UNESCO might have wondered whether it would be left like some beached whale on the shores of forgotten hope. Yet it was to demonstrate a remarkable ability to survive, tenacious in its will to contribute and luckily unaware of the future's own malicious schemes for its undoing. When Richard Hoggart spent time in Paris as an assistant director-general in the 1970s, he remembered the words of the delegate from Mali about the organization's important oral-history program. "When an old man dies in one of our villages," the delegate said, "a whole library disappears." Hoggart kept his own zeal and sanity intact by staying in touch with all the extraordinary grassroots activity UNESCO carried on and never forgot the "global misery, endurance, and courage" of the humanity it served. Awed by the "many different kinds of strength and resilience people can show," Hoggart recognized how UNESCO still maintained that "sense of worldwide involvement and common brotherhood" that had been its original mission.[54]

In viewing the history of UNESCO's relationship with the United States and exploring the public and official interactions, that deeper historic presence should not be forgotten. Although bedeviled by big-power politics, derided as a do-gooding dilettante, and often treated by the West with "amused scorn" if noticed at all, UNESCO or "the UNESCO question" will not go away. It has survived the impossible dream of its founders and the betrayal of their support; it has survived the 40 years of wandering in the desert of nationalism's disdain. Rooted in the endurance, courage, strength, and resilience of those whose welfare it represents, UNESCO will be out there building the defenses of peace whether or not the United States stands by its side. Because the wild, foolish expectations of the founders were the right ones. That the United States gave up on them before UNESCO did is the history that must now unfold.

NOTES

1. U.S. Congress, House Committee on Foreign Affairs, *Membership and Participation*, pp. 2–3, 54.
2. *Ibid.*, pp. 3–4, 10.
3. Benton, pp. 1–3.
4. Karp, p. 32.
5. Benton, pp. 1–4.
6. "Membership and Participation," p. 55.
7. Hoggart, p. 27.
8. Benton, p. 2.
9. Hyman, p. 342.
10. Markel, pp. 43–44.
11. Beichman, pp. 201–2.
12. *Ibid.*, p. 204.
13. Beichman, p. 15.
14. The characteristics of the ideal international civil servant were defined by C. W. Jenks in Hazzard, pp. 20–22, 248–49, and *passim*.
15. "Membership and Participation," pp. 8, 24, 43–97.
16. Hoggart, pp. 42–44.
17. "Membership and Participation," pp. 5, 29.
18. Hoggart, pp. 51–54.
19. "Membership and Participation," p. 4.
20. Benton, pp. 2–4.
21. Hyman, p. 341.
22. Karp, pp. 34–35.
23. Hoggart, p. 23.
24. Ninkovich, p. 112.
25. *Ibid.*, pp. 75, 97–98.
26. Blanchard, pp. 2–3, 21–72.
27. *Ibid.*, pp. 19, 65, 108, 99–120; Hyman, p. 397.
28. Blanchard, p. 116; Hyman, pp. 314–15, 318, 344–66.
29. Blanchard, pp. 19–57, 72, 76–77.
30. Hyman, p. 367.
31. William Preston, Jr., "Shadows of War and Fear," in Reitman, *passim*.
32. See Powers, pp. 297–98; Hyman, pp. 350, 375–77, 381; Ninkovich, pp. 82–85, 121, 125.
33. Hyman, pp. 314, 328, 375–76, 424–25.
34. *Ibid.*, 338.
35. Laves, pp. 3–11.
36. *Ibid.*
37. Ninkovich, pp. 75, 129.
38. Hyman, pp. 337, 384.
39. Sewell, *UNESCO and World Politics*, pp. 43, 52; Sewell, "UNESCO: Pluralism Rampant," p. 142.

40. Hyman, pp. 339, 360, 375.

41. Ninkovich, pp. 116–34.

42. *Ibid.*, pp. 96, 120, 167.

43. Sewell, *UNESCO and World Politics*, p. 90; "pluralism rampant" is the title of Sewell's chapter in Cox and Jacobson; the UNESCO constitution is reprinted in Appendix A.

44. *Ibid.*, pp. 34–82, 125; Karp, pp. 18–25.

45. Sewell, *UNESCO and World Politics*, pp. 62, 99.

46. Blanchard, p. 23.

47. Wete, p. 2.

48. Coate, p. 4.

49. *Ibid.*, pp. 4–5, 8.

50. Ninkovich, 97–99; Sewell, *UNESCO and World Politics*, pp. 105–7; Laves and Thomson, p. 36.

51. Laves and Thomson, p. 42; Sewell, *UNESCO and World Politics*, pp. 126, 135; Benton, p. 6.

52. Sathyamurthy, p. 155.

53. *Ibid.*, p. 46.

54. Hoggart, pp. 17, 21.

VI. POLITICIZING UNESCO IN THE U.S. AND ABROAD: COLD WAR INTRUSIONS, 1946–1960

A. Information and Mass Communication

As the first director-general, Julian Huxley of the United Kingdom seemed singularly absent-minded about the Cold War realities that accompanied the birth of UNESCO, for his goal was to develop "the higher activities of mind and spirit" in a search for "a world civilization." In doing so, Huxley hoped to reduce, if not end, the influence governments might have over UNESCO policies and free the secretariat and staff to get on with the fulfillment of the preamble's idealistic objectives. His successor, Jaime Torres-Bodet of Mexico, also pledged adherence to the "spirit of universalism" which UNESCO would stimulate as the conscience of mankind and by engaging in "a crusade for truth and tolerance." Huxley and Bodet represented one of three influences affecting UNESCO in the first decade and a half of its existence, the voice, one might observe, of original intent.[1]

However, the trio contained other voices less attuned to the universal spirit of international cooperation, representative instead of the national interests and popular patriotic chauvinism UNESCO had been designed to overcome. William Benton, representing the United States' vision of world preponderance in mass communications, believed the "great stakes of diplomacy now involved the winning over of 'peoples.' "[2] Although he insisted that it would be done by the U.S. media "in the interest of the well-being of all mankind," it represented a projection of propaganda directed against the Soviet Union's perceived initiation of "psychological warfare on the United States all over the world."[3] Indeed, U.S. policies threatened to make UNESCO a partner in that anticommunist endeavor. The minds of men were already being designated not as UNESCO's arena for peace, but as the battleground for East-West ideological conflict. Minds were of too "prime importance" to be left to international meddling.[4]

Within the United States, a third, virulent strain of commentary challenged the very concept of UNESCO. Domestic anticommunism cared less about intellectually pacifying the world than isolating their country from its infections, the quarantine approach as opposed to the missionary. Their premise was simple and emphatic: one loyalty undivided and incompatible with any other. Adherence to UNESCO thus meant disloyalty to the United States, since the two were "completely antithetical." A retired U.S. Army major general told Congress that UNESCO was "designed to break down Americans' faith in American government and dilute American loyalty and patriotism to American institutions." He reminded the politicians that America had gotten along without the U.N. system for 150 years.[5] Benton's allies in UNESCO and elsewhere, however, were more sophisticated and felt that such "hostility or indifference . . . would help betray . . . millions of people to the demagogues of Soviet aggression."[6]

The role of the Third World. It would be historically remiss to ignore the early role of the Third World. Standard accounts of the Truman-Eisenhower presidencies tend to cast the narrative in terms of the U.S.-Soviet antagonism, believing it to be the all-encompassing framework of analysis. But that is one more example of the ethnocentric egotism of both big-power protagonists. Their failure of perception should not be ours. While the world watched the shell game of communism and communism's containment, the missing pea may well have been hidden in the third shell of national liberation. Robert J. McMahon has made a strong case, in fact, for the view that the "single most dynamic new element in international affairs during the 1950s was the emergence of a vigorous, broad-based, and assertive nationalism throughout the developing world . . . the most significant historical development of the mid-twentieth century."[7]

On the one hand, this phenomenon represented an expansion of UNESCO's concern with Third World issues and a tremendous target of cultural opportunity for its work. On the other hand, it signified the geopolitical expansion of Cold-War opportunism so that UNESCO would again be competing with the East-West rivals for access to the minds of men. Additionally, apart from UNESCO's subversion by the ideological priorities of the Cold War, it faced further political pressures to define its technical assistance activities in terms of repelling communism's economic advance. Moreover, burgeoning superpower competition further endangered UNESCO's nonpartisan efforts to assist the nonaligned.[8]

As McMahon sees it, the Eisenhower administration "grievously misunderstood and underestimated . . . the force of Third World nationalism." Blinded by the macro-distortions of anticommunism, Ike and his secretary of state, John Foster Dulles, oversimplified the realities, suspecting that the surge of liberation was the red tide of revolution and aligning the U.S. government with "inherently unstable and unrepresentative regimes" which upheld a dead status quo. The memory of that failure of understanding and support certainly affected subsequent Third World attitudes in international organizations, and, most seriously, affected the U.S. approach to cultural relations and the presence or absence of its support for the UNESCO idea.[9] While the State Department ostensibly managed foreign-policy relations with the tumultuous Third World, the national security/intelligence agency bureaucracy, through covert action and counterinsurgency, added a large, unaccountable, and deceptive presence to the social engineering UNESCO was trying to undertake on a global scale. The national security mentality, of course, asks only how other people and UNESCO can serve the U.S. national interest, never what the U.S. can do for or learn from them.[10]

UNESCO could not sit on the sidelines spouting "shallow generalities about the unity of mankind" while all this was going on. It, too, had a mission and a moral authority, as Huxley and Torres-Bodet kept insisting. Though the environment was not exactly to its liking, there was no point in waiting for the atmosphere to clear. The Cold War was a fact of life; cultural relations were being affected and distorted by the U.S. containment policy abroad and anticommunism at home. Ambivalence and distrust of UNESCO had already surfaced, and would taint its performance and integrity and affect the U.S. involvement as well. Much of the world was experiencing a fundamental convulsion of change, complicating UNESCO's pursuit of the common welfare. However perilous and uncertain it may have seemed, there was no alternative but to begin, and if UNESCO took its preamble seriously, that beginning would surely have something to do with change in the realm of ideas.

The "free flow" of information. During the forty years of the U.S.-UNESCO relationship, information and flow have been the essential, divisive political issues between them. Mass communications and the "free flow of ideas" represented U.S. initiatives that claimed to be the necessary instruments for creating mutual understanding and human solidarity. In its withdrawal from UNESCO in 1985, the United States insisted that UNESCO had betrayed its commitment to free flow and had supported a variety of proposals that would control, manipulate, distort, or censor that stream of unimpeded, enlightened messages. Part of UNESCO's bad press in the U.S. stemmed directly from its perceived hostility to a free press and to the information concepts of a free society. It is important, then, to assess UNESCO's commitment to the circulation of ideas in terms of its aims and to compare that mandate with the U.S. definition of it.

If UNESCO was indeed to break down the barriers of ignorance, mistrust, and hostility, and to accelerate the intercultural communication promoting peaceful relations, it had to acknowledge the reality of cultural diversity and the right of all people to address each other on relatively equal terms. Free flow, of course, meant reducing obstacles to the movement of ideas, but it meant more than dissemination. It also signified "discovery," as James Sewell has argued, "the promise [of] practical access to the media by diverse spokesmen and that [their] respective views would be heard."[11] UNESCO believed in a "two way flow resulting in a mutual assimilation of cultures."[12]

Given the principles of universality and cultural democracy, UNESCO could not align itself with any of the world's competing ideologies, and it most certainly would have violated its charter by imposing one system of information values on the rest of the world. Since it had been asked to reduce the tensions that propaganda of all sorts had aggravated, UNESCO had a further responsibility to the quality of information being circulated, a global concern since the end of World War I and one that Hitler had made critical. That war of words, still far from being disarmed, demanded attention. Since much of that defamatory, malicious, and false information stemmed from the disruptive force of national chauvinism, UNESCO even had a mandate to reduce the many passions of self-interest that blocked the interchange of more peaceful signals of mutual regard and accommodation. Free flow connoting mere quantity might simply exaggerate the tainted character of the information being disseminated. Yet blocked by the prohibition on any interference in areas essentially within a nation's domestic jurisdiction, UNESCO could only serve as a communication network and clearinghouse for the exposure of the higher standards to which it was dedicated and hope to gain their legitimacy as the accepted norms for the exchange of information.

The United States had a somewhat more parochial definition of universality and cultural integrity, based on its belief in the unimpeded, free flowing dissemination of the information gathered and produced by its free-enterprise organs of mass communication, with the growing capacity to dominate the global market. As the British had suspected in 1945, "free flow" and "free markets" were used mainly to disguise commercially advantageous exports as First Amendment principles. The open-door tradition was to be consummated by the creation of an information empire in which all other cultures would be passive recipients of news, information, film, and other instruments of influence over ideas and values, distributed from the United States. UNESCO was simply to eliminate any barriers, allowing that distribution without interference or interruption.[13]

Nor did the official U.S. position accept the idea of quality control of content; the infiltration of infamous material would either be offset by the competition of a free market or be eliminated by the responsible ethics of the industry itself. The free-flow philosophy thus restated Woodrow Wilson's dream of "making the world safe for democracy" but framed it in terms of free-enterprise information ideology. It also revived the concept of the melting pot as a global opportunity for Americanization by information hegemony.

These two divergent approaches to free flow and cultural interaction—the U.S. demand for free-enterprise domination and UNESCO's commitment to pluralism, balance, and reciprocal exchange—marked their first major political controversy. This sputtered along, unresolved, perhaps worsening, until the Third World explosive reaction against Western media dominance revived the issue in the 1970s. While that criticism received immediate scorn in the West as an extreme, implausible attack on freedom of the press, it had roots not only in the interwar proposals for information regulation, but in the postwar environment of concern about media responsibilities to the national and international communities. The United States and its media backers pursued unrestricted international free flow amid choruses of opposition at home and abroad, none of it orchestrated by UNESCO.

The Hutchins Commission. The Hutchins Commission on Freedom of the Press, backed by Henry Luce's fortune and University of Chicago support, issued its findings in a report and a series of monographs in 1946. The findings of this think tank of experts, under the chairmanship of University of Chicago president Robert Maynard Hutchins, concerned with the dangers to a free press as traditionally understood, are critical to understanding the media industry's hysteria over similar concerns emanating from the Third World. The commission's alarm at conditions in 1946, in fact, would have increased over time, since trends then under way have only worsened.

Revolutionary changes in communications technology and economic structure, the report concluded with dramatic certainty, did endanger freedom of the press by vastly reducing access to it and placing "individuals and the public interest increasingly at the mercy of private agencies controlling the great mass media." Noting the media's susceptibility to "an environment of vested beliefs," its "bias as a commercial enterprise," and the influence of advertisers, the commission wondered whether the press should not be compared to a common carrier clothed with a public interest and thereby bound both to provide the community with balanced news coverage and not to pollute the information environment by the "corruptions of a conscienceless publicity," the distortions of rancorous malignity, or the degradation of culture. Obviously influenced by the recent deluge of global misinformation, the Hutchins' experts suggested that "false propaganda or outrageously false reporting especially about international situations affecting peace might be so far overt, demonstrable, and pernicious as to demand and admit legal remedy."[14]

Clearly distinguishing speech from press, the commission defined the latter as an "institution of . . . civilization," and "like other service professions, of grave concern to its users and the community." The free market did not guarantee that truth would survive the competition of ideas. According to the report, that market lacked both "structure and integrity" and did not naturally prevent "large numbers [from being] deceived, injured, or degraded." Even in the United States, constitutional law expert Zachariah Chafee asserted, most state constitutions held the press "responsible for abuse of that right." As Supreme Court Justice Felix Frankfurter once declared, "Freedom of the press is not freedom from responsibility for its exercise; responsibility for its abuse was imbedded in the law."[15]

Suffusing all the commission's deliberations was an overriding solicitude for the nature of community and its moral cohesion, an anxiety that would remain an obsession among newly liberated countries struggling to achieve their own sense of national unity and purpose. They, too, would emphasize a need for information that would empower them "to take effective action" which would not undermine their culture, that is, for "coherent and reliable" communications supporting "the social fabric." To attain this end, the U.S. experts suggested an independent board of citizens to monitor press performance, but concluded that government regulation would be appropriate if self-administered codes proved inadequate to rectify abuses that were "poisoning the wells of public opinion." In its final "summary of principles," the commission affirmed that "clearly a qualitatively new era of public responsibility for the press has arrived."[16]

Forty years later UNESCO was bitterly abused for daring to believe that those same opinions might be given international credibility. Still, UNESCO might have been more wary about providing a free market for their discussion had it absorbed the earlier press reaction to the Hutchins reports. Apart from a few hardy expressions of support from editors, the media reaction ran from "so what" to predictions of press censorship and government control, even though the latter were expressly rejected in the conclusions. That nothing else happened demonstrates the media industry's authority to neutralize and suppress any expression of criticism attacking its primary assumptions. Yet later the press would point to the Hutchins commission itself as an example of the freedom of expression they represented and defended around the world. They were not yet ready to admit that free flow in the ocean means freedom for the shark and death for the minnow.[17]

Mass-media imperialism. The 1946 Hutchins Commission episode was a precursor to the international freedom of information conference held at Geneva in 1948. The U.S. media industry may have expected its critics there to receive the same summary dismissal, but such short shrift was not to occur. Though heartened by the bilateral guarantees of press freedom the U.S. wrote into treaties and proposed for foreign aid and technical assistance, the press leaders should have recognized the unique isolation of their own ideological absolutism. Not only did the wartime allies not support the American position fully, but they also were ready to restrict the publication of "false information" (France) and restrain the "irresponsible perversion of or suppression of the truth" (Great Britain). After all, both nations had barely survived their subversion by Nazi propaganda in the uncontrolled free market of ideas. And both England's BBC and France's new constitution bespoke regulatory attitudes requiring more accountability than the U.S. was willing to concede.[18]

Other nations, such as India, wanted UNESCO to "correct the common tendency of organs of mass communication to distort the truth." In its own investigations the State Department had also discovered that the United States had historically "recognized other governments' right to control information," as, of course, it did itself in numerous ways. When Argentinean President Juan Peron closed *La Prensa* in 1951, the State Department called it "an internal matter," since the U.S. wanted to ensure Peron's commitment to their "cold war alliance."[19]

Other ambiguous activity preceded Geneva. In May 1946 the U.N. Human Rights Committee created a subcommittee under Eleanor Roosevelt to evaluate freedom of information and the press, and to adopt resolutions pertaining thereto. Truman urged the General Assembly to support free flow by getting rid of all barriers to it. And William Benton, aided by industry representatives, planned to carry the U.S. position forward with a strong delegation to the Geneva Conference. Like the eager missionaries they were, the free-flow advocates could not imagine the world not adopting their bible of beliefs. However, dissenters were everywhere, and not just in the Eastern Bloc. Numerous, unaligned smaller countries felt threatened and maltreated by the superior resources and power of the U.S. press and wire services. Using the term "cultural imperialism,"[20] these nations, according to journalism professor Margaret Blanchard, "ardently disliked United States journalistic practices" and were determined, despite the effects of war and underdevelopment, to safeguard their own infant information industries from media predators and protect their people and institutions from distorted reporting.

Some had more specific grievances—Arabs who claimed the Americans were pro-Zionist for example—but the general atmosphere, including the Latin Americans, was one of anger at their abuse by "professedly democratic correspondents." Nor did they want to get caught in the middle of a Cold War information battle between East and West.[21]

The Europeans also remained unconvinced. France talked about "mass media imperialism." The British considered the free-flow proposals "an effort to spread U.S. culture by a massive media network." The Soviets, partially in response to U.S. propaganda directed to eastern Europe, favored resolutions against "war-mongering and the spread of false information" and Yugoslavia in the U.N. and Poland in UNESCO attacked the spread of "misinformation." References to the Hutchins Commission report were not uncommon, and media critic Alan Barth added an American voice to the U.N. clamor when he agreed the U.S. media had practiced "some pretty serious excesses, banalities, outright untruths and offenses against decency and good taste."[22]

Nowhere was the complaint against unequal resources more painfully true and obvious than in the allocation of the world supply of newsprint, a perfect example of the relationship between financial power and free-market dominance. The United States, an independent UNESCO study confirmed, had over 60 percent of all the newsprint available. To war-devastated nations seeking to re-establish newspapers that had been reduced to a few paltry pages, this discrepancy, and the sight of the swollen size of their U.S. competition, must have embittered their fruitless appeal for an equitable share of this scarce material necessity.[23]

By 1948 the Marshall Plan supported further imbalance by its specific provisions "to help promote the circulation of American publications and American ideas in Europe." American wire services also experienced extraordinary increases in business, the Associated Press serving 1,493 media abroad by 1949, the United Press moving from 485 to 1,058 customers, and the International News Service (later to merge with UP) going from 100 to 495.[24] Publishers could also turn in blocked currencies for dollars through Marshall Plan regulations.[25] Hollywood, meanwhile, had achieved a foreign audience of 110 million weekly, compared to the 90 million domestic viewers, a market that represented the difference between profit and loss. The newsweeklies also experienced large foreign-circulation increases.[26] There was no doubt that the flow was moving freely, but it was doing so in only one direction.

The Geneva Conference. Given this situation, it is not surprising that when the Freedom of Information Conference met in Geneva in 1948 to draft conventions symbolizing global unity on the major facets of the all-important principle of the free flow of information it failed to negotiate agreements acceptable to all. The world in its diverse needs, complex cultural aspirations, ideological divisions, and still unforgotten memories of the immediate and dreadful inferno of unregulated propaganda, could not yet devise international accords on a topic so close to every country's sense of well-being. In short, the topic had been traumatically politicized, in spite of, or perhaps because of, its designation by the U.N. General Assembly as "the touchstone of all freedoms to which the United Nations is consecrated."[27]

The U.S. delegation initially viewed the conference as largely successful, since they felt they had been able to "seize and hold the initiative in the ideological field." However, the conference's four major draft conventions contained legal restrictions or philosophies of regulation that the United States delegation and later the government itself could not accept. And, in fact, the ratification process in the U.N. subjected the tentative results to such diplomatic nitpicking that the issue was consigned to international limbo for some time to come.

Some of the support the U.S. received at the conference represented anti-Soviet reactions combined with the influence of American economic aid. But the 1949 U.N. debates on freedom of information "clearly revealed how few supporters the American ideal of freedom of the press had around the world."[28] This result was not a "communist victory"; the East Bloc states had neither the votes nor the allies to overturn the U.S. position. The effective opposition, then as later, came from the nonaligned nations of the Third World, and much of it originated in the sense of inequality and imbalance in resources and coverage those countries were experiencing.

U.S. media distortions. As the U.S. media industry saw victory slipping away, its own paranoia began to taint its version of the events. Ignoring the realities of the debate and frightening itself with the menace of Soviet-sponsored obstruction, the press began a campaign "primarily political" and "grossly exaggerated and distorted," even "demagogic," to repudiate the conventions the U.N. had under consideration. Domestic anticommunists suspected any U.N. treaty on the subject would have the force of supreme law and threaten U.S. freedoms, as Senator Bricker charged. This "communist conspiracy" interpretation of information issues was to resurface as an American press axiom in its subsequent response to the communication reforms proposed in UNESCO in the 1970s.[29]

"Exporting the First Amendment" had been a political priority for U.S. foreign policy in the postwar years, but had reached an ideological impasse. It could not be legitimated as a set of principles in international law. Still, this did not mean the United States had to abandon the crusade either in theory or in practice. The U.S. simply took its self-interests to a new organizational entity. UNESCO, though conceived of as a technical, barrier-reducing agency promoting free flow and mass communications in reaching human understanding, was that next arena. When politics obstructed progress in the U.N., the U.S. could utilize UNESCO to monitor the content of dissemination and "combat the effects of any harmful propaganda." It could also "attempt to stamp out any form of discrimination liable to hinder man's cultural development" even if such efforts "necessarily had political aspects." Yet the United States expressed surprise and shock when other nations brought their information priorities to the same forum. The Americans seemed to think this "politicized" UNESCO.[30]

In terms of the realities of free flow, the United States continued to press its postwar advantages in technology, resources, and size. As Julian Behrstock has noted, the communications revolution kept on adding greater significance to the questions concerning media "rights and responsibilities." Satellites, television, and electronic and computer instrumentation heightened the global disparities in equipment and access, while decolonization and threats of nuclear extinction stimulated demands for equality and control of aggressive propaganda. The cycle of animosity over Western dominance that voiced the resentments and fears of the information underdogs would surely return. The pity of it all was in America's failure to understand the meaning of the original confrontation stemming from its own cultural blindness. Systems of communication are culturally based and biased, as rooted in historical experience and national development as are the people themselves.[31]

Ideological warfare. The propaganda and practice of free flow that entered UNESCO's stream of consciousness as a U.S. intrusion had an unfriendly, equally political, partner, the propaganda of ideological warfare. Both served U.S. foreign-policy interests and both wanted to inform the world about the American Way of Life and to recruit adherents to it.[32]

The media seemed unaware of its own self-interest, and the U.S. government characterized its overseas information program as an instrument of the truth, providing "spiritual nourishment" to the unenlightened.[33] In the Cold War "battle for the minds of men," however, the free flowing free market of ideas, as important an ideological weapon as it was, could not do the job alone. Even the U.S. government understood that the economics of media industry life would narrow its reach to the limits of profitability and often carry content not serving the re-educational purposes of the national interest. William Benton, the driving administration force behind the origins of the Voice of America (VOA) and the United States Information Agency (USIA), first had to convince his country's media industry, however, since they and their congressional allies considered government information operations to be a deeply suspect competition with free enterprise and likely to besmirch all information with the stigma of government propaganda.[34]

The campaign to free information from the grip of its entrepreneurial managers took all of Benton's experience in advertising salesmanship, and it proceeded slowly and unevenly at first. Organizing ex-OWI and OIAA personnel for political action, lobbying the American Society of Newspaper Editors (ASNE), and bringing in big name witnesses, such as Eisenhower and Walter Bedell Smith, for congressional testimony, Benton played up two crucial themes. Government activities would supplement, not supplant, commercial news: It would fill in the gaps. More important, he argued that handcuffing publicly run endeavors in the struggle for men's minds would be an act of "unilateral information disarmament."[35]

The AP and the UP temporarily suspended their services to the State Department as an act of protest. Some congressional conservatives wondered whether State was not too infected by "commies" to oversee an American news operation. And the Smith-Mundt Information and Educational Exchange Act (introduced May 6, 1947) stimulated over 100 speeches in a "bitter and long debate" before it finally became law, a milestone in the creation of a permanent peacetime government propaganda apparatus (later the USIA). Its passage was one element in the Cold War initiative between the Truman Doctrine and the Marshall Plan.[36] Even after Benton's legislative victory, the media remained involved in the public sphere of news management. The VOA contracted out 75 percent of its operations to NBC and CBS until October 1948. Later it struggled for sufficient funding and respect since it still had to overcome the opposition stereotypes of "screwballs" dishing out "balderdash." Neither the public nor the State Department were yet focused on, or at all expert in, designing and executing a program of foreign information and cultural relations.[37]

Having put in place the machinery of propaganda at home, Benton and the State Department next turned to UNESCO, an obvious and potential ally in influencing men's minds. On what basis, however, could the U.S. expect UNESCO to join its anticommunist struggle, and what reasoning or illusion allowed the U.S. to believe that some such ideological crusade was consistent with UNESCO's founding principles and not an outrageous act of politicization? Frank Ninkovich describes the process in its crudest formulation when he argues that "UNESCO was temporarily transformed into a mouthpiece for the expression of American ideological interests" and "pressured to carry out American foreign policy."[38]

According to Ninkovich "under the guise of internationalism, the rhetoric of idealism masked the pursuit of power."[39] If one accepted the Cold War assumption that communism's skillful propaganda machine was waging a psychological war for the same minds the United States needed to convert, then the worldwide struggle for freedom and democracy was as much UNESCO's task as it was an American imperative. One simply had to believe that human understanding could only be achieved under U.S. notions of freedom and democracy to make that essential connection, and to be convinced that "truth" remained the basis for both the U.S. and UNESCO's information activities. Mass communications and free-flow doctrine would make the UNESCO operation technologically effective and ethically supreme, and would free the United States from the onus of itself being held responsible for cultural imperialism.[40]

Universality. The Cold War interpretation of UNESCO's role emphasized the universality of the free world, but universalism itself rebutted this analysis. Critics believed the organization should not be aligned with any political bloc or become any nation's truth squad. True universality meant respecting and tolerating the diversity of all cultures, improvising contacts between them, and building bridges of understanding across the chasms of difference. Both Eleanor Roosevelt and Archibald MacLeish wanted UNESCO to ease East-West tensions by mass communications that promoted "friendly international cooperation," not the reverse.[41] Julian Huxley also opposed any mass-information programs that stimulated "sectarian and national interests" and spread "false, distorted, or incomplete information."[42] The debate involved serious disagreements about the quality of free-flowing mass communications and their relationship to the defenses of peace UNESCO had an obligation to construct.[43]

How far would tolerance for self-determined pluralism in the international community reach, and would it extend to societies not yet "free"? And how would UNESCO balance any campaign against communism with the latter's desire not to be victimized by war-mongering propaganda and the sensationalist hysteria it observed in the American press? As early as 1946 William Benton hoped UNESCO would create a world radio network to beam its messages of peace by shortwave across national frontiers. While it did not then catch on, the U.S. revived the idea in 1950 during the Korean War. However, Benton believed that it would not serve its purpose "if it were managed by an international organization in which communist Bloc countries participated."[44]

The U.N. General Assembly condemned war-mongering in 1947, and UNESCO's subsequent conference in Beirut in 1948 debated similar resolutions in an East-West context of division. There, the first important anticommunist address by the U.S. chief delegate, George V. Allen, drew the Cold War line by asserting UNESCO could "tolerate every idea except intolerance," and argued that human understanding could develop only in democratic societies. In 1949 UNESCO's educational activity in Germany's western zones led the three East Bloc members to charge it was trying to turn that population against them as part of America's Cold War foreign policy. At the 1949 Cleveland meeting of the U.S. National Commission, George Allen again attacked the ideal of universality in a bi-polar world. "There can be no compromise with either political or intellectual dictatorship," he proclaimed, and UNESCO had a "vital role in making right prevail over wrong both in the United States and universally."[45]

By 1950 UNESCO had enlisted reluctantly in the U.N.'s defense of South Korea although anxious to stay distanced from joining the U.S.-backed Korean campaign of truth. Secretary of State Dean Acheson urged UNESCO to clarify for the world the "brutal" nature of the communist attack that had been "obscured or distorted by communist propaganda." To the editor of *Foreign Affairs*, the issue was clear: The world and UNESCO had to choose between democracy and communism. The question of China's membership in UNESCO also divided UNESCO that same year when a resolution to expel the Kuomintang Government as no longer representative went down to defeat.[46]

B. Anticommunism

As the U.S. increasingly politicized UNESCO, it was increasingly viewed as generating, in Benton's phrase, a "Marshall Plan for Ideas" that would "close the mental gap between the United States and the rest of the world," just as the economic reconstruction was doing in Europe. Both Benton and Truman insisted UNESCO must choose between the two Cold War ideologies and "find a way to tap all the resources of the free world, and to learn to use every means of mass communication to tell the glorious story of freedom." The organization could not remain neutral, indifferent, or aloof, but rather must recognize its role as a "political instrument in the cold war," since the U.S. and UNESCO had certain goals that were "identical." And Benton still hoped UNESCO's radio could "pierce the Iron Curtain by broadcasting from Germany." Instead of being a bridge between people or furthering international understanding, UNESCO was to expose communist aggression, undermine communism, and "integrate the free world." The self-righteous and parochial U.S. view assumed, therefore, that UNESCO would promote peace by stimulating the very divisions and animosities that led to war. And if the organization did not see it that way, Benton predicted it would be "doomed to ineffectuality."[47]

U.S. anticommunism in UNESCO also went further afield in search of the enemy mind. In addition to opposing the entry of some communist-led states, the U.S. tried to block the membership of international NGOs representing the communist world.[48] It believed UNESCO's fundamental education program would help "block communism," and led an unsuccessful effort to have UNESCO revise Soviet and other textbooks to make them "fair and objective." Yet the Americanization pressures fell short of their objectives. Nations within UNESCO, including France and England, resented the politicizing of policy and the abridgment of the ideals of "universalism and neutrality." The director-general and other member states limited UNESCO's involvement in the Korean War to refugee aid, education about the U.N.'s role, and postwar reconstruction assistance.[49]

By failing to convert UNESCO wholeheartedly to its own foreign policy agenda, the United States had to rethink its attitudes and options. One reaction was that of partial disengagement, as Sewell points out, "on the grounds UNESCO had refused to make itself relevant to the 'real' world."[50] Another was to emphasize the strictly technical, functional projects with limited aims, ones that would operate below the ideological level yet still support the themes of Truman's Point 4 program of world-wide assistance to underdeveloped countries. A third option represented a shift to "statist" or political control of UNESCO policymaking. The U.S. backed a British amendment that turned Executive Board members into government representatives rather than spokesmen of their discipline or individual conscience. But when the Soviets joined UNESCO in 1954 and Eastern European states returned after their Korean War absence, the U.S. then argued that UNESCO should be essentially and necessarily nonpolitical.[51]

While those tendencies signified a certain disillusionment with internationalism as a viable weapon of U.S. Cold War policies, they also reflected the suspicion and distrust that McCarthyism had directed toward international organizations and their American staff. In that view, UNESCO was not the government's Cold War ally but already its subversive enemy.[52]

The anticommunist crusade locked internationalism in a dual embrace of favor and tough-minded disdain. While urging it to confess to ideological bias for the U.S. national interest, anticommunism could just as easily knock internationalism around for its supposed intransigent subversive behavior. Caught between these two extremes, the victim can only emerge confused, as did the two major international victims, the U.N. and UNESCO. Managed in their early years as if they were the urban machine of a big-city boss, at the same time they suffered the abuse and intellectual attack usually reserved for political pariahs. Anticommunism politicized UNESCO abroad and at home, and in each case dealt its integrity and purpose serious, if not permanent, damage.

The betrayal of internationalism. A U.S.-inspired administrative Armageddon swept over the U.N. system in its founding years. Virulent and destructive in its effects, it represented the first great betrayal of internationalism in the name of national-security political interests. Not only did this obsession with disloyalty wreak havoc in the U.N. organizations and destabilize them, but it also damaged the public perceptions of them and thereby vastly diminished their symbolic legitimacy, perhaps forever. As Shirley Hazzard has argued, this was a battle over the soul of the international ideal, whether it could resist consigning itself to the "ownership" of any one country and survive with its charter and principles intact. Neither the U.N. nor UNESCO was able to withstand the "corrupt and clandestine provisions" of servitude to which the U.S. witch hunt dispatched them. Nothing they have done or left undone has so maimed their spirit or effective function to the same degree as this initial assault, one that set the pattern of politicization for years to come while leaving the United States free to denounce any country imitating its malevolent practices.[53]

The immense power and financial resources of the U.S. added an often undeniable authority to its political demands, however "childish and demeaning" they might be. Compliant and even cowardly concessions to the nation's anticommunist paranoia seemed premised on the certain punishment that might follow a refusal to obey. The iron fist of financial threat strengthened the velvet glove of suggestion, an irresistibly persuasive force given additional credibility by the hint of withdrawal. And its manic nature seemed underscored by U.S. warnings to the U.N. not to capitulate to "debilitating national pressures" from others.

Imagine what presumptions of guilt these newly formed international organizations had to overcome to avoid facing a serious funding crisis or worse. If they employed "disloyal" or suspect Americans, they could bring into disrepute their entire program on the rotten-apple theory of administrative integrity. That argument also assumed that the security of the United States could be threatened by an international organization that hired "unrepresentative Americans." The U.N. and UNESCO might also suffer attack for harboring "nest[s] of communist spies" or engaging in "espionage and subversion" themselves. Holding some two-thirds of all headquarters positions at the U.N. and elsewhere, U.S. citizens or delegates were naturally at the heart of the personnel issue and its susceptibility to manipulation by domestic politics.[54]

The challenge to an international civil service. What the United States challenged was the international civil-service ideal, a concept of independence and objectivity that imagined a singular devotion to the internationalism the official duties demanded. Inscribed in the several charters, this idea postulated freedom from interference by any government dictating national norms for employment suitability. Hiring would seek to secure only the "highest standards of efficiency, competency, and integrity." But how would those words, especially integrity, be interpreted in an atmosphere in which suspicions of subversion raised doubts about association with internationalism itself? The loyalty-security program, now deeply entrenched in the U.S. government, was expanding into more and more areas.

In 1948 a State Department visa official charged that "hundreds of foreign agents" were in U.N. jobs as cover for subversive activity, an accusation Secretary of State George Marshall flatly denied. But U.N. Secretary-General Trygve Lie had already asked for passport checks on U.S. employees of the U.N. attending a Paris meeting, and the FBI had reported 42 with derogatory information in their files. In January 1949 the U.N. and the U.S. began an FBI-managed collaboration formalized in a fall secret agreement to screen all U.S. applicants for U.N. jobs and eliminate any persons about whom the secret investigations had turned up "adverse information" unknown, of course, to the individual involved. According to Hazzard, this marked "the ascertainable point at which the international secretariat delivered itself conclusively, in its earliest years, into the hands of national interest."[55]

In the fall of 1952, Senator McCarran's Internal Security Subcommittee and a New York Grand Jury coached by Roy Cohn pursued the theme of subversive U.S. infiltration at the U.N., investigations that exposed the secret U.S.-U.N. agreement and faulted it for not removing "an overwhelmingly large group of disloyal U.S. citizens." The press, meanwhile, featured stories of "Sinister Doings at the U.N." and "Nixon Blames Democrats for Reds in U.N." On January 9, 1953 President Truman's Executive Order 10422 established the International Organizations Employee Loyalty Board (IOELB) to oversee the employment of Americans in all U.N. agencies, a screening process of inglorious reputation that remained in place until declared unconstitutional in 1984. As a symbolic flag of surrender, the U.N. gave the FBI office space and fingerprinting facilities in its headquarters building in New York, as though J. Edgar Hoover had the right to set up shop on international territory and impose his standards of acceptable conduct therein.[56]

A devastating impact ensued as the pervasive U.S. scrutiny sapped morale, ruined careers, encompassed the "extirpation of quality," and established the precedent of government-controlled civil servants. Suspicion proliferated as informers went to work and opponents of the process faced dismissal for daring to object. Loyalty to the secretary-general at the U.N. or to the director-general at UNESCO became a necessity, a U.S.-encouraged elevation of authority which the United States found objectionable in the 1980s. Abusive interrogations, secret dossiers, and blacklists imposed a further chilling effect on morale, and all this intrusive surveillance discouraged the very administrative qualities the international civil service had sought to establish. Noncooperation and reliance on the Fifth Amendment were tantamount to a confession of guilt. "Stealth, expediency, and platitude" by the leadership encouraged a demeaning timidity characterized by "fear, cowardice, indifference and bureaucratic restriction," all of it adversely affecting "competence and integrity." Distrust might even be generated by foreign birth or "contact with communist nationals" also employed at the U.N. A stagnant conformity antagonistic to individual or idiosyncratic initiative was bound to follow.[57]

In spite of opposition by some other member states and legal findings by administrative tribunals and International Court justices against the policy, the United States won both U.N. General Assembly and UNESCO General Conference approval for its position. The FBI stayed in place through 1954 and the IOELB screened some 4,000 persons in the first sixteen months of its existence. From 1953 until 1958 director-general Luther Evans at UNESCO found his tenure "plagued" by the issue and his inconstant, concerned temporizing with wholehearted commitment to his government's approach probably lost him its backing for his re-election. In 1956 a Senate Committee report still identified UNESCO as "by far the worst danger spot, from the standpoint of disloyalty and subversive activity among Americans employed by international organizations."[58]

In the late 1970s Richard Hoggart described "the greatest obstacle to the emergence of a secure and true international civil service" to be those very same procedures set in motion by the U.S. insistence on political clearance and by then widely imitated.[59] That a democracy espousing freedom of speech and association in its Bill of Rights and proclaiming the validity of a global free market in ideas should transgress its own Constitution to betray an international ideal has its own terrible sadness. Even as Hoggart deplored this political disruption, its reversal had begun when Dr. David Ozenoff refused to submit to IOELB evaluation to take a position with the World Health Organization (WHO). Initiated in 1970, the federal court case he brought came to decision in September 1983. Judge John McNaught at the District Court level and the Circuit Court of Appeals in September 1984 unanimously found the screening process to be an unconstitutional violation of First Amendment rights, because the "standards for ascertaining loyalty" were "unconstitutionally broad" and penalized " 'advocacy' of unpopular views." This reassertion of constitutional principle that validated as well the independence of an international civil service occurred as the United States prepared its withdrawal from UNESCO for, among other reasons, failing to uphold standards of administrative competence and integrity.[60]

Both the Truman and Eisenhower administrations described their anticommunist inquiries into UNESCO as necessary defenses of it, a kind of high level protective custody against the grassroots impulse to lynch internationalism on the spot. The process would reassure the public that the suspect organizations, "dangerously subversive" as they seemed, were, in fact, staffed and run by loyal Americans who would not use their positions for "aiding the overthrow" of their own country. While there was a certain public clamor among the disenchanted chauvinists locally, the political leadership's posture of supportive concern for UNESCO may have been somewhat specious since the politics of anticommunism had an establishment priority, as covert Cold War initiatives suggested. William Benton had, after all, cleaned out the suspects from the State Department earlier and secretly. And other programs made evident how large an arena anticommunism could muster for its performance. Shirley Hazzard came closer to the truth when she reported the world's reaction as one that recognized "an unscrupulous right-wing campaign to discredit democratic thought and practice, led by cynical demagogues and supported by a variety of reactionary groups."[61]

The United States agenda of anticommunism, therefore, had a broader purpose than a simple house-cleaning at UNESCO to allay popular mistrust. The government also desired to place reliable people in the crucial positions affecting ideological control of UNESCO's policies, in order that those appointees should loyally serve the U.S. national interest. Cold War cultural policies also dictated a wide surveillance over the free market in ideas to prevent its contamination by alien systems of belief. The McCarran-Walter Act in 1952 defined some seven hundred reasons for denying visas or entry papers to foreigners and ceded enormous power of refusal to the bureaucratic interpretive authorities. The very idea of a people-to-people scholarly or scientific exchange seemed to excite a xenophobia lest America be "swamped by invaders from Europe." And U.S.-Soviet exchanges raised the question whether a Russian not a "bona fide" scholar should not have to register as a foreign agent under the Foreign Agents Registration Act of 1938.[62]

In 1963 Roger Revelle could write that during the 1950s it had been "almost impossible to hold an international scientific conference in the United States due to visa and immigration barriers," and claimed it was "still difficult," with China and East Germany "very tough still."[63] Cultural exports also fell prey to suspicions of subversion: Both books and paintings might be tainted by content and the political orientation of the writer or artist. A State Department art exhibit sent abroad ran into political opposition when a large percentage of the artists represented turned up on the attorney-general's list (as members of suspect organizations).[64] The State Department denounced the International Organization of Journalists' proposed code controlling the spread of false information as "ninety percent Communist" yet the group unanimously passed a free-press resolution. Even the word "cultural" carried suspect connotations.[65] Appearing in the Smith-Mundt legislation title, it had to be replaced by the less controversial "educational" to satisfy congressional critics.

A free-flow challenge. Free-flow concepts also took a beating from anticommunism on the home front. A tougher, more inclusive government classification program in 1951 widened the arena of official secrecy. The ASNE waged

an unsuccessful campaign to exclude Tass reporters from the congressional press galleries while both the State and Defense Departments did
exclude them from some of their news briefings. The Justice Department
opposed entry of communist reporters who wished to cover U.N. sessions, restricted their movements, and hoped to prevent their engaging
in "extracurricular, subversive, or propaganda activities, or agitation
against the U.S." while in the country. The U.S. press itself fired journalists named by congressional investigating committees or noncooper-
ative with them and raised no outcry over the political trials of domestic
Communist Party leaders accused of "publishing and circulating,"
namely fostering the free flow of their own writings. In Margaret Blanchard's view, these actions made the international information positions
of the United States "collapse under the weight of their own hypocrisy."
Her conclusion that "Americans never willingly have shared freedom of
expression with persons whose beliefs might alter their society" seems
to have been substantiated by history time and again.[66]

While the political leadership suffered from bipolar focals and nativist anxieties with all its access to foreign-policy intelligence and the realities of multilateralism, the grassroots population formed its views of
the international world at a much lower level of awareness. Battered by
the propaganda of un-Americanism, often reared in an isolationist atmosphere, and politicized by a variety of patriotic orders, public opinion
had little sustained knowledge of or interest in international affairs and
organizations, themselves "so far removed from the daily experience of
most citizens." As late as 1976 expert estimates suggested less than two
percent of them were "fully knowledgeable" in the area of foreign affairs
as a whole and only fifteen percent sustained any interest in international news. Nor would they be informed by a free press that allotted
some ten percent of total space to coverage of it.[67]

Lacking any clear or accurate perspective, mass belief about UNESCO
would, therefore, be shaped by lobbies of one sort or another manipulating powerful emotional symbols to confirm and strengthen the deep-
seated, free-floating stereotypes already ingrained in the unwary public
at large. The latter could also be expected to exhibit similar forms of
"cultural protectionism" as its foreign counterpart. Having lost much of
its own local way of life to outside national forces and still desiring
power over its own destiny, it might seek that sense of control in attacks
against further foreign (international) influence. And it would probably
opt for simple and certain solutions. The United States National Commission, the authorized pipeline of information about UNESCO to its
grassroots constituency, would not necessarily offset either traditional
attitudes or entrenched pressure groups. As a coalition of voluntary and
professional organizations, its intellectual superstructure might remain
distanced from the very public it needed to influence.[68]

Anti-internationalism. A concerted attempt to destroy popular confidence in internationalism followed years of propaganda directed at a U.S. consciousness already sensitized by hysterical revelations of a communist presence in Washington and Hollywood. In 1950 Senator Joseph McCarthy named as communist sympathizers individuals working for the U.N. and UNESCO, including Dorothy Kenyon, a member of the U.N. Commission on the Status of Women. A lawyer and former New York Municipal judge, Kenyon had been, according to McCarthy, "a member of twenty-eight communist front organizations." Philip Jessup, also named by McCarthy, was twice attacked for his connections to the Institute for Pacific Relations, itself under investigation, when he was named to U.N. positions. Others suffered similar attacks even while being denounced by the Soviet Union and the People's Republic of China for policies they had supported. Investigation of suspects in the Government Printing Office tainted the U.N. since the GPO had contracted to publish U.N. materials. Other allegations of un-Americanism tainted the licensed newspapers in occupied Germany, the Voice of America for its literature failing to give "a true picture of American life," and books distributed in the overseas educational exchange program that did not meet "U.S. foreign policy objectives."[69]

Martin Dies charged that the U.N. was a "reservoir of espionage agents," while Congressman John Rankin deplored "improper activities by U.N. representatives." Some State Department wartime overseas personnel also came under the "investigatory inquisition" for alleged pro-communist activities. Combined with the McCarran and N.Y. Grand Jury inquiries in 1952, these sensational accounts of subversive activity in the international arena fostered a continuing popular distrust for the U.N. system in years to come. Anticommunism turned the idealistic expectations that internationalism had generated at war's end into a profound and bitter disappointment.[70] No wonder President Eisenhower noticed that "there has been . . . a lot of suspicion about UNESCO . . . in many quarters in the United States."[71]

Not all this uneasiness stemmed from the publicized accounts of subversive infiltration. Some Americans distrusted UNESCO's educational mandate, believing it taught un-American doctrines to their children. In the fall of 1951, a particularly virulent form of this paranoia broke out in Los Angeles. Charges that the public-school pupils of that district were being indoctrinated with "daily doses of Communism, Socialism, and New Idealism" repeatedly dominated school-board meetings and newspaper headlines. The center of attention was a Los Angeles school district teaching-aid pamphlet entitled "The E in UNESCO." The pamphlet was designed by UNESCO to explain the role the organization played in education around the world, to make children aware of its global perspective.

An assortment of critics—members of "The Liberty Belles," "The Native Sons of the Golden West," and other patriotic groups—led the offensive while the League of Women Voters, the PTA, and like-minded allies fought back. The opponents of internationalism also claimed UNESCO intended to "abolish parochial schools" and that the U.N. favored birth control and displayed a flag "almost identical" to that of the Red Army.* Concerned about public reaction to an impending bond issue and the political fall out, the school board rescinded the pamphlet's distribution. The school superintendent assured the voters his term as director of the American Association for the U.N. would soon expire.[72]

The American Legion led a similar attack against UNESCO, stimulated by conservative, patriotic, and business distaste for international cooperation. The Daughters of the American Revolution joined, as did the U.S. Chamber of Commerce, which published "A Study of UNESCO" in 1954 opposing the organization. *American Mercury* magazine ran critical articles while right-wing publisher Henry Regnery distributed books such as Chesley Manly's *The U.N. Record*, and Devon-Adair publishers contributed V. Orval Watts's *The United Nations: Planned Tyranny*. But the Legion campaign best symbolized the widespread antipathy stimulated by long-standing grievances even though they were unrelated to the truth about UNESCO. According to the Legion, UNESCO had hired "many people" with communist-front affiliations, had advocated world government and tried to advance it by infiltrating the schools, had attempted to "undermine national loyalties," might effectively "interfere in the American school system," and had displayed "atheism or anti-religious bias" in its work.[73]

As a result of the political atmosphere and the American Legion's congressional influence, President Eisenhower appointed a distinguished panel in 1953 to investigate the charges and report their findings. Although their conclusions completely repudiated the accuracy of the indictment and cleared UNESCO of all accusations, the Legion's National Convention passed a resolution calling on the government to dissolve the U.S. National Commission for UNESCO.[74] In 1956 the House Committee on Foreign Affairs again heard the same complaints, and its 1957 report again absolved UNESCO of all allegations of subversive activity, although the committee believed it was "reasonably certain attempts have been made by the communists to penetrate the organization," but with "no perceptible success." Instead of demeaning UNESCO, the Congressional Report concluded, the nation should unite with and support it as an agency committed to free democratic institutions. UNESCO's principles, it said, were "in conflict with the Communist totalitarian ideology"

*In the controversial 1987 ABC-TV miniseries "Amerika," the troops that invade the United States march under the banner of the United Nations' flag.

and the organization could help the United States "combat Soviet misinformation."[75]

Racism. While UNESCO's subversive image aroused the most prevalent popular antagonisms, another ideology surfaced to challenge its unique peace-building mission. Though not as intense as the Cold War concepts of anticommunism, racism opposed the UNESCO programs that promoted racial understanding and betterment. And in succeeding decades, racist theories re-emerged in neo-fascist forms linked to apartheid and a world anticommunist endeavor still upholding white supremacy. Nor were race and subversion ever clearly distinct from each other in America's own monitoring of dissent, as J. Edgar Hoover's campaign against Martin Luther King would symbolize. The FBI's COINTELPRO covert operations to repress the civil-rights and Black nationalist movements further corroborated the U.S. racist bias.

In its intellectual manifestation of respectable science, racism donned eugenics trappings and paraded a genetic fatalism that had earlier applauded the Nazi sterilization program of the 1930s. The eugenics movement in the U.S. had, after all, set an example to subsequent world action with sterilization legislation as early as 1907 in Indiana, and in 30 other states by 1928. A tradition of "racial preventive medicine" that railed against those designated genetically inferior or subnormal in intelligence, often the poor and the Black, thus existed in the United States for most of the twentieth century. Its proponents obviously resented an international organization like UNESCO that proposed racial equality and the termination of racial barriers to the attainment of full human dignity.[76]

Determined to diminish the tensions that create conflict and human division even in the midst of Cold War rivalry and the arms race, UNESCO sponsored numerous collaborative symposia and studies analyzing issues of peace, national stereotypes, and race. Its "Statement on Race," which appeared in 1950, and the collection of nine essays entitled "The Race Question in Modern Science," published in 1956, indicated the direction UNESCO was taking.[77] Otto Klineberg's chapter on "Race and Psychology" evoked a full rebuttal from Professor Henry Garrett, chairman of Columbia University's Psychology Department and a spokesman of the new eugenics. Denying Klineberg's assertions that environmental and cultural factors determined racial and ethnic disparities, Garrett argued against "racial intermixture and its debilitating effects." Civilization, he claimed, could progress only where racial separation existed, because scientific statistics, he asserted, proved the existence of racial inferiority.[78]

Both academic and general racism in America continued to confront civil rights, Black national independence, and the UNESCO forum for racial equality which supported both of them. In the 1970s, Roger Pearson, William Shockley, and Arthur Jensen were still stressing the relevance of the genetic theories that denied the validity of affirmative action as "reverse discrimination."[79]

C. Culture

The American preoccupation with mass communications as the preferred connection to the popular consciousness of its overseas audience exaggerated the emphasis on speed, information, and the one-way movement of influence. Education and culture with their slow, indirect, long-range consequences building on exchanges, elite influence, training, and a reciprocal understanding, never seemed as dramatic or measurable as libraries, radio broadcasts, films, tapes, or, later, television. The mass media delivered instantaneous messages: Education and culture worked with people. Culture and information thus competed and often operated at cross purposes. The information image machine with its tendency to propagandize might indeed undermine the educational/cultural objectives that tried to reduce the oversimplified stereotypes distorting the "general flow of sympathy" between peoples. And too often, as shall be seen, the United States favored information (USIA) over cultural relations, just as it did in UNESCO.[80]

UNESCO's origin had been a utopian yet necessary invention in international cooperation, and the attempted elevation of educational and cultural relations to the forefront of world diplomacy was equally adventurous. Both represented the growing intensity of international contacts, as technology, communications, and economic interchange reduced the distance between the world's diverse populations. Confronted by a shrinking sense of space and the increasing abuse of it, numerous countries realized the significance of greater understanding and perspective about their neighbors. Political, economic, and military affairs had always dominated the elite transactions among diplomatic offices, but now diplomacy needed to respond to a new context of culture.

In 1945 the world thus witnessed an explosion of cultural concerns with the birth of UNESCO and the simultaneous commitments by nations to the cultural component of foreign policy. It was obviously a large agenda of expectation.

The tensions between idealism and national and political self-interest played out dynamics of struggle within countries similar to those in UNESCO. As a latecomer to cultural relations, the United States was least well prepared for their influence on foreign policy. Yet there were high hopes for the successful integration of culture. William Benton, one of the postwar architects of this diplomatic initiative, believed the U.S. ready to "confront the differences and variety" of other cultures and "to come to know other people." He denied the presence of an impulse to convert or standardize the world by imposing any nation's cultural influence on others.[81] As Robert Blum wrote later, the purpose was "for understanding ourselves better and seeing ourselves as others see us."[82]

Nonetheless, cultural relations seemed destined for neglect rather than the attention and nourishment they deserved. Conceived in an atmosphere of war and Cold War struggle, their growth was often subordinated to other national interests and pressures. The first adverse circumstance was perhaps the "politicized" and "propagandized" world into which cultural foreign policy made its debut. Designed to offset the Nazi propaganda preceding World War II and to serve the military operations of the allied offensive in it, cultural relations could never totally free themselves from this initial association with psychological warfare and information aggression. This tended to link educational and cultural affairs to the short-term objectives of U.S. foreign policy, and to be judged then for effectiveness in terms of their immediate impact upon "foreigners." The anticommunist campaigns that followed perceived culture as negative and reactive. Nor could there be a truly reciprocal exchange in a program that featured the attractions of the American Way of Life as a piece of salesmanship. U.S. cultural policy often looked like the country was trying to win a popularity contest. Culture, in this sense, was strictly an export.[83]

Technical aid. Development assistance, technical aid, and all the transfer of skills supposed to consummate modernization also distorted the cultural component of foreign policy. Viewed as economic progress, these programs were not as narrowly self-serving as anticommunism, yet they too could vitiate the goals of international understanding and good will. U.S. "know-how" has its own culturally bound attitudes, seldom open to change. The development specialists viewed cultural effectiveness in terms of a technical Americanization of the recipients, a narrow education in skills. Technical assistance programs have always involved a cultural assault, and, as Charles Frankel has argued, are "rightly seen as programs for radical social, psychological, and moral change." Just as communications aroused fears of "cultural imperialism," so technical transfers stimulated cries of "development imperialism."[84]

To practice a culturally oriented foreign policy it was necessary to moderate the systemic racial intolerance that desensitized the U.S. foreign-policy establishment to the world's underdeveloped majority. As George Shuster noted, the U.S. had a sorry record on "the theory and practice of race relations," which he considered "a serious handicap."[85] In the late 1960s, Arnold Beichman described the State Department's "disdain" for the members of its United Nations mission in New York, symbolized by the department's contemptuous comment that "they're the tacticians for whom the ultimate reality is the Afro-Asian majority." Beichman believed, perhaps naïvely, that the U.S. should send leaders to U.N. agencies who could relate to the "poor and disadvantaged" majority, individuals with a "known involvement with social concerns, with liberalism, and a record of having articulated great social issues." Such diplomats might minimize the "distortion and friction in cross-cultural communications and operations."[86] Reciprocal cultural understanding might have avoided targeting neutralism as a crime or denigrating nonalignment as pro-Soviet, instead recognizing their integral relation to national independence and development.[87] However, the State Department, long dominated by a Europe-first outlook and antagonism to the Soviet Union, did not, to say the least, adjust easily to the complex realities of the Third World.[88]

Even when professionally designed, cultural-relations policy faced other pitfalls that threatened its integrity or minimized its impact. A miasma of congressional distrust enveloped the word "culture" and initiatives in its name often met indifference or hostility. As a component of the annual appropriations package, education and culture inevitably were measured in immediate foreign-policy objectives. Rarely evaluated for their own worth, with no strong domestic constituency behind them, these policies were easily blamed for not resolving the endemic anti-Americanism that continually stung the U.S. self-image as benefactor to the world. And other federal agencies had their own cultural messages serving specialized interests with goals that differed from those of the State Department. Even more important, an official cultural relations outlook could never approximate in size or influence the thousands of contacts carried on around the world by private and unofficial sources. As the great proponent of free flow and free-market doctrine, the United States produced cultural/educational exports that dwarfed those of the government's own projection overseas. "Deliberate exchange," as Charles Frankel stated, was "only a drop in the bucket."[89]

In this somewhat difficult and ambiguous environment, U.S. foreign-policy cultural relations took their cue from the Cold War. Frank Ninkovich found that by 1950 "cultural programs of all kinds" had become "deeply committed to waging" that bipolar struggle, a development of which UNESCO had become acutely conscious. The Fulbright educational exchange program, for example, despite its high reputation, had its anticommunist component as well. Not wishing to cede control of this facet of cultural reciprocity, the U.S. created, according to Ninkovich, "an overseas American educational imperium" supported by binational foundations with American majorities keeping them out of foreign control. Fearing an inundation of "reds" from eastern Europe under the exchange program, the government adopted visa and security checks for scholars entering from communist-controlled nations. And the United States confused education and indoctrination by identifying "liberal and anticommunist principles . . . [as] functional equivalents" that all candidates should absorb while studying at American universities.[90]

Built-in bias against African, Asian, and Latin American exchanges also occurred when Congress tied their funding to the surplus foreign currencies that had mostly accumulated in the European world. In 1955 the Eisenhower administration backed a high-level "cultural presentations" effort abroad in symphony, ballet, theater, and jazz again as a Cold War counter-offensive against the Soviet influence. U.S. art exhibits overseas in this era also represented not "artistic considerations" but the soft sell for official policies. When the Belgian Congo crisis exploded, in 1960, the U.S. supported an educational/cultural grant to the U.N. to "forestall" Soviet activities there.[91]

Restrictions on the entry of foreign scientists, already mentioned, showed how anticommunism restricted both the free market in ideas and the concept of reciprocity in cultural relations. But at the same time other exchanges served the Cold War ideology. By 1960 the Defense Department's program of military training for foreign officers had trained more than three times as many people as there were scholars in the Fulbright and Smith-Mundt operations combined. As a result of this warped view of cultural policy, a 1959 survey of the American image abroad, "As Others See Us: The United States Through Foreign Eyes," presented a generally negative indictment, an anti-Americanism, according to Frankel, "with numerous strands," most of which evidenced resentment against a victimization by mass market and technological intrusions and "cultural imperialism."[92]

The covert side. The indictment could have been much stronger. The National Security establishment had a program under way from war's end that rivaled and subverted in principle everything that the United States proclaimed about both its commitment to UNESCO and its development of cultural relations as a humanistic adjunct to the conduct of its foreign policy. Rather than help build the defenses of peace in the minds of men and learn from other cultures, the U.S. had sheltered and admitted the very Nazi war criminals whose atrocities had just so shocked the world community, a policy, moreover, that violated the Nuremberg principles, the U.N. Charter, and the express will of the American Congress — apart from its own repulsive ethical dimension.

Initiated in the same years in which the U.N. and UNESCO were first established with America's enthusiastic support, the rescue of war criminals had intelligence and national-defense objectives, tied to anticommunism and space research. The former included sharing wartime anti-Soviet secrets the Nazis had developed and providing access to anti-Soviet forces for guerrilla warfare in, and the hoped-for liberation of, eastern Europe. By a National Security Council secret directive, a special intelligence operational unit, the Office of Policy Coordination (OPC), came to life in 1948, essentially bypassing the CIA and, of course, Congress. Besides moving Nazi "assets" into the United States as refugees or POW's with sanitized records, the OPC planned "subversive political actions" behind the Iron Curtain. "Operation Paperclip," meanwhile, brought in the educational exchange component, Hitler's ex-rocket scientists, under forged papers with incriminating material deleted. Both the CIA and the Defense Department also had exceptions under the immigration laws to bring in one hundred ineligibles a year.[93]

With a budget over half that of the CIA (an irony in terms of UNESCO's paltry finances), the OPC "waged an undeclared war" against the Soviet Union while army intelligence facilitated the Nazi escape to Latin America, with help from the Vatican. As time went on, the OPC set up fronts including Radio Liberty, organized refugee Committees of Liberation, laundered money, secretly financed cultural organizations, and stimulated internal purges by campaigns of disinformation in Poland and the U.S.S.R. Its Nazi refugees broadcast American propaganda on Radio Free Europe and Radio Liberty. Although the guerrilla subversion against the U.S.S.R. was compromised and failed completely, the information and scientific exchanges must be rated as Cold War successes. Like all such operations, they maintained their secret identity by cover-ups and "routine purges" of the files, and obstructed justice with the assistance of the DOD, FBI, INS, State, and CIA (which, in the early 1950s, superseded the OPC, taking over responsibility for covert operations).[94]

Having sampled the attractions of covert cultural operations in the immediate postwar period and shown its willingness to recruit war criminals as freedom fighters, the national-security and intelligence systems pre-empted much of this new arena of international influence. The world to which UNESCO conveyed its messages of peaceful and mutual understanding had, in a sense, been hijacked by U.S. national interests ready to project a secret intelligence imperialism as part of the free-flow/free-market format that it had insisted UNESCO adopt. This New World Intelligence Order mocked the ideals of self-determination, cultural autonomy, and the independence of ideas, and reintroduced the false and distorted propaganda of distrust that had been the very poison leading to World War II. And this program compromised the State Department's openly administered educational and cultural outreach as well, since its hidden dimension seemed merely to be the function of those many agencies of information that form and define the free market in ideas. Favored with immense resources, these CIA-led intrusions into UNESCO's field of operations had endless congressional funding for their cultural activities that neither UNESCO nor the State Department could ever obtain on its own. The U.S. obviously preferred secrecy while waging its ideological offensive on behalf of freedom.[95]

As pieces of its world-wide involvement in the shaping of men's minds came to light in the late 1960s and 1970s, the evidence portrayed an immense, covert presence in networks of newspapers, news agencies, radio broadcasting, book publishing, periodicals, and "other communication entities." Many of these were wholly owned CIA "proprietaries." Others were financed, in whole or in part, by CIA fronts in the foundation world or by CIA-created dummy corporations. Dozens of other organizations active in the international arena also received generous, concealed support, while hundreds of individuals in the news and information business became CIA agents or contract employees. By direct ownership and subsidy, by infiltration and financial control, by assigned or edited manuscripts, the CIA "channeled information and misinformation" to unknowing consumers of ideas. Students, intellectuals, scholars, educators, labor-union leaders, businessmen, and other molders of opinion were enlisted in the cause or received support from it.[96] From 1953, when Allen Dulles set it in motion, until the mid-1970s, when public exposure somewhat limited its pervasive reach, CIA media operations had spent billions of dollars to propagandize the world on behalf of policies the U.S. government wished to promote, while UNESCO fought to overcome illiteracy and sponsored conferences on mass communications and peace and disarmament with vastly fewer dollars to spend.

Among prominent assets penetrated or subsidized were the Congress for Cultural Freedom, the National Student Association, the AP and UPI, CBS, *Time*, the Copley Press and Copley News Service, the *Rome Daily American*, the Foreign News Service, and Forum World Features. Radio Free Europe, Radio Liberty, Radio Free Asia, and Radio SWAN beamed their propaganda broadcasts across national frontiers as CIA fronts, a mass-communications management of minds William Benton would have admired. According to later revelations, the CIA "never hesitated to manipulate the output of its foreign based assets," disinformation and "black" propaganda serving political goals. If there was "blowback," where the foreign-disseminated false material appeared as news in the U.S. press, that was a result the CIA could not control. Yet it was inevitable, since its proprietary foreign news services provided material to numerous media in the United States.[97]

More aggressive covert paramilitary operations were also available to ensure by coups and counterrevolutions whatever could not be established by the "free" flow of information. Almost every president from Truman to Reagan announced a "doctrine" upholding the right of unilateral intervention to preserve regimes from the anticipated criminality of defection from the "free world."[98]

The workings of the State Department. The United States withdrew from UNESCO with numerous criticisms of the latter's administrative failures as though its own cultural activities had been above such negative interpretation. While an evaluation of the CIA's forays in the cultural field is beyond the scope of this work, an analysis of the State Department's cultural relations efforts suggests that the field itself has often been resistant to standards of efficiency and achievement.

The United States simultaneously regarded cultural relations as a significant component of its foreign policy and treated it as the ugly stepchild of the State Department's bureaucracy. It was important enough to be swept into "the foreign policy mainstream" because of its considerable stature as an ideological influence in the contest for men's minds. Yet it never attained recognition for the overall perspective it could give to the formulation and execution of policy. Nor did it ever overcome the traditional service prejudice against it as somehow irrelevant and inconsequential to the main business of diplomacy. In this regard, culture fell into the same neglected category as the United Nations and multilateral affairs generally—time consuming, bothersome, lacking high visibility and domestic impact, off the main track—an arena where large efforts produced small results usually measurable only in the long run. Cultural relations, therefore, tended to be rated by their information or propaganda dimension, and were often confused with it.[99]

The primary complaint about the nation's management of its educational and cultural activities was the failure to see them as essential or to recognize the significant role they could play in international relations. There was no "clear understandable U.S. government policy as to the role of these cultural relations in our national policy," a role described as "muddy," "complex," "cloudy," and "fuzzy."[100] The lack of recognition seemed particularly apparent among the State Department's top leadership. Perhaps the country's past experience had not equipped it for "world leadership" in the cultural arena, but this deficiency had been noted by Benton in the late 1940s and had still not been repaired by the 1960s. The exchange program remained an "orphan."[101] "In sum," Charles Frankel noted, "international relations have a technological and scientific setting, and an altered political and sociological context, which have pushed educational institutions, scholarly investigation, and the communications of intellectuals across the border to the foreground of international affairs." If these did not receive sustained and forceful support, the government would be "ignoring the factor which, as much as any, will affect its long range destiny in the international area."[102]

Although cultural relations did not receive attention as the flower of U.S. foreign affairs, they nonetheless grew and proliferated like weeds. By the 1960s, some 25 government agencies played educational or cultural roles overseas, while another 98 organizations contributed to some aspect of foreign technical or educational services. The State Department's lack of interest in the face of this spreading diversity only heightened the problem of lack of coordination or focus.[103]

The relationship between information and communication on the one hand, and education and culture on the other, remained ambiguous. In the propaganda and military battle against the Axis menace, the two components had been administratively united, then co-equal bureaus in the same division, and finally separated in a compromise that left them both in a strangely illogical position to contribute most efficiently and effectively to the government's foreign-policy goals. No one seemed satisfied with the original coalition of information and culture, their influence, or the erosion of the latter's integrity by the taint of propaganda.[104]

In a 1953 reassessment with on eye on McCarthyism, John Foster Dulles created an independent United States Information Agency (USIA) to strengthen the Cold War anticommunist propaganda campaign against the Soviet Union and detach this psychological activism from State. Culture had been destined for the same separation, but the Senate, led by William Fulbright, insisted State should retain oversight of this field and that it be separated from the onus of shared authority with information. The State Department took back its educational/cultural bureau, but all the overseas representatives got assigned to the USIA for administrative oversight and were supervised by the USIA's Public Affairs officers who were trained in mass-media and public-relations activities. That is to say, propaganda and its immediate impact were their main concerns.[105]

Equally odd was the USIA's autonomy from State, since the name of the information game was the active promotion of State's foreign-policy agenda, while education and culture, with their slow, long-term consequences, did not fit into the department's emphasis on dealing with current issues as they arose. Embassy officials looked upon cultural affairs "as a footnote" to their other responsibilities, while USIA programs tended to "embarrass and compromise" the activities undertaken by the cultural attachés. AID's larger presence in education and training marched along on its own as did similar programs administered by Labor, the Office of Education, the Children's Bureau, and other units of the federal government.[106]

While these problems plagued the coordination and execution of policy, leadership and staffing also diminished the management of cultural affairs. Cultural attachés, from the very beginning in 1938, have never been well qualified for their positions. Foreign-service professionals continued to regard the field as "not a competitive career interest." Philip Coombs found evidence that cultural affairs did not stimulate upward advance in the ranks. From 1945 until 1960 not a single official from that division rose to be an ambassador.[107]

But can a country not capable of administering and coordinating its own cultural foreign relations bring vigor, excellence, initiative, and requisite support to its multilateral commitments in the same sphere of interest? UNESCO did not have the U.S. media attention or popular recognition that the U.N. achieved by its location in New York City. Nevertheless, it did have the early advantage of American co-sponsorship, and the U.S. National Commission for UNESCO linked the foreign-policy establishment to a network of organizations devoted to the implementation of UNESCO's cultural agenda.

Initially, therefore, the organization did attract the leaders and talented professionals it deserved at the State Department's UNESCO desk, in the U.S. delegations to UNESCO and to its conferences, and in those U.S. nationals recruited to its Secretariat. It seemed to have achieved instant status as the fulfillment of liberal cosmopolitanism's greatest hopes. Disillusion, however, lay just ahead, as UNESCO entered its winter of isolation amid the Cold War ideologies it could not contain. The U.S. National Commission under Milton Eisenhower reluctantly became an instrument of the government's anticommunist national interest, one that approved for UNESCO service only those truly representing "an American point of view." The Truman Doctrine's repudiation of compromise with the Soviet Union embarrassed the initial U.S. delegations to UNESCO that had supported the organization's willing acceptance of all the world's diversity. By 1955, if not sooner, the U.S. National Commission had converted to a Cold War view, although by then the State Department had substantially restricted its input to policy and personnel.[108]

Joining the UNESCO team had great liabilities for foreign-service regulars, and the system inhibited a strong U.S. presence at UNESCO. Any foreign-service or Civil-Service people picked for UNESCO assignments had to regard their employment there as short-term and inconsequential. Although William Benton had urged the State Department in 1946 to choose top young appointees whose long-term tenure at UNESCO would enhance their influence and experience, the bureaucratic realities dictated otherwise. Under U.S. Civil Service and Foreign Service regulations, any individual posted to a U.N. agency would lose seniority and pension rights of accrual after three years. As a result, UNESCO service tended to enlist officials at the end of their careers or those simply on temporary loan between other more attractive department positions.[109]

Critics point to a growing disarray by 1960, both in the United States' management of its cultural relations in general and in its UNESCO relations in particular. "After enthusiastic support for UNESCO at the start," Philip Coombs wrote, "the United States interest dwindled, the efforts to recruit good quality Americans for UNESCO work were at best spasmodic, the formulation of United States positions on UNESCO matters was largely relegated to people far down in the bureaucratic hierarchy, and in the face of Cold War pressures the American preference for bilateral action grew steadily stronger."[110] Support for UNESCO had become a minor part of the overall purpose of U.S. foreign policy. Delegations to UNESCO general conferences received "inadequate instructions," and the UNESCO issues no longer seemed to be "matters of major concern" to the State Department leadership.[111]

The U.S. National Commission, despite some excellent individuals, did not serve as a coordinating force as originally expected. U.S. government responsibility for all the various activities in the field was not yet centralized and lay "scattered among federal agencies and within State," without "strong leadership" over policy. Cultural attachés overseas languished in an administrative limbo and long-range purposes remained a low priority.[112]

It should have been otherwise. "Cultural relations," George Shuster admonished, were now "at a stage of development which will require the very greatest intelligence and even venturesomeness." It would be the job of the next decade of political leadership under John F. Kennedy and Lyndon B. Johnson to meet that challenge, to subject cultural relations to some "vigorous experimentations."[113]

UNESCO's own operations. While the United States struggled to bring coherence to its bilateral and multilateral foreign cultural policies, UNESCO was busy defining its own institutional character and purpose. Its open-ended constitution had to be given operational meaning, the structures of governance had to be made functional, and program objectives had to be assigned priorities. As the conscience of mankind devoted to the search for peace and security, UNESCO still had its mission—to do the most practical good in a world starved for all the necessities of knowledge it could dispense. Nor could it avoid the fact, as Richard Hoggart has argued, that "almost any question to which UNESCO turns has a political character." UNESCO realized it could not be trapped in what Hoggart has called a "technical cordon sanitaire." Concern for the ethical dimensions of human experience meant it had to consider always the value implications of everything it did.[114]

Manipulated by Cold War ideological imperatives, politicized by anti-communist intrusions into its personnel policies, caught up in communications issues serving Western commercial interests, and dominated by the power of the U.S.-oriented Western bloc, UNESCO still fashioned a program of action that fulfilled many of the expectations of its founders. In fact, Assistant Secretary of State Francis O. Wilcox in his 1956 congressional testimony contended that "UNESCO's work in fundamental education alone . . . would more than justify its existence." Not controversy, nor tension, nor conflicts of interest absented themselves from the process of development in those days. But they were then regarded not as evidence of UNESCO's incompetence or weakness, but as signs the organization was confronting the most significant problems of its culturally diverse constituency.[115] As an arena for the redistribution of scarce resources and the reassessment of international norms, UNESCO's history had always included a continuing effort to balance these competing claims and fashion novel resolutions of them.[116] The problem was not a new one when it came to the attention of the Reagan administration.

Inspired and led by four director-generals between 1946 and 1961, each of whom brought his own special interpretation of the UNESCO idea, the organization established the major themes that were to guide its progress in succeeding decades. In the first place, the founder's idealism continued to sustain a commitment to building the defenses of peace by a persistent struggle against "intolerance, prejudice, racism, and apartheid." As the new nations of Asia and Africa became members, these goals received an impelling urgency, resulting from memories of former discriminatory colonial subjugation. International understanding always had a proper place at UNESCO's table. Second, and closely connected, the advance and circulation of knowledge remained a high priority, from the fight against world illiteracy to the sharing of nuclear research. This was based on UNESCO's correct assumption that education improved both local and international citizenship and reduced intolerance of others, and, finally, that all intellectual endeavor now demanded global cooperation. An equally important objective involved the reduction or elimination of all technical, legal, economic, and political barriers which prevented access to or from the free flow of ideas. That goal, in turn, stimulated the preservation of the world's heritage of ideas and encouraged their interchange to broaden cross-cultural appreciation of the achievements each society had manifested over the ages. All of these had as a premise maintaining and advancing human rights, since the denial of human dignity had always been the first abuse in the rise of aggressive group behavior everywhere.[117]

Ignorance, inequality, and bigoted isolation spawned the mistrust and aggression UNESCO was mandated to reduce. But poverty and backwardness had also taken their toll on the human capacity for mutual understanding and peaceful cooperation. Poor people and poor nations locked into deprivation did not have the time, energy, or resources to engage in the dynamics of "civilized" intercourse or sustained international reconciliation. UNESCO's peace-building mission, therefore, had to include development assistance and technical support to relieve the intellectual and scientific homelessness in two-thirds of the world. Properly managed this aid would sustain the integrity and autonomy of the recipients, preserving their cultures from the disruption and devastation of rapid, unthinking, unresponsive modernization by any powerful self-interested agency from the outside.[118]

As these purposes became manifest, UNESCO's administrative procedures established themselves. The director-general's importance was crucial in an organization whose centrifugal tendencies each additional member state exaggerated. Centralization of power steadily accompanied both the growth in numbers and the expansion of program responsibilities. The Executive Board, overseer of policy and function, remained in Western hands until the influx of Third World nations after 1960. It served effectively only when the Western majority remained seriously engaged, and reflected the strength of their UNESCO missions and chief delegates. The West had made it a body of government representatives to ensure the security of their own national interests and in expectation of their long-term control of it.

In the UNESCO Secretariat the Anglo-Saxon countries took command of three strategic departments—budget, personnel, and administration—where the U.S. and the U.K. held down international spending. The biennial General Conferences approved programs, resolutions, and "rule creating and supervisory" legislation prepared by the staff and delegate missions, conferring legitimacy or denial of it to a wide variety of issues and principles. They expressed the idealistic aspirations of UNESCO's multitudes for standards of international conduct most nations had not yet attained as well as the expressions of emotional anguish over the distribution of the spoils that others had already acquired.[119]

The professional skills fueling and directing UNESCO's ambitious plans for world improvement had their source in the staff and in the numerous nongovernmental organizations (NGOs). The NGOs represented voluntary nongovernmental associations, independent nonstatist elements capable of balancing self-serving national political interests. Numbering some 400 by 1956, their presence defined a third force of influence.[120]

UNESCO evolved its initial programs on a trial-and-error basis from some 150 projects presented in the first year. Among the notable achievements by 1956 were: Arid Zone Research; the Center for European Nuclear Research; the East-West Mutual Appreciation Cultural Study; the Scientific and Cultural History of Mankind; The Hague Convention to protect cultural property in War (1954); the Copyright Convention (1952); the reduction of costs and obstacles to the free circulation of educational, scientific, and cultural information; clearing-house activity; many symposia, seminars, and monographs in the social sciences dealing with racism, nationalism, intolerance, tension-creating phenomena, and peace and disarmament; participation in the U.N. Program of Expanded Technical Assistance and Development Programs; Arab Refugee Aid and Training; and numerous projects supporting bibliographic statistical abstracting, museum, library, curricula, scientific, and cultural and archaeological preservation centers and services. UNESCO was not without its failures, yet so extensive and manifold were its activities that a *New Yorker* cartoon visualized it as "UNAZO: The United Nations A to Z Organization."[121]

Problems. Despite this considerable record of achievement, UNESCO still found many intractable problems that sapped its strength and its original mission. The politicization that surrounded its founding remained an ever-present danger. Nor had UNESCO freed itself from manipulation by ideology or superpower rivalries. It had had little success moderating Cold War differences or other regional antagonisms, and it had not yet been able to elevate National Commissions to significant levels of political support. National sovereignty had ceded little to international claims, and the U.N. General Assembly, itself politicized and financially distressed, dumped its own insoluble problems on UNESCO for further discussion and action. Threats of financial revenge by its major donors drastically limited UNESCO's resources. Yet the charges of excessive costs rang a singularly false tone, given an evaluation of the spending priorities of the restrictionists themselves. The United States, for example, gave General Lucius Clay $16.5 million for German re-education when UNESCO's total budget was $8 million. The Voice of America alone had a $30 million budget.[122] In terms of support for foreign projects, unilateralism won every time. In 1962 Philip Coombs estimated that the United States' own cultural relations efforts in every area received eighty times the UNESCO budget.[123]

However, no nation had yet abandoned UNESCO except South Africa, whose departure in 1956 marked its displeasure with the racial priorities of an organization hostile to apartheid. After Stalin's death, the Soviet Union turned to "peaceful co-existence," a doctrine that revived its sense of international participation. East European nations, whose membership had lapsed during the Korean War, rejoined. The People's Republic of China remained an outcast as long as U.S. pressure controlled membership qualifications on behalf of the Taiwan regime. Regional blocs attained a permanent place in the political maneuvering at general conferences as the membership expanded. Between 1947 and 1954 UNESCO grew from 28 to 73 countries, a figure that included the former Axis powers which joined after their "re-education." All of this created the "rampant pluralism" that James Sewell described as UNESCO's essential "pattern of influence."[124]

How did the United States evaluate the achievements, failures, and changing nature of UNESCO? The Cold War and communication issues had left suspicions about multilateralism's usefulness, and the U.S. posture toward UNESCO was as confused as its attitude toward culture in its own foreign relations. Most of the organization's projects did not reach a level of importance that aroused much interest. As Sewell noted, "UNESCO policy areas identified with only a few of the objectives the United States was pursuing intensely."[125] Both the Soviet Union and the U.S. were skeptical about issues whose salience was acute for nations of the Third World. In spite of the inroads of anticommunist discontent with UNESCO, Congress remained supportive. A series of congressional hearings in 1953, 1954, and 1956 concluded that the legislative branch was "firmly convinced that the United States should continue to give its full and vigorous support" to UNESCO, with a cautionary proviso that the country would also "more forcibly seek to promote activities and programs which emphasize the concepts of free democratic institutions, particularly in those agencies where such concepts are in conflict with the Communist totalitarian ideology."[126]

As they listened to UNESCO's expert and professional champions from the NGOs and the National Commission, U.S. legislators heard an impressive array of positive testimony: the significant fight against illiteracy; the crucial studies relating education and culture to technical assistance in over 30 countries where free, universal, compulsory learning was under way; the support for and utilization of NGOs; the contributions to free flow, freedom of information, and international understanding; and support to the International Council of Scientific Unions and the International Geophysical Year. These statements apparently convinced Congress that UNESCO had had a successful first decade.[127]

Yet the U.S. vision remained bounded by a narrow definition of accomplishment. UNESCO was judged by the degree to which it helped create "free citizens," able "to maintain free, stable governments" and help the U.S. "combat Soviet misinformation." If nonaligned nations sought their own destiny outside the parameter of the U.S. model, how would the United States deal with UNESCO's value? And what about American cultural policy if powerful antagonistic pressure groups turned against internationalism in a country where a decade of involvement with UNESCO had made little or no impact on public opinion? Polls indicated that "the substantial majority of the American people . . . [were] unaware of the organization and its program."[128] So the dynamics of America's relationship to UNESCO stayed constant, a strange, potentially dangerous combination of "paradox, ambivalence, contradiction, and thwarted idealism," as T.V. Sathyamurthy has characterized them.[129]

Conclusion. An uneasy future lay ahead. Eisenhower's "rash and counterproductive actions" toward the "vigorous, broad-based and assertive nationalism throughout the developing world" would be bequeathed to both the Kennedy administration and UNESCO in a decade marked by civil-rights agitation, national liberation, gender and generational protest, and the Vietnam War. The simplistic answers to world problems that had categorized most issues as Cold War big-power conflicts would be inadequate responses to the explosion of national self-determination in the U.S. and abroad. Neither COINTELPRO nor covert actions could contain these claims to independence and equality, though both would make the attempt. In all international organizations, the new nationalism would struggle against Western domination, viewed as "collective colonialism," and threaten to overrun the "constructive channels" of change into which the West had so far managed to safely divert it.[130] Preoccupied with their own agenda of identity and development, the nonaligned countries were "willing to accept help from anyone without

subscribing to the philosophy of the donor." Aggressive ideological propaganda tended to make them only "more non-aligned and more cautious" about the relevance of Cold War divisions.[131]

The United States and its allies, meanwhile, did not adjust well to
these unexpected events; Third World grievances were written off as irrelevant. The United States would learn, however, that the containment
of communism and the U.S.S.R. could not be applied to the containment
of people protesting the maldistribution of wealth and power. New initiatives would be a requirement of successful international influence in
the 1960s, and would surely demand something more imaginative than
the donning of green berets.

NOTES

1. Sathyamurthy, pp. 97–98, 100–102, 105–14.
2. Hyman, pp. 320–21, 337.
3. Ninkovich, p. 135.
4. Markel, pp. 3–4.
5. Sathyamurthy, p. 159.
6. Laves, p. 3.
7. McMahon, pp. 456–57.
8. *Ibid.*, pp. 453–72.
9. *Ibid., passim.*
10. Barnet, *passim.*
11. Sewell, *UNESCO and World Politics*, p. 97.
12. Sathyamurthy, p. 46.
13. Blanchard, *passim*; Hyman, pp. 320–21, 397; Benton, pp. 4–6; U.S. Congress,
House Committee on Foreign Affairs, *Membership and Participation*, p. 8.
14. Hocking, pp. 126–29, 135–68.
15. *Ibid.*, pp. 10, 80–89, 91–118.
16. *Ibid.*, pp. 19–21, 129–32, 162, 168, 174, 182–91; the statement of principle was
No. 11 of 15 enunciated.
17. Hyman, p. 396; Blanchard, p. 88, fn. 171 at 98.
18. Blanchard, pp. 64–67, 70, 72, 89, 134, 358–61.
19. *Ibid.*
20. Laves and Thomson, p. 116.
21. Blanchard, pp. 63, 68, 157, 167, 169, 225–26, 228, 274–77, 289.
22. *Ibid.*, pp. 129, 133, 137, 160, 190, 287, 345.
23. *Ibid.*, pp. 171–73, 191–92.
24. C.D. Jackson, "Assignment for the Press," in Markel, pp. 180–95.
25. Markel, p. 42.
26. Markel, n. 24.
27. Blanchard, pp. 174–208; Behrstock, pp. 172–74.
28. Blanchard, pp. 175, 180–82, 184–88, 192–94, 196, 209–11, 236–41, 246, 289;
and see Hyman, pp. 395–402.
29. Blanchard, pp. 268, 270, 285–86, 290–91, 401–2; and see Behrstock, p. 173.
30. Blanchard, pp. 330–31.
31. Behrstock, p. 176; and see Blanchard, pp. 401–2.
32. Ninkovich, p. 122;

33. Markel, pp. 33, 35, 38, 39.
34. Hyman, pp. 314–15, 318, 329, 344–47, 351–53, 363, 383–84, 387, and see Blanchard, pp. 99–105;
35. Hyman, pp. 383–84, 430; Ninkovich, p. 134.
36. Blanchard, pp. 122–27.
37. W. Phillips Davison, "Voices of America," in Markel, pp. 170–71, 178–79.
38. Ninkovich, p. 149.
39. *Ibid.*, pp. 167–68.
40. See Ninkovich, p. 135; Sathyamurthy, p. 160; Karp, pp. 50–88.
41. Ninkovich, pp. 151–54.
42. Sathyamurthy, pp. 23–33.
43. See Karp, pp. 50–88; Sewell, *UNESCO and World Politics*, pp. 109–11.
44. Hyman, pp. 330–31, 337, 355, 368.
45. Karp, pp. 63–88.
46. Sewell, "UNESCO: Pluralism Rampant," pp. 162–64.
47. Sewell, *UNESCO and World Politics*, pp. 97–98, 140–42; and see Laves and Thomson, p. 43; Hyman, p. 356, Sathyamurthy, pp. 45–47, 68; Sewell, "Pluralism," pp. 163–64, 167–68.
48. Lawrence S. Finkelstein, "Conference Document: Is the Past a Prologue," pp. 27–28, 34.
49. Laves and Thomson, pp. 59, 80, 230, 271–72, 276; and see Coate, pp. 9–11, 13.
50. Sewell, *UNESCO and World Politics*, pp. 149–51.
51. Sewell, "Pluralism," pp. 167–68.
52. See Sathyamurthy, pp. 36–48, 165.
53. For the U.N. story see Hazzard, pp. 15, 73, and *passim*; for UNESCO, see Behrstock, *passim*.
54. See Hazzard, pp. 56, 73, 80–81, 84; and Behrstock, pp. 21, 54, 126–27.
55. See Hazzard, pp. 15–16, 20, 27; and Behrstock, pp. 10–13, 16, 28–29, 154.
56. See Hazzard, pp. 14–51; and Behrstock, pp. 17–23.
57. Hazzard, pp. 30–112.
58. Behrstock, pp. 23–25, 54–66, 144–46.
59. Hoggart, pp. 44–50.
60. Behrstock, pp. 38–46, 51–52.
61. Hazzard, p. 30.
62. Ninkovich, pp. 99–100, 103, 105, 111, 121, 125, 147.
63. Revelle, p. 127.
64. Hyman, pp. 376–77, 381, 383, 471–73.
65. Blanchard, p. 79.
66. *Ibid.*, pp. 169–71, 230–32, 374–86.
67. Markel, p. 213; Markel and March, pp. 55, 99, 121–22.
68. Metz, pp. 380–81.
69. Latham, pp. 201–2, 273–75, 277–79, 303, 308–9, 345–47, 352–53, 355.
70. Goodman, pp. 165, 187–88, 254, 260; see also Harper, passim.
71. Behrstock, p. 51.
72. Caughey, pp. 165–66.
73. Sathyamurthy, pp. 155, 159.
74. Laves and Thomson, pp. 331–32, fns. 22–25 at 412–13.
75. U.S. Congress, House Committee on Foreign Affairs, "The United Nations Specialized Agencies," pp. 1–9, 26–33.
76. Mehler, "A Comparison of American and Nazi Sterilization Programs," pp. 2–15; Mehler, "The New Eugenics," pp. 18–23.

77. Mowlana, pp. 136–37, 140–41; and George N. Shuster, "The Nature and Development of U.S. Cultural Relations," in Blum, p. 29.

78. Mehler, "The New Eugenics"; Garrett, pp. 1–7.

79. Mehler, "The New Eugenics"; and see Gould.

80. See Frankel, *The Neglected Aspect of Foreign Affairs*, pp. 30–33, 88, and *passim*; Frankel, *High on Foggy Bottom*, pp. 20–25; Ninkovich, p. 119.

81. Hyman, pp. 320, 355, 368.

82. Robert Blum, "The Flow of Peoples and Ideas," in Blum, pp. 3–4.

83. Frankel, *The Neglected Aspect*, pp. 61–62, 89, 97, 102–3.

84. Frankel, *High on Foggy Bottom*, pp. 21–22; Frankel, *The Neglected Aspect*, pp. 69–70, 90–95.

85. Shuster, "Nature and Development," in Blum, p. 29.

86. Beichman, pp. 100, 159, 164.

87. Sathyamurthy, pp. 169–70.

88. McMahon, *passim.*

89. Frankel, *The Neglected Aspect*, pp. 52–60, 63–66, 68–70.

90. Ninkovich, pp. 139, 141–44, 148, 162, 168, 174.

91. Coombs, pp. 144–46.

92. Lowry and Hooker, pp. 43, 65; and Frankel, *The Neglected Aspect*, pp. 52–60.

93. Loftus, pp. 38–160, *passim*; see also the TV documentary on PBS, "The Nazi Connection," aired in New York City on February 24, 1987; and see *Covert Action Information Bulletin*, Number 25 (Winter 1986).

94. *Ibid.*

95. See Ninkovich, pp. 163, 176–77, 179.

96. See *Congressional Quarterly Almanac*, 1967, pp. 360–61; *New York Times*, February 26, 1967; February 20, 1976; December 25, 26, and 27, 1977; *Washington Post*, February 18, 1967; *Los Angeles Times*, February 26, 1967; Carl Bernstein, "The CIA and the Media," *Rolling Stone*, October 20, 1977; Frankel, *High on Foggy Bottom*, pp. 160–63.

97. *Ibid.*

98. Barnet, *passim.*

99. See Ninkovich, pp. 113, 115; and Frankel, *The Neglected Aspect*, *passim.*

100. Lowry and Hooker, pp. 43–44, 58–62.

101. Hyman, pp. 387, 398, 430; Coombs, pp. 143, 151–53; and Blum, "Flow of Peoples," in Blum, p. 19.

102. Frankel, *The Neglected Aspect*, p. 79.

103. See *ibid.*, p. 10; Coombs, p. 149; Frankel, *High on Foggy Bottom*, p. 30.

104. Frankel, *The Neglected Aspect*, pp. 16, 19–20, 25–38.

105. *Ibid.*; and see Coombs, p. 144.

106. *Ibid.*

107. Shuster, pp. 10–11, 35; Coombs, p. 151; Interviews with John E. Fobes, February 5, 1987; Richard Nobbe, February 5, 1987; Henry Kellerman, March 19, 1987.

108. See Ninkovich, pp. 103, 105; Sathyamurthy, pp. 157, 160–62; Karp, pp. 66–88; Sewell, "Pluralism," p. 154; Finkelstein, "Is the Past Prologue," p. 34.

109. Hyman, pp. 371, 429, 544–45.

110. Coombs, p. 150.

111. Sewell, "Pluralism," p. 165; Sathyamurthy, p. 160; and Laves and Thomson, p. 314.

112. Wilson, pp. 101–2; Lowry and Hooker, pp. 75–76; Coombs, pp. 150–51.

113. Shuster, p. 40.

114. Hoggart, pp. 162–64.

115. Laves and Thomson, 192.

116. Sewell, *UNESCO*, p. 196.

117. See Mowlana, p. 137; Laves and Thomson, pp. 86–101, 117, 122, 128–30, 136–37; Sewell, UNESCO, pp. 138, 171–185.

118. Laves and Thomson, pp. 52–53; Sewell, *UNESCO*, pp. 189—-90; Coate, pp. 9-10.

119. See generally, Lawrence S. Finkelstein, "The Political Role of the Director-General of UNESCO," *passim*; Coate, pp. 110–13; Laves and Thomson, p. 80; Sewell, *UNESCO*, pp. 135, 168–69, 189–90; Hoggart, pp. 174–75, 177, 181, 187, 190–91; Sewell, "Pluralism," pp. 144, 150–51, 158–62; Cox and Jacobson, pp. 9–10.

120. Sewell, "Pluralism," pp. 160–62; Laves and Thomson, pp. 86–101.

121. See Sewell, *UNESCO*, pp. 171–85, 189–90; Laves and Thomson, pp. 45–59, 86–101, 117, 122, 128–30, 133–40; Hoggart, p. 174; Sewell, "Pluralism," p. 152; Karp, pp. 89–166; Sathyamurthy, pp. 18–19.

122. Sathyamurthy, pp. 44, 62–63, 86–87, 117, 249; Sewell, *UNESCO*, p. 146.

123. Coombs, p. 177.

124. Sewell, "Pluralism," pp. 145–47, 165–68, 173–74.

125. *Ibid.*, p. 165.

126. *Ibid.*, p. 174; "The U.N. Specialized Agencies," pp. 3, 5, 19–25.

127. *Ibid.*

128. "The U.N. Specialized Agencies," pp. 506.

129. Sathyamurthy, pp. 155, 163; Sewell, *UNESCO*, p. 235.

130. Cox and Jacobson, pp. 371–436; and see Cuddihy, *passim*; McMahon, pp. 456, 472.

131. Sathyamurthy, p. 169.

VII. CHALLENGE AND CHANGE CONFRONT COLD WAR CONCEPTS: THE 1960s

Conceived in postwar idealism, UNESCO found itself quickly succumbing to the imperatives of Cold War anticommunism during its initial phase of operational life. Liberal hopes locked into Western patterns envisioned the universal potential of the U.N. system as a way to reproduce their values and attitudes around the world. But UNESCO also developed a mind of its own. Maltreated and ignored in great-power rivalry, UNESCO and its Third World adherents entered the 1960s with plans and objectives that would redefine the terms of co-existence set forth by the Western powers.

The U.S., by the same token, had become aware that its ideological game plan failed to address most issues of significance to the less developed countries and that something had to be done or an explosion might result.

As the mythology of peace had exalted the postwar yearning for international cooperation, the folklore of development sanctified the subsequent collaboration of the 1960s. Both presented themselves as symbols of a new dedication to the common cause of international progress and human betterment, while blinding their followers to self-serving realities. "Building the defenses of peace" had turned into a mass-communications nightmare of nationalistic propaganda aided and abetted by free-market principles. "Development" was to have an equally ambiguous career beneath its veneer of charitable assistance. As Denis Goulet observed, that seemingly objective program of welfare modernization represented as well "the attacks of a technoculture which disdains their [the recipients'] most cherished self-images as puerile and obsolete."[1] Development could betray as well as fulfill the hopes of the Third World, just as the mass media had done in the 1950s. And in each case, UNESCO had the same role to play, evaluating the quality and content of the proposed program of relief and restoration and trying to hold it accountable to its intended beneficiaries. The issue in both decades was local control and local access to the decision-making process, that is, who would manage the world's information and development systems and in whose interests?

President Kennedy and New Cultural Relations

As the paradigm of UNESCO's mission shifted, so, too, did the United States model of foreign cultural relations. In a similar resurgence of idealism, the Kennedy administration attempted to reinvent the entire format by which the American people made themselves understood abroad, learned about others, and thereby came to know themselves better. In typical Kennedy style, the heavy think-tank battalions led a *Blitzkrieg* of change against a well-defended institutional bureaucracy. The momentum carried through Lyndon Johnson's term of office, but met strong resistance from the State Department, the Congress, and the lobbies of popular "patriotic" paranoia.

However well-intentioned the effort, the Democratic presidencies lost the possibilities of achievement in the morass of Vietnam. As so often has happened in American history, war aborted reform. Cultural relations and the UNESCO association remained unfinished business to be settled by later administrations less interested in these dimensions of foreign policy.

The United States, UNESCO, and the U.S. National Commission for UNESCO all believed in the early 1960s that they were entering a new era of hope and achievement that would reflect the contributions each had to make to the welfare and security of the world. And they anticipated undertaking this vast project, with its immense cultural consequences, together. Soon after taking office, John F. Kennedy remarked that the whole field of education and culture needed "imaginative policy directions, unification, and vigorous direction."[2] When he became the first president to invite a UNESCO director-general, René Maheu, to a White House meeting, the symbolic gesture seemed to signify his government's commitment to the international organization.[3]

Responsive to the American initiative and sensing its own revival as seventeen new African states became members, UNESCO leaders believed they were witnessing the torch being passed to a new generation. When James Sewell described the history of this period, he entitled his chapter "Regeneration."[4] The U.S. National Commission also seemed to sense "the newly developed stature" of its international agency and its "dynamic" abilities to function well. "No skepticism now existed about "UNESCO's work and necessity," USNC stated. And the Commission anticipated that a resurgence of its power and influence would follow.[5] As 1961 began, the old idealism had returned: It seemed almost like 1946 again. But this time the goal appeared less elusive. Development carried such practical, technical connotations that its subversion by ideology and politics could not yet be imagined in that early enthusiasm.

Under John F. Kennedy, the U.S. government was apparently ready to accept the existence of the emerging nations of the Third World and to readjust somewhat its foreign policy toward a dialogue with them. When his close adviser Averell Harriman asked, "What course do we want events to take"? Kennedy responded by determining to "manage history" and somehow find the power and resources to do so. His was a policy-producing administration, and its break with the past was most noticeable in those programs that signified an orientation to the Third World nationalisms that Eisenhower had largely neglected. Kennedy's commitment to U.N. organizations that were responding to the less developed world substantiated his willingness to play a strong international as well as bilateral role in the formulation of a better global community.[6] In an early 1961 address, the new president called for a "U.N. Decade of Development" in which UNESCO would have a large contributory role to play.[7] Kennedy gave international bilateral backing by creating the Agency for International Development (AID), the Alliance for Progress, the Peace Corps, and the Food for Peace Program, all of them designed in one sense to stimulate and serve the national developmental needs of the Third World countries.[8] However, as we shall see, all of these programs had another side, a commitment to the assumptions and priorities of the Western, capitalist notion of democracy.

Utopian rhetoric marked by "frenzied enthusiasm," similar to that which had accompanied UNESCO's founding, again characterized the plunge into a development syndrome. Wearied of the monolithic anticommunist abstraction of the Eisenhower-Dulles approach, with its dogmatic dismissal of neutralism as treason against the "free world," the Kennedy intellectuals prepared to disengage America from Cold War crusades steeped in militarism and to recognize the postcolonial world as the pluralist, autonomous ally it could be. The compelling catchwords of freedom and diversity once more echoed from academic halls and State Department corridors. In May 1961 Dean Rusk told the Senate Foreign Relations Committee, "We seek, above all, a world of free choice in which a great diversity of nations, each faithful to its own traditions and its own genius, will learn to respect the ground rules of human survival. We do not wish to make the world over in our own image and we will not accept that the world be made over in the image of any society or dogmatic creed. Against the world of coercion, we affirm the world of choice."[9]

This ideology of self-determination (albeit with a substantial reservation) received additional encouragement in a subsequent presidential speech at Berkeley, California. Kennedy proclaimed his country's alignment with "the profound tendencies of history" that were moving the world toward pluralism and national variety in an irreversible trend toward independence. The U.S. and those new revolutions could proceed together "within a framework of international cooperation [where] every country can solve its own problems according to its own traditions and ideals." At the USIA, Edward R. Murrow had similar ideological hopes for a new future in which his information services would "explain the American role in a diverse and evolving world" instead of "expounding free-enterprise" propaganda. In *Foreign Affairs*, John Kenneth Galbraith emphasized that the critical necessities of any nation's development included sizable educational improvements, increased social justice, responsible administration, and "a purposeful theory of national planning." UNESCO, possibly, could lead in the training and enlightenment of the human-resources sector of that economic modernization. All in all, the Kennedy administration responded to the "revolution of rising expectations" by a commitment to closing the economic gap between the North and South. Since the president admitted that "six percent of the world's population . . . cannot impose our will upon the other 94 percent," reducing that gap would have to be a process of mutual and equitable negotiation. Failure to address the issue or resolve the maldistribution of wealth and power would just as clearly turn rising expectations into, in Arthur Schlesinger's words, 'a revolution of raging envies."[10]

Rhetoric and Reality: Some Contradictory Tendencies

Some hidden "profound tendencies of history" did not, however, support the self-assured, even glib, theorizing of the Harvard-MIT brain trust which inspired this rhetoric of free choice in autonomous development. A closer examination of its context, for example, reveals one major reservation, the ever-present anticommunism, a qualification Secretary of State Rusk made with his usual terse frankness. The United States would still oppose any tendency for the Third World "to be made over in the image of any society or dogmatic creed." The choice Rusk offered was really no choice at all. Although Kennedy's Berkeley speech condemned the monolithic model the communists offered the world, the freedom of choice in the American design simply assumed "the processes of democratic reform" would be elected. Accordingly, he pledged U.S. military support for such systems of development "against disruption and intervention."[11]

Although Kennedy's theoreticians defined the dynamics of modernization in much more comprehensive terms than the limited technical assistance that had dominated U.S. foreign aid since Truman's Point 4 program, they did not always foresee the cultural complexities that could inhibit such schemes of social restoration.[12] While recognizing the potential for "explosiveness" in altering "entire social structures and ways of thought and life" and in changing men's minds, they did not describe the political and cultural policies that would actually have to accompany the aid to make it, as Frankel urged, "culturally penetrative" and acceptable to those experiencing it.[13] Nor did they guarantee that either the State Department's educational and cultural relations office or the American mission to UNESCO had the resources, staff, and time to manage the export of modernization in the appropriate context. There was not even an assurance that Congress was prepared to go along. Was there the national "discernment and creativity," as Denis Goulet put it, to bring this about? He doubted it: "Can the increased opportunity for a full life . . . be conveyed from an industrialized source in a crisis of personal and collective unfulfillment"? The odds were against it, since, in spite of their impressive technological supremacy, the developed nations "have in the main failed to bring wisdom to their social structures and human relationships."[14]

What the Kennedy think-tankers had not yet realized was the idea of balance and equal exchange in all cultural relations, the same concepts that had once bedeviled the mass communications debate and would do so again. Frankel's analysis predicted the failure of aid if it remained "project oriented" and did not explore the "political, ethical, and anthropological" context in a two-way educational dialogue. Only if two moral systems spoke to each other in a continuing exchange would the aid work.[15] Unless the development aid had, therefore, a high-level commitment to advancing educational objectives first and foremost, the intended beneficiaries would likely see it as "cultural aggression, witting or unwitting."[16] In that case, those perceptions would sooner or later emerge in the commerce of international debate scorning the hands that aided it and demanding a more equitable, culturally respectful order of things in the future.

Another profound historical tendency inhibiting the development decade was America's own tradition of foreign aid. Like mass communications, it combined the principle of benevolence to others with a self-serving commercial advantage decked out in free-market doctrine and accentuated by anticommunism. More often it supported short-term national political goals and military ends rather than the long-term benefits accruing to the supposed beneficiaries. As one U.S. expert explained, "It is likewise, I believe, the right of a great capital-exporting nation, always adhering to the principles of the U.N. charter, to parallel in its external activities the pattern of its internal economy."[17] The rhetoric of international assistance duplicated a defense of the mass media's global supremacy as it called upon the World Bank to promote "the free flow of private capital" by the "removal of all obstacles" to it. The elimination of all "deterrents to the free flow of private capital" by the international agency of finance would thereby "renew the lush economic growth of another day." Preaching free trade and an Open Door abroad, while practicing restrictive economic policies of advantage to its own industry and agriculture, America's development aid package would not be likely to escape the restraints a powerful free-enterprise economy would demand.[18]

Modifications in Foreign-Aid Concepts

As the Kennedy planners modified the priorities in foreign aid, moreover, its impact induced greater national hysteria and economic damage than the less intrusive, more haphazard experiments of the Eisenhower era. It required a more extensive educational and cultural apparatus to attain viable patterns of growth. Memories of UNRRA and Marshall Plan successes proved deceptive, since their achievements had restored preexisting industrial economies and had helped by grants rather than loans. Truman's Point 4 inaugurated a decade of spasmodic technical assistance keyed to defense against Soviet intervention. Narrowly focused on the export of American know-how and increasingly military in nature and political in purpose, it had by 1960–61 become primarily short-term back up to friendly governments and defense-related materials, and had little to do with the instigation of "self-sustained" growth or with the support for nationally conceived, endogenous economic expansion. Chaotically administered, ineffectual, and fragmented, the aid program experienced four organizational transformations and eight directors during Eisenhower's two terms of office. The Kennedys viewed it as a deformed relic of the Cold War and were determined to change it.[19]

Intimations of reform had already surfaced in the late Eisenhower years. Making the long-term aid segment of the total assistance program more effective, enhancing the United States' position in Third World economies, increasing the low-cost access to foreign raw materials, and improving the U.S. export of industrial and agricultural products all motivated the shift toward reform. The toll of Cold War expenditures also played a role, especially in the turn to greater multilateral involvement by U.N. agencies responsive to U.S. influence and policies.

As the U.S. balance of payments became increasingly unfavorable, in part owing to Common Market competition, this served as an additional pressure for change. The United States was finding its international aid obligations more burdensome and desired to ease this financial strain and the payments deficit through multilateral programs that spread the responsibilities among other nations. The late 1950s thus produced the World Bank's International Finance Corporation (1957), the U.N. Special Fund (1959), and the International Development Association (1960), while the United States created the Development Loan Fund (1958) and the Inter-American Development Bank (1960). All these ventures had a mission that supported U.S. foreign economic-policy objectives. By the "demonstration effect" of its loans, the IFC would stimulate the free flow of private investment capital by proving "development loans could be highly profitable." The IDA and the Special Fund would build infrastructures, whether "revenue producing" or not, and train people in services that would create an opportunity atmosphere for both private and public investment.[20]

In gaining public recognition and value, IDA's proponents stressed its value in "meeting the Soviet economic offensive" as well as involving a wider community of lenders in that operation. Obviously the free flow of private capital in its search for "highly profitable" returns did not venture forth to spur less developed countries economically forward without the international ground work of preparation beforehand. Economic free flow, like information free flow, moved in one-way channels designed to maintain established systems of power. The result, according to James Sewell, often exaggerated the problems of development rather than solving them and tended to engender, in the nonrecognition of the local cultural context, "continuing conflict" among those involved, rather than a "habituation in agreement." The LDCs remained dissatisfied with free flow as such. Private investment would have to return, besides profits to the lender, "higher per capita real income, a higher standard of living, . . . justice, and economic independence."[21]

The self-sustained growth of the Agency for International Development made it look like a Third World country receiving bilateral aid. While it brought under one roof Eisenhower's disparate collective of assistance, it could not disentangle itself from the prior subservience to military assistance and anticommunism. If it was more unified and theoretically pure, a suspicious Congress and the consequent political appeasement of its fervent right-wing coalition kept its purposes and its resources narrowly circumscribed. Congressman Otto Passman, chair of the Foreign Aid subcommittee of the House Appropriations Committee, still derided "the spenders, the dreamers, the internationalists," while Senator Bourke Hickenlooper put through a 1962 law requiring aid to be cut off to nations expropriating corporate property "without prompt, adequate, and effective compensation." In his survey of AID's early years, Arthur Schlesinger described it as "sluggish and . . . ineffectual" during a time of "turmoil and frustration." At the end of the decade the interpretation was even more dismal, but from a Third World point of view.[22]

The development boom, whether bi-or multilateral and however well-intentioned, was always a boomerang, returning substantial benefits to the donors who preferred to call them "by-products" of their foreign-aid programs. In Eugene Black's description of "development diplomacy," aid served the national economic interest by the promise or threat of its presence or absence and by the terms of self-enrichment attached to the bounty it distributed. Not intended to "make friends," as John Foster Dulles affirmed, foreign assistance "look[ed] out for the interests of the United States." It opened markets, aided exports, stimulated investment, and provided low-cost raw materials and essential minerals. In Percy Bidwell's succinct summary, it also ensured "that neither nationalistic policies nor Communist influences deny American industries access on reasonable terms to the basic materials necessary to the continued growth of the American economy."[23]

The AID development loans (not grants), for example, required repayment in dollars earnable by selling commodities whose price level and stability the U.S. controlled by its opposition to producer agreements. Tied loans also forced the recipients to spend the money for U.S. exports. Import quotas and tariff preference barriers further limited the power of less developed countries while the $3 billion annual subsidies to American farmers expanded their access to foreign markets. Debt service, meanwhile, confirmed the stagnation implicit in unequal bargaining power and resources. (This mounting Third World debt was to become, perhaps, the most compelling problem of the late 1980s.) The disparity of outlook began appearing at the United Nations Conferences on Trade and Development in 1964 and 1968 where the U.S. opposed most Third World demands. A development policy combining "aid pressure and exclusion" had the LDCs wondering whether they had been delivered from Cold War ideologies only to be unlucky participants in the ruthless realities of free-market capitalism, where political interventions favoring the powerful lay hidden in the "automatic" processes that market proclaimed.[24]

UNESCO and the Kennedy initiatives. UNESCO took the Kennedy initiatives at face value, just as it had done with the preamble to its constitution. It could hardly do otherwise. Declarations of high purpose had been its inspiration and translating them into effective programs the cross it had always borne. (American Blacks had used the 14th Amendment in much the same way, slowly moving its constitutional impact from corporate protector to foe of inequality and state sanctioned segregation.) UNESCO also realized it had an obligation to act since the development process was bound to be a transforming and massive educational and cultural experience for most of its members, whether UNESCO participated or not. Minds would certainly be affected regardless of motives; they might still be somewhat prepared by the small but deliberate attempt the organization could make to build defenses against the unequal onslaught of change.

Nor could UNESCO neglect its role as a parliamentary forum for the less powerful to influence the international climate of opinion and propose alternative values for consideration there. It had always served a symbolic purpose, one that the Americans had taken full advantage of in their own propagandizing of global attitudes from 1946 on. Since the United States still retained extraordinary influence even when uninterested in or unaffected by multilateral affairs, UNESCO may even have hoped to turn development enthusiasm into formal U.S. overall support, just as mass communications once had done. And the diversion of development must have come as a relief from the rigid Cold War preoccupations characterizing so much of the U.S. UNESCO experience.

However, the new U.S. development programs did not necessarily suit UNESCO's original mission, dispel inner disagreements about its priorities, or eliminate the politicization that had so long characterized its pursuit of peace. It could be argued that promoting development was a form of "peace building," on the premise that rising standards of literacy and living inculcate a capacity to understand others and become more peaceful as a result. And if economic growth occurred, the population might then have the self-confidence, resources, and identity to pursue mutual international affairs as equals. The proponents of intellectual cooperation in UNESCO, focused on high-level professional interaction, were less enthusiastic and regarded the practical projects as a somewhat tawdry digression from the educational and cultural exchanges, seminars, and conferences that flavored their academic life.

Development, like the concept of peace, had a limitless frontier of need, and as UNESCO's membership steadily enlarged, the expanding demands for relief vastly complicated the equitable assignment of priorities. The "task expansionists" included both the NGOs that received subvention funding and the LDCs. A process of bloc and individual bargaining, log-rolling, and horse-trading thus became characteristic of project formulation. The threat of centrifugal disaster and budgetary inflation now loomed ever larger, held in bounds by the centralizing powers of a strong director-general and the fiscal discipline of the eleven or so restrictionist nations (mostly Western, but including the Soviet Union) that dominated finances by the size of their assessments.[25]

As a fact of Third World life, development inevitably spawned politicization, but that was not limited to program and budget alone. The real political issue involved the differing interpretations of development among UNESCO's members. The United States and its industrialized allies believed it to be a technical, nonpolitical dimension of the organization's good-works agenda. UNESCO would be responsible for sustaining and improving the infrastructure once maintained by the colonial regimes. In that view, the attention to economic modernization reduced the possible intrusion of contentious political issues into UNESCO's arena. Even if the United States lost its voting majority, therefore, the organization's programs would still enhance the patterns of development the nation was pursuing by bilateral relations and through its influence in other U.S. agencies, such as the IMF, the World Bank, and GATT. If this structure of power faltered, the rich countries could conduct their economic planning in smaller units of control like the OECD and the Group of Ten.[26]

UNESCO's Own Perspective

The Third World and UNESCO's Director-General, René Maheu, had an alternative perspective that envisioned a less technical goal and sought in the process of development some redistribution of the world's wealth and power. At the very least, these UNESCO voices resisted being overwhelmed by the "technocratic avalanche" the separately financed United Nations Development Program's funding might unleash. External financing and support for U.N.-organized development projects by voluntary contributions endangered UNESCO's independence and enhanced the control of development assistance by the industrialized North. Development theory by Third World adherents stirred politically sensitive dreams of a more equitable international economic order. As the newly liberated nations emerged and formed alliances in their common impoverishment, they recognized the connection between economic backwardness and exploitation and communications stagnation.[27]

The reformation of global economic relations demanded access to information resources: LDCs needed media power to cement their own mutual allegiance to take action as a united movement. They would not be able to influence the center of world economic power until they had first "promote[d] a greater interchange of ideas among themselves" and that meant freeing themselves from their communications captivity to Western media. Since these media did not provide the coverage promoting information flow among the nonaligned or much care to do so, the LDCs would obviously have to create their own. Only later would they fight the battle over the serious imbalances in world information power that diminished their ability to wage convincing attacks on the hostile economic environment they wished to change. To the West's surprise, therefore, development led to the idea of a New International Economic

Order and, in turn, to the New World Information and Communication Order. The decade of development triggered rising expectations the U.S. had not expected.[28]

The UNESCO development mission had its origins in the postwar U.S. and U.N. responses to world economic conditions that might foster international anarchy, especially, in the U.S. view, if manipulated by communist intervention. In the 1949 Point 4 program and in the 1950 U.N. Expanded Program of Technical Assistance, UNESCO added an educational and training component, but that area remained small during the decade of the '50s. With the U.N. Special Fund (1959) the World Bank's IDA (1961), and the UNICEF decision to support education, UNESCO greatly enlarged its funding and functioning in education for development. It assisted governments to generate proposals for Special Fund support, served as an experimental laboratory for the assessment of educational ideas, and fought energetically to reduce the 700 million illiterates in the world community. In educational planning, teacher training, and institution building, UNESCO's activity, according to historians, was "salient, effective, professional and non-political." Once, UNESCO had been attacked as not relevant to the real world for its failure to enlist in Cold War ideological battles. In the '60s this relevance to the real world could not be doubted.[29]

Responding to the development of human resources as a precondition of economic progress, UNESCO broadened its involvement, thereby stimulating opportunity and achievement in education, science, and mass communications. A convention against Discrimination in Education in 1960 helped open the field to a wider participation (the United States did not sign it). René Maheu attended the first U.N. Conference on Science and Technology in 1963 and made UNESCO a key player in imagining the applications of science in enhancing and facilitating growth, something the Non-Aligned Movement (NAM) members were quick to understand. Thereafter, UNESCO took initiatives and planned studies in hydrology, oceanography, geology and seismology, man and the environment, land-use, and conservation.

All of this culminated in the 1970 Man and the Biosphere program with projects all over the world. Not only did this activity imply a commitment to "planetary management" that preserved resources still undeveloped for future generations but it also distributed the subsequent scientific knowledge as a giant information bank for the benefit of those countries where such exchanges otherwise would not have occurred. A computerized scientific statistical system called UNISIST, for example, developed between 1967 and 1971, collected and circulated this scientific information in bibliographies and abstracts. By the early 1970s UNESCO was supporting development in 119 countries and had 317 large-scale projects under way, and an additional 65 teacher-training programs. It had also provided $80.5 million in technical assistance to

50 engineering colleges or institutes during the 1960s. In India, an experimental satellite-assisted education program was beaming instruction to 5,000 villages. Encouraging learning and access to the tools of knowledge, UNESCO remained a symbol of hope for Third World nations trying to mobilize their human resources to escape from an underdeveloped past.[30]

Other UNESCO activities supported cultural pride, preservation, and understanding on the theory that a sense of dignity and autonomy is also an essential ingredient of the national well-being that should accompany development. Social-science research and publications examined the internal cultural dynamics that affected modernization. Population and family-planning studies provided crucial information on their linkage to economic growth. Comparative cross-cultural studies and projects, such as the publication of the multi-volume *History of Africa*, stimulated the recognition and diffusion of national and racial achievements. At the same time, the visible outstanding examples of those historical contributions to the world's aesthetic betterment came under UNESCO's protection. Saving the Abu Simel and other Nubian monuments from the waters to be stored behind the Aswan Dam represented the most spectacular of these rescue efforts. Other such initiatives followed in Venice, Indonesia, Cambodia, and Florence after its 1966 floods, and the program received world-wide authority in the 1972 Convention for the Protection of the World Cultural and National Heritage which listed important sites in the United States as well (although the U.S. had not yet signed as of late 1973). These continued a preservation mandate that had already produced the 1954 Convention for the Protection of Cultural Property in the Event of Armed Conflict (to which the U.S. is not a party). UNESCO also sponsored research on techniques of conservation and restoration at some ten regional centers and had dispatched 250 experts to 64 countries to help rehabilitate various cultural sites and monuments.[31] As Julian Behrstock concluded, these achievements demonstrated "UNESCO's capacity to perform the valuable work foreseen for it in the Constitution."[32]

The Special Role of Mass Communications

If UNESCO could combine its dedication to peace with its promotion of development and integrate education and culture into programs enhancing each, then it was bound once more to turn its attention to mass communications, recognized by all as a critical instrument of mutual understanding and of national economic growth. The free flow of educational, scientific, and cultural information had always been close to UNESCO's charter. It had never ceased trying to reduce the technical and legislative barriers to the circulation of knowledge, which included assistance to libraries and museums and the exchange and sponsorship of experts in the relevant professional fields. As nonpolitical as all this had seemed, that consensus did not carry over into the mass media whose enormous free-flowing influence had long excited political reverberations in many quarters. Free flow meant one thing to a librarian and something else to the corporate owner of a media conglomerate, the difference, perhaps, between knowledge for learning and knowledge for profit.[33]

Since Director-General Maheu had started his UNESCO career as director of its office of communications, his familiarity with the issue ensured its position on his agenda when he became the organization's leader. He had been present when the 1948 U.N. Conference on Freedom of Information reached a political impasse over the proposed conventions and resolutions concerning the responsibilities of the media. The U.N. had shelved the whole subject as hopelessly contentious and handed the question to UNESCO, which had its own obligation to act because the U.S. had insisted on mass communications as one of its major divisions of interest. While fending off a U.S. compulsion to politicize that arena, UNESCO had not neglected the relevance of mass communications to its overall goals.[34]

However, the technical opportunities never succeeded in driving out the charge of "politicization," since the nature and content of the information flows remained of prime importance to all. In 1956 after the Soviet Union's entry, UNESCO's ninth General Conference at New Delhi passed "a resolution . . . inviting member states to direct the mass media toward the cause of peace and international understanding."[35] In 1958 President Eisenhower made a "historic speech" to the U.N. General Assembly concerning a peace proposal for the Middle East in which he urged that the United Nations engage in "systematic monitoring" of inflammatory radio broadcasts in the area and "examine complaints" from countries who considered the propaganda threatening to their national security. The U.N.'s Economic and Social Council's subcommittee on freedom of information had been surveying the spread of "false or distorted information" harmful to international understanding since 1953. In an August 1960 article, Chester Bowles had advocated a "pledge by all nations to refrain from agitating propaganda within Africa and end all efforts at direct or indirect subversion" as a way of sanitizing the atmosphere for the emerging new nations there.[36]

Raising these issues, ones that clearly recognized the need to defend people from distorted and disruptive propaganda and implying the right to receive international protection from it, brought the discussion closer to the basic question of national sovereignty over the air waves. It was a problem satellite space communications would soon make urgent. And it aroused the same fears of victimization by superior technology already stimulated by the mass-media debate over balanced flows. It was also linked to the practice of jamming, a defensive sovereign remedy for unwelcome broadcast intrusions that the U.N. General Assembly had condemned in 1950 by a 49-5 vote as an interference with free flow, the right to receive information, treaty agreements, and ITU conventions. Still, even though contrary to international law, legal jamming survived in two exceptions permitting nations to block "incitements" and for self-defense. The issue remained unresolved. Anyone recalling Nazi broadcasts might condone jamming hostile propaganda that subverted morale or led to rioting and bloodshed, as Eisenhower's and Bowles's recommendations suggested. Do nations have an international right to invade each others ether with whatever messages they wish to disseminate? The 1960s had to come to grips with that question.[37]

While the content of mass communications thus continued to receive attention, UNESCO went about its technical support efforts. Based upon its belief that free flow did not become a right equally possessed by all unless they had mass media of their own, and recognizing that the latter would also stimulate development, UNESCO initiated a variety of useful projects. It set standards of attainment for the number of newspapers, radio receivers, and cinema seats a nation should possess and helped them build to that level. Training for reporters and broadcasters and expert support for the expansion of facilities followed. At 1961 and 1963 conferences UNESCO supported the creation of national news agencies and helped set up regional arrangements for pooling their services. Between 1961 and 1963, UNESCO, the U.S. National Commission, and the U.N. all affirmed the relationship between mass communications and the prospects for self-sustained development. A new era of investigation and action was, however, waiting in the wings as these activities progressed. UNESCO and the Third World once again found their goals overrun by the technological pace of change. In 1963 Intelsat opened the age of satellite information flows while the less developed were still playing catch-up in the print and broadcast media.[38]

Space and Satellites

According to Julian Behrstock, "space communication with its capacity for instantaneous world wide transmissions . . . put UNESCO itself into orbit," namely, the political one. While Behrstock rightly relates satellite activity with an intense, widespread offensive by the satelliteless countries, he is wrong in assuming mass-information issues had ever left the political agenda. But space did give them a new dimension of concern and anguish as the LDCs, closing somewhat the disparities of media power, found themselves suddenly and totally outdistanced, further behind than ever. The Space Communications Conference in 1965 issued a finding that UNESCO published which revealed the impact the new technology was having on the organization and its members.

UNESCO, the report urged, should now "move beyond the techniques of communication to 'a common concern with the content of what is transmitted.' " The statement noted that satellites enabled "the mass media to reach and influence a vast audience" requiring them, therefore, "to be used for the benefit of all."[39]

In 1969 Lord Ritchie Calder sounded a similar alarm. Citing broadcast satellites as "one of the most serious problems of our age," Calder claimed they would make it "virtually impossible" for the receiving countries "to enjoy cultural self-determination." The lands they had liberated apparently did not include the ether above them.[40]

Apart from the sudden intrusion of direct satellite broadcasting into the debate over media responsibilities, false and distorted information, war propaganda, and information flows threatening national cultures continued to arouse international anxiety and discussion. An international right of reply and correction, for example, had evolved from the common practice of many states (the U.S. being an exception) into an idea suitable for U.N. action. Both justice and self-defense supported the individual's ability to counter false and distorted information. At the 1948 Geneva Conference a draft convention had paved the way for a 1952 "reply communiqué" that went into force in 1962 after getting the requisite signatures.[41]

War propaganda remained a more difficult problem to solve mainly because it had become identified as part of the Cold War struggle, with the Soviet Union championing its elimination and the United States in reflexive opposition behind its absolutist free-press barricade. During the Kennedy years, however, the 1962 Disarmament Conference addressed the issue once more. While both big-power antagonists took their usual positions at first, the United States shifted ground, ending its seventeen-year stand. A draft six-point declaration, as Whitton and Larson describe it, "called on all states to adopt within the limits of their constitutional systems appropriate practical measures including legislation to give effect to a declaration against war propaganda." Designed to strengthen peace and disarmament by increasing friendly relations and cooperation among peoples and states, the agreement collapsed after the Soviets changed their position with counter-proposals the United States would not accept.[42]

As Whitton and Larson point out, the two big-power extremes on the ideological spectrum did not typify the attitudes of most nations, many of whom favored government controls. Since the U.S. Neutrality Act itself prohibits the commencement in the U.S. of hostile actions against another nation with which the United States is "at peace," and the U.S. has long restrained "radical incitements" in the press, it would seem logical for it to support the Nuremberg Principles condemning war propaganda. None of the U.N. conventions on the issue would have affected the constitutionally protected rights of the press. Nor would free-flow/

free-market doctrine overcome propaganda since the same experts argue correctly that truth would not necessarily be part of the flow, its appearance, if it occurred, would not necessarily be in time to avert war, and free flow itself would not counter a sustained campaign of incitement. The 1967 Outer Space Treaty seemed to agree since it contained provisions against the dissemination of war propaganda by satellite broadcasts.[43]

Media Responsibility and Cultural Protectionism

Two 1966 International Covenants also addressed media responsibility issues, one on Civil and Political Rights, the other on Economic, Social, and Cultural Rights. Articles 19 and 20 of the former spoke to the "special responsibilities" that accompanied the exercise of individual rights and included legal prohibitions against war propaganda and "the promotion of national, racial, or religious hatred constituting an incitement to discrimination, hostility, or violence." The second covenant gave states authority to "conserve, develop, diffuse, and protect" their cultures, including in it the right to restrict the free flow of information that "threatens culture." Among the justifiable restrictions were those over advertising and program standards. Both covenants (not signed by the United States) thus evidenced an international obligation to reduce the unrestricted flow of information to protect social order, basic values, and cultural autonomy and diversity. If the U.S. considered these odd ideas to make binding as practices among nation states, their own cultural protectionism was less blind.[44] In 1962 U.S. postal legislation required "the interception of all mail originating in a foreign country except sealed letters and mail to schools, libraries, professional institutions and government agencies if determined by the Secretary of the Treasury to be communist political propaganda." Delivery could take place only if the person addressed then specifically requested it.[45]

The theme of cultural protectionism in U.S. hands, while derided and opposed when practiced by Third World nations or introduced as acceptable international practice, had a vibrant, unilateral offensive quality none of those participants ever imagined. What surfaced as postal legislation at home reflected a willingness to defend American values wherever they might be threatened. The decade of development to which UNESCO devoted its energies was once more a decade of U.S. intervention, beginning with Cuba in 1961 and ending with Vietnam. The 1965 Dominican Republic invasion, however, best signified the way the United States exported its cultural protectionism abroad with New World Diplomatic Orders to suit itself. The Johnson Doctrine, justifying the Dominican foray, claimed the authority to intervene against the left even if it came to power in free elections. The United States had proclaimed the right of "collective self-defense against foreign ideologies."

If this was an integral part of American cultural relations, a sort of bottom line by which to measure the interaction of the nation with other cultures, it also symbolized the intense interest the United States did have in the values and attitudes adopted overseas. The government certainly realized how important it was to change men's minds, the same mission UNESCO had been authorized to achieve. Beyond intervention, therefore, a foreign cultural-relations policy had other less unilateral and less violent forms to take and still included the commitment to international understanding and cooperation through UNESCO and by other peace-building activities. During the 1960s these hopeful aspects of cultural good-will continued to receive sustained American attention. What the U.S. failed to include was an equally vigorous effort to change its own mind.[46]

U.S. Cultural Relations under Kennedy

Like a boat adrift, foreign cultural relations never had a secure intellectual or political anchorage in the government, in its natural constituency of the academic and professional intelligentsia, or among the public at large. Conceived as an immediate response to Nazi propaganda and diverted toward anticommunist containment thereafter, the field of culture was still seeking a full and authentic position of importance in foreign policy when the Kennedy administration came to power. Besides the desire to overcome its haphazard and fragmented management in the 1950s and give it a "New Frontier" of purpose, the Democrats also recognized that recent global developments accentuated the need for a clear and comprehensive reorganization of the cultural arena. The Cold War had settled into a nuclear deadlock; the supposed monolithic communist bloc had developed a polycentric character; and national liberation from a colonial past had made the global setting more diverse, complex, and challenging than it had ever been before. The egalitarian principles of international law and the democratic parliaments of international life challenged the elitist management of international affairs. As Seán MacBride has said, there were now many voices in one world, new claimants to shared authority insisting on pluralistic bargaining over the definition of the issues and the division of the spoils. Mutual understanding had never been more important, and cultural relations were the key to it.[47]

The momentum for change had been accelerating since 1956, and the excitement for ideas and reform under JFK seemed to suggest that the cultural orphan might finally win adoption as a legitimate child of U.S. foreign policy. Thirty-five advanced nations had organized systems for cultural interrelations by 1958, a sign of their significance. The Morrill Report on "The University and World Affairs" in 1956 had proposed raising the status of State Department cultural activities to the level of an assistant secretary and giving them more substantial funding. The Congressional Legislative Reference Service in 1959 deplored the lack of co-ordination, but the White House had taken no action at that time. In 1959 the publication of *As Others See Us* detailed in "a barrage of in-dictments" a pervasive anti-Americanism abroad that undermined the execution of the country's foreign policy and its standing in public esteem.[48] After Kennedy's inauguration "a spate of expert reports" and a 1961 State Department Task Force all noted the degree to which cul-tural relations had "fallen far short" in performance and achievement. The American Assembly's 1956 analysis of *The Representation of the United States* abroad was updated in its 1962 evaluation of *Cultural Affairs and Foreign Relations*. Walter H. C. Laves had authored a 1960 re-port, *Toward a National Effort in International Education and Cultural Affairs*; its importance was underlined by Laves's reputation in the field and his association with UNESCO.[49] The Brookings Institution followed in 1964 with Charles Frankel's incisive and critical study of *The Ne-glected Aspect of Foreign Affairs: American Educational and Cultural Policy Abroad*.[50] If think tanks of experts were ever to effect major re-forms, surely this concentration of intelligence and insight had created the conditions for successfully moving cultural relations to a higher plane of priority.

The many evaluations did not omit UNESCO from the scope of their inquiry. They called upon the government to give it a larger share of at-tention in formulating its foreign policy. The organization should be "vigorously supported" as "an invaluable center of consultation, in-quiry, and documentation" and as "a frugal investment" that had as-sisted U.S. policy "in many ways."[51] Experts in education urged the United States to "endorse more fully" UNESCO's efforts in that field as they were "particularly beneficial to American education."[52] Overall, the government was advised to apply itself more energetically to coop-erating with "international and regional organizations, and particularly strengthen U.S. leadership in UNESCO" and "participate more vigor-ously" in its affairs.[53]

As a center of and clearinghouse for the world's professional knowl-edge in education, science, and culture, UNESCO had "highlighted the key issues" in those fields, drawn up standards for taking "remedial action," and defined solutions for correcting the imbalances between the more and less developed worlds. Its major utility, according to Charles Frankel, lay in its ability to "remove suspicions of 'cultural impe-rialism.' "[54] But UNESCO could also achieve results by international collaboration that no single country could do by its own efforts, espe-cially in the area of science, the most intensely cooperative discipline by the very nature of its work.

The United States National Commission for UNESCO aired a similarly enthusiastic call for change and underlined the necessity for improve-ments in its affairs as well as those of the State Department. The times had become more critical, since development demanded a "greater sense of immediacy and purposefulness" than intellectual cooperation had. The struggle for peace, as the USNC saw it, would be overwhelmed by "illiteracy, poverty, disease, alienation, . . . famine, the gap between the rich and the poor, and urbanization." Shifting its focus from the minds of men to the quality of life, the commission spoke of the "crisis" that added "unprecedented urgency" to UNESCO's tasks, yet it also believed that the extraordinary tempo of scientific discovery and modern communications would yield answers to those intractable problems. Resolving to correct "the great vacuums of information about UNESCO," attract another hundred NGOs to UNESCO-related projects, mobilize the private sector for effective support, and improve its liaison with State, the USNC foresaw its own reinvigoration by additional staff and resources.[55]

It might well have imagined that outcome since the common consensus of the Kennedy experts envisioned the "need to double or treble" the U.S. cultural effort within the next three to five years, with expenditures rising from 1962's "gross outlays of 50 million dollars to 200 million by 1966 or 1967." In terms of total national-security spending, even these outlays would not significantly raise the educational and cultural budget much over its former level of 1 percent of that figure, but it was a beginning.[56]

The New Frontier and Cultural Foreign Policy

The restless activism so characteristic of the New Frontier was, moreover, to leave its mark on foreign policy and its cultural component. Having documented the startling deficiencies of management, coordination, and implementation in culture's various international relations, the Kennedy administration took charge in a series of administrative and policy decisions remarkable for the range of their attention. JFK and his reformers in quick succession created the position of assistant secretary of state for educational and cultural affairs, made State by executive order the coordinator of all activities in those areas, reorganized cultural relations on a geographic basis to stimulate their connection to the country desks and make them a more attractive career opportunity, "enlarged and upgraded" the State Department's office of science advisor with a bureau director for international scientific affairs and increased the number of embassy science attachés to seventeen, created the U.S. Advisory Commission on International Educational and Cultural Affairs, appointed former UNESCO co-founder and ex-U.S. Senator William Benton as the government's representative to UNESCO with ambassadorial status for the first time, and met with UNESCO's director-general as a signal of U.S. interest and support.[57]

At the same time, the entire program of Fulbright educational exchanges received a thorough-going review, culminating in the 1961 Fulbright-Hays Mutual Educational and Cultural Exchange Act. This legislation "broadened, regularized, and coordinated" the process and emphasized its reciprocal nature by using the word "mutual" in the title. Its purposes included both the objective of balance in the exchanges, a necessity in all cultural activity including information and "the development of friendly, sympathetic, and peaceful relations between the United States and other countries of the world." To underscore this renewed commitment to international cooperation and to the then 71 international organizations, the U.S. was sending out delegations to their conferences at the rate of one a day in 1962. A year later Kennedy made his "Strategy of Peace" speech specifically denying any desire to impose a "Pax Americana" on the world and calling for an end to the arms race, a test-ban treaty, and a search for mutual understanding between the U.S. and the U.S.S.R.[58]

An atmosphere of clarity and vision also seemed to envelop the bureaucracy of foreign policy at Foggy Bottom. In his survey of State Department responses to Kennedy reform imperatives, Philip Coombs listed seventeen different proposals for improving cultural relations. In terms of the problems they attacked, these projects would have focused on "human resources" as essential to any AID and Alliance for Progress development support; invigorated and coordinated the private sector's involvement in education, science, and culture; improved the teaching of language and world affairs at all levels of American education; stimulated exchanges with the Third World; enlarged and upgraded all U.S. cultural activities overseas, including the nation's schools and colleges there; and "reorganized and strengthened" the Bureau of Educational and Cultural Affairs and its mission to UNESCO. Overall the State Department seemed ready to "clarify and articulate the basic philosophy, concepts, and guidelines" of its foreign cultural relations. It was, as Coombs described it, "a big effort" and one that would require "time and effort" to bring about successfully.[59]

It was most certainly a projection of the president's own intentions and ideals. In his meeting with Director-General Maheu shortly before his assassination, Kennedy had said to him, "Tell me what you want the United States to do for UNESCO? I want a strong UNESCO. How can we help?" And Maheu had replied, "I want your intellectual understanding and support and comprehension of UNESCO, your perception and insight into UNESCO and its problems." According to Benton, who was present, the director-general left the White House "inspired and grateful." It is a mark of what the U.S. and UNESCO have lost to compare that dialogue with the rancorous, mean-spirited exchanges characteristic of Ronald Reagan's international outlook and understanding.[60]

Charles Frankel and the Early Johnson Years

Kennedy's death, Lyndon Johnson's accession to office and his re-election, and the administration's confrontation with the civil-rights movement at home, as well as the growing quagmire of Vietnam, must have disrupted and diverted the cultural initiatives set in motion in 1961. Yet the enthusiasm for reform did not entirely wane under LBJ. In the summer of 1965, for example, he appointed Charles Frankel as assistant secretary of state for educational and cultural affairs. Frankel had been an astute, knowledgeable critic of their troubled disarray and LBJ's choice for the position implied agreement with his analysis and an interest in seeing further effective change.

On his arrival Frankel found that much work still needed to be done. He discovered an "inadequate understanding . . . of the nature of his job, a residue of congressional suspicion toward the entire program, and deep-seated problems of policy and administration." Frankel still saw the necessity for disengaging cultural relations from the "psychological warriors" and "technicians" of development assistance and leading it into the promised land of mutual understanding. Americans, he believed, had not yet "internalized the habit of international cooperation" and were not yet ready for "international intellectual disarmament" in their cultural affairs. Between 1965 and his departure in 1967, Frankel tried to restore to the conduct of cultural relations its long-range view outside the "competitive and cold warish" boundaries of its customary location. And most of all, he wanted to make the United States "educated up to its position in the world" and the American people "less ignorant of themselves." In its breadth and sensitivity this vision represented an unusual outlook, almost prophetic in its anticipation of the disasters awaiting a nation ignoring the message of regeneration, and a rare point of view at such levels of government administration.[61]

Apart from the stimulation and direction his own leadership could supply to State Department attitudes and practices, Frankel determined to put his energy behind the reform of international education, as if that might return the U.S. and UNESCO to the idealism of 1945 and counteract the anti-Americanism military intervention and covert operations had induced over the years. He particularly hoped to "end the subordination of international education to public relations . . . , reduce the parochialism of American schools," and cultivate "two way exchanges" (the old idea of balance). A key to effecting this change was to be the creation of a "Corps of Education officers" assigned as embassy attachés. In addition, Frankel urged Secretary of State Rusk to free cultural-affairs officers and education and culture as a whole from their subordination to propaganda. A third element of the package involved amendments to the McCarran-Walter Immigration Act that would ease visa restrictions impeding the free flow of exchanges of "scholars, scientists, and artists from Communist countries" and, of course, cut down on the red-tape delays in granting waivers.[62]

Lyndon Johnson seemed prepared to jump on Frankel's bandwagon. At a Smithsonian Institution event honoring the founder and its anniversary, LBJ spoke in the exalted manner reminiscent of those testimonials to UNESCO's own creation. It needs to be quoted at some length:

> We know today that . . . ideas, not armaments, will shape our lasting prospects for peace; that the conduct of our foreign policy will advance no faster than the curriculum of our classrooms; . . .
>
> That is why I have directed a special task force . . . to recommend a broad and long-range plan of worldwide educational endeavors. . . .
> First, to assist the educational effort of the developing nations . . .
>
> Second, to help our schools and universities increase their knowledge of the world and the people who inhabit it. Third, to advance the exchange of students and teachers who travel and work outside their native lands. Fourth, to increase the free flow of books and ideas and art, of works of science and imagination. And fifth, to assemble meetings of men and women from every discipline and every culture to ponder the common problems of mankind.
>
> In all these endeavors, I pledge that the United States will play its full role.

René Maheu believed the Smithsonian address represented "the ideals of UNESCO" and the organization's Executive Board was reported to be "impressed and hopeful."[63]

There seemed to be no immediate reason not to be. Johnson followed up with a White House Conference on International Cooperation in December 1965, and in his message to Congress in February 1966 the president described his proposals in education as the "moral equivalent of war" and "at the heart of the United States' international relations." The country, he stated "expected to learn as well as to teach." The sleeping giant bureaucracy seemed indifferent at first. As Frankel recalled, "they somehow gave the impression that the meeting [on the Smithsonian speech] was an interruption of more important business," while "the budget people . . . were also fundamentally unconvinced that anything was going to happen."[64]

Backing Away: The Vietnam War as a Factor

In September 1966 Senator Fulbright predicted "a dim future" for international educational and cultural exchanges as long as the Vietnam War continued, and LBJ's inspiring project did not even receive a reference during the congressional debate on appropriations for the cultural-relations budget that year. The USIA, meanwhile, opposed the idea of education attachés in the embassies—probably because they were seen as competitive with its control of the cultural-affairs officers — and the Congress took no action on the International Education Act. AID reported that it saw "no future" for education in its activities. When Congress finally examined the plan for education officers, the House committee rejected it after a five-minute debate, and only one senator bothered to attend the committee hearing on the same topic. Hostility to exchanges had also surfaced when some members of Congress expressed their outrage over grants to opponents of the Vietnam War. Senator McClellan claimed "the country had had too much of all this international business" in responding to the education legislation. Soon thereafter Charles Frankel described the International Education Act as "a dead letter."[65]

If a spasm of life still twitched in the concept, it evidenced itself only in the October 1967 Williamsburg World Conference on the Crisis in Education where Johnson repeated the themes he had so boldly proclaimed at the Smithsonian. At Paris the UNESCO Executive Board now realized this was evidently all talk and that there would be no follow-up to the earlier initiatives and little was said about them. In Frankel's view, educational and cultural affairs still lacked the essential ingredient of political appeal, since their long-range consequences could never demonstrate "evidence of effectiveness" in the immediate terms policy and national interest demanded. Yet the larger catastrophe of Vietnam had played an important role in the demise of cultural reform, as Fulbright had asserted. Frankel had watched the "souring of the Washington mood" owing to the war and the protest against it. At the November 1966 UNESCO General Conference, he reported the "untold damage" it had done to the U.S. reputation. U.N. Secretary-General U Thant had even taken his attacks against U.S. intervention in speeches to the American people. Obsessed by the war, the administration and Congress had little interest in other areas, especially those that had traditionally been low priority. Even within the bureaucracy not much had changed. Coordination of cultural affairs remained "faulty"; any major reorganization seemed unlikely, however desirable; the Budget Bureau could not fathom the location of international education "outside the framework of technical development or the promotion of the American image"; and policies still had to be defended in terms of their short-run benefits. Recognizing the stalemated prospects for change, Frankel resigned his post at the end of 1967.[66]

Resurgent Anticommunism

Although Vietnam and bureaucratic passivity and entrenched self-interest had helped fossilize the remnants of change, anticommunism and antagonism toward multilateral affairs also conditioned the American outlook. Kennedy's public rejection of a "Pax Americana" and the initiation of an era of détente did not necessarily affect the long established and customary suspicions both the executive and legislative branches still harbored for subversive activities at home and abroad. And international organizations that included both Communist states and Third World nations pursuing policies embraced by the Soviet bloc or receiving aid from it suffered from the guilt-by-association syndrome infecting the American view of the world.

A Senate hearing in 1963 symbolized the political excitement one "subversive" misstep could set in motion. A UNESCO pamphlet, "Equality of Rights between Races and Nationalities in the U.S.S.R.," brought about an extensive review of that organization's direction and purpose because of the public clamor that had arisen over the deposit of this supposedly misleading Soviet assessment in U.S. libraries as a UNESCO publication. According to the State Department, the Soviet study was "a vehicle for political propaganda" and violated UNESCO's principles. Senators Church of Idaho and Carlson of Kansas reported "considerable opposition" to UNESCO and "public pressures on Congress" to eliminate U.S. contributions to the U.N. Although Assistant Secretary of State Lucius D. Battle said UNESCO had generally "resisted Soviet efforts," had published "hundreds" of objective studies that no one had criticized, and had received protests over only some 2 percent, judgment about the agency tended to be based on the appearance of any "tendentious" Soviet actions or materials the United States considered propaganda.[67]

The Soviet analysis of its racial equality and the U.S. condemnation of UNESCO for printing it may have reflected not just the superpowers' ideological rivalry, but also some considerable U.S. embarrassment as well. What with the FBI's surveillance of Martin Luther King, ghetto riots, civil-rights protests, and COINTELPRO disruption of Black activists, the theme had a sensitive raw quality for the U.S. government. The distinguished black historian John Hope Franklin, then serving an eight-year term on the Fulbright Board during the 1960s, recalled the FBI coming in to report on candidates for the award. The agent would question the "fitness" of the nominee to represent his country abroad if, for example, they had discovered evidence "he was seen going to a party where there were Negroes." Franklin had to be vigilant, he remembered, lest the subject of subversive racial attitudes and behavior lose the country numerous good people for the overseas exchange program.[68] All candidates for any U.N. agency employment were, of course, still subject to security investigations by the International Organizations Employee Loyalty Board.[69]

Other signs of un-American paranoia carried on the Cold War behavioral patterns of earlier decades. Charles Frankel witnessed a labor leader rejected for an overseas speaking engagement because the State Department had "adverse information" about him, largely "loose innuendo." Frankel's proposed invitation to a Cuban dancer aroused concern because the department felt it might arouse congressional opposition to an East-West trade agreement under negotiation. And, as previously noted, opponents of the Vietnam War became unworthy candidates for educational exchange grants in some congressional eyes. In 1967 *Ramparts* magazine's exposé of CIA covert cultural operations publicized the apparent subordination of many representatives of the American intellectual community to Cold War considerations defined by the intelligence agencies. The discovery tainted the cultural relations of the United States, revealing them to be secret schemes to promote ulterior national purposes rather than the open opportunities for mutual understanding they pretended to be. J. Edgar Hoover still had the kind of influence he exhibited when setting up shop at the U.N. In 1967 a détente-inspired consular treaty with the U.S.S.R. proposed an increase in consulates in both nations. The Senate did not ratify the treaty when Hoover charged the Soviets would greatly expand their espionage activities under it. Not until Lyndon Johnson was able to announce Hoover's approval of the treaty did the Senate proceed with its ratification.[70]

While the American Legion and the DAR did not stir up popular anti-communist opposition to the U.N. and UNESCO during the 1960s, the grassroots continued to display its muscles on issues involving the "reds." Below the surface of the hippie outrage, youthful protest, urban riots, and civil-rights and anti-war marches that dominated the headlines of that tumultuous decade, a slow, steady increase of fundamental conservatism was under way. In the Goldwater candidacy the American Enterprise Institute, the Young Americans for Freedom, and the John Birch Society demonstrated a new political coalition, one that broadened in the late 1960s and 1970s.[71] During the Kennedy-Johnson years, conservatism indicated its continuing interest in "changing the American mind" and anchoring it in free-enterprise economics and anticommunism. When Tshombe led the Katanga secession from the newly liberated Belgian Congo, for example, conservatives backed the Katanga Lobby and called its military arm "freedom fighters." Ever since 1953, the California based China Lobby had had an immense political influence over American foreign policy toward the mainland government. With a Committee of One Million that was able to attract 339 congressional signatures for its advertisements, the lobby traumatized China Policy into a hostile rigidity exploiting trade embargoes, travel restrictions, CIA overflights and propaganda broadcasts, and a military alliance (SEATO) designed to isolate the People's Republic of China.[72] In terms of U.N.-UNESCO policies, this intransigent opposition had made the United States itself an increasingly isolated voice against the admission of China to those two bodies in spite of their designation as organizations open to universal membership. The U.S. Congress passed almost annual resolutions denouncing recognition of the People's Republic or its seating in the U.N., and some members threatened to force the U.S. to withdraw should that government be admitted. In 1961 recognition was still a decade away.

Meanwhile, the House Un-American Activities Committee and the Senate Internal Security Committee kept an investigative watch over Americans that organized themselves to help build the defenses of peace in the minds of men. UNESCO's peace and disarmament studies were essential and required elements in its assigned educational mission, yet both committees regarded this whole field of interest as suspect and an instrument of Soviet propaganda. In the 1984 hearings on the U.S. withdrawal from UNESCO, Dr. Harold Jacobson noted the irony and inconsistency of this attitude on the part of the United States. Not only did the latter have the world's "largest arms control community," but its social scientists led in the exploration of the subject and courses in peace had become common components of university curricula.[73]

The 1960 investigation of the National Committee for a Sane Nuclear Policy (SANE) and the 1961–62 hearings on the Women's Strike for Peace indicated, however, the intervention into and politicizing of the free-market debate voluntary associations wished to conduct with the American public. It was a taboo that even threatened their discussion of the test-ban proposal, an avowed aim of the Kennedy administration.[74] Some years later the State Department blocked a conference on "perception as a factor in arms control agreements." that U.S. social scientists and UNESCO planned to conduct, because U.S. policy remained hostile to such UNESCO-sponsored explorations of these issues.[75]

A Reassessment

As the Johnson administration came to a close with its own foreign cultural policies still in limbo and a war devouring its energy and resources, it decided to conduct a major reassessment of all its relations with international organizations, obviously including UNESCO. Perhaps it was aware of the violence still abroad in the world. By 1968 there had been "379 instances of armed conflict since 1945," 150 of them big enough to affect all of the international community and 70 invoking U.N. attention.[76]

Perhaps this National Security Council survey reflected the growing disquiet the United States was feeling as it lost control of its automatic majorities in the U.N. and UNESCO to new Third World coalitions of voting power. Intimations of a growing U.S. estrangement and disengagement had been signaled even before that control had declined. And official attitudes and political options needed to be evaluated in terms of the contemporary costs and benefits to the national interest. For UNESCO the NSC study represented the first "national policy study in which relations with UNESCO . . . [were] viewed in the overall context of U.S. foreign policy" and was "the only comprehensive, authoritative statement of United States policy towards UNESCO ever produced by the U.S. Government in the history of U.S./UNESCO relations," according to Richard Nobbe of the State Department's UNESCO Bureau.[77]

A sense of the government's view had already come to light in Assistant Secretary of State Battle's 1963 Senate testimony. Unlike the unguarded and enthusiastic comments of the academic and professional supporters or even of the Kennedy admirers of UNESCO, the State Department's outlook sounded like the sober, more cynical realism of a diplomatic bureaucracy evaluating a poor relation regarded as spendthrift, undependable, and inept. "We are re-examining our complete participation in this organization," Battle warned, and there were "many parts of the UNESCO program with which we are heartily in disagreement." Although it was still to the country's advantage to remain a member, Battle also noted that there were "many areas in which I have serious doubts." U.S. participation was to be reviewed "with great care."[78]

If the assistant secretary had been "very disturbed" about UNESCO, what improvements did UNESCO have to make to allay those misgivings? Budget, management, and program concentration headed the list as they almost always had and would continue to do. UNESCO should cut back on meetings, conferences, seminars, youth gatherings, tendentious publications, and polemical as opposed to scholarly studies, programs duplicated by or competitive with other U.N. agency work, and the support of NGOs that could be self-sustaining. Projects should not be allowed to run on and should be subject to more critical evaluation. Supportive toward the education sector and scientific investigations such as oceanography, Battle (or the State Department) never seemed to acknowledge the vast expanse of need or the political imperatives demanding some sort of global demonstration if UNESCO was to make itself known and a felt necessity to its diverse, scattered constituency. Nor was the question ever asked whether UNESCO should not be doing more rather than less on a budget comparable to that of an American university.[79]

The United States was unwilling to admit its starring role as a featured actor in the UNESCO drama. The "we" versus "they" pose seemed an odd caricature of the American claim to world influence and leadership, carrying on as the pathetic hand-wringing victim of organizations it had founded and dominated. As the U.N. system took on new members, in fact, more energy and input were required to master the politics of these more complex forms of international cooperation, but the United States reduced rather than strengthened its leadership. Battle's testimony did refer to certain omissions in that respect, such as failure to follow up after general conferences, problems with the quality of U.S. representation, exclusion of the U.S. National Commission from active participation in policy and personnel issues, and lack of contact between the American permanent delegation and the director-general. All true, yet rarely rectified. It symbolized the difficulty that the UNESCO operation had in self-renovation, something endemic to the government's administration of all its cultural relations. Better to reform UNESCO than point the finger at itself. When Lucius Battle concluded his appearance, he hoped that the State Department's current re-examination of UNESCO policy would give it "a clear conception of what we are trying to do within it as a nation." He must still be waiting.[80]

Lyndon Johnson's more comprehensive policy-planning analysis of 1968 indicated the government's continuing uneasiness about UNESCO and the United States role in it, yet, like Battle's forlorn hope for change, it, too, "was never adopted by the National Security Council and, in fact, had limited impact," as Richard Nobbe reported in his review of all the government studies. Directed and authored by Dr. Henry Kellerman, himself a veteran of five years at UNESCO as head of the U.S. permanent delegation (1956–61), and informed by the contributions of all the government agencies "with major responsibility for UNESCO," the Kellerman report expertly addressed itself to the three major concerns that needed serious and intelligent rethinking. UNESCO's twentieth anniversary, its shift of focus into development-supported activity, and its rapid expansion in size during the last decade all suggested the usefulness of this reassessment, the kind of critical, objective review academic accreditation regularly requires.[81]

The policy-planning staff, therefore, took under serious reconsideration "the focus and cohesion" and "the priority objectives" of the program; the organization's adaptation to "the requirements of an expanding, changing program" to ensure a "realistic balance between UNESCO's aspirations and capabilities"; and the effective mobilization and management of U.S. participation "strengthening it at all appropriate levels." Who would argue with these criteria? Nor would anyone oppose the evaluation of projects to determine which, if any, did "exceed UNESCO's competence." Nor could there be objection to a desire to see the programming be "responsive to the interests of all member states." What is startling is the often official uninterest in carrying any of the findings or recommendations into the realm of action; the United States behaved like a general evolving strategies of battle for an offensive that never took place.[82]

Although the Kellerman report has not yet been declassified for historical research, Richard Nobbe's summary of its purpose and contents indicated the conclusion. "There were apparently no issues sufficiently grave to call for extreme actions, such as withdrawal or suspension of U.S. payments . . . ," but the United States would not want to give "unqualified support to all UNESCO activities." Implications of confusion and internal disagreement were apparent in Nobbe's comment that the policy proposals "did not lend themselves to concrete action and that there were strong differences of opinion on various portions of the study by the U.S. mission and the Bureau of International Educational and Cultural Affairs which were papered over."[83]

There must have been other items of history that were papered over as well such as the government's long ambivalence toward culture and UNESCO; its early elimination of the National Commission from the scene of the action; its failure to manage, coordinate, or focus its own foreign cultural relations effectively; and its use of the U.S. delegation to UNESCO General Conferences as a repository of reward for party hacks. Bureaucratic amnesia may also have buried the early and now customary politicization of U.S. personnel practices by security testing and the continuing overview of UNESCO as a tool of the U.S. national interest abroad. And one cannot forget the irony of John F. Kennedy's question to René Maheu as that decade of anticipated change got underway, "I want a strong UNESCO. How can we help?"[84]

UNESCO's Increasing Autonomy

Seen as an isolated member of a large conglomeration of international organizations, UNESCO's rapidly increasing autonomy from U.S. control seemed to have been an accurate assessment of its status. While the United States claimed to be losing multilateral influence there as pluralism became the dominating factor, that trend was, in fact, more illusory than real, as Robert Cox and Harold Jacobson have argued in their account of the *Anatomy of Influence*. The "pitiful giant" syndrome has had a useful career as a cover story, after all, as a supposed abandonment of power that has wished to conceal the locus of its still impressive command. As the raucous, strident, and even reckless voices of the newly liberated nations demanded redress, it made more political sense to disguise the presence of American control to avoid the open denial of their clamorous calls for equality of wealth and decision-making authority.[85]

When those vigorous expressions of nationalistic self-assertion began to dominate various international forums, the more powerful countries could also deride and denigrate the rhetoric as irrational and extremist, manifestations of hysteria rather than frustration. At the same time, the U.S. and its industrialized allies could direct UNESCO's attention to the technical, functional, and purely scientific activities that would help build the necessary infrastructures of growth still determined by their control of resources. As Cox and Jacobson have concluded, the developed states "have sought to direct the international agencies with a large membership from less-developed countries into a more exclusive preoccupation with development assistance, since they no longer wished to use them for issues of concern directly to themselves."[86]

In this process, the United States "appeared to be more retiring," as an active influence in UNESCO but "seen from the perspective of the whole system of interagency relations" where the U.S. retained its power over funding and policy decisions in, for example, the UNDP and the voluntary donations, it still exercised "ultimate control . . . even though it was seldom asserted directly." According to the Cox-Jacobson analysis, "international organizations could provide only the services that governments would accept and the levels were determined by the decisions of a few of the most powerful states." Looking at this complex of power in the early 1970s, the two authors noticed the increasing dissatisfaction among the LDCs with that straitjacket of autonomy and minimal level of service. If they demanded more of UNESCO and kindred agencies, Cox and Jacobson suspected, the powerful would "diminish the role" of such organizations and confine them to an ever greater number of "low salience tasks." But they could not have foreseen the withdrawal of the United States from UNESCO. In the 1960s still in a controlling situation, the U.S. felt UNESCO could not do it any damage.[87]

As a wider perspective illuminates the relationships of power between the U.S. and UNESCO, it also suggests some of the missing elements that would have made for a more successful and enduring collaboration. Compared to the U.S. mission at the United Nations (USUN), for example, the American delegations to UNESCO lacked the kind of national reputation, talents, and qualities of leadership those representatives possessed. Nor were they often notable professionals from the educational, scientific, and cultural communities. The chief delegate never had the same direct access to the president and was not regularly accompanied to conferences by select members of Congress as at the U.N. The USUN also had enough independence to dissent from State Department policies once or twice a session and remained in the public eye by geography, press coverage, and almost daily briefings to gatherings of citizens. USUN had the recognition and the constituency UNESCO never developed.[88]

By 1968 the United States and UNESCO seemed to have established the rhythm and style of their uneasy collaboration, one that marked the twentieth anniversary of their relationship. Two moments of surprising American enthusiasm had been counterpoised against a backdrop of official indifference sometimes verging on disdain. In each case, the U.S. national interest had expected UNESCO to serve it well, first in the mass communication of American liberal values as the road to peace and later as the international instrument of American orchestrated development policies that promoted the traditional Open Door dynamics of economic expansion. Disillusion with collective activity set in early in both instances when neither the Cold War nor the constructive channels of economic growth proved that appealing to UNESCO's diverse member states still seeking something more than ideological anticommunism and permanently inferior economic status for their own national futures.

A second identifiable strand in the U.S./UNESCO association concerned the connection between the former's foreign cultural relations and those similar multilateral efforts directed through UNESCO. In twenty years of trying and after dozens of expert professional evaluations suggesting new directions, the educational and cultural policies still remained captive to propaganda, public relations, and technical-assistance activities. Unable to set its own cultural house in order, the United States transferred its frustration with the problem to its international ally. Continually finding fault with UNESCO's administration and direction, the U.S. ignored its own ineptitude and confusion. In the interplay of these dynamics, a third dimension of historical repetition added its ominous partnership to the equation. Domestic political support for internationalism's finest goals failed to attain the effective influence over policy its coalition of professional organizations should have produced. The opponents of global participation in all its cultural manifestations, on the other hand, linked their diatribes of isolationist distrust to the traditional grassroots emotions of anticommunism, nativism, and America First. With mass opinion about UNESCO unformed and misinformed, the lobby with access to Congress and the executive branch, the resources to attract public notoriety, and the themes of subversion to which Americans usually responded would undoubtedly carry the day. The explosive events of the 1970s in UNESCO were about to provide the occasion for that political opportunity to take place.

NOTES

1. Denis Goulet, "The Cruel Choice: A New Concept in the Theory of Development," quoted in Hazzard, pp. 229–33.
2. Lowry and Hooker, pp. 43–44.
3. Hyman, pp. 547–48.
4. Sewell, *UNESCO*, pp. 200–201.
5. United States National Commission for UNESCO, *Getting America Behind UNESCO, passim.*
6. Hilsman, pp. 23, 57, 249.
7. Sewell, *UNESCO*, pp. 201–4.
8. Schlesinger, pp. 168–70, 204–5, 465–66, 508–9, 593–95, 605–9.
9. *Ibid.*, pp. 587–89, 609–13.
10. *Ibid.*, pp. 587–91, 612, 615–19.
11. *Ibid.*, pp. 613, 617.
12. *Ibid.*, pp. 587–89, 593–600.
13. Frankel, *The Neglected Aspect*, pp. 90–91.
14. Hazzard, pp. 229–33.
15. Frankel, *The Neglected Aspect*, pp. 90–95.
16. Frankel, *High on Foggy Bottom*, pp. 21–23.
17. Sewell, *Functionalism and World Politics*, pp. 93–94, 199.
18. Kolko, pp. 56–81.
19. Schlesinger, pp. 585–87, 591–92; see also Kolko, p. 70.

20. Kolko, pp. 56–81; and see Schlesinger, p. 590.

21. Sewell, *Functionalism and World Politics*, pp. 111, 115, 208, 222, 227–34.

22. Schlesinger, pp. 589–600, 610–11.

23. Kolko, pp. 65, 70–72, 79, 56–81, *passim*.

24. *Ibid.*; and see Rohan Samarajiwa, "The History of the New Information Order," in "World Forum," pp. 111–12.

25. Sewell, "Pluralism," pp. 159, 161; see also Coate, p. 13.

26. Sewell, "Pluralism," pp. 144, 160; Cox and Jacobson, pp. 412, 428–32.

27. Sewell, "Pluralism," pp. 144–45, 160.

28. Samarajiwa, "History," in "World Forum," pp. 110–11.

29. Sewell, *UNESCO*, pp. 202–4, 217, 228–31; see also Finkelstein, "Conference Document," pp. 31–32, 37–38; Coate, p. 10.

30. Sewell, *UNESCO*, pp. 223, 230–31, 235–50; Hoggart, pp. 31–38. Sewell, "Pluralism," pp. 145, 160; U.S. Congress, House Subcommittee on International Organizations, "UNESCO: Challenges and Opportunities," pp. 39, 43–45, and Appendix 1, "UNESCO and the U.S. National Interest, A Statement by the U.S. National Commission for UNESCO," June 1974, pp. 71– 74, 78; Behrstock, pp. 167–69.

31. Finkelstein, "Conference Document," p. 39; Appendix 1, "UNESCO and the U.S. National Interest," pp. 74–77; Sewell, "Pluralism," p. 152; Sewell, *UNESCO*, p. 251.

32. Behrstock, pp. 167–68.

33. Appendix 1, "UNESCO and the U.S. National Interest," pp. 68–69.

34. John E. Fobes statement in "World Forum," pp. 163–64; Fobes Interview, February 5, 1987.

35. Nordenstreng with Hannikainen, p. 7.

36. Whitton and Larson, pp. 183–84;

37. *Ibid.*, pp. 207, 210–19.

38. Sewell, *UNESCO*, pp. 256–61; Fobes, "World Forum," pp. 163–65; Wete, p. 3; MacBride, abridged edition, pp. 31, 56.

39. Nordenstreng with Hannikainen, p. 14.

40. Sewell, *UNESCO*, p. 261.

41. Nordenstreng with Hannikainen, p. 169.

42. Whitton and Larson, pp. 187–93, 234–42, 245–48.

43. Nordenstreng with Hannikainen, p. 169.

44. MacBride, p. 140; Raube-Wilson, pp. 116–19, 125–27; Nordenstreng with Hannikainen, p. 169.

45. Whitton and Larson, p. 205.

46. Franck, pp. 70–71; Lowry and Hooker, p. 44.

47. See Beichman, p. 181.

48. Lowry and Hooker, pp. 44, 58–62, 65.

49. Coombs, pp. 152–53; see also Shuster, pp. 14, 24.

50. Frankel, *The Neglected Aspect*, p. viii.

51. Shuster, pp. 22–23, 27, 33.

52. Wilson, pp. 102–9.

53. Coombs, pp. 153, 157.

54. Frankel, *The Neglected Aspect*, p. 130.

55. United States National Commission, *Getting America Behind UNESCO*, *passim*.

56. Coombs, pp. 165–66.

57. Frankel, *The Neglected Aspect*, p. 36; interview with Lucius D. Battle, April 27, 1987, Washington, DC; Lowry and Hooker, p. 42; Revelle, pp. 136–37; Kranish, pp. 15–16.

58. Coombs, pp. 153–54; Beichman, p. 64; Hilsman, p. 347.

59. Coombs, pp. 154–55.

60. Hyman, pp. 547–49.

61. Frankel, *High on Foggy Bottom*, pp. 10, 20–29.

62. *Ibid.*, pp. 33–34, 36, 40, 66, 70, 128.

63. *Ibid.*, pp. 42, 127.

64. *Ibid.*, pp. 42–44.

65. *Ibid.*, pp. 66, 70, 76, 130–31, 134, 166, 191, 197, 200.

66. *Ibid.*, pp. 64, 128, 175, 196, 199, 206, 223–24; Franck, pp. 117, 154–57.

67. U.S. Congress, Senate Foreign Relations Committee, "Activities and Procedures of UNESCO," pp. 2–5, 21, 32.

68. Interview with John Hope Franklin, May 1, 1987, New York, NY.

69. Behrstock, pp. 35–46.

70. Frankel, *High on Foggy Bottom*, pp. 44, 139, 160–63; Beichman, p. 208.

71. Saloma, pp. xvii–xviii, 3; Morgan, *Washington Post*, January 4, 1981.

72. Hilsman, pp. 253, 261, 267, 292–95, 298–99, 306–7, 309.

73. U.S. Congress, House Foreign Affairs Committee, "U.S. Withdrawal from UNESCO," pp. 253–54.

74. Goodman, pp. 437–42.

75. House Foreign Affairs Committee, "U.S. Withdrawal from UNESCO," pp. 253–54.

76. Beichman, p. 31.

77. Nobbe, p. 1, and *ibid.*, "Annotated Bibliography," p. 1.

78. Senate Foreign Relations Committee, "Activities and Procedures of UNESCO," pp. 1–3, 19–22, 32.

79. *Ibid.*

80. *Ibid.*, pp. 14–17, 25–26, 31–32; Beichman, p. 118.

81. Nobbe, "Annotated Bibliography," p. 1; interview with Dr. Henry Kellerman, Washington, D.C., March 19, 1987.

82. *Ibid.*

83. *Ibid.*

84. United States National Commission, *Getting America Behind UNESCO*, passim.

85. Cox and Jacobson, pp. 432–33.

86. *Ibid.*

87. *Ibid.*, and p. 412.

88. Beichman, pp. xiv, xv, 7, 22–24, 81, 131–32, 136, 140, 171. The American presence in the International Telecommunications Union suggests what salience can create in attitude and effort toward a U.N. agency. One example will suffice. Before the 1963 Extraordinary Administrative Radio Conference that was to establish regulations for the spectrum, the United States determined to dominate the proceedings. For two years the government prepared its case aided by the Rand Corporation, Lockheed, General Electric, and other multinational entities. GE alone committed 200 of its staff to the project. Successfully coordinating and managing this multitude of private-sector and government bodies through an InterAgency Radio Advisory Committee and the FCC, the delegation easily triumphed at the conference. It was a demonstration of administrative skill, technical virtuosity, and political influence that the United States never assembled for any UNESCO agenda. Harold Jacobson, "ITU: A Potpourri of Bureaucrats and Industrialists," in Cox and Jacobson, pp. 69–73, 81.

VIII. BACKLASH AND REACTION: THE ROAD TO WITHDRAWAL, 1968–1981

Having faced its own domestic turmoil and dissent in the 1960s, the United States may have expected the world to become more manageable in succeeding years. The failed liberal enthusiasms inspired by the Kennedy-Johnson era had renewed a commitment to internationalism and had ostensibly offered the newly liberated nations emerging from colonial subjugation the promise of development and American technical assistance. But although the country's foreign cultural relations had attained a new sensitivity, it was seldom sustained either in effective reorganization or in changed bureaucratic attitudes. Had the anticommunist crusade in Vietnam not intruded, the Democratic presidencies might well have believed they had accomplished a difficult transition between the bipolar geopolitics of the Cold War to the multipolar realities of détente. And UNESCO might have been the beneficiary of an American willingness to see that it succeeded, as Kennedy had promised Maheu. Instead, the United States and UNESCO entered the third and most tumultuous time of their association in a world that was becoming more complex, crisis-filled, and finally resistant to U.S. control.

As the Republican conservatives under Richard Nixon came to power in the 1968 election—after the assassinations of Robert Kennedy and Martin Luther King, Jr., the international scene was preparing a series of surprises that would overwhelm the U.S. and UNESCO by the frequency and intensity of their onslaught. Primary among these was the resurgence of the Third World entering a second, more demanding phase of its postcolonial liberation. Its rising expectations had not been satiated by the sugar-coated pill of development aid. Quite the contrary, since it could not redress long-term inequities in world trade nor ensure equality in the process. The encroachment of modernization with all its technological subversion also undermined cultural traditions and revived fears of neo-colonial subordination. The psychological and emotional response of people determined to eliminate every stigma of their colonial past gave their relations with the industrialized elite a dimension of passion and pride quick to resent the patronizing gestures of superiority. Nationalism in the face of big-power resource monopoly inspired the creation of effective balances through blocs, regional collaboration, and the nonaligned movement. The Third World agenda for an international economy represented demands similar to those the Western countries had already acceded to domestically, namely agricultural price stabilization and subsidy, anti-trust style protection against competitive malpractices, regulation of public interest industries, and forms of welfare for the poor and disabled. The Third World, therefore, exhibited an extraordinary combination of hope, dissatisfaction, and euphoria about the politics of the 1970s.[1]

Ironically, the established powers radicalized these moderate ambitions for justice by calling them a New International Economic Order (NIEO). The LDCs quickly realized the significance of information to their own unity before the global audience. Like dissidents before them, they felt trapped in a communications ghetto that excluded them from world opinion and influence. The seventies would witness, therefore, a sustained struggle to create a balanced free market in place of the distorted one dominated by the commercially advantaged, technologically superior forces of the industrialized North.

The Struggle for a Balanced Free Flow

This challenge was regarded in the West as a New World Information Order of Soviet-inspired and ill-conceived design rather than as a call for equal access and the reciprocal exchange of information. Proposals to readjust the international economy and its communications marketplace became critically divisive issues at the U.N. and in UNESCO during this decade of confrontation. Since mass communications were part of its original mission and one the United States had introduced from the start, UNESCO was a natural forum for the drama of debate and negotiation between the two contending forces within its membership.[2]

The Third World challenge to the old international system of power, wealth, and influence gained strength from numbers and from elevated levels of anxiety. And connected with the anxieties of the 1970s came a succession of economic crises shattering confidence in the world's capacity to adjust and survive. Henry Kissinger warned that the world was entering "a dark age of debt and deprivation." Inflation, recession, and the OPEC oil price controls exaggerated the strains and tensions plaguing relations between the have and have-not nations, and spawned a further sense of desperation and urgency.[3]

At the same time, unsettled issues of regional interaction and delayed liberation intruded themselves into the international parliamentary arena. Since 1947 the Middle East crisis had festered without a successful resolution. The six-day Arab-Israeli War of 1967 was followed by the Yom Kippur conflict in 1973. UNRWA had supplied relief and educational assistance to Palestinian refugees since 1949 with help from UNESCO, thereby opening it to charges of giving aid and comfort to Israel's enemies, the Palestinians. The middle eastern military and political impasse moved the battle to symbolic arenas where the war continued to be fought in the theater of world opinion. As territories shifted hands, UNESCO became the scene of many Arab proposals and resolutions of condemnation regarding cultural heritage monuments now under their enemy's control. This regional Cold War politicized UNESCO just as U.S.-Soviet tensions had done.[4]

Africa also had its time bombs of delayed independence, particularly Namibia, whose right to national existence had been stalled since 1947. South Africa, which had withdrawn from UNESCO in the mid-1950s, defied U.N. sanctions to give up control of Namibia, and this stimulated the rise of SWAPO as the national liberation movement that would seek recognition and support from UNESCO. Apartheid's premier rank as the embodiment of racism kept it on UNESCO's agenda, while the racist colonial regimes of Portugal and Rhodesia fostered further struggles for freedom echoing within the United Nations system.[5]

Resenting its loss of influence in the U.N. and in UNESCO, and soured on international affairs as its losses in Vietnam brought about its withdrawal, the United States faced its world involvements with more suspicion and hostility than ever before. The "assertive nationalism" of the Third World introduced new standards of global behavior which the U.S. found threatening. Opposition began to form within the U.S. linking the conservative free-market advocates committed to anticommunism and isolationism with the multinationals concerned with maintaining world-wide influence. Joining the coalition were the liberal proponents of international press freedoms and communications dominance. These lobbies presented an unusual array of political hostility toward UNESCO as an agency that harbored the voices of change. When joined by the Israeli lobby, angered by Arab initiatives, their combined outrage represented a powerful U.S. antagonism UNESCO had never before confronted. A short-tempered congressional impatience with UNESCO and other U.N. agencies also surfaced. Personified by a House member who asserted that the United States would "not tolerate their abuses," Congress developed the habits of threat, financial sanction, and even withdrawal as disciplinary proceedings to bring multilateral organizations in line with U.S. national objectives. UNESCO's defenders found it difficult to make their case for support in the face of this combination of resources, power, and political skill.[6]

If UNESCO did not notice this rising tide of American discontent, it was perhaps because the State Department portrayed an indifferent attitude toward UNESCO affairs. UNESCO naturally recognized the ongoing U.S. concerns with budget, program, and administration, but those had never been critical enough to suggest severe sanctions of any kind. As UNESCO's membership underwent a tremendous expansion, however, sheer size and the adjustment to it imposed new problems of management and direction on the agency: A quantitative leap had its natural qualitative fall-out of transitional difficulties. The concurrent appearance of both the Israeli issue and the information dispute resulted in endless diplomatic bargaining and meant UNESCO had to face unexpected political pressures at the same time it was undergoing its own crisis of administrative adaptation. More than ever before UNESCO was becoming a sitting duck, derided for its ethical aims, ignored because of its intellectual mandate, criticized for its operational failures, and disliked and feared for its questioning of the international status quo and its helping to legitimize collective new standards of conduct. Like the U.N. itself UNESCO had the ironic reputation of being both "powerless and dangerous."[7]

No issue in the 1970s made UNESCO seem more dangerous than the proposed New World Information and Communication Order (NWICO), a quest for communications equity that created a decade of "strident confrontation." When Secretary of State George Shultz, announcing the U.S. intention to withdraw, claimed that "trends . . . led UNESCO away from the original principles of its constitution" so that it now "served the political purposes of member states," it was the NWICO he was concerned with, more than anything else. America's powerful media corporations reacted to the NWICO campaign in "rage, panic, and considerable bias," as one journalist described it. They further stimulated a popular, official sense of outrage that left objective response beyond possibility. The NWICO had, in fact, attacked a hegemonic principle by which the press and the government had jointly invented reality in the United States for many years. The free press and the free marketplace of ideas had become, thereby, unquestioned, common-sense assumptions having the status of myths and, as such, immune from critical analysis. When the NWICO broke through the "structuring silences" protecting this myth, it faced the consequences for itself and UNESCO.[8]

Shultz was, of course, dead wrong in his charge that UNESCO had departed from its original principles. Grappling with the role of information and mass communications in fact represented a reaffirmation of them. As UNESCO had long before discovered, building the defenses of peace in a politicized, propagandized, violent world was often seen as an attack on the national interests of states engaged in militarism, imperial domination, and aggressive ideological warfare. But to subordinate itself to the mundane tasks of technical assistance would have been, as Richard Hoggart has noted, an abdication of responsibility to its "high-minded constitution." By the 1970s, the world had grown smaller, more crowded, and more fragile—a planet verging on irreparable damage, pushed to the edge by human abuse. It needed immediate attention to overcome global defects which in turn required intergovernmental, cooperative action. UNESCO's Man and the Biosphere program, the 1972 U.N. call for joint consideration of the world environment, its 1974 focus on world population, and the International Geophysical Year all testified to this overriding priority. Did not the quality and circulation of information represent a similar global responsibility? Preventing the pollution of minds merited the same attention as other noxious influences on man and earth.[9]

Thus UNESCO had several roles to play in these various international efforts. It always had to be there, as Hoggart suggested, to provide a larger context in all applications of economic, scientific, or technical reconstruction around the world. In all endeavors, UNESCO's educational mission provided the understanding that protected the "needs and rights" of the affected communities from groups to national units. Since information had deeply penetrative cultural power, UNESCO had an obligation to protect these same interests from the media's international impact. Even more so, since mass communications had become the major instrument affecting the mutual understanding UNESCO was created to promote. The United States, however, never had the desire to grasp that elementary constitutional principle governing UNESCO's behavior.

But the U.S. government resisted reform by the popular majorities in UNESCO's global parliament. The media interests that the U.S. defended were ready to engage in "flagrant fabrication" to maintain their communications supremacy. This political, polemical reaction mirrored the ideological attack UNESCO had undergone soon after its founding and from an identical quarter. The American media believed they had the same right to set international standards for world information and communications practices as J. Edgar Hoover had had when he defined the personnel policies of international organizations years before.[10]

The gathering storm over mass communications that national liberation and development initiatives had unleashed in the 1960s accelerated in intensity throughout the succeeding decade. According to Kaarle Nordenstreng, its historical evolution encompassed three different aspects. From 1970 to 1976 the Third World aggressively sought to reverse U.S. and Western domination, and introduce new international norms regarding media content, balanced coverage, reciprocal exchanges, and technological equality. Focusing on the right to seek and impart information as well as the right to receive it, these proposals fostered the democratization of access to mass communications and its social accountability to the people it addressed and served. The reform movement also demanded an equitable share of the spectrum as a global resource held in trust for all nations, not simply for those who had got there first. Noting that "neither the structures of communication nor the messages transmitted . . . [were] neutral in a free market," the Third World challenged the objectivity and fairness of the status quo, and argued that it led to information dependence and exploitation. The fear that communications might revive a cultural colonialism inspired the attempts to protect a nation's airwaves from unwanted or unsolicited intrusions from foreign-controlled sources. Cultural autonomy and protectionism thus connected the proposed NWICO to the vigorous national feelings of people who resented the stigmas of past subordination, finding them unwelcome attributes of a free-flowing marketplace run by the industrialized and corporate elite. None of these themes contradicted UNESCO's goals for international exchange of ideas and values. Nor did they diverge from UNESCO's peace-building mission which concerned itself with the content of international communications and disarmament in the war of words.[11]

The Role of the Non-Aligned Movement

For six years the Non-Aligned Movement (NAM) and its newly liberated allies met, studied, analyzed, conferred, and formulated resolutions and declarations of concern expressing the intent to change the existing structure and content of international mass communications. Beginning at a Montreal meeting in 1969, the intellectual resistance to outdated authority maintained pressure for change and involved the UNESCO general conference as early as 1970. Approving studies and research into information issues at that time, UNESCO thereafter became the forum for their discussion and advancement. While much of this debate focused on structural or technical improvements which built up national and regional strengths in the field, UNESCO meetings also dealt with professional standards, journalistic responsibilities, and codes of ethics, taboo topics for the U.S. In 1972 UNESCO voted curbs on satellite broadcasting; this represented the principle of "prior consent" by the receiving nation, holding that it had the right to assert its people's sovereignty over their own air waves. Canada and Sweden, incidentally, not the U.S.S.R. or the Third World, proposed this legal theory of cultural protectionism, a position given international status in UNESCO's two covenants on rights drafted in 1966. The U.N. General Assembly passed a similar resolution, but the United States cast dissenting votes in both organizations.[12]

Between the 1973 NAM summit meeting in Algiers and the 1976 UNESCO general conference in Nairobi, the controversy became more heated and intense. A draft declaration on the mass media which originally contained a code of ethics (later dropped) attracted extremes of support and opposition that seemed capable of tearing UNESCO apart in the process. The draft declaration, in spite of the world-wide attention it had received and its links to both national and international traditions supporting media accountability, inspired only anger and anguish in the United States. A fiercely aggressive free-market lobby, the World Press Freedom Committee (WPFC), was formed in 1973, determined to moderate or terminate any proposals limiting the absolute freedom and independence of the Western media giants. The specter of government controls, communist-dictated principles, and a totalitarian subjugation of the press inflamed the public and industry to which the WPFC addressed its campaign. While Nordenstreng has described the 1970 to 1976 years as an offensive by the less developed countries, this interpretation does not do justice to the Western initiatives. Once the WPFC organized the opposition, it kept the NWICO movement under close surveillance and issued its own version of events. When the "Zionism is Racism" resolution, which had passed at the U.N., appeared in the draft declaration of the NWICO as an area which deserved media support, the U.S. and thirteen other delegations walked out of that 1975 meeting. Western pressure succeeded there and in the elimination of the journalist code of ethics as well.[13]

As UNESCO's 1976 Nairobi General Conference neared, the U.S. threatened to withdraw from the organization if the Mass Media Declaration endorsed unacceptable press standards. Thus the then newly appointed director-general, Amadou-Mahtar M'Bow of Senegal, faced a disastrous General Conference, the first ever to be held in Africa, unless he managed to negotiate a successful resolution of the issue with the diplomatic skills and persuasive bargaining for which he later became famous. Apart from the political jockeying it conducted, the United States continued its own technological offensive. By the end of the decade, the U.S. and the other communication leaders still dominated "satellites, the electromagnetic spectrum, . . . use of the airwaves, telecommunications, microelectronics, remote sensing capabilities, direct satellite broadcasting, and computer related transmissions," according to Francis N. Wete.[14]

The second phase of the communications controversy that Nordenstreng dated from 1976 through 1977 as a Western-led, media counterattack had probably begun as early as 1973, and its supposed termination in 1977 had more to do with tactical cunning than with a strategic withdrawal from the information order's front lines. Confrontation with the Third World majorities had, in fact, been a United States policy position since the latter had attempted to "widen the circle of international decisionmaking" and introduce a new era of "international ruledrawing." That OPEC-induced euphoric sense of Third World power had indeed created after October 1973 a radically new tone in U.N. parliamentary relations. Ambassador Daniel Patrick Moynihan's "union-busting tactics" attempting to break the back of Third World demands had not been notable diplomatic successes. Henry Kissinger had also censured the "alignment of the non-aligned," as though the unity of the powerless had some subversive quality. After two years of negligible influence in multilateral forums from 1974 until 1976, the U.S. found itself increasingly isolated and typecast as the villain of neo-colonialism, especially in Africa. It had opposed General Assembly resolutions against the Portuguese army's Mozambique massacre in 1973, opposed all three resolutions concerning Rhodesia, voted against the arms embargo against South Africa (the only "no" vote), allowed the import of Rhodesian minerals (particularly chrome) in violation of U.N. obligations, and continued the export of arms to Portugal and South Africa. By 1976 the United States had to face the reality that confrontation stimulated resistance and threatened its economic positions abroad. It was time to try the softer diplomatic line of selective negotiation with certain Third World nations.[15]

A similar shift from coercive confrontation to adaptive cooperation occurred at UNESCO in 1976 and in the four succeeding years of the Carter administration. While not abandoning its opposition to the Mass Media Declaration, the U.S. appeared more willing to make concessions on certain issues and consider additional support for communications development in the Third World.

Postponing the day of reckoning to the 1978 conference to allow for further negotiations and a less politicized atmosphere, the director-general bought time by his astute lobbying of the African, Asian, and Latin American delegations. In 1977 the Senate Foreign Relations Committee indicated a new direction by urging the government to recognize the information imbalance and to promote additional communication facilities in the less developed countries. The implied deal involved an end to what the U.S. head delegate to UNESCO called "restrictive declarations" and the start of a "Marshall Plan of Telecommunications." At the same time the MacBride Commission began its exhaustive investigation of "all the problems of communication in contemporary society," in the hope of discovering common grounds for agreement on their solution. Director-General M'Bow's foreword to the commission's published findings, *Many Voices, One World*, convincingly connected this project to UNESCO's mission when he wrote:

> Communication is at the heart of all social intercourse. Whenever men have come to establish regular relations with one another, the nature of the systems of communication created between them, the forms these have taken and the measure of effectiveness they have attained have largely determined the chances of bringing communities closer together or of making them one, and the prospects for reducing tensions or settling conflicts wherever they have arisen. . . . It is essential that all men and women, in all social and cultural environments, should be given the opportunity of joining in the process of collective thinking thus initiated . . . , each people must be able to learn from the others, while at the same time conveying to them its own understanding of its own condition and its own view of world affairs. Mankind will then have made a decisive step forward on the path of freedom, democracy and fellowship.[16]

The Draft Declaration, meanwhile, arrived for consideration at the UNESCO General Conference of 1978 revised by a Drafting and Negotiating Group searching for consensus on international principles acceptable to all. The issues, it must be remembered, had been the subject of world-wide concern since the end of World War I, and the devastation to human understanding and good-will that irresponsible and distorted communications had inflicted on the global community had repeatedly underlined the necessity for further progress in media accountability. By 1978 the majority of developed nations were "ready to negotiate the text" of the forthcoming declaration, but the U.S. press and its representatives remained antagonistic and paranoid, ever suspecting the worst and projecting this point of view in their dispatches about UNESCO. However, their anticipation of disaster did not prevent the member states or the U.S. from unanimously approving by acclamation the Mass Media Declaration at the 1978 meeting. Emphasizing the same themes that the MacBride Commission would restate in 1979, the declaration presented a "carefully balanced" statement of media goals and obligations, all of them consistent with U.N. principles and Western free-press values. It had been a remarkable achievement, for UNESCO had created this agreement, as Kaarle Nordenstreng has stated, on "one of the most difficult problems of cultural policy of our time."[17]

Had the world finally and really settled on the goals that mass communications would seek to pursue down through the future? Certainly it had taken a daring step forward and, for the world, that in itself was a rare and startling accomplishment. In the exhausted aftermath of their long politicized struggle, both sides claimed victory, a natural self-regarding evaluation in any such evenly balanced outcome. But the proclamations of success also forecast the possible unraveling of the agreement. Conflicting interpretations of the meaning of the stated principles might rekindle old animosities. The deal, described by Nordenstreng as "trading ideology against cooperation" depended on several ensuing actions for its own effect on subsequent communications developments, namely, the level of U.S. aid, the willingness of the U.S. to accommodate the Third World's interest in balance, the acceptance of the 1978 declaration by the American media, and the survival of a political administration in Washington that favored cooperation over confrontation.[18]

Between 1978 and UNESCO's 1980 General Conference at Belgrade, the atmosphere of mutual accommodation remained hopeful but uneasy. The Mass Media Declaration and the forthcoming MacBride Commission report each had its critics. On the one hand, the U.S. media industry felt the declaration had violated UNESCO's charter, representing "a doubtful, if not dangerous instrument" of regulation. It remained utterly opposed to any international standards that endorsed the idea of the media's social responsibility. Afflicted by its enduring anticommunist outlook, the U.S. media kept viewing the NWICO as a Soviet-sponsored attack on press freedoms, despite all the evidence to the contrary. Director-General M'Bow's effective intervention against Soviet draft initiatives, in fact, went unrecognized and unreported.[19]

On the other hand, Third World member states attacked the MacBride Report as too Western. They feared it foretold a "deceptive cooption" by technical assistance, leaving them vulnerable to domination by an unchanged power structure. At the U.N. and at UNESCO meetings in 1979 and 1980, those Third World voices continued to deplore information's status as a commodity, upholding its importance as a social tool that supports humane and progressive goals which would "enfranchise not condition" its users.

Carter Administration Optimism

The Carter administration, meanwhile, made preparations to fulfill the plan promoted at UNESCO's 1978 General Conference. Testifying before the House Subcommittee on International Organizations in 1979, John E. Reinhardt, who led the U.S. delegation the year before and headed the U.S. International Communication Agency (ICA), affirmed the government's commitment to U.S. leadership both in providing communications assistance and in influencing the direction the NWICO would take. At Belgrade in 1980 these policies came to fruition. The Marshall Plan idea received permanent form as the International Program for the Development of Communications (IPDC). Its organization excluded the corporate world from membership and consigned the West to a minority position in its administration. Sarah Goddard Power, deputy assistant secretary for human rights and social affairs, spoke afterward in Detroit of the official optimism the U.S. delegation had felt after the Belgrade conference. In summary, the U.S. had blocked "Soviet-inspired ideological approaches" to communications in UNESCO by introducing the IPDC's "practical nonideological approach," a move she believed would realign the more moderate developing nations with U.S. policies. As she also pointed out to her corporate audience, the information issue was no small matter to their export ambitions. That industry was now the second biggest one in sales abroad at an annual figure of $75 billion the previous year. The Carter administration believed, therefore, that the United States had made substantial progress between Nairobi and Belgrade, had shifted the direction of the communications struggle from ideology to "concrete development opportunity," and had positioned itself for further leadership of information issues in UNESCO.[20]

While the U.S. had obviously been influential in the UNESCO debates during the Carter years, it had not seriously affected the media's sense of outrage and hostility nor had it attempted to reduce the Third World's continuing interest in restructuring both the international economy and the pattern of global mass communications. The Mass Media Declaration and the MacBride Commission Report, like other national and international statements of high ideals, now served as constant reminders of a changed order of things. As long as they existed, they would remain ethical guidelines to which those disaffected by the status quo could appeal. The U.S. communications industry looked upon them as a loaded gun for use against them. The real loaded gun, however, was the information advantage that the Western media used to falsify and distort realities at UNESCO and in the Third World, the best example being the disinformation they circulated about the Belgrade conference itself. Misrepresented by the press and disillusioned by the U.S. failure to provide the funding the IPDC required, the Third World once again agitated for further reforms by multilateral collaboration on behalf of the NIEO and the NWICO. The timing was inauspicious. The mean-spirited enmity of the U.S. had clearly been revealed in its coverage of the 1980 General Conference. A dirty fight was looming and would receive extraordinary official U.S. support as the political dynamics of the electoral process brought to power a right-wing Reagan administration determined to confront the Third World, undermine international cooperation, and export its free-market principles to the entire world.[21]

As UNESCO and other U.N. organizations became theaters of combat over the nature of the international economic and communications orders, a third major issue rose to prominence creating further conflict and controversy. For want of a succinct definition, we can call it the search for a New World Social Order, one that would remove all remnants of colonial inferiority, fulfill the ambitions of all peoples for self-determination and independence, and eliminate the psychological and emotional debasement of humanity instilled by discrimination, racism, and apartheid. National liberation and full social equality had, of course, been on the international agenda of promised reform at least since Woodrow Wilson's Fourteen Points. Other declarations and covenants since World War II and the collapse of the old imperial system had continually raised expectations of political and racial equality which had not been honored. The "assertive nationalism" that Eisenhower had ignored, as Robert McMahon suggested, achieved stunning victories in the 1960s, however, and transferred its struggle for full autonomy to the U.N. and its multilateral allies, where voting majorities attracted world attention. Descendants of slave owners and beneficiaries of an imperial past, still engaged in the slow recognition of their own racial discrimination, did not understand the deeply felt outrage among Third World nationals. The tempo and content of proffered reform attuned to the self-interests of the U.N.'s Western industrial elite had not, therefore, appeased that anger as the 1970s began. The decade thus became the setting for history's long delayed revenge in a drama of liberation and racial redemption.

Although the highlight of this spectacle featured an Arab-Israeli dispute within UNESCO, no narrow interpretation can fully explain its symbolic fury or the havoc it inflicted on an organization already damaged by the disinformation the Western press was scurrilously disseminating about the mass-communications issue: The 1974 anti-Israeli resolutions passed by UNESCO's General Conference, in fact, stimulated charges of politicization that had deeper effects on public opinion than the information debate. The bitter campaign of one-sided propaganda established the idea of politicization as a degenerative defect within UNESCO, and politicization remained thereafter a way for critics to explain and condemn any UNESCO activities with which they disagreed.

The 1970s had a unique historical pattern within which the attack on Israel must be understood. With its newly found political voice, the Third World was ready to remove the last vestiges of colonialism and support the national liberation movements still ensnared in its grasp. UNESCO's mandate to remove the bonds that restricted human dignity and development made it a natural arena of support for such activities. It could give the various movements observer status at its functions and lend them educational, scientific, and cultural assistance as repressed or refugee freedom fighters on their road to independence. But this also put UNESCO on a collision course with Portugal, South Africa, Southern Rhodesia, and, of course, Israel, where the PLO represented the Arab demands for a national homeland. A series of resolutions against racism and apartheid emanating from UNESCO's forum symbolized the Third World's drive to mobilize world opinion and gain legitimacy for social reform. In the 1970s an intense atmosphere of "planetary bargaining" began. The oil crisis, the U.S. distraction and defeat in Vietnam, South Africa's refusal to give any ground, and the Middle Eastern impasse all produced heightened expectations and frustrations among the Third World majority. That the United States had become isolated and on the defensive gave additional impetus to these demands.[22]

Racism, apartheid, and anti-colonialism had been concerns of UNESCO since its founding, but the focus of attention narrowed in the 1960s. It was not a sudden deviation from its activities that suddenly erupted in Israel's direction in 1974. Arab hostility toward Israel was of long standing, although earlier instances of nationalistic antagonism had simmered unnoticed under the greater intrusion of Cold War hostilities during UNESCO's first twenty years. The military conflicts among that region's contentious neighbors, however, ensured the reappearance of the ill-will. In 1954 that opportunity was all but made certain when UNESCO formulated and passed the much-needed Hague Convention for the Protection of Cultural Property in the Event of Armed Conflict. If war reoccurred and the signatories to that agreement seized territory, UNESCO had an obligation to protect the cultural heritage therein. That intervention, if it took place, would undoubtedly appear political to one side or the other since a nation's monuments, shrines, and artistic representations have immense political symbolism. Since the convention itself was not clear on the issue of archaeological excavations in lands acquired by war, the 1956 UNESCO resolution did expand the meaning to prohibit them.[23]

UNESCO's stand on racial issues was highlighted when South Africa withdrew from the organization effective at the end of 1956. It had resented being attacked for apartheid at the 1954 General Conference. In spite of the Executive Board's plea for it to remain a member, South Africa recognized UNESCO would not abandon its struggle against racial discrimination and prejudice, and made its departure final. It was words alone—statements and resolutions deploring certain racial attitudes and practices—that caused South Africa's pullout; UNESCO's constitution forbade intervention "in matters of essentially domestic jurisdiction."

At the 1960, 1962, and 1964 General Conference sessions, UNESCO emphasized the right of all people to self-determination, arguing that only those liberated into freedom could fully benefit from the education, science, and culture that UNESCO promoted. The organization also resolved to help them "overcome the harmful after effects of colonialism." Beginning in 1965, UNESCO went further in supporting the right to independence when the U.N General Assembly asked its specialized agencies to deny aid to colonial powers refusing to grant their subject people freedom. Sanctions on assistance to and exclusion from UNESCO activities for Portugal, South Africa, and Southern Rhodesia followed in 1966, and the organization again claimed that "all forms of colonialism and neo-colonialism [were] threats to international peace and security and . . . crimes against humanity." The same pattern of condemnation occurred in 1967 and 1968.[24]

Israel, the Arabs, and Jerusalem

A point of view consistent with UNESCO's goals had evolved, therefore, before the Israeli issue surfaced and had a general relevance to it. Liberation from foreign occupation and rule of whatever kind promoted autonomy and equal rights, the basis of mutual understanding and intellectual and moral solidarity, and should be supported. The six-day war between Israel and the Arab States in 1967 involved a foreign occupation of seized territory thereby violating the principle of autonomy. But the Arab-Israeli controversy focused first on the symbolic issue occasioned by the unification of Jerusalem under Israeli control and its subsequent archaeological excavations there. The 1974 resolutions, then, dated their specific origin from the events of 1967 and had had a seven-year history during which then Director-General Maheu had worked to calm the passions on both sides and temper the conflict of interests, a struggle for which he rarely received public credit. Since all the combatants had signed the Hague Convention, UNESCO had the authority to intervene; but since the convention's statement on archaeological digs was ambiguous, there were different interpretations of it. And since the UNESCO Executive Board had been made up of government representatives after the 1954 U.S.-British instigated constitutional change, their participation in the archaeological dispute was necessarily political rather than professional.[25]

Over the nine years of festering Arab-Israeli relations (1967–1976), the director-general operated a form of intellectual peace-keeping force that, despite some setbacks and crises, returned UNESCO and the participants to an uneasy truce in which their vital interests had not been compromised.[26] What had been compromised was UNESCO's standing in the United States, in some U.S. NGOs, and among the intellectual community that supported Israel, none of whom recognized or appreciated the process and outcome the director-general had pursued and achieved.

The historical context in which the director-general sought his objectives was extremely complicated and contentious. The U.N. General Assembly and Security Council resisted the seizure of territory by military means as a violation of the charter, and Jerusalem had standing in the cultural heritage of the world as well as being the particular embodiment of the Muslim and Jewish past. The 1956 resolution on archaeological excavations was only a recommendation, and Israel's legal obligations remained unclear. Nevertheless, the pressures for UNESCO to intervene came from near unanimous Executive Board decisions enhanced by large General Conference majorities. Experts did not agree on the "status" of Jerusalem or the degree to which excavation inflicted "damage" on a site or its surroundings. Urban renewal and high-rise development in Jerusalem, meanwhile, also threatened to alter the traditional aesthetics and environment of the city. And through all of this the Arabs remained infuriated and the Israelis intransigent. The symbolism of archaeological tampering aggravated the fact of occupation and Arab displacement, while Israel's unilateral actions flaunted the principles of international mediation and collaboration.[27]

The director-general steered a course of careful implementation and exhaustive expert investigation thereby avoiding crisis intervention and upholding intellectual and scholarly guidelines as the UNESCO secretariat's procedural approach. His offer of technical assistance which would satisfy the goal of UNESCO's presence in Jerusalem won Israel's acceptance, only to be turned down by Jordan and Lebanon because it implied Israel's legal authority over the occupied territories. But Maheu's excellent relations with the Arab delegations to UNESCO helped control the issue's explosive quality. According to former Deputy Director-General John Fobes, Maheu "kept it from blowing up."[28] He negotiated other political pitfalls almost as skillfully. He carefully and cautiously initiated inquiries among the occupied Arab populations to see whether their rights to "national identity" and cultural autonomy were being respected. Recognizing the complexity of UNESCO's assigned "full supervision," Maheu had not yet reported back when the anti-Israeli resolutions passed in late 1974. Other elaborate, even exhaustive surveys of UNESCO's NGOs in the early 1970s investigated their connections to countries practicing racist or colonial policies with a view to

ending UNESCO's involvement with those NGOs collaborating even in-
directly in the maintenance of such conditions. In 1972 the General Conference gave observer status to African liberation movements recognized
by the Organization of African Unity. Israel must have known that the
PLO would soon receive such status.[29]

Seven years of stalemate over the archaeological digs and a longer period of increasing concern over the status of people subjected to colonial
rule or foreign occupation had, therefore, set the stage for the 1974 resolutions. But their immediate origin had to do with the revival of the
Middle East conflict in the Yom Kippur war of 1973 and the Arab-initi-
ated OPEC oil crisis of that same year. Those two critical events added
an immense emotional dimension for the Arab nations, victimized by
military loss and buoyed by sudden economic dominion. Thus, the resolutions against Israel were neither unexpected nor especially striking.
And had not Director-General Maheu been ill and unable to keep the lid
on the issue through his close diplomatic relations with the Arab delegations, even less of an uproar might have taken place.[30] UNESCO was
not the only parliamentary body stricken by intense political upheavals
during the excitements of the crisis erupting between 1973 and 1975.
During that same period, the U.N. was dealing with Mozambique,
Southern Rhodesia, and South Africa (with the U.S. in dissent). The
Vietnam debacle, Watergate, and the congressional reassertion of authority in the War Powers Act created political turmoil in the U.S. The
Non-Aligned Movement took its strong stand on mass communications
at the Algiers Conference in 1973. The World Press Freedom Committee,
the Trilateral Commission, and the Heritage Foundation all originated
that same year as responses to the uncertain impact national and international policies might have on the world status quo. Arafat visited the
U.N. in the fall of 1974 where the PLO received observer status. Meanwhile, a serious economic recession afflicted the world between 1974
and 1975. That UNESCO manifested this political hysteria abroad in the
world only in the 1974 resolutions and had restored the position of Israel in the organization by 1976 would seem to suggest its stability and
resistance to serious politicization rather than the reverse.

The Executive Board and General Conference castigated Israel for its
failure to comply with recommendations urging an end to the archaeological excavations and proposing monitoring of educational and cultural life in the occupied zones, and asked the director-general to cut off
UNESCO assistance to Israel. But the real sanction was the exclusion of
Israel from the European region. This action left Israel without an administrative home, one in which every other nation had been placed. A
unique exclusion of this kind, which the Executive Board agreed to
solve at the 1976 General Conference, represented a symbolic shaming
of Israel by its opponents. While the temporary exclusion did offend the
principle of universality, Israel had once opposed West Germany's

membership and the United States had successfully prevented the People's Republic of China's entrance into the U.N. and UNESCO until 1971.[31] As David Landes, representing the New York Committee for an Effective UNESCO, admitted in a 1976 congressional hearing, politicization of many issues was nothing new in UNESCO. "Our hands are not clean," he testified, for the United States had often rounded up votes for its "political advantage," and he concluded "that's embarrassing—history usually is."[32] Moreover, even this action disturbed none of that country's vital interests nor its continuing archaeological excavations.

History, of course, is never embarrassing to the United States since it manages its national interest and foreign policies without regard to History. Nor does the U.S. believe its own past conduct ever represents a historical precedent determining the contemporary conditions it later finds objectionable. The impact of Arab national interests on UNESCO policies in the 1970s was thus unaffected by past U.S. Cold War politicization campaigns. Similarly, criticism of the NWICO proposals was unaffected by the earlier U.S. manipulation of mass communications in UNESCO. With this amnesia, political outrage was not far behind. The Congress seemed to think the nation had been taken hostage by Middle Eastern extremists.

Although Roger Coate has argued that the Israeli crisis in UNESCO was "short lived," it permanently and wrongly affected U.S. public and congressional perceptions of UNESCO.[33] It did this in several ways. In the first place, the anti-Israeli sanctions helped implant the image of a politicized UNESCO deeply into the consciousness of important U.S. constituencies. They felt thereafter that hostile and irresponsible forces somehow controlled the organization and used it for purposes alien to its mission. They assumed that politicization was both novel and unnatural, and hostile to U.S. interests. In the second place, the issue had a traumatic effect on crucial segments of the professional cultural elite that had been among UNESCO's strongest supporters. The shock of Jewish scholars and scientists when UNESCO attacked and shamed the Jewish state, and the uneasiness academic people felt over the apparent intrusion of politics into objective, scientific studies (archaeology) transformed enthusiasm and commitment into anger and disillusionment. The 1976 congressional hearing aired these grievances. David Landes likened the anti-Israeli sanctions to an "excommunication" that was "discriminatory and selective," one that created "a serious question of conscience" lest UNESCO's advocates in the United States become "dupes and accomplices" in the action. He believed it would "tear apart the educational, scientific, and cultural community in the United States" and "set friend against friend."[34] Dr. Miller Upton, an educational consultant and president of Beloit College for twenty-one years, represented the U.S. National Commission and reported that the 1974 resolutions "have caused a deep and widespread disquiet in the intellectual community." He claimed to have personal knowledge of nine professional organizations representing 2.5 million members that had "taken formal actions" against the anti-Israeli stance, another nine with 1 million that had "discussed it," and, in all of them, there had been "consistent condemnation."[35]

The U.S. scientific community symbolized the extraordinary backlash that had swept over UNESCO's most involved and dedicated partners. The National Academy of Sciences "deplored" the resolutions and "urged" the government to "reverse the trend" that "dissipated" UNESCO's "potential for service." Even more significant was the action of the American Academy of Arts and Sciences, which appointed a committee to study the "political misuses" of UNESCO and to compile a full historical, documentary record about the recent actions. The AAAS hoped to "mobilize the world intellectual, scientific, and artistic" community to oppose the politicization and restore the organization to its original "effectiveness." As Richard Nobbe has concluded, Professor Daniel Partan's lengthy and exhaustive examination of the Arab-Israeli dispute in UNESCO "perhaps more than any other single document about UNESCO, . . . contributed to a serious erosion of support for UNESCO among the American intellectual community."[36]

Nevertheless, neither those scholars nor their professional organizations put out a call to boycott UNESCO or deny it United States funding. Indeed, Partan's research had been "highly selective" and did not try "to present the very considerable body of solid evidence that most work of the UNESCO General Conference and Executive Board continues to be carried out in a fully responsible fashion squarely within UNESCO competence in the fields of education, science, and culture."[37] And if the 1976 congressional hearing had circulated, Professor Roger Revelle's statement in it would have carried much weight. Revelle, chairman of the Joint Committee on UNESCO of the AAAS and the National Academy of Science and professor at Harvard University's Center for Population Studies, reminded his colleagues and the members of the House Committee that "the United States brought politics into UNESCO." Professor Revelle also recalled from his service on three U.S. delegations to UNESCO that "the principal objective of the chief delegate was to keep the words 'peaceful co-existence' out of all UNESCO documents as they were invented by the Russians."[38]

The anti-Israeli resolutions had a third unfortunate consequence in arousing the hostility and suspicions of a Congress determined to reassert its authority over foreign policy in the post-Vietnam era. In 1974 Congress banned further U.S. funding to UNESCO until the Israeli exclusion from the European region had been resolved to the satisfaction of the United States. In an organization whose budget never approximated the demands upon its resources, such intimidation naturally had an influential political impact. However, an unexpected, ironic aftermath put pressure on the United States to pay its dues since default would lose it voting rights in the 1976 Nairobi General Conference considered crucial for the U.S. position on mass communications. As it turned out, UNESCO carried out the Executive Board recommendation to solve the regional question and the ban terminated in 1976. The policy, nevertheless, promoted a bad congressional habit and set an example of financial bullying responsive to internal political dynamics that threatened the welfare and future of all international organizations heavily dependent on the U.S. contribution.[39]

Withdrawals and Sanctions

Withdrawal from a U.N. specialized agency as an ultimate sanction of national interest had also developed as a U.S. multilateral policy, though it was not yet aimed at UNESCO. The International Labor Organization (ILO), founded in 1919 as "Versailles' answer to Bolshevism," had undergone early U.S. politicization after the Soviet Union's entry in 1954. A decade of Cold War ideological rivalry quieted down, however, after the 1963 Test Ban Treaty and the beginning of détente. A congressionally imposed ceiling on the U.S. contribution in the 1950s and a ban on funding the ILO in 1970 indicated the government's willingness, to enforce its policies and express its displeasure through unilateral devices of an extraordinary nature. George Meany's AFL-CIO played the most decisive role in the political lobbying that helped determine U.S. actions affecting the management and direction of this organization. According to Robert Cox, the AFL-CIO could both "block Director-General initiatives or undermine his authority in setting ILO policies."[40]

In 1977, under renewed pressure from George Meany, the United States withdrew, citing four major problems, among them "selective concern for human rights" and "politicization." The Library of Congress's Congressional Research Service described the U.S. initiative as a consequence of "Meany's antagonism toward the European trade unions and his longstanding opposition to Soviet bloc participation in the ILO" attitudes that "shaped the overall American approach to the organization." Meany's death and the apparent, though disputed, changes in the ILO led the U.S. to return in 1980. The example was to encourage the practice and suggest its utility as an easy diplomatic weapon for the U.S. to wield. The ILO analogy to UNESCO, of course, was a thoroughly unfortunate and misleading one, as the Congressional Research Service pointed out.[41]

The financial sanctions against UNESCO and the pull out from the ILO represented the hard-line, confrontational approach to multilateral affairs that the United States adopted in the 1970s. Both of them indicated the influence powerful lobbies could exercise in defense of their vital interests. In a country where public awareness of foreign affairs rarely reached a critical mass and where commitment to international collaboration had always been defined as an extension of the American Way of Life, concentrations of wealth and power wielded unusual authority over the agenda of public debate and the formulation of public policies. The media industry's domination of the mass-communications issue illustrated this ability, for it controlled public perceptions of the NWICO and of UNESCO's management of it to the near total exclusion of all competing points of view. The World Press Freedom Committee (WPFC), in addition, organized and marketed the media's self-interested position with remarkable skill and impact after its formation in 1973. Had the Israeli, labor, and media lobbies been alone in the field, UNESCO would have had trouble enough presenting the realities of its program in the face of this hostile opposition. However, a far more powerful coalition had appeared on the political scene, one determined to alter forever the country's attitudes toward international cooperation. UNESCO was to be its first victim.

Conservative Pressures

Vast in size, with millions of dollars to spend, the ultra-conservative and right-wing networks thought of themselves as a "second culture" in what Irving Kristol described as a "war of ideas."[42] Among the many targets of their wrath, the United Nations and its numerous agencies ranked high and were the favored enemies on the Heritage Foundation's hit list. Unlike UNESCO's mission, the right wing's international purpose aimed to build the offenses of free market, unilateral chauvinism in the minds of men and accustom them to hate the idea of mutual understanding and solidarity achieved through multilateral cooperation. Julian Behrstock has called their attitude a "systematic, wide-ranging bias against the UN," promoting the belief that the world would be a much better place without it.[43] Their "long term strategic dimension," as an analyst of these "ominous politics" has argued, proposed to subvert the conventional liberal wisdom that had informed U.S. national and international affairs since World War II and destroy the legitimacy of its policies. By the time the Reagan administration took office, a massive ideological campaign to change the hearts and minds of the country's citizenry had been under way for a decade or more. It made the earlier grassroots superpatriotic anticommunism look like the horse and buggy era of nativist bigotry.[44]

While the reactionary resurgence dated back to the draft Goldwater movement of 1964, its corporate, think-tank, and foundation supporters had long exercised influence in public affairs. What was new about the 1970s reincarnation of purpose and power was its acceleration of activity, its far-reaching propaganda impact, its immense financial resources, its linkage and influence over Republican Party politics, and its aggressive new organizational members led by the Heritage Foundation. Formed in 1973, the latter quickly became the epitome of the skilled manipulation of opinion in the marketplace of ideas, and it served as the prototype of that larger assembly of some 70 groups setting the context of debate as the 1980s arrived.[45]

The manifestations of dissent and civil disobedience popularizing the voices of the nation's and the world's submerged majorities had challenged the old order everywhere in the '60s and had shocked the conservative elite. The liberal response of more government at home and more multilateral organizational activity abroad had further outraged conservatism's doctrinal assumptions. Nor had its spokesmen been pleased with détente, which had violated their anticommunist principles and threatened the supremacy of "Fortress America." The international economy had also appeared to be falling apart while the Third World's vigorous demands for control of its own strategic resources attacked the free-market domination of U.S. corporations. The Committee on the Present Danger, as its name suggests, had characterized the immediate future as filled with peril. Even the Trilateral Commission, also formed in 1973 as an Eastern Establishment effort to manage the world more effectively, had warned of the harm that lay ahead. The Trilateral's Executive Committee report of 1974 clearly summarized the mounting concern. "The international system is undergoing a drastic transformation through a series of crises," the statement read.

> "Worldwide inflation reflects, transmits, and magnifies the tensions of many societies, while the difficulties produced by the abrupt change in oil prices are accompanied by the entry of major new participants onto the world scene," it continued. Describing the situation as a "critical" turning point in world history, the Trilateral analysis predicted "serious strains," an "alarming deterioration" in international relations, a "high risk of global anarchy," and the threat of a "long term disaster" that could end the United States' global "hegemony."[46]

As the answer to these challenges, the Heritage Foundation had extraordinary resources and the power to affect public opinion, political decisions, and national policies. Backed by founding right-wing millionaires Joseph Coors and Richard Mellon Scaife and with an annual budget of $10 million by 1982, a staff of 90, "a network of some 450 research groups and 1,600 scholars and public policy experts," this activist think tank placed its average piece of literature in the hands of "7,000 Congressmen, administration officials, journalists, and major donors" as well as turning out articles for editorial and op-ed circulation. Its opinion-influencing program had developed to the point where it had 400 titles published between 1980 and 1985. With close links to such network groups as the Institute for Contemporary Studies (founded by Edwin Meese III and Caspar W. Weinberger) and financially supported by 87 of the top Fortune 500 corporations, Heritage balanced this panoply of elite associates with grassroots support totaling some 130,000 paying members. And it did not neglect the mass-communications avenue of influence, marketing and promoting its ideas through the broadcast media.[47]

Was it any wonder that this array of professional talent with such endless funding behind it had a tremendous edge in the public-relations contest with the U.N. and UNESCO? Fomenting a new illiteracy about the programs and value of international organizations, the Heritage Foundation propagated the doctrine of a failed U.N., a U.N. that had proven its inability in all nine key areas that had been its mission from disarmament and peacekeeping to health and human rights. And Heritage claimed its secretariat suffered from every bureaucratic defect ever catalogued from inefficiency to corruption.[48] Titles in the series on the U.N. underline the point of view expressed: "How the U.N. Aids Marxist Guerrilla Groups" and "The Model U.N. Program: Teaching Unreality." The United Nations Association of the United States (UNA) tried to rebut the distortions, misrepresentations, and factual inaccuracies. Elliot Richardson, then its president, for example, wrote Frank Shakespeare about one such piece of propaganda, complaining that it was "shoddy sensationalism at its worst" and that "its inaccuracies are legion and its accusations border on the libelous."[49] But disputing the disinformation of the Heritage U.N. assessment project required a far more advanced system of public education and publicity than conservatism's critics could muster. Scaife alone was bankrolling Heritage with donations of up to $1 million a year, and supporting some 110 "ideological" organizations of an arch-conservative, New Right orientation. By one estimate, he had provided $100 million to these causes in the twelve years before 1981. According to Karen Rothmeyer's research in the *Columbia Journalism Review*, Scaife had been able to "establish group after group" that through "layer upon layer of seminars, studies, conferences, and interviews" was setting "the national agenda of debate." When the Heritage Foundation pamphlet "For UNESCO, A Failing Grade in Education" dismissed that organization's efforts, it was because UNESCO never had the backing Richard Scaife gave to its opponents.[50]

As the conservative network gathered strength and influence between 1968 and 1981, its ideology found expression in the Nixon and Reagan administrations, two California-based political forces with California's peculiar right-wing doctrinal prejudices. Antagonistic to internationalism, these presidencies were likely opponents of UNESCO in any case and even more so if UNESCO appeared to challenge the dominant free-enterprise anticommunist values they cherished. The only free-market maxim these conservatives deplored was the free market in ideas. In its report to the incoming Reagan government in November 1980, the Heritage Foundations's *Mandate for Leadership: Policy Management in a Conservative Administration* advised the Reagan team to understand "the reality of subversion and [to put] emphasis on the un-American nature of much so-called dissidence." The priorities espoused by *Mandate's* recommendations also upheld the axiom that "individual liberties are secondary to the requirement of national security and internal civil order."[51]

During the Nixon years, the administration's policies toward UNESCO exhibited a scornful disinterest rather than an overt antagonism. Still, the U.S. members of the UNESCO Secretariat did feel the chill wind of neglect as the Kennedy-Johnson enthusiasm gave way to the colder hostility of the new Republican leadership. A 1972 National Security policy-planning document dealing with UNESCO was rumored to have had a presidential comment scribbled on it to the effect that "This outfit's no good, let's gut it." Although the evidence remains classified, the impression NSC people gave to the U.S. staff at the headquarters in Paris was a largely negative one.[52] Richard Hoggart recalled the nature of the U.S. appointments to UNESCO's Executive Board in those years as symbolic of the administration's attitude. "In Nixon's Presidency," Hoggart wrote, "the USA put on the Board two successive people so ill-equipped that one could only ascribe their nominations to gross ignorance or contempt for the organization's purposes."[53] Even the State Department's assistant secretary for international organization affairs admitted to a congressional hearing that one of them was the "nadir" of all U.S. representatives, but he happened to be Pat Nixon's cousin. Besides being inexperienced and often political hacks, the U.S. Executive Board appointees had little or no time in service there. In fact, they rotated in and out in the early '70s at the rate of about one a year. Often chosen at the last minute with no prior briefing, delegates to the General Conference included one individual so late being selected that he flew off "without his briefcase."[54] As the Nixon administration underscored its indifference to UNESCO by the nature of the representatives it sent there, it took an even more aggressive attitude toward the U.S. National Commission, the supposed locus of influence on policy and UNESCO's main funnel of publicity to the nation's citizens. From 1970 on the USNC budget and staff steadily eroded. From fifteen in that year, the number dropped to four or five by 1978. In the Reagan years it would be eliminated entirely. UNESCO was obviously losing the connection to its grassroots constituency in the United States by the government's deliberate subversion of its only institutional support network.[55]

In other areas that helped determine United States relations with UNESCO, the same ritualistic pattern of high-level study, congressional investigation, and professional testimony by experts continued to be repeated without any major impact on business as usual or reform initiatives. It could not have been a mating dance since nothing ensued, but its symbolic character, as the right wing gathered momentum, had an increasing similarity to a dance of death. The first evaluation under Nixon may have been an effort to forestall an attack by two enemies of UNESCO with considerable political clout, Representative John Rooney and George Meany. Questions about UNESCO's importance to the U.S. had also arisen among the White House staff. Former Ambassador Woodward headed the evaluation team that had from December 15 until February 1 to prepare the report, based on some 100 interviews with individuals in Washington and Paris. After assessing the positive and negative aspects of UNESCO's varied programs and administrative functions, the findings, according to Richard Nobbe, "demolished many of the spurious charges against UNESCO and cleared the air." In Ambassador Woodward's own later recollections, the important contributions UNESCO made in science had carried great weight and aided the U.S. in fields where it evidenced a strong national interest. Woodward's study also valued the role UNESCO played in providing a neutral setting for the exchange of scientific ideas with other countries and notably with those with which the United States had no contact such as North Korea. Noting the significant activities in fighting illiteracy, the preservation of monuments, and the physics center as well, Woodward felt that the U.S. certainly got its money's worth from its membership.[56]

Urging the government to "continue to participate energetically in UNESCO," Woodward's study proposed "thirteen specific recommendations for strengthening U.S. participation" at the Paris-based organization. It is hard to estimate the impact of those recommendations in light of the record of indifferent and politically oriented actions undermining that very participation. Richard Nobbe's annotated bibliography of the document claims many of the reforms took effect and briefly improved the U.S. position at UNESCO. Yet elsewhere in his analysis of the numerous reviews on UNESCO, Nobbe argues that all of them "have had little impact on guiding the overall U.S. posture towards UNESCO," and even when a temporary strengthening of U.S. involvement occurred, it took place "in the absence of a national policy."[57]

State Department testimony by Assistant Secretary for International Organization Affairs Samuel Lewis at the congressional hearing in 1976 echoed the positive assessments in the Woodward report, recognized the complexity of the political situation at UNESCO, praised Director-General M'Bow, and criticized the U.S. for its failure to maintain a more effective presence there. Lewis also distinguished political actions by member states that aroused U.S. resentment from the work of the organization, its director-general, and its Secretariat. Noting the criticism of some allies that the financial sanctions punished UNESCO for the behavior of other governments, Lewis suggested the withholding may have had counterproductive results. The United States, he said, had "almost always gotten progress" on policies it had pursued in UNESCO before

1974, and he saw no reason to abandon the field to others, particularly the Soviets whose delegations were larger, more experienced, and more aggressive than those of the U.S. And this was especially true when mass-communications initiatives threatening the U.S. position needed to be opposed.[58]

With sophisticated understanding and insight, the assistant secretary explained to the committee that the Israeli uproar reflected the unsettled and acrimonious nature of the Mid-East crisis; that the archaeological excavations were "a fairly tricky question" for which Israel had some responsibility and in which UNESCO had a mandate to act; and that behind the scenes diplomacy at UNESCO would probably resolve that issue. Two of his conclusions deserve to be remembered as a counterpoint to the Reagan administration's dismal evaluations to come. "M'Bow," Lewis affirmed, "deserves the highest praise for his statesman-like efforts, [and] his behavior in an extremely difficult and trying situation can serve as a model for emulation by all international civil servants." In a more restrained analysis of his own country's record, the assistant secretary admitted, "it may well be that over the years we have given, as a government, less priority to this agency than perhaps it deserved."[59]

No such restrained commentary issued from the intellectual, scientific, and professional experts or the U.S. National Commission in their chorus of complaint over the management of its UNESCO relationship by the United States. Even as the government was relegating the USNC to its terminal impotence by budget and staff reductions, a plaintive and poignant refrain of proposals for reform kept pace with its demise. Since the State Department had shut itself off from any significant influence over policy emanating from this aggregation of grassroots associations years before, their expectations had an unreal, fanciful quality. The USNC seemed not to understand its intellectual disenfranchisement. Had its members been 1960s radicals, they would have rioted in protest.

Support for UNESCO

Historians of the U.S. withdrawal from UNESCO should honor the efforts of the UNESCO constituency for its devotion to internationalism and the persistence of its struggle. Its rebukes to the official world catalogued the deficiencies of the status quo that the right-wing reaction was to exploit. In 1976, 1982, and last in 1984 the National Commission rallied to UNESCO's side, pleading for the U.S. to make changes that never came. The 1976 recommendations serve as a prototype of these urgent and hopeful proposals:

UNESCO, they said, was indispensable, essential to any country wishing to be part of the world community. "Interdependence," these

UNESCO supporters pointed out, was "a fact of life." They also argued that the difficulty reaching agreement reflected the world's diversity and was not UNESCO's fault, that politics were no more "inflammatory and divisive" in UNESCO than in any national legislature, and that the budget was a modest one by any standard of judgement. Above all, the United States had to give a much higher priority to UNESCO affairs in contrast to the haphazard, inattentive policies of the preceding years. What needed to be done? The U.S. National Commission had the following recommendations for the State Department:

1) Appoint top-quality people to head the delegations.
2) Give the mission leader ambassadorial rank.
3) Send professional, talented staff members to Paris with multilateral experience and emphasize the length of their assignment there.
4) Select distinguished experts as delegation members.
5) Improve the staffing in Washington.
6) Coordinate all the agencies involved in UNESCO areas.
7) Bring the NGO groups into more active participation.
8) Support the U.S. National Commission with additional staff and funds and use it effectively especially by consultations on policy and personnel with access to the Secretary of State.
9) Embark on long-range planning to recruit staff for UNESCO and its programs in the field.

If these reforms occurred, then the U.S. would have the professional continuity and expert assistance to have an active future at UNESCO. It could seize the initiative and propose programs rather than constantly blocking or vetoing policies generated by others.[60]

In 1979 the comptroller general of the United States confirmed the disarray in the management of the nation's UNESCO policies and produced "a long list of shortcomings." Among them, his report noted, political issues had led the U.S. to neglect "the agency programs"; the U.S. had "proposed few new initiatives" and had become focused instead simply on the budget issue; the government did not "coordinate and oversee" its involvement in program activities; and "frequent turnover" of personnel and "inadequate" briefing of conference delegations diminished the U.S. influence in UNESCO. Nor was the government able to oversee adequately either the "financial management or new issue areas" of the organization. The recommendations proposed "long-range strategies" to correct these defects and, according to Richard Nobbe, led to "some improvements in the management of U.S. participation in UNESCO."[61]

The deficiencies of the multilateral component of overall U.S. foreign policy would not seem to be insurmountable, but the reforms depended upon a certain political will and direction above all. Given the supposed administrative skills the U.S. prided itself on possessing, the execution of these changes in management and policy formulation seemed a relatively easy task. It was not complicated, for example, by the explosion in size from which UNESCO had suffered nor the diversity of style and interest 161 countries brought to the decision-making process at the Paris headquarters. Nor did the United States have to deal with the planning and follow-up for biennial conferences devising global programs of improvement, research, and scientific collaboration and establishing international guidelines to which all nations might adhere. And UNESCO, as fair-minded critics agreed, did not have the sole responsibility for its functional quality, since the operations it directed succeeded or failed according to the joint commitments and support it received from member governments, NGOs, the National Commissions, and the world's intellectual experts. Compliance with UNESCO's activities still depended on the willingness of innumerable political authorities at the local, national, and regional level to give effect to the decisions their representatives at Paris had reached. UNESCO obviously needed all the help it could get and then some.

In the late 1970s, evaluations of its performance by those most closely associated with its work found UNESCO to be a struggling organization plagued by administrative problems but successfully achieving most of its goals. As Roger Revelle put it, criticism of UNESCO was easy since it was "a big, bumbling, heavily bureaucratized, overcentralized, frequently inept, and often frustrating agency." But then he added "if it did not exist, it would have to be invented."[62] Richard Hoggart, who spent five years as an assistant director-general, made a similar assessment, critical of its operational malfunctions but admitting that "in spite of all its weakness, it is still an immensely valuable organization." But if UNESCO was "sick," as Hoggart claimed, what were the ailments and what had caused them?[63]

Governments themselves, especially the U.S., had afflicted UNESCO with three long-standing administrative disabilities. Few, if any, states supported the ideal of an international civil service, and the Secretariat staff remained hostage to national "clearance" and direction that put political reliability ahead of competence. Governments also mistrusted UNESCO's wide-ranging search for truth and the free exchange of ideas, especially those with ethical, philosophical, political, or religious overtones. UNESCO was required to respect these national sensitivities, avoiding any semblance of intervention into "matters essentially in the domestic jurisdiction" of states. Still, its experts tried to expand the boundaries of knowledge and intellectual freedom against these barriers of conservatism and intolerance. And finally, the inevitable politicization, present from the founding, used UNESCO to advance interests or programs which would benefit individual governments rather than the international community.[64]

Neither the National Commissions nor the NGOs had successfully offset the strong governmental presence in UNESCO affairs. As the U.S. example had made clear, National Commissions did not influence official policy to any great extent, and most, Hoggart discovered, were "neither strong nor effective." While the NGOs had the capacity to provide independent, informed, and nonpolitical balance to UNESCO's operations, few of them stood on principle in disputes and their many professional experts and consultants did not exhibit a "strong and articulate" point of view toward UNESCO's dilemmas. Development programs had also turned many of these professionals into cautious technicians avoiding the "intellectually contentious," as Hoggart described it. They did not help UNESCO set priorities in terms of its ideas, and collaborated in purveying much sentimental humbug about peace and mutual understanding.[65]

Other difficulties of management and leadership common to bureaucracies tempered the efficiency and effectiveness of the organization's activities. Director-General Maheu had "enormously extended the powers of the post" in the face of UNESCO's rapid expansion and the need for centralized direction.[66] Yet he also had too little power as governments restricted UNESCO's reach by their own interference in Executive Board policy formation and by their political demands. If he was a tyrant to the Secretariat staff and threatening to its morale, he was also tyrannized by the influence of competing national and regional interests. The balance between generalists and specialists, tenured and short-term contract appointments had not yet been achieved. Setting priorities among projects remained elusive and program evaluation inadequate so that the focus and later assessment of results did not fully serve to advance UNESCO's goals and self-understanding. But both staff and leader had enough "intellectual distinction," diplomatic ability, and administrative competence to make UNESCO "important and worthwhile overall."[67]

As he came to the end of his exhaustive survey of the organization he had served for five years, Richard Hoggart gave his own prescription for its future well-being. "The western democracies," he wrote, "need to give UNESCO much more support." They erred in treating it with scorn and indifference and they needed to "listen to the developing world and take it seriously," for they had not yet responded sensitively to either the NIEO or the NWICO. "Emphasizing the "intangibles" UNESCO could offer the world and the long-run nature of its contribution, Hoggart hoped the West would recognize those values and stand by them. Even as he wrote, however, forces in the United States were preparing to abandon UNESCO rather than stand by and improve it. "Intangibles" in the long run meant nothing to those enemies of Hoggart's international dream.[68]

NOTES

1. Cox and Jacobson, pp. 428–36; Franck, pp. 13–14, 87, 184– 204; Maynes, pp. 804–19; Farer, pp. 79–97; Amuzegar, pp. 547–62.

2. Samaragiwa, "History of NWICO," in "World Forum," pp. 111–12; Schiller, "Decolonization of Information," pp. 35–48; Nordenstreng with Hannikainen, *passim*; Mowlana, in "World Forum," pp. 138–39.

3. Shoup, pp. 109, 115–39, 142–45; Kissinger, *passim*, and pp. 886–87; Markel and March, pp. 1–20.

4. Partan, *passim*; Franck, pp. 205–23.

5. Shoup, pp. 125–35.

6. *Ibid.*, pp. 109, 136–39, 141–45; Behrstock, pp. 156–59; Saloma, *passim*; Morgan, "Conservatives," *Washington Post*, January 4, 1981; Partan, *supra*; see also Coate, pp. 18, 29–30.

7. Hoggart, *passim*; see also House Subcommittee on International Organizations, "UNESCO: Challenges and Opportunities," *passim*; Maynes, p. 804.

8. Wete, pp. 3–4; Banks, pp. 30–51; see also MacBride, p. 15; and see Parenti, *passim*.

9. Hoggart, pp. 160–61; Hazzard, pp. 233, 236; Nordenstreng with Hannikainen, p. 180.

10. Hoggart, pp. 164–69; Nordenstreng with Hannikainen, p. xiii.

11. MacBride, p. 15 and *passim*; Nordenstreng with Hannikainen, pp. 7–9, 79–106; Wete, pp. 3–4; Hocking, *passim*.

12. Nordenstreng with Hannikainen, pp. 7-14, 85; Raube-Wilson, pp. 121, 124–25; Sewell, *UNESCO*, p. 261; Schiller, "Decolonization," p. 45.

13. Nordenstreng with Hannikainen, pp. 9–14, 79–113; Schiller, "Decolonization," pp. 36–39; Coate, pp. 16–19.

14. Wete, pp. 3–4.

15. Maynes, pp. 807–13; Farer, pp. 84–96.

16. MacBride, pp. 9, 12, 14; Nordenstreng with Hannikainen, pp. 17–19, 98–122.

17. Nordenstreng with Hannikainen, pp. 19–21, 120–32, 134–38.

18. *Ibid.*, pp. 5, 26–28, 41–42.

19. *Ibid.*, pp. 29, 32, 36–38, 128–30, 137; Coate, pp. 19–20.

20. Nordenstreng with Hannikainen, pp. 20–21, 26, 41–43, 45–46, 48–56; Coate, p. 21; Banks, pp. 78–84.

21. Nordenstreng with Hannikainen, pp. 737–38 and fn. 124, p. 52; Wete, pp. 4–6; Mehan, p. 163; Hughes, "Twilight," pp. 30– 32, 41–48; Franklin interview, May 1, 1987. See also Part III.

22. Farer, pp. 79–96; Hughes, "Twilight," p. 31; Lyons, Baldwin, and McNemar, pp. 81–92.

23. Karp, pp. 69–71; Blanchard, p. 277; Partan, pp. 11–13, 18–19.

24. Partan, pp. 113–23.

25. *Ibid.*, pp. 11–75.

26. Sherry, pp. 756–57, 759, 764–65, 769.

27. Partan, pp. 11–75; Hoggart, pp. 75–81.

28. Fobes interview, February 5, 1987; Partan, pp. 95–100.

29. Partan, pp. 133–63, 169.

30. Fobes interview, February 5, 1987.

31. Partan, pp. 64–65, 77–93, 95–100, 103–10; Hoggart, pp. 75–81; Coate, p. 18.

32. House Subcommittee on International Organizations, *UNESCO: Challenges and Opportunities*, p. 54.

33. Coate, p. 18.

34. *UNESCO: Challenges and Opportunities*, pp. 24–27.

35. *Ibid.*, pp. 29–30.

36. *Ibid.*, pp. 47–49; Nobbe, p. 3.

37. *UNESCO: Challenges and Opportunities*, p. 30; Partan, p. vi.

38. *UNESCO: Challenges and Opportunities*, pp. 65–66.

39. Finkelstein, "Conference Document," pp. 27–28, 35; Coate, p. 18; Finkelstein, "The Political Role of the Director-General of UNESCO," p. 19; Jean Gerard, "Statement" in "Conference Report," p. 18; Hufner and Naumann, p. 10.

40. Cox, pp. 103 and 102–36.

41. Congressional Research Service, Library of Congress, "U.S. Withdrawal From the International Labor Organization: Successful Precedent for UNESCO?" in Senate Committee on Labor and Human Resources, "Human Resources Impact of U.S. Membership in UNESCO," pp. 133, 147, 152, and 123–59; interview with former Ambassador Woodward, March 19, 1987, Washington, D.C.

42. Morgan, *Washington Post*, January 4, 1981.

43. Behrstock, pp. 158–59.

44. Saloma, pp. vii and *passim*.

45. *Ibid.*, pp. 3–84; Morgan, *passim*.

46. *Ibid.*; Shoup, pp. 103–4, 109, 115–17; see also Markel and March, introduction.

47. Saloma, pp. 15–20; Morgan, *passim*; Behrstock, pp. 156–59.

48. Behrstock, pp. 158–59.

49. William C. Powell, Director of Public Information, UNA to Marcus J. Albrecht, May 5, 1982; Elliot Richardson to Frank Shakespeare, September 27, 1983; see also "The Heritage Foundation and the United Nations: Whatever It Is—I'm Against It," (part of a series of analyses and rebuttals to the Heritage Foundation U.N. assessment Project by the Southern California Division, UNA-USA, January 1983).

50. Saloma, pp. 26–31; "Heritage Foundation and the U.N.," *passim*.

51. Saloma, pp. 15–16.

52. Fobes interview, February 5, 1987.

53. Hoggart, p. 104.

54. "UNESCO: Challenges and Opportunities," pp. 13, 61, 65; Hoggart, p. 61.

55. Fobes interview, February 5, 1987; Nobbe interview, February 5, 1987.

56. Nobbe, "Annotated Bibliography," p. 2; telephone interview with Ambassador Robert Woodward, Washington, D.C., March 19, 1987.

57. Nobbe, "Analysis of Past and Present Reviews," p. 3; Nobbe, "Annotated Bibliography," p. 2.

58. *UNESCO: Challenges and Opportunities*, pp. 2–15.

59. *Ibid.*, pp. 8–14, 16–17.

60. "United States Participation in UNESCO: A Report by the Special Committee to Study Representation in UNESCO, May 1976," in *UNESCO: Challenges and Opportunities*, pp. 86–98; see also *ibid.*, pp. 17, 31, 33, 38, 61.

61. Nobbe, "Annotated Bibliography," p. 5.

62. *UNESCO: Challenges and Opportunities*, p. 38.

63. Hoggart, pp. 13, 17, 23.

64. *Ibid.*, pp. 42–75.

65. *Ibid.*, pp. 83–109.

66. *Ibid.*, p. 148.

67. *Ibid.*, pp. 112–34, 136–59; see also Finkelstein, "Conference Document," *passim*; Finkelstein, "Political Role," *passim*.

68. Hoggart, pp. 190–91, 194–96.

IX. THE UNITED STATES EXITS, 1981–1985

The conservative coalition with its antagonism toward the United Nations and international cooperation in general was, indeed, waiting in the wings and gathering force. Between 1977 and 1981, however, the eye of that hurricane of opposition passed over UNESCO giving it a false sense of security. In post-Watergate American politics, Jimmy Carter's Democratic presidency interrupted the progress of conservatives and maintained a more liberal, flexible, accommodating approach to the issues erupting in UNESCO's forum and elsewhere. Even if the State Department did not really reverse the benign neglect to which it had assigned its UNESCO relations, the Carter appointments and the Carter approach suggested a greater attention to and leadership of multilateral affairs and Third World demands, even a kind of understanding of them. Part of this attitude probably represented a global sophistication that members of the Trilateral Commission and Council on Foreign Relations brought with them into the Carter administration when filling important foreign-policy and national-security positions in it. Recognizing the many strains that were undermining the old international order and the consequent need for "a renovation of the entire international system," this leadership cadre had its eye on the constructive channels into which the discontent of the less powerful could be directed "without abandoning the control of action to them." They were ready to negotiate and bargain in the pluralistic centers of accommodation the U.N. system provided, and perhaps even learn "adaptive behavior" there. And they certainly recognized the Third World's strategic and economic importance to their own country's security and well-being.[1]

But Jimmy Carter also seemed to sense the deeper emotional and psychological realities accompanying the postcolonial era of national independence abroad and the liberation movements at home. At least in his appointments, he realized the importance of gestures to those feelings. John Hope Franklin has described one of those Carter innovations, the only such experiment of its kind in U.S. history. The Advisory Board on Ambassadorial Appointments, on which Franklin served for two years, consisted of people from all walks of life, ordinary individuals as well as renowned, with black and women members. They were to nominate three candidates for any post without regard to anything but their qualifications and, according to Franklin, not once did the individual's politics come up for discussion. To UNESCO the Carter administration sent Esteban Torres as permanent representative with the rank of ambassador (1977–79), and Barbara Newell, a prominent educator, followed him (1979–81). Andrew Young became the ambassador to the U.N. And at the National Commission for UNESCO, John Fobes, former deputy director-general, took charge as the chairman of that organization after he left UNESCO. The ambassadorial rank and the diversity and talents of the people appointed indicated the government's strong support for multilateral collaborations and UNESCO's importance. And the delegations to the 1978 and 1980 General Conferences sustained this point of view.[2]

These representatives did not applaud everything UNESCO did nor did they fail to defend the U.S. national interest in some bitter disputes, but they did not picture the United States as a victim of evil forces and they did not bully their equals in international organizations with threats of financial sanctions or U.S. withdrawal. On the single most controversial issue at the end of that decade, the NWICO, the United States position had survived intact, the Soviet resolutions on mass communications had been rebuffed, the Mass Media Declaration and the MacBride Commission report had protected free-flow and free-market doctrines, and the good-faith offer of increased technical assistance through the IPDC had indicated the U.S. recognition of imbalance in the structures and resources of the world's media affairs. In addition, the Arab-Israeli conflict remained quiescent.[3]

In looking back on those years, Esteban Torres, now a California congressman, believed that UNESCO had changed in a positive way and that United States attitudes toward it had much improved. Barbara Newell had similar feelings. She believed that the U.S. was on the verge of a new opportunity to restore its status among Third World countries and regain its leadership in international organizations. The civil-rights gains at home, the recognition of them in U.S. staffing of its multilateral commitments, the continuing appeal of U.S. science and "know-how," and the Soviet invasion of Afghanistan seemed significant trends in Newell's analysis. Director-General M'Bow's "effective leader[ship]," as Torres saw it, and his support for the Carter initiatives, aided by the African caucus he led, also pointed to a better U.S./UNESCO relationship. The United States had not ignored that activity and had supported M'Bow's reelection as director-general. However, the optimism and the illusions of 1980 proved to be short lived.[4]

History, of course, should have warned all the enthusiastic reformers that their spasms of change sat precariously atop the ingrained, age-old traditions. Habits of indifference and attitudes of antagonism among the State Department bureaucracy were sure to outlive the temporary Carter infusion of new leaders with new ideals. And if an Esteban Torres or an Andrew Young did not panic over Third World rhetoric in international organizations, that did not mean the racial animosities and ideological resentments of others had abandoned the field. Even more important, the Carter administration could not undo in four years what had been gathering momentum for twenty. Only crackpot fanatics believe that history or organizational practices and policies reverse direction overnight, or easily, or without long and continued attention, as UNESCO would try to explain to the Reagan ideologues who set one year timetables for acceptable and thorough reform.

The U.S./UNESCO relationship and the role of the U.S. National Commission had not, therefore, been turned around, but a start had been made, and, as Barbara Newell argued, a "window of opportunity" existed. On the main points of political controversy, the United States had accomplished much; in a sense, the war had been won. Two ominous and uncontrollable events, however, would hide that victory from the nation that had achieved it, and Carter could do little about it. The U.S. media, obsessed by the NWICO rhetoric and the very suggestion of public accountability, continued their campaign of disinformation and attack. They were apparently pursuing a scorched-earth policy to ensure that discussions of mass communications issues would never again recur in UNESCO forums. At the same time, their control of news in the United States "socialized" the readers "to view . . . [UNESCO] with disregard."[5] The right-wing conservative coalition, meanwhile, was ready to assume political power and begin dismantling the nation's international obligations. Like the general staffs they imitated, both hierarchies of power were making plans to fight the last war, as if nothing had changed. UNESCO, basking in the improved relations of the Carter era, was thus poised between the Scylla of public indifference and the Charybdis of potential right-wing assault with the media interest in it conditioned by self-interest over the communications issue.

If the United States relationship with UNESCO had often been characterized more by pretense than by effective support, the Reagan administration stripped that pretense away and offered fanaticism instead. The single-minded pursuit of UNESCO, now a target of opportunity, did not appear as a preconceived international mugging because both the media's manipulation of opinion and the State Department's posture of neglect had largely prepared the way. Conditioned to believe UNESCO guilty as charged, even by irresponsible zealots, mass opinion could not believe UNESCO innocent of the accusations or the perpetrators responsible for the wrong doing they had so nefariously brought about. The whole affair, in fact, had the character of those political trials in which opponents of government policies are rounded up as dangers to the state security, tried before excited and prejudiced juries in an atmosphere poisoned by McCarthyism at its most reckless, and convicted quickly and without redress. And there were other similarities in the staged presentation of fairness and due process whereby the defense had its meaningless day in court amid the prosecution's protestations that justice must be upheld. While the anti-UNESCO cabal did not don hooded sheets and hang the organization from a tree, they accomplished the political equivalent and blamed the victim for it. As an example to other delinquent U.N. organizations, UNESCO's fate also had its role to play in creating a chilling effect, the popular term for cost-efficient random intimidation that suppresses dissent on a wider scale.

But UNESCO would never have become the objective of Reagan's right-wing campaign if the latter had not had a coherent and comprehensive philosophy opposed to multilateralism in general and UNESCO in particular. As the Heritage Foundation's *Mandate for Leadership* made clear, the conservatives proposed a new global order of their own. It would restore free-enterprise/free-market values and enforce them by unilateral action or through policies determined in U.N. agencies controlled by the U.S. and its allies. Deregulation and privatization were key support systems enhancing the power of the large corporations at home and overseas. Development aid would also depend on the receiving nation's commitment to private-sector growth and activity. At the same time, the Reagan administration reduced its multilateral aid to new lows and cut its assessed payments to the U.N., scorning the World Court's jurisdiction and the rule of international law. It displayed little faith in international treaties, refused to sign the Law of the Sea Convention after its ten-year negotiation by four previous administrations; it tied votes cast in the U.N. General Assembly to bilateral U.S. aid prospects, indulged in the unilateral use of force in Grenada and Nicaragua, threatened to leave the ILO, FAO, UNCTAD, and the IAEA. The Reaganites illustrated the full context of their return to an American exceptionalism in all its isolationist, nativist, and provincial intensity. To the extent they accepted international organizations, they thought of them as a private club of the virtuous whose prestige and power ruled over the less distinguished. With its Third World majority and its uninhibited rhetoric promoting the re-regulation of the international order, UNESCO was obviously not the kind of club in which the U.S. could feel comfortable.[6]

The demands the Reagan administration made on international organizations also had a curious self-serving quality, for UNESCO had to meet standards of behavior the United States was unable or unwilling to adopt in its own sphere of operations. Free flow was a good example. Ronald Reagan did not believe in it. Greater government secrecy, higher classification guidelines, intelligence agency exemptions, visa and immigration controls over the free market in ideas, emasculation of the Freedom of Information Act, OMB-imposed reductions in the collection and dissemination of statistics and data of all kinds, funding cuts to archives and libraries, and the surveillance and intimidation of dissent in and outside the government characterized a hostility to the free exchange and flow of ideas already obstructed by the monopolistic control over communications the media industry maintained.[7]

Budget discipline rated further skepticism, as anyone familiar with the U.S. deficits and budgetary inflation under Reagan might imagine. UNESCO's spending was a pitiful drop in the bucket of U.S. expenditures in any case. Herbert Schiller has estimated the cost overrun of one nuclear submarine to be the equivalent of UNESCO's total annual budget. An even more startling comparison was produced by the Grace Commission report on government financial waste and mismanagement. According to that study $424 billion could be saved in three years through cost-cutting reforms in the United States government operations. this amount represented the dues the U.S. would pay to UNESCO in 1,000 years of membership. Chairman Peter Grace — himself a conservative — concluded that "the government is run horribly." As Professor Hans Weiler observed, "the U.S. government . . . seems a rather odd candidate for leading a worldwide crusade against bureaucratic waste and inefficiency." In the year the U.S. withdrew from UNESCO, the former's budget increase was 10.8 percent over the previous year, UNESCO's was 6 percent. And UNESCO managed its global responsibilities with less spending than a major U.S. university.[8]

The Reagan administration, furthermore, wanted the equivalent of a Security Council veto in organizations whose majorities represented members of the Third World. The specious U.S. plea for an equitable treatment of itself as a minority (the minority-rights justification) through a variety of procedural gimmicks should be compared to its domination of other U.N. organizations, such as the World Bank, where no such gratuitous concern for uninfluential minorities had been evidenced. And its outcry over Third World blocs has seemed hypocritical when measured against the West's own power centers of unified authority such as OECD and the Geneva Group, not to mention the influence its wealth and resources made possible.[9]

Conceived as part of a larger conservative campaign against the U.N. system as a whole, aided and abetted by Heritage Foundation members and their right-wing political allies from California, and sustained by disinformation and double standards of judgment, the assault against UNESCO, much like any military invasion of a hostile country, passed through three main stages. In fact, some analysts of the operation have described it as knocking off the Grenada of the United Nations.

In the first phase, the incoming administration prepared its plans, assembled its forces, and softened up the beach-head. From 1981 through 1983, a full-scale attack demolished UNESCO's standing and reputation, and cut off pockets of resistance in UNESCO and in the United States. After the actual withdrawal had been announced, a proclamation of victory one might call it, the political occupation administered a program of re-education intended, like all such oversights, to bring the conquered territory into ideological line with the victors. Or so it was said. In reality, the U.S. never put the terms or the timetable of acceptable reform within reach of the victim. The U.S. departure at the end of 1984, therefore, suggests a better definition of the exercise as a punitive expedition much like those of gunboat diplomacy days when the Marines landed in China to administer a sound thrashing to an insubordinate native population.

Some indications of the forthcoming campaign had surfaced before the Reagan inauguration and others followed quickly in the first months of the new conservative era of government. The president himself had supposedly expressed opposition to UNESCO when he was governor of California, but even if he had not, his close links to the right wing in that state and elsewhere aligned him with the anti-U.N. ideology that the Heritage Foundation expressed with such passion.[10] The Republican platform and the lengthy volume of briefing materials Heritage had prepared promised a much harder line toward the U.N. Nor was this a temporary reaction to the Democratic internationalism that Carter had pursued, as the Republicans' 1984 platform confirmed. It warned that "Americans cannot count on the international organizations to guarantee our security or adequately protect our interests." Noting that "many members consistently vote against us," the platform continued that "President Reagan . . . has put the United Nations on notice that the United States will strongly oppose the use of the United Nations to foster anti-semitism, Soviet espionage, and hostility to the United States." Applauding the rejection of the Law of the Sea Convention and telling the U.N. it was not welcome in formulating policy for Antarctica or outer space either, the statement told the U.N. members the U.S. would "monitor their votes and activities . . . [and] Americans will no longer silently suffer the hypocrisy of many of these organizations."[11]

Because UNESCO had the worst rating among the numerous international agencies, the incoming cadre of Reagan appointees marked it for immediate attention. David Stockman, who was to direct the Office of Management and Budget (OMB), argued in an early position paper during the transition period that the United States should withdraw from UNESCO since it advocated "pro PLO policies and . . . support for measures limiting the free flow of information."[12] In January 1981 Stockman's OMB recommended that UNESCO receive no funding and the State Department reduce its involvement in other international organizations. Other officials exhibited hostile or quizzical attitudes toward UNESCO, among them Elliott Abrams, the first assistant secretary of state for international organization affairs who apparently accepted the idea of a U.S. withdrawal at this time. The State Department did strike UNESCO from its 1981 draft budget, but somehow the funding was restored. As these events transpired, the Reagan administration proceeded to downgrade the U.S. National Commission even further by additional staff reductions. The experienced UNESCO hand John Fobes did not receive a reappointment as chairman. His replacement was James Holderman, president of the University of South Carolina. Unknown to Holderman, a plan to phase out the National Commission had been formulated, but Elliot Abrams convinced him to take the chairmanship on the grounds that no withdrawal was in sight and the USNC still had an important role to play. USNC was already being "privatized," for Holderman largely had to supply his own staff support. As the government's UNESCO agenda unfolded, Holderman was later to admit that he had been lied to.[13]

The UNESCO Bureau in the government, meanwhile, was suffering from excessive mobility and seemed in its homelessness to represent the disarray in and even an underlying ill will toward educational and cultural affairs. In an unfortunate and highly symbolic reorganization in 1978, President Carter had assigned responsibility for those activities to the International Communication Agency (ICA). This transfer under Executive Order 12048 had placed the information or propaganda agency formally in charge of education and cultural matters, the final subordination of those policies to the immediate national interests that information was designed to serve and that had been resisted ever since World War II. The move may well have represented the government's belief that its interest in UNESCO's programs had now so narrowed down as to exclude everything except the mass-communications issue.[14]

According to the 1984 congressional staff study on the U.S. withdrawal, however, the UNESCO Bureau had moved to the office of Social and Humanitarian Affairs by 1981. In that year a reorganization created a combined Office of Communications and UNESCO Affairs under a deputy assistant secretary for political affairs. In late 1983 the bureau moved once more, again with striking symbolism, to an office headed by a deputy assistant secretary for private sector affairs. Had the U.S. not withdrawn, one wonders where the UNESCO desk might have moved next.[15] On the other hand, the pro-UNESCO members of that bureau may have been trying to hide from the opponents of internationalism scattered throughout the State Department — Alan Keyes, Jeane Kirkpatrick, Roger Brooks, Gregory Newell, and others.

As the anti-UNESCO hostility began appearing in policy and personnel decisions within the government, two other developments in early 1981 contributed to the organization's further deterioration in official and public esteem. Both of them had their origin in the continuing international discussions about mass-communications issues. That in itself was enough to stimulate a conference at Talloires, France organized by the World Press Freedom Committee and its Western media allies to combat the NWICO and open an aggressive campaign on behalf of the free-press/free-flow definition of global information standards. In turn, congressional hearings supported this revived attack on UNESCO and the NWICO and that led to a congressional decision to impose financial sanctions against UNESCO should any of its activities threaten a variety of free-press values upheld by the United States. The Western victories at Belgrade in 1980 and the achievement of consensus there had disappeared overnight in a blaze of renewed panic and confrontation. The conservative coalition within the executive branch thus picked up powerful media and legislative allies early on in their campaign against UNESCO. They knew, therefore, that the press would remain uncritically hostile to UNESCO and give their own position uncritical support. They also knew the Congress was in an antagonistic mood over the NWICO issue. The conservatives could go forward with this renewed assurance of dominating the debate.[16]

A UNESCO-sponsored conference on the protection of journalists in February 1981 was the immediate cause of the latest round of controversy between the West and the rest of the world. An idea that had germinated in 1957 and been given added significance by the death and disappearance of reporters in various trouble spots since then, the protection proposal aroused all the acrimony that the larger NWICO had earlier developed. Seen by the Western media as one more step to identify, license, and thereby control journalists, they insisted on participating in the meeting with a view, according to Kaarle Nordenstreng, of seeing that it came to no conclusions. And it did not, but the U.S. media interests there did come to one, "to take initiative" and "a united stand against the campaign by the Soviet bloc and some Third World countries to give UNESCO the authority to chart the media's course."[17]

The Talloires Conference of May 15–17, 1981, in which 63 delegates from 21 countries participated, terminated "the strategy of accommodation," as one friendly observer described the previous seven years, and revived the ideological hard line opposing any modification of the absolutist free-press position. And it pictured UNESCO's NWICO initiatives as "a step toward Big Brother control over human lives similar to that pictured in George Orwell's frightening novel."[18] The U.S. was again exporting the First Amendment and demanding its acceptance as a world standard of press authority. The congressional hearings took an equally one-sided view of the information dispute and peddled exaggerated claims of imminent danger should the NWICO order proceed apace. The invited range of witnesses certainly did not represent a free market in ideas. Three House members who drafted the hostile resolution, two U.S. government officials, including Elliott Abrams, and "six industry and news media" spokesmen appeared as opponents of UNESCO and its mass-communications activities; one person defended the NWICO "after all the other witnesses had been heard and the resolution already endorsed," and the *Washington Post* and the *New York Times* gave his testimony no notice at all. His attempt to clarify the realities by insisting UNESCO did not plan to "license journalists or regulate the press," therefore, did not have any impact in the U.S. But his statement did appear in *The Times of London* and he recalled that its "story from Washington . . . varied so drastically from American coverage that . . . [it] appeared to be covering an entirely different hearing."[19]

The State Department witness, Assistant Secretary Abrams, provided the historical context that sparked the congressional decision to threaten sanctions. Arguing that the NWICO meant government dictation of media content and "restrictions on Western news agencies, advertisers and journalists," Abrams linked the New World Information and Communication Order to the New International Economic Order and told his audience that the U.S. rejected "the radical restructuring of the international economic system that would necessarily follow.[20] The ensuing legislative action laid down the terms of future U.S. funding of UNESCO. The "Beard Amendment" (Section 109 of the State Department Authorization Act for fiscal year 1982-83, PL 97–241) would cut off U.S. support to UNESCO "if that organization implements any policy or practice the effect of which is to license journalists or their publications, to censor or otherwise restrict the free flow of information within or among countries, or to impose mandatory codes of journalistic practice or ethics." The legislation also required the secretary of state to report annually to Congress about UNESCO's status under the terms of liability set forth. In the fall of 1981 Ronald Reagan added a further somber warning that UNESCO's time was running out. Referring to the Talloires declaration and encouraging "a broad and rich diversity of opinion" as the only way to overcome information imbalance, the president advised that "we do not feel we can continue to support a UNESCO that turns its back on the high purposes this organization was originally intended to serve."[21]

The controversy that the Carter administration believed it had largely resolved by the time the Belgrade Conference had ended had now resumed with greater ideological intensity and a U.S. determination to impose its will by financial sanctions or worse. And the misperceptions and misinterpretations of the NWICO were as much the currency of U.S. press analysis as they had been in the 1970s. As a further confirmation of the shift in U.S. strategy, the Reagan administration also welshed on the promised support for the IPDC. Since this was a major instrument with which the Third World could build the "broad and rich diversity of opinion" that Reagan claimed he favored, the government's refusal to sustain its commitment revealed the hypocrisy of its rhetoric. At the January 1982 Acapulco meeting to inaugurate the program, the United States offered a mere $100,000 "in the form of expert services" and not a penny in cash, although other countries promised substantial contributions.[22]

Inequality of access to public opinion continued to bedevil UNESCO and its defenders in 1981 and later. Director-General M'Bow denied that his organization advocated "state control over the press" and said he opposed both "foreign domination and internal domination" because he "would act always in support of democracy and the freedom of the press." This point of view circulated in the London-based *South* magazine, a small monthly. The Smith-Kline transnational corporation, on the other hand, sponsored a four-page supplement for the U.S. editions of *Time* (February 1, 1982) and *Newsweek* (February 8, 1982) that told the readership of "Danger at the U.N." In contrast to M'Bow's low-key declaration in support of freedom, the Smith-Kline ads described a "UNESCO-sponsored coalition of tyrannies and their accomplices hatching elaborate plots to muzzle free world news media, all in the name of alleged 'omissions' and 'imbalances' in coverage." The ads spoke of Third World "extortion" and "bureaucratic coercion" that the industrial world would resist through their control of "coveted technologies and vital capital" and by "selectively offering and withholding our markets, skills and capital" until the LDCs abandoned their schemes for new international orders. Unilateral hard ball had an appeal that multilateral negotiation obviously lacked, and one aspect was its power to manipulate the ideas people adopted toward the U.N. and particularly UNESCO.[23]

As the media industry, its advertising supporters, and their legislative representatives in Congress coalesced behind the right-wing Reagan conservatives in 1981, the latter's unsparing denunciation of UNESCO began to have an impact on other segments of elite opinion. Reaction to international events had prepared this elite emotionally for the Heritage Foundation propaganda about the United Nations. Global crisis and Third World demands had produced from the 1970s a deep anxiety about the shape of the future and the nation's ability to establish its direction and control its agenda. And anticommunism's pervasive influence still led many Americans to believe the Soviets were behind all the disquieting developments that disturbed them. The Ad Hoc Group on U.S. Policy toward the United Nations, which had formed in 1975, best symbolized the latent high-level unease that could easily be aroused against UNESCO, reminiscent of the way some German industrialists had turned against the Weimar Republic. The Ad Hoc membership, including the former Democratic secretaries of state, Rusk, Vance, and Muskie, issued a position paper in October 1981 that evaluated the U.S. and the U.N. relationship and called for "A Policy For Today." It revealed a spectrum of influential thinking that spelled further trouble for UNESCO.[24]

Postulating a deepening popular "disenchantment" with the U.N. (more likely their own), the Ad Hoc group deplored the "politicized behavior" there that undermined its ability to act in "an impartial and effective manner." The policy statement called for a return to "useful dialogue and constructive action" instead of the "grossly biased resolutions" the Third World introduced. While recognizing certain positive contributions of the latter (joining with the West mainly), the Ad Hoc members criticized majority tyranny, which often meant to them the "radicalized" majority. On certain issues the policy document was clearly not aligned with Heritage, for it understood there were faults in the international economic order, that the U.S. was "among the least generous" in the percentage of its GNP it gave to development aid, and that Namibia should be independent of South Africa. But when it evaluated UNESCO, it was back in the Heritage camp. "UNESCO," it concluded, "presents perhaps the most troubling case of retrogressive ideology and biased politics." The Soviet menace re-emerged as the main impetus behind the NWICO aided by "some Third World governments" and the NWICO meant "government controls" over all aspects of the mass media. The report noted the Senate's 99-0 vote against the idea of a new information order and the Beard Amendment, and applauded the administration's support for the Talloires Declaration. "The time has come," the Ad Hoc group suggested, to reassess the capacity of UNESCO, and certain other U.N. agencies, to function compatibly with their declared ideals and purposes." If "politicization, or gross inefficiency" could not be remedied by U.S. efforts within the organization (which the group preferred) then "we should not exclude the possibility of withholding financial support or even withdrawing from the agency."[25]

This high-level analysis and the other public investigations and statements during 1981 indicated that the range of ideas that circulated about UNESCO had been significantly narrowed to exclude all the organization's positive contributions and achievements from public awareness and debate. Even those most well informed on foreign-policy issues had apparently accepted the media industry's version of the issues, an interpretation that by then had developed the character of unquestioned gospel truth. UNESCO was trying to kill the First Amendment. Nor did historical perspective have any role in illuminating the nature of past political abuse and misuse of UNESCO by the nation that now leveled accusations of gross politicization at the Third World. A country that refused to acknowledge the realities of its own past could be equally blind in other areas. Passing over its own administrative incompetence and budgetary mismanagement, the U.S. falsely attacked UNESCO for violating the very standards it so cavalierly disregarded itself. Totally lacking context and distorted by disinformation, the UNESCO debate had reached its final form by the end of 1981. The subsequent evaluations would have to overcome the presumptions and prejudices that had been instilled by then. The United States had won the propaganda battle and having so manipulated everyone's minds, it could treat UNESCO any way it wished. The stunning irony of this achievement was that the United States, having proved that the free market in ideas did not exist, attacked UNESCO for planning to destroy it.

The Termination Operation

Although UNESCO's photograph and fingerprints had not been circulated for display in U.S. post offices as a most-wanted public enemy, it had attained that status in the notoriety the media had instigated. And the Reagan administration, aware of that favorable climate of opinion, could now move on to more aggressive measures. The candidate chosen to head the termination phase of the operations was a young right-wing political advance man named Gregory Newell. With close connections to and backing from the White House, Newell became the assistant secretary of state for international organization affairs with an apparent mandate to deal with UNESCO. His office thereafter became a headquarters of hostility to the U.N. and UNESCO with which Heritage Foundation staff could share outlook and policy proposals. In the view of those who followed the final stages of the U.S./UNESCO relationship, Newell's appointment represented a preordained decision to pull out. It was simply a matter of building to a dramatic climax for the entertainment of the audience and extracting an Aristotelian lesson from the tragedy. At any rate, an ideologue had charge of the production and his direction of it apparently had but one end in view.[26]

The unequal contest between the contending sides over U.S. policy toward UNESCO became even clearer during 1982. Newell, of course, now had oversight of UNESCO affairs and seemed determined to remove from effective influence any members of the IO staff that understood the history and the value of the UNESCO relationship. Newell did not want an institutional memory to inhibit the policy position he had decided to adopt. He also prepared to cut off funding for the U.S. National Commission to lessen its opportunity to organize the network of professional societies that had the widest knowledge and most favorable assessment of UNESCO's activities over the years. At a later date, he apparently disrupted and destroyed the accumulated files covering the 40 years of the commission's life, obliterating its own history in the process—a preemptive form of historical revisionism not congenial to the free flow of ideas. His Heritage Foundation allies, meanwhile, began their massive U.N. assessment project that would amount to some 60 "Backgrounders" (pamphlet-size pieces), three lecture series, three books, fifteen "executive memos," and seven book-size "U.N. Studies" by the end of 1986. Given Heritage's vast financial resources and distribution system, a further propaganda windfall would skew the public perception of U.N. affairs as Newell was orchestrating the U.S. withdrawal from UNESCO.[27]

Opposing this powerful mobilization of official design and popular influence would not be easy. Where were the big battalions of support? Was there a mouse that could roar? If history was any indication, UNESCO itself had been able to generate strong, if often erratic and ineffective, support over the years. Would there be an Archibald MacLeish, a William Benton, a Charles Frankel, or a John F. Kennedy now that UNESCO needed him? And would the professional, intellectual, and academic community be able to offset the Heritage Foundation and conservative alliance with its mastery of public relations. There was even an outside chance that the UNESCO Bureau and certain congressional staff might commence a small, concerted foray of fact-finding and expose the truth. If they did, one major obstacle still remained: What major media outlet would publish and disseminate it?

That question did not seem to have a high priority among the pro-UNESCO activists. They remained philosophically committed to the free market in ideas their opponents had already abandoned and, therefore, they conducted their campaign as though a fair-minded, reasonable evaluation of the issues would somehow automatically reach a wide audience and influence policy. Nor did they seem to realize that their consideration of the pros and the cons of U.S. participation in UNESCO simply provided an additional hearing for the cons, since the pros were essentially D.O.A.—dead on arrival—in the then unfavorable marketplace supposedly open to all. Like the tree falling in the woods with no one present to hear it, the favorable recommendations to stay in UNESCO kept crashing down on the public consciousness with a thundering silence.

The first such effort of thoughtful reappraisal took place at the Columbia campus of the University of South Carolina June 1–3, 1982. Its president and host, James Holderman, chairman of the U.S. National Commission, arranged and sponsored this special meeting of his organization. The conference report described the event as "A Critical Assessment of U.S. Participation in UNESCO," the first overall study of that participation "organized by and for the American public since 1960." Of the 150 individuals from the "academic, business, and government communities (including the U.S. Congress)" that received invitations, 93 attended. Both Jean Gerard, U.S. Ambassador to UNESCO, and Director-General M'Bow were present and gave major addresses. A historical overview, panel commentary by experts, and discussions among five working groups completed the thorough agenda the meeting had been called to conduct. At the end came a unanimous recommendation by all five groups "that the United States not only continue to remain a member of UNESCO but that the effectiveness of U.S. participation in the work of the organization be increased." It was a rallying cry of advance and determination.[28]

One need only read over the professional analyses by U.S. experts on U.S./UNESCO relations going back to the late 1950s, evaluations and recommendations that became monotonous in their understanding of UNESCO's value and their calls for greater U.S. leadership, to be overwhelmed by the ironic and poignant nature of this last cry for help. If a quarter-century had not changed the State Department's or the president's commitment to this indispensable international organization, would they now respond and reverse those years of benign neglect? With Ronald Reagan in the White House and Gregory Newell as assistant secretary of state for international organization affairs, it did not seem likely. Even sadder was the conference's expectation that the National Commission would emerge from the South Carolina meeting like a phoenix from the ashes of executive indifference and play the role designed for it by the UNESCO constitution. Would a vigorous advocate of planning and policy formation overseeing the State Department's management of its UNESCO affairs be welcomed by the very people who had cut the National Commission staff to shreds, soon to end its funding entirely?

What then did the "critical assessment" mean? How does anyone interpret the event without dismissing it as a cynical charade or a distraction from more covert purposes underway elsewhere? The historian is fascinated by its millenarian aspects, the assembled throng awaiting the second coming of international cooperation like the true believers they were. Certainly the published report represented the finest short collection of material on the UNESCO experience and the U.S. involvement in it that can be found. And there were other valuable documents as well: M'Bow's inspiring evocation of UNESCO's mission, his summary of its achievements, and his clarification of the issues that had been distorted by controversy; and the surprising testimony to some of UNESCO's activities by Jean Gerard, who later became a determined force for withdrawal. If expert assessments and academic conferences determined the course of history . . . yet they fit the Reagan definition of acceptable behavior: not "politicized," over-budget, or grossly mismanaged.[29]

Published as No. 9287 by the State Department that fall, "A Critical Assessment" in all its comprehensive and spirited coverage of UNESCO's full dimensions did not make front-page news—the whole complex story rarely does. Nor did it apparently have any influence on policy. On the other hand, it did not appear in the obituary columns. The news that UNESCO did make in November 1982 represented, instead, the return to coverage as usual by the mass-communications professionals who attended or wrote about the Fourth Extraordinary Session of UNESCO's General Conference (November 23–December 3), which met to adopt the medium-term plan for the succeeding years. Analyzed by George Gerbner, dean of the Annenberg School of Communications and reviewed by Ed Herman (in Part III of this book), the press attention to the manifold business of the meeting was inadequate, biased, misleading, and superficial, and as usual focused on NWICO issues as though they were the only subject on UNESCO's agenda. No one reading the media accounts ever knew about the other thirteen major programs that represented the great majority of UNESCO's activities. And the messages conveyed about the mass-communications issue in UNESCO were hostile, negative, speculative, and strident anticipating consequences that the "actual resolutions and official actions" of the conference did not support at all.[30]

When 1983 began, the last year before the withdrawal announcement in late December, the patterns that would determine that decision had become well established. Perhaps the most important involved the contest between truth and propaganda, and a second significant aspect concerned the relative status of education, science, and culture as opposed to that of mass communications. Ever since UNESCO's founding, those two struggles had characterized the setting for the U.S./UNESCO relationship and for the management of the United States' own cultural relations. It should not be forgotten, of course, that a U.S. initiative led by William Benton had introduced mass communications as one of the four main objectives for which UNESCO had responsibility. And propaganda had clashed with culture ever since World War II as opposing strategies in the U.S. foreign-policy approach toward other countries. No critic had analyzed the contrasting goals and values of these two dissimilar projections of the national interest more intelligently or fully than Charles Frankel in the 1960s. His plea to upgrade cultural relations and insulate them from the public-relations, image-making, self-serving nature of the propaganda sector had not succeeded in elevating the educational, scientific, and cultural dimensions of U.S. foreign policy to their rightful place. The same dynamic competition, of course, overtook UNESCO in the 1970s, when mass communications increasingly absorbed the attention of the member states reacting against the very dominance it had achieved as a public and private purveyor of U.S. culture and values.

Since education, science, and culture had consistently lost out to mass communications, and the latter had remained the favored instrument with which to project the national interest, the outcome of their struggle in 1983 had, in a sense, already been decided by history. Regardless of the benefits the former might bring the U.S. or the world, and regardless of UNESCO's achievements in those areas, their status and significance could not compare with the favored image and power of mass communications. The advocates of UNESCO and its contributions in "ESC," therefore, had no more influence than they had had in promoting those areas within the State Department, nor did they have the ability to influence men's minds on a scale comparable to that of the mass media. Although they had the backing of the truth, that was no advantage over propaganda in the war of ideas. But they did continue to fight for UNESCO, establish a record of its positive contributions, and rebut the disinformation that appeared in the columns and editorial commentaries of the mass-circulation press.

In early 1983, two events gave the pro-UNESCO group a reason for guarded optimism that the U.S. could still adjust its differences with the organization and remain a member. One of them should not have been trusted. At the February 3 meeting of the U.S. National Commission, Gregory Newell told the gathering that he "fully supported" the conclusions of its 1982 "critical assessment" review, namely that the U.S. remain a member and upgrade its participation. His statement was consistent with the government's actions at UNESCO's Extraordinary General Conference Session the previous November when it had been part of the consensus approving the medium term plan and 1984–85 program.[31] But it was not consistent with the purpose of his appointment or the actions he had taken toward the USNC. The second and more dramatic indication of support for UNESCO came from the State Department. Because of the Beard Amendment, it had to file reports concerning UNESCO's treatment of the various mass-communication problems that could have brought about financial sanctions. Had this analysis received widespread publicity, it would have recast the terms and the tone of the UNESCO debate and even made the withdrawal more politically hazardous.

The judgment rendered by State mainly cleared UNESCO of the charges against it and declared it a fit member of the U.N. community worthy of the government's continued involvement. Apart from any other considerations about their value, UNESCO and its programs "for the most part contribute to broad U.S. foreign policy goals and particular U.S. educational, scientific and cultural interests," the executive summary declared. Even the "highly controversial activities," it noted, "relate to a minority of UNESCO programs" (8 percent at most). Even in the communication area, the department concluded that "UNESCO is not, at this time, implementing any policy or procedure proscribed by Section 109(a) of Public Law 97-241." There were even "many UNESCO communication programs [that] do not pose any problems for the U.S." and the U.S. and its allies had defeated some "anti-free press ideas and programs," the licensing of journalists had "disappeared from UNESCO agendas," while the Secretariat had "recently taken care over a range of issues to avoid initiatives which might lead to confrontation with values and interests of importance to the U.S. and other democratic countries." That sounded like a clean bill of health and the final conclusion confirmed it. Reviewing the Second World Conference on Cultural Policies held in 1982, the executive summary indicated it "did not adopt resolutions critical of U.S. cultural industries and did endorse the principle of the free flow of information. These developments," the report insisted, "indicate an improved atmosphere within UNESCO toward U.S. free press values."[32]

In addition to dispelling the myths the media fostered about UNESCO's Soviet-led threats to world press freedoms, the State Department review also treated the politicization issue in a much calmer manner. "U.S. interests are generally well served by UNESCO programs," it stated, "which are, for the most part, non-political and which can most effectively be pursued through international cooperation." While mentioning the Arab-Israeli conflict, it noted that "the problem was resolved," and no further challenge had occurred. Even the budget and management issues seemed not so serious. Although UNESCO had not yet met the U.S. insistence on no budgetary growth, its next projection had held to 4–6 percent and "management reforms" were underway and "evaluation procedures" had "improved." This assessment agreed with a U.S. General Accounting Report of 1979 that concluded, "we regarded management procedures to be unique and forward looking compared to other U.N. agencies examined; and further as having the potential for improving the effectiveness of U.S. participation in UNESCO. . . . After closer study of UNESCO planning and budgeting processes, we believe they are conceptually sound and permit progress toward improved disclosure of program aims and their financial implications for member governments." At the time it was issued, the Stated Department's Bureau of International Organization Affairs considered it to be "fair and accurate."[33]

In February 1983, the idea of withdrawal seemed ridiculous to the authors of the report to Congress. In a section on "U.S. Goals and Objectives" they found UNESCO to be "a major forum for U.S. multilateral diplomacy," a place "to promote U.S. (and Western) values and methods — particularly in the Third World." The national interest would be "best protected by participating vigorously to avoid conceding the ideological/political struggle within UNESCO to those with opposing ideals which could contribute to a world environment increasingly hostile to U.S. interests." A sense of the opportunities to shape the world's educational, scientific, and cultural development and win acceptance for U.S. methods and values in those areas through membership in UNESCO permeated the analysis. And U.S. proposed norms and standards had been and would continue to be established and accepted internationally, the report suggested. Nor were the detailed economic benefits the U.S. gained from its membership ignored, including UNESCO's spending 40 percent of the value of the U.S. dues in the United States.

That the U.S. could be an effective influence at UNESCO was not just a State Department pipe dream, in spite of the years of indifferent success. At the Fourth Extraordinary General Conference in November 1982, it had, in fact, negotiated some 50 amendments to the draft communications program which succeeded in numerous free-press/freeflow activities being recognized and established as goals.[34] The February 1983 evaluation thus joined dozens of other testimonials that had confirmed UNESCO's advantages and utility over the years. The U.S., oddly enough, was guided to its withdrawal by sign posts that confirmed the importance of staying in. Pro-UNESCO advocates may not have been able to withstand yet another favorable notice that year!

In June 1983, however, the State Department announced that yet another "review of relations with UNESCO" would commence, even though it had just produced a full such assessment for the Congress three months earlier. Were the right-wing conservatives like some gambler on a losing streak, determined to keep rolling the dice of investigation until they won with a negative report? Were there personnel changes under way to help create more critical findings? One wonders. The U.S. National Commission had no indication at the time that anything ominous was under way. According to Leonard Sussman and other members of the commission, "the Director of UNESCO affairs at the State Department in July 1983 informed [them] . . . that the purpose of the review was to secure positive improvements in UNESCO's behavior, not to pave the way for withdrawal."[35] This was a strange justification, since the U.S. had already benefited from "positive improvements" because of the Beard Amendment, its own negotiations, and M'Bow's skillful multilateral diplomacy from 1976 on. And it had testified to these improvements in evaluations of the 1982 Extraordinary General Conference and in the favorable assessments of UNESCO delivered to Congress that February. Another search for ways to secure changes in UNESCO was not, therefore, indicated by the evidence that State had already submitted nor was it suggested by any understanding of the world situation in the 1980s.

As Professor Majid Tehranian has pointed out, a different set of economic and political realities confronted the United States in the 1980s, and it should have recognized them and adjusted its policies accordingly. OPEC, a sponsor of the NIEO, had lost "much of its momentum" and its unity. The Third World itself, assuming it ever voted as a bloc, had become "far more stratified and divided," and had generally adopted "a new mood of reasonableness" to attain the legitimate demands for change that its members had sought more angrily in the 1970s. As Director-General M'Bow has argued, the LDCs "have always sought to arrive at a consensus acceptable to all in order to promote and consolidate international cooperation within the organization. I must say, that in every issue where there has been conflict, the principle of consensus has prevailed." That process had certainly been working since 1976 in the give and take of the negotiations over the NWICO.[36]

By the summer of 1983, however, the U.S. government still seemed to view the world and UNESCO through perceptions rigidly fixed by the realities of the 1970s and held in place by the doctrinal obsessions of its conservative leadership and the vivid and irresponsible apprehensions of the media industry's lobby. What the Reagan administration seemed to be seeking, when it spoke of "positive improvements" in UNESCO, was not a search for consensus, moderation, and reasonableness which had largely been achieved, but a radical restructuring of the organization to restore U.S. control and domination, to turn the clock back to the late 1940s and early 1950s. Not unimaginable in the context of other right-wing conservative fantasies that projected domestic agendas for a return to the days of Adam Smith, Horatio Alger, the Robber Baron Era of unregulated monopoly power, and social insecurity for labor and racial minorities. But given the nature of international life where U.N. organizations represented the sovereign authority of some 161 members whose political and economic priorities had to be acknowledged and adjusted, the U.S. desire to impose its will lacked contextual sense. It represented another sign that the nation sought unilateral power in multilateral environments.[37]

The decision to re-examine UNESCO and possibly reopen old wounds must have been a disquieting preliminary to the forthcoming UNESCO General Conference that would be held that November in Paris. Much of the State Department maneuvering was, of course, common knowledge at UNESCO, whose staff must have wondered what was coming next. In July Jean Gerard and Gregory Newell met with Director-General M'Bow and, according to Gough Whitlam, then the Australian ambassador to UNESCO and a member of its Executive Board, delivered an ultimatum to M'Bow. As Whitlam recalls, Gerard and Newell wanted UNESCO to cut or end "all the programs bearing upon peace and justice." Although those fields are at the core of the organization's constitutional mission, the conservatives in the United States had always regarded them as Soviet initiatives and propaganda, and UNESCO programs there further convinced them that the organization had been "politicized" and was conducting activities extraneous and irrelevant to its technical functions. The director-general could not, of course, "disregard . . . [his] constitutional mandates" unless the Executive Board and the General Conference authorized him to do so. He told Gerard and Newell they should make their case there "rather than bring covert pressure to bear upon him."[38] M'Bow might also have asked them if they thought UNESCO should not support the free market in ideas.

Another warning signal came in October. Jeane Kirkpatrick, who certainly spoke for the Reagan government, in testimony to Congress described the administration's "profound disapproval of UNESCO" because it had "succumbed to politicization, . . . created obstacles to a free press, . . . discriminates against Israel, and . . . is utterly indifferent to fiscal restraint."[39]

By the time of the General Conference, therefore, it was clear that UNESCO was under intense surveillance of a still vague and ill-defined character, as though it were a political refugee of suspect leanings trying to obtain a United States visa. Several things could now have a decisive impact on future developments, always assuming that the decision to withdraw had not been made in January 1981 or earlier. Who would lead the United States delegation to the conference and under what directions from the White House and the State Department? What sort of record would M'Bow and the General Conference establish? And finally, what kind of U.S. evaluation of those events would follow? It seemed to have been agreed by all that a critical watershed had been reached, one that would surely determine the future of the U.S./UNESCO relationship.

According to a number of accounts of the events at the 22nd General Conference of UNESCO, the United States achieved an important, if not stunning, success. Combined with the progress that had been made since 1976, a new era in the history of U.S. participation could well have been expected to open. Leadership such as had not been visible since the days of Kennedy and Benton had demonstrated intelligence, mastery of the complex negotiations, and diplomatic sensitivity. UNESCO, in turn, had staged a conference that revealed a remarkable ability to achieve consensus and to reduce contentious and divisive ideological conflict. On two of the three questions that affected the future relationship, therefore, the Paris meeting returned positive and hopeful answers. But the U.S. government saw none of this or regarded it as irrelevant and treated the events at Paris as another UNESCO failure. The delinquent organization remained an object of suspicion and deep distaste to the conservative coalition. An announcement of intent to withdraw followed in December and the departure itself came one year later.

The State Department chose Edmund P. Hennelly to head the delegation to the General Conference. A staunch Republican and Heritage Foundation member, Hennelly also represented international business as a vice-president of the Mobil Oil Corporation. As a self-made man, Hennelly may have had conservative views on economic issues, but he was independent, strong-minded, and fair. From his knowledge of the global scene, he understood the complex political realities that affected multilateral negotiations. He could be counted on to go to Paris with an open mind, recognize the bargaining position of his opponents, and defend the U.S. national interest with skill and intensity. He had no desire to impose U.S. values on the world, but he would come home with the best deal he could obtain for his country. And he was willing to criticize what was wrong with the U.S. side of the UNESCO relationship and try to improve it. Having been appointed to the U.S. National Commission soon after the Reagan administration took over, Hennelly knew the issues, the sorry state of the USNC in building support for UNESCO, and some of the politics behind the U.S. dissatisfaction with UNESCO affairs. He realized that there were forces in the administration hostile to international cooperation and determined to undermine support for it, but he accepted the appointment in the belief that, if he achieved the agenda of reform the U.S. had demanded, the country would honor its implicit pledge to remain an active and leading member of UNESCO. It is clear that he never would have represented the United States had he known that the withdrawal had already been "wired" by Newell and his White House allies so that the administration's participation in the conference was simply a showcase cover for a preordained decision. He would come to regard his experiences at Paris, the repudiation of his efforts and postconference assessment, and the timetable for withdrawal as indications of just such a misleading scenario.[40]

While there were some duds and poltical ideologues in the delegation Hennelly led, he considered it overall to be a strong and experienced one. Still, he alone gave it the character and direction that returned such favorable results for the United States. That a Heritage Foundation maverick rededicated his country to the international ideals of UNESCO as their relationship was about to end gave that departure an ironic and implausible context. Hennelly's plenary speech and his leadership did just that. Not that he neglected the policies the U.S. had been defending in UNESCO for a decade; but he recognized as well the need for international cooperation, the existence of "the many good things . . . [and] excellent programs" for which UNESCO was responsible, and the professionalism and dedication of UNESCO's secretariat. And after listing the "deep concerns" the United States still had over communications, politicization, human rights, bureaucratic centralization, and budgetary growth, Hennelly said he was "convinced that this conference can lay those concerns to rest." He pledged his delegation would "listen to your points of view" and "make every effort to reach consensus" by consultation, debate, and reasoning together. "We can rekindle the dream of our founders," Hennelly concluded, "It is still possible."[41]

Indeed it was, as Hennelly discovered in the course of his deliberations at Paris. Among the numerous signs of that spirit of accommodation and forward progress was the mutual respect and friendship Hennelly and M'Bow developed. That in itself seemed remarkable since the United States brought a hard-line position to its demands for change that were backed up by its threatening posture of preconference intimidation and intimations of political boycott should UNESCO not measure up to those standards. The director-general must have sensed the hope and understanding Hennelly exhibited in his plenary speech and in his negotiations, the expectation that things could be worked out. And M'Bow and Minister Tel of Lebanon, the conference president, responded accordingly, as did other representatives from the Third World. As a result, not only did Hennelly and the U.S. delegation work expertly and hard, but other nations matched that effort to ensure a positive outcome. Ending two days ahead of schedule, the Paris meeting conducted its business with unusual dispatch, the consequence of the decline of ideological rhetoric and political harangues as well as the motivation for concrete accomplishment.[42]

By any reasonable considered judgment, the United States no longer had just cause for terminating its relationship with UNESCO. It had not attained every one of its goals, however, since 160 other countries also had a hand in the outcome. But in the few weeks the meeting encompassed, there had been greater adjustments of attitude and behavior than, say, the United States had achieved in reforming the foreign cultural relations of its own State Department over twenty years. There would be an inevitable "catch-22" reaction by the right-wing conservatives in the U.S., of course, since they would always be able to denigrate the reform effort as a contrived, meaningless, and momentary response to stave off the impending punishment the U.S. had promised. UNESCO changes supposedly had neither substance nor the guarantee of future commitment to the new era of tranquillity and consensus. This paranoid view of UNESCO as an unredeemed and potential offender would have entailed its lengthy parole under right-wing surveillance and would have been fully rehabilitated only when it met the ideological preconceptions of a national political minority. And that was an absurdity on its face.

Edmund Hennelly, on the other hand, offered results and an opportunity for continuing progress. His assessment of the conference listed in detail the evidence for his optimism. It had been "among the least politicized and the most constructive from the U.S. point of view in recent memory"; in fact, it obtained "the most positive results in ten years." As he advised the USNC, "Israeli credentials were not challenged, anti-Israeli rhetoric was muted or non-existent, Soviet peace propaganda was contained, and the debate on Grenada represented a plus for the United States." Hennelly reported that no threat to freedom of the press had developed, that the NWICO had not dominated the discussions, and that the U.S. had even won recognition for issues in mass communications it considered important, namely the "watchdog role of the press in opposing abuses of power and state censorship as a block to the free flow of information." On the plus side, the delegation leader mentioned, in addition, a U.S.-favored distinction "between individual rights and concepts such as 'peoples rights' " that was to receive further study; the watering down to the point of inoffensiveness of Draft Resolution 14 that purported to establish international codes of conduct for multinational corporations; favorable positioning of the U.S. representation on all five major committees including the one on informatics and the election of a U.S.-backed candidate as president of the Executive Board with Ambassador Jean Gerard elected as vice-president of it; and, as already suggested, a "non-polemical and business-like" atmosphere throughout the meetings. On the crucial budget issue, the U.S. did not achieve its zero-growth target, but the Nordic compromise "reduced overall UNESCO spending for the next two years by $12 million," and the director-general "recognized the validity of U.S. principles and positions on budget matters." Not only did these victories represent solid and skillful diplomatic advocacy by the U.S. at drafting and negotiating sessions, they also signified astute and sustained leadership by M'Bow that made possible those concessions to the U.S. interpretation of UNESCO priorities. M'Bow clearly must have played a large role in the dramatic movement on such issues as the budget.[43]

Hennelly's analysis of the minus side of the U.S. balance sheet suggested what M'Bow and UNESCO had accomplished, for the United States' positions did not all win early or enthusiastic support even in the West. Because the zero-growth-rate figure had not been reached, the Reagan administration ordered a no U.S. vote on the Nordic compromise, the sole negative vote that was cast. On the location of the next General Conference site at Sofia, Bulgaria, the U.S. in opposition lost again, this time by 98 for, 22 opposed, and 8 abstentions. Hennelly also believed that UNESCO still did not utilize the private sector sufficiently in its programs, that procedures needed more improvement, and that certain activities in all of UNESCO's sectors might yet exhibit an "anti-Western spirit" without continued close "vigilance" in the future. Concluding that the conference had been a "clear plus for the U.S." Hennelly's survey of results assumed that "a new beginning has been made"; if that same vigor was applied again "much more progress can be made."

Most if not all of the Western allies registered their strong approval of that view. The Israelis, in particular, wanted the U.S. to stay in. So did the CIA and the USIA. And it was not just because of the conference achievements. On the outside, as Hennelly well knew, the United States could not defend Israel, take advantage of world scientific collaboration, form and influence educational, human-rights, and information policies, spread its values, or gain access to the markets created by UNESCO activities. And Hennelly did not count on other Western nations to defend economic advantages the United States had gained through UNESCO if it abandoned that field to them.[44]

Ambassador Jean Gerard confirmed Hennelly's evaluation of the conference. In November 1983 she too offered a favorable estimate of the proceedings. "We can take pride in the work and in many of the accomplishments of this General Conference," she said. "It has been marked, in many instances, by agreement on issues about which such agreement has not always been easy. Most important," she predicted, "I believe we have laid the groundwork here for greater efficiency and effectiveness in UNESCO's programs."[45] Had it not been for the policy review being assembled under Gregory Newell's direction, which kept the door open to further reconsideration by the Reagan administration, UNESCO could have believed the crisis had passed and its relationship with the United States had survived intact. Yet there was one other unsettled issue that might also threaten the "new beginning" Edmund Hennelly had proclaimed. Was the mass-communications industry ready to report these new realities to its audience of readers and was it willing to abandon its distorted coverage of UNESCO and give its story equal access to the free market of ideas the industry controlled?

On November 8, 1983, meanwhile, while the 22nd General Conference was meeting in Paris, the USNC wrote its response to the policy investigation Newell had initiated that June. Still assuming that the purpose had a rational objective in evaluating the costs and benefits of U.S. participation, James Holderman, the USNC chairman, once more took a stand behind "reform from within, . . . strong American leadership . . . and . . . a revitalized National Commission" which could "improve the management of our relations with UNESCO" by means of "more resources and a concerted effort by the private sector." Referring again to the positive recommendations of the USNC conference in 1982, Holderman wrote Newell that "our recent survey reaffirms last year's conclusion" i.e., "remaining in . . . and increasing our impact there." And this represented another "unanimous" agreement among the national associations the USNC had consulted. Some of them had even "quantified the specific benefits of UNESCO membership" and "the anticipated costs of withdrawal." Since USNC and its associated members were, in fact, the major participants in UNESCO's fields of operations, their influence on policy should have carried great weight if the government thought those fields had any connection to the national interest, as had once been believed at UNESCO's founding.[46]

Educational, scientific, and cultural affairs had, of course, little meaning to the conservatives managing the attack on UNESCO. By mid-December the withdrawal had been set in motion, an act that disregarded the results of the 22nd General Conference, Hennelly's favorable assessment of it, and the substance of the latest internal UNESCO policy review. The U.S. National Commission recommendations apparently had no influence at all. Once the government decision had been announced, it would dominate that ensuing year as a national initiative reluctantly adopted by the Reagan administration in the face of a decade-long UNESCO failure to reform. The three themes that formed the basis for the withdrawal decision had an extraordinary appeal to the political culture in the United States. Simple to grasp, emotionally appealing, and framed without regard to the history or the complexities behind the U.S./UNESCO relationship, these slogans took command over the marketplace of ideas almost without opposition. As Senator McCarthy had known, reckless accusations smearing the reputation of the victim in a campaign of innuendo and deceit resisted almost any rebuttal, especially when the charges made the headlines and framed the nature of the news. In this case, as Ed Herman indicates in his analysis below, the media accepted the government line as the truth and carried almost no alternative interpretations. Given their own self-interest, they probably had little interest in doing so.[47]

The trio of charges described by Newell as a "persistent pattern," were "irrelevant politicization of the programs that should be its most important; an endemic hostility toward the basic institutions of a free society, especially a free market and a free press; and the most irresponsible and unrestrained budgetary expansion in the United Nations system." Withdrawal would not bring any adverse consequences to the United States, Newell asserted, since there were "few if any UNESCO activities, the important functions of which cannot otherwise be fulfilled." Intellectual and scientific cooperation would continue "in other channels if need be." Newell must have been imagining a bilateral future. Even more ethnocentric was his finding that "given the fact that neither culture, commerce, nor world science can proceed meaningfully without the participation of U.S. nationals and American institutions, cooperative arrangements . . . will surely be activated—and on a healthy non-ideological basis."[48]

As Newell fleshed out the main outline of his argument, other exaggerated and inaccurate descriptions of UNESCO completed the mythical and ideological image he was creating. "UNESCO programs and personnel are heavily freighted with an irresponsible political content," he stated. Disarmament studies (claiming they were no "proper concern" of UNESCO!) had a "pro-Soviet bias" or were "naive and simplistic."

Human rights had been "infected with Soviet and statist concepts" of collective rights; anti-Israeli attitudes were "deeply-rooted"; UNESCO "parrot[ed] the product of an extreme and unproductive posturing on Southern Africa issues"; the U.S. was "regularly pilloried" at UNESCO which was "relentlessly hostile to our ideals"; the NIEO and NWICO represented a "compulsively statist . . . Orwellian nightmare—complete with 'Big Brother' ' "; and "atrocious" management was to be made worse by personnel practices favoring the disadvantaged and ex-colonial states. Evaluating his own review as unprejudiced and not indicating the positive recommendations it contained, Newell claimed he had made a good-faith effort to change UNESCO and failed. "Experience shows," he concluded, "that the United States cannot change UNESCO substantially if it remains a member.[49]

Since conservative ideology and a unilateral definition of the national interest seemed to be the consuming passions of Newell's global vision, he dismissed the "foreign policy costs" as minimal, did not care what other countries might think or do, and believed the action would "have a salutary effect on other U.N. system agencies." Regarding the educational, scientific, and cultural community as simply another "special interest," Newell argued it, like any other such domestic lobby, would have to give way to the national interest.[50] Lawrence Eagleburger, through whose office the memo traveled to Shultz, had a more restrained, even cautious evaluation and recognized that "some serious negative consequences" would follow the U.S. withdrawal, especially the inability to oppose international standard setting, rebut the "radical concepts" in various areas, contain Soviet influence, and defend Israel. Nor was he at all certain that alternative strategies for collaboration in UNESCO's fields would be easily discovered; rather, that task would be "a major undertaking." In the end, while finding the decision to withdraw "a close call," Eagleburger recommended it should proceed, but, unlike Newell, left the door open to cancel the planned exit "if UNESCO adequately reforms itself" during the coming year.[51]

On December 16, 1983 while the State Department was acting on the Newell memorandum of the 13th, the U.S. National Commission held its 47th annual meeting. It heard Edmund Hennelly's positive analysis of the General Conference, reviewed its own previous assessments as well as those of the U.S. Mission to UNESCO and the State Department, and on the basis of all this evidence voted 41-8 to stay in, the eight negative votes representing Reagan appointees.[52] On the morning of that meeting, however, an editorial supporting withdrawal had appeared in *The New York Times*. The coincidence seemed remarkable. Not only did it undermine the commission's position, but it apparently had been the product of a State Department leak that angered and surprised Shultz, who was not yet aware of the Newell initiative. Enlisting *The New York Times* with all its national influence in the Newell-orchestrated withdrawal once more revealed the unequal conditions that prevailed in the free marketplace of ideas. The USNC's evidence and assessment received no such notoriety or circulation in that same newspaper.[53]

The tempo of activity and disinformation accelerated during the final weeks of 1983. Newell was prepared to tell the National Commission only that the administration was studying its options. Eagleburger had promised Holderman that no decision would be made without a full review to which the USNC would have access, and the commission wanted to see it and have it published (a free-flow-of-information concern). The review itself, while not yet fully completed, had been prepared by the UNESCO career professionals in the State Department. Although it criticized UNESCO, it also upheld continued U.S. participation and membership in the organization. Parts of it had been or were about to be leaked to congressional members and their staffs, and the USNC was determined to get a copy. Newell's conclusions, therefore, were in conflict with the substance of the policy study which was likely to become public knowledge. In response, Newell did two things. He organized an off-the-record press briefing and a campaign to manage the UNESCO news in the media. And second, he had to prepare (or have written) a summary of the policy study that would resolve the cognitive dissonance between the substantive materials and his own interpretation of them.[54]

On December 22 and 23 the final stages of the decision-making process took place. Shultz made his recommendation and the president approved it. In between, the Canadians urged the United States not to withdraw, Canada's plea that the U.S. take no unilateral action until "it consults extensively with its friends and allies" received no consideration as the Reagan administration rushed to make its announcement before the year ran out. The secretary of state notified Director-General M'Bow on December 28 and Gregory Newell held his off-the-record briefing the next day.[55] In these various exchanges, the outline of the following year's strategy began to take shape. It suggested that the internal struggle to define U.S. policy toward UNESCO was still under way, although the overall framework gave UNESCO little or no opportunity to meet the U.S. demands for reform.

The primary and overriding limitation on a successful resolution of the crisis was the Reagan administration's insistence that UNESCO had only one year to satisfy the United States. The 1983 General Conference had ended just before the U.S. notice of withdrawal; anther meeting would not be held until 1985. The director-general and the Executive Board could act, but no confirmation of those policies by the assembled member states could occur until 1985. Apart from that, the timetable of turning around a 161-member organization in one year or less with all the procedural complications seemed totally unrealistic. But if it was to work, UNESCO would have to have early and full notice of the bill of particulars from the United States. It needed to know what exactly had to happen to abort the U.S. withdrawal. Whether the U.S. would assist in the process of change beyond setting forth its complaints would also help determine the outcome, since the United States still had administrative skills and leadership influence to expend if reform was, in fact, a high priority.

A second almost as serious obstacle to meeting the U.S. requests related to the nature of the accusations themselves. They had no specificity and described a subjective perception more than an objective reality, "politicization" being an excellent case in point. Since global political values and priorities differed and since 95 percent of UNESCO's programs did not suffer from the problem, how would the organization satisfy a nation that found it intolerable that politics existed at all in UNESCO, especially when that country had engaged in politicization itself and still did so elsewhere? And how could UNESCO overcome the judgment that it had an "endemic hostility" to free-market economics when its members encompassed the whole range of economic theory, and when regulation of economic activity on behalf of the public welfare was a common practice even in the United States? The answer to the UNESCO question, of course, existed in the U.S., not in UNESCO, just as the answer to McCarthyism rested in the mental apparitions and political hysteria of the senator himself, not in the reality of communism in the United States. And when Gregory Newell wrote about Orwellian nightmares of Big Brother, those were his paranoid delusions, not the programmatic experience of the organization he attacked. The resolution of the crisis, in effect, was a simple one; get Newell out of the State Department.

Although the timetable and the accusations implied that the United States did not seriously consider the possibility of remaining in UNESCO, there were political forces which favored that outcome and the right-wing conservatives still had to play out the hand they had dealt. Their own cards included access to the White House, congressional allies, a Heritage Foundation propaganda campaign of support, and a compliant accessory to their plans, the U.S. media. But voices in the State Department, the Congress, and the UNESCO constituency urged moderation and fairness; a flicker of hope still existed. In Shultz's memorandum to the president, for example, he described a possible agenda of reform that narrowed the focus of expectations. But it did not become public knowledge or known to UNESCO until Newell so informed M'Bow on July 13, 1984, over halfway through the year. The minimum changes Shultz set forth were three: "assurances, reinforced by structural and procedural changes, that political diversions will be curtailed; concrete movement toward changes in the structure of UNESCO, to eliminate suppression of 'minority' (U.S. and Western) views; [and] management and budget procedures that will produce genuine program evaluation and fiscal integrity." Whatever these meant in detail and whether they were reasonable is not the question here; they at least gave notice of a minimum. "Should we see progress," Shultz advised, reconsideration might be recommended.[56]

Under-Secretary Eagleburger, meanwhile, proposed a monitoring panel to evaluate the reform process and act as a brake on the rush to withdraw that Newell was pushing ahead. James Holderman became its chairman, but the original purpose quickly disintegrated when Newell succeeded in stacking it with a pro-administration majority hostile to UNESCO.[57] Robert McFarlane's reply to Shultz on December 23 also called for a review panel and, more important, urged the State Department to "expend every effort to effect meaningful changes over the next year" in UNESCO. In doing so, McFarlane said that the president wanted Shultz to consider "significant upgrading of our representation in UNESCO . . . [and] begin appropriate notification and consultations with our allies and interested organizations."[58]

All of this apparent open-mindedness contrasted with Gregory Newell's assertion in his December 29 press briefing that UNESCO was incapable of making the necessary changes. He certainly seemed unwilling to help it do so, for his Bureau of International Organization Affairs (IO) took two months to justify the withdrawal and refused to participate on the thirteen-member temporary committee the Executive Board had established to promote essential changes. Ambassador Jean Gerard now took a similar line. In May 1984 she told the UNESCO Executive Board that "the U.S. government would not define terms of negotiation, 'when we are not negotiating.' " And Deputy Assistant Secretary of State for International Organization Affairs Jean Bergaust explained that "we have not and do not intend to present UNESCO with a formal list of demands as we believe UNESCO reforms are a matter between the body of member states and the Secretariat."[59]

These conflicting approaches to the issues of instituting appropriate change within UNESCO suggested that IO was stonewalling and subverting a higher level decision for the United States to take an active role in influencing the preferred outcome in the organization, and was probably protected in this by allies in the White House. This strategy risked discovery, however, by leaks, congressional disclosure, or investigative reporting by the press. On January 23, 1984 the London *Guardian*'s Washington bureau representative revealed the discrepancies between Newell's summary analysis of the State Department's U.S./UNESCO Policy Review and its overall conclusion that the evidence did not support the case for withdrawal. Although Long Island's *Newsday* carried this story, the major U.S. media did not run it. But *Editor and Publisher* on February 4 did expose a Newell plan to manage the information that would reach the public about the UNESCO issue. Citing a December 16, 1983 confidential memorandum, the trade weekly said, "The State Department attempted to wage a campaign to manipulate the press in order to generate public support for its recommendation that the United States withdraw from the United Nations Educational, Scientific and Cultural Organization." According to the secret memo, Newell had planned a "strategy of withdrawal" which included planting friendly articles and letters to the editor and using "private sector individuals" in the process.[60] Newell need not have worried. As Ed Herman has demonstrated, the U.S. media consistently carried the "party line" the government publicists put forth and interpreted the UNESCO story the way jackals attack the carcass of a dead animal.

Since the U.S. National Commission had been effectively isolated and rendered impotent, the monitoring panel packed with a Newell majority, and the media observed to be reliable allies behind the withdrawal campaign, the anti-UNESCO right-wing coalition had to consider only two other potential hazards: the U.S. Congress and the reformers at work within UNESCO. The former might still uncover the truth and give it the airing it deserved, and the latter might still demonstrate the organization's capacity to rejuvenate areas that needed attention. History did not suggest that either would upset Newell's applecart. The truth that Congress and its staff would seek out resided in layers of reports and investigations that had accumulated over the years, all testifying to the benefits of membership and the importance of continued U.S. participation. And that information included the revelations of ineptitude and neglect that had characterized the management of the government's UNESCO relations. In the latest such round of collective wisdom "83 U.S. embassies and consulates around the world and 13 federal agencies" declared themselves opposed to withdrawal.[61] In its 1984 report to Congress required by the Beard Amendment, the State Department had again corroborated the findings of its 1983 advisory, namely no activities in the mass-communications field "pose any active, direct threat to a free press."[62] Yet none of these conclusions and recommendations had become a significant part of the free market in ideas or that segment of it that influenced national policy formulation.

Congress, nevertheless, actively involved itself in another valiant effort to rescue the UNESCO experience from the disinformation that surrounded it. Extensive hearings took place in April, May, July, September, and December 1984. The Committee on Foreign Affairs dispatched two staff study missions to Paris, one from February 10 to 23 and another to the May and September-October Executive Board meetings. Their investigations and analyses offered a wealth of historical perspective and contemporary insight. In addition, the House Committees on Foreign Affairs and Science and Technology asked the U.S General Accounting Office to review UNESCO's "management structure . . . , personnel system . . . , program management . . . , budget development and presentation . . . , [and] expenditure controls."[63] In the hearings, the majority of witnesses, communications, resolutions, and statements supported the U.S./UNESCO relationship and urged the U.S. to stay in, but this had been true of all such surveys of expert opinion that had been informed by the experience of participation in one or another of UNESCO's many activities and had followed the organization closely. Not that they did not have criticisms and suggestions for improvement, but they knew the importance of the work. Negative testimony and adverse assessments came largely from Owen Harries, resident associate at the Heritage Foundation, Charles M. Lichenstein, senior fellow there, Gregory Newell, and Jean Gerard, and from the materials they submitted which mainly echoed the Heritage-Reagan administration interpretation of UNESCO's failings. What the impact of all this investigation may have been can only be judged by its inability to reverse the withdrawal decision or even have it postponed for one year. The UNESCO constituency and the numerous associations on the U.S. National Commission had never had the resources, standing, or political clout to block a powerful, politically connected lobby, and that was still true in 1984.[64]

The two staff study missions were models of historical research and investigation whose findings made clear the seriousness of the U.S. decision and the strange sequence of events that was taking place in 1984. They also provided authenticity to the views of the educational, scientific, and cultural community whose position was corroborated by the near unanimous opposition of UNESCO's member states to the U.S. unilateral withdrawal. The reports noted the following significant patterns in the methods the State Department had pursued. It had not exhausted other alternatives to withdrawal or cooperated with its allies in any coordinated reform initiatives; it had not consulted with other governments, Congress, or the USNC associations before making its decision; it had not improved its own representation at UNESCO, given its affairs a high priority, or strengthened the National Commission and used it in developing policy; it had not developed any "plan and strategy to mobilize international support and in effect conduct a 'major campaign' to turn UNESCO around in 1984," as the National Security Council under McFarlane had twice recommended; it had not assessed the impact of withdrawal on relations with other nations or on Soviet influence in UNESCO; and it had not provided a survey of the alternatives in educational, scientific, and cultural cooperation that would replace those abandoned by the departure from UNESCO.[65]

In terms of the evidence for such a drastic step, the staff reports also faulted the administration and found the charges against UNESCO to be misleading, even spurious and often not based on a comprehensive evaluation of programs. Politicization had not been set in perspective, for example, or assessed as a factor in many areas. Disarmament studies represented under 1 percent of the education budget, and the policy review had admitted that peace research and arms control were legitimate fields for UNESCO to investigate. On the collective versus individual-rights issue, the congressional staffers found people's rights to be a further stage of evolution in protecting rights and not competitive with traditional liberties. The genocide convention and the Holocaust would have supported that conclusion. The report pointed out the U.S. failure to ratify a variety of international human-rights conventions and UNESCO's active human-rights committee. Nor had the work in education with Palestinian refugees or members of national liberation movements been politicized. On these three issues (disarmament, collective rights, refugees), the staff study mission believed that there "seems to be an attempt to denigrate the organization's performance on extraordinarily weak grounds," since some $2 million of $186 million of spending might even be considered as "politicized."[66]

Three other problems raised similar doubts among the congressional investigators. Statism as a misnomer applied to the NIEO and the NWICO had no great presence in UNESCO. The mass-communications debate, they found, had diminished greatly in intensity and by 1983 was "not much of a problem," and they recalled that UNESCO activities in that area had "never triggered a suspension of payments." While they found "some evidence for criticism" in budget and management practices, withdrawal was not an appropriate response. Staff incompetence, leadership styles, vacancies, morale problems, and cronyism were, after all, the life blood of bureaucracies, and always required attention. The report challenged the idea that UNESCO had been guilty of "unrestrained" budgetary expansion and found a new attitude already in place. As to the government's management of its UNESCO relations, conclusions similar to those that had been leveled since the 1950s reappeared in the staff study. The U.S., it argued, had helped create the conditions it criticized "by default" and made "unrealistic demands" and adopted "out of date strategies" because it did not change as the multilateral system did.[67]

In the second of the two staff studies, which observed most of the events of 1984, the actual reform process came under close scrutiny and raised further questions about U.S. motivations and purposes. As has been noted, both Shultz and McFarlane endorsed a timetable of action and a minimum set of changes that UNESCO would have to meet, while Gregory Newell had scoffed at the very idea of reform in UNESCO and taken no action to spell out conditions or involve the State Department in attaining them. Instead, he had written a misleading summary of the policy review and planned a covert campaign to manage the news about UNESCO and the withdrawal. His objective seemed to be to avoid a specific list of grievances and let the more general accusations circulate as final judgments UNESCO had not addressed. Since the United States "had no clear set of goals and strategy for reforming the Organization," as the staff report concluded, UNESCO was left to imagine what they might be and embark on reform unguided by its major critic. In May, already late in the year for significant change to occur, both the director-general and the Executive Board acted. M'Bow established five working groups to examine "budget techniques, recruitment and staff management, program evaluation, public information, and critical analysis of the program." The Executive Board in turn created a thirteen-member temporary committee "to recommend measures for reforming UNESCO and to review UNESCO programs as well as administrative and budget matters." The staff study considered this a "significant benchmark in UNESCO's reform process"; it was the first ever such committee. In addition to these efforts, the director-general cooperated with the GAO survey of management and budget issues, "many of which" also drew the attention of the temporary committee and the working groups. Although much of this self-analysis aimed to make UNESCO operate more efficiently, responsively, and effectively, and with zero-budget growth, a streamlining of procedure undoubtedly overdue, some of it also met U.S. programmatic concerns and attempted to reduce or eliminate the most contentious ones.[68] But these approaches, as useful and important as they were, did not guarantee that UNESCO would emerge as an instrument of the U.S. national interest or as a clone of the Heritage Foundation. And they did not yet privatize the multilateral world.

As UNESCO struggled with its internal administration, it must have wished the Reagan administration had the same understanding of the difficulties that that entailed as did the members of the congressional study mission. The latter compared UNESCO's efforts with the legislative process in the House of Representatives, an incremental procedure "where comprehensive change over the short term is rarely possible." And when anything did happen, it required "time and mobilization of interests, compromises, and votes on paragraphs, sections, and titles of bills." The report recorded the opinion of one UNESCO ambassador who said, "the United States was trying to change in one year problems that had accumulated over 30 years." Would that UNESCO had asked for the same amount of time as the United States had so far taken to reform its own cultural relations and to restore the U.S. National Commission to its original stature and purpose. Yet as the staff evaluated what had happened in UNESCO, it found that "the reforms made in 1984 are encouraging," even though some of them could not be fully evaluated until after the General Conference of 1985.[69]

Gregory Newell, on the other hand, may have been disturbed by the encouraging developments underway in UNESCO. No one can say for certain, but on July 13, 1984 he wrote Director-General M'Bow a long letter establishing a new set of requirements, the first time the United States had submitted specific proposals to UNESCO. And by now there were only five months left for the organization to meet these demands. Newell talked about the need for "profound reform" and listed three changes that were of "fundamental importance." They were, "first, creation of a mechanism to ensure that, in major matters, UNESCO decisions and programs enjoy the support of all geographic groups, including the support of the group that contributes the major part of UNESCO's budget; second, a return to concentration on UNESCO's original purposes, with which we can all agree; third, the assumption by member states of their rightful authority in the organization, through the strengthening of the General Conference and, in particular, its Executive Board." Newell also reminded M'Bow that "budget and management changes . . . are of basic importance in achieving these objectives."[70]

According to Newell, UNESCO's system of consensus decision-making and the Draft Negotiating Group did not adequately protect minority interests (namely U.S. interests) since it could not reconcile "fundamentally different points of view on vital questions." Newell, of course, wanted a U.S. veto should contentious issues arise or even better the elimination of them altogether, which was apparently the Heritage Foundation's interpretation of the free market in ideas. His letter suggested that "issues would be decided only upon the basis of full agreement among all the geographic groups," and no budget would pass without the approval of those contributing at least 51 percent of the funds. The return to UNESCO's original purposes meant that the organization would "pursue those core activities which are widely agreed upon, and abandon those that divide us," so that "programs and themes that are a source of contention" would be eliminated. What Newell wanted to remove from UNESCO's agenda were "uncritical and simplistic approaches to disarmament, economic theorizing, and global standard-setting." And UNESCO should never again be a "partisan participant in existing quarrels" as Newell imagined it had been over collective rights and the NWICO.[71]

On points one and two, therefore, the U.S. wanted to control both the discussion of issues and their possible development as programs or international norms. Contention, it must be noted, affected a small minority of UNESCO's total activities, had always existed in multilateral organizations representing governments, and was an innate part of all human intercourse. Newell's view was the simplistic one and totally ahistorical and, if anything represented a new international order, it did, for Newell was attempting to universalize in UNESCO the right-wing, unrestricted, free-market, privatizing theories of a political minority in the United States. As the staff report assessment noted, these latest proposals "practically speaking were beyond UNESCO's reach within a 1-year period, and unrealistic in terms of their broad acceptance by UNESCO member states." The two U.S. demands on weighted voting, for example, did not even attract Western nation support. One of them suggested that "85 percent of UNESCO Board members . . . approve recommendations on UNESCO's program and budget, if no consensus could be reached."[72]

The third policy proposal restoring the authority of member states in the General Conference and Executive Board and reducing the power of the director-general spoke to member governments not UNESCO! Richard Hoggart has described the low level of interest UNESCO attracted in the West, which viewed it "with amused scorn" if noticing it all, and has noted the common tendency of "not taking the organization seriously." And Hoggart had called for the West to give UNESCO "much more support."[73] The director-general's influence had grown enormously over the years and been encouraged by the United States and others, as the U.N. secretary-general's power also had been, for example, in the "leave it to Dag" syndrome. René Maheu had established this dominance, a necessary response to the increasing size of UNESCO as well as to government disinterest and neglect. That power, of course, had done more to support Western priorities than the governments themselves, as M'Bow's recent skills in negotiating consensus had proved. Maheu and M'Bow, as Hoggart has argued, "made UNESCO work as a large organization." But there were obvious administrative weaknesses and imbalances that needed to be redressed, and while some of them dealt with internal Secretariat problems, the larger ones had to do with member government attitudes and commitments, especially those of the United States.[74]

Newell's July 13 letter restored the ideological component of the U.S./UNESCO dispute to its position of dominance and diminished the management and budget issues to their ancillary role. Zero-budget growth had been pledged by the reform groups within UNESCO and numerous proposals for administrative redesign were on the table, some awaiting the 1985 General Conference. But they were not the focus of the Heritage Foundation attack, although their presence added the illusion of hapless and hopeless mismanagement, an image that outrages conservatives when they are not reminded of the Pentagon. The July agenda, however, was less a movement for reform than an ultimatum, like Hitler's message to Poland in 1939. UNESCO and its member states would have had to surrender and, in a sense, accept a United States occupation of their organization for the indefinite future. And the Third World could never have raised another contentious issue offending that country or its conservative coalition. There was, therefore, as Roger Coate has observed, "little change ... in 1984" in the status of the "profound reform" Gregory Newell had required as the minimum program for continued U.S. participation. It came as no surprise that the withdrawal took place as scheduled in December 1984.[75]

Both the media and the Heritage Foundation, however, continued pounding nails into UNESCO's coffin after Newell's July announcement so that no inkling of its battering by hostile forces would escape into the marketplace of ideas. Director-General M'Bow, realizing he and UNESCO had no access to the U.S. press, hired a public-relations firm to try to get their story across. Imagine his audacity. The Heritage Foundation used this attempt to raise $75,000 to combat it. Heritage President Edwin Feulner, Jr. circularized his membership to help fight "this corrupt, anti-Western organization" with its "high-powered public relations campaign, and sixty major liberal groups lobbying Congress." They threatened, Feulner warned, to "make short work of our withdrawal from UNESCO" unless money came in to "defeat the pro-UNESCO lobby."[76]

On August 9 the U.S. National Commission called a press conference in New York City and Washington, D.C. to publicize the historical analysis of the issues it was then making available as a national "Advisory." The USNC report covered twenty-three areas that had been presented as the heart of the controversy between the U.S. and UNESCO. In thirty pages of documented rebuttal, the advisory challenged the Reagan administration line, disputed its facts, and dispelled its disinformation. Two experts with impeccable credentials, Leonard Sussman and Edmund Hennelly, spoke and answered questions. Ed Herman's analysis of the media response to this dramatic free-market confrontation suggests its futility when power is centralized and motivation is absent. What coverage there was, Herman finds, "was so superficial and trivializing as to amount to de facto suppression."[77]

The media were not the only ones to ignore the U.S. National Commission, which remained throughout 1984 a potentially dangerous antagonist because of its experience and access to the sixty national organizations comprising its nongovernmental membership. While not at all the powerful pro-UNESCO lobby that Feulner described to frighten his own supporters, the USNC had the capacity to expose the lies and propaganda the government circulated and raise hell about them. It had, therefore, not only been decimated by staff and funding cuts, but had been edged aside as the State Department's consultant on UNESCO affairs and replaced by a monitoring panel lacking similar experience and a grassroots constituency. The congressional staff assessment expressed surprise and chagrin that the administration had "undercut the potential for maximum reform by failing to utilize" the USNC and appoint its "eminent scientists, educators, and professionals in culture and communications" to various delegations to Executive Board meetings during 1984. This "indifference to the role the Commission should play in developing U.S. policy in UNESCO," the report stated, "has been counter to the legislative will of the Congress." And exactly what Gregory Newell intended.[78]

On November 9, 1984 the monitoring panel made its report. It had had three or four meetings since convening in April, had sent representatives to the two Executive Board meetings in Paris, and maintained a low profile. Newell's control of the appointments to it foreshadowed its conclusions, but Holderman, Davidson, and some others worked hard to give the report balance. Still it lacked any sense of UNESCO's history, simplified the complex background of politicization in the organization, maintained a naïve belief that a noncontentious core area existed, described the Third World resolutions as "shibboleths," decried the tyranny of the majority, and accepted the Heritage anticipation of bad tendencies in UNESCO without proof of their existence. The executive summary concluded in favor of withdrawal.[79]

A miasma of suspicion about UNESCO's finances poisoned the atmosphere of deliberation about the organization's future during 1984 as well. Although a United Kingdom audit regularly inspected the accounts and the 1979 GAO investigation had reported favorably on UNESCO's financial procedures and management, the forces hostile to the organization wanted another survey, perhaps in hope of discovering irregularities or corruption of some sort. The press certainly speculated on these possibilities, which the final GAO report released in December 1984 did not confirm.[80] Nor did it confirm gross mismanagement or financial irregularities, but rather it established what Hoggart and other insiders knew. There was plenty of room for improvement, particularly as to duplication and evaluation of programs, accountability in expenditures, oversight by governing bodies (i.e., which member governments control), personnel recruitment, budget presentation, payroll controls, and "the Secretariat's responsiveness to external auditor recommendations." Nothing sensational, quite the opposite, and "no budget mismanagement in any legal sense," mostly requests for administrative adjustments that any large bureaucracy might need. The propaganda of negative expectations in the media, however, had largely made these innocuous findings irrelevant.[81]

A postscript to the disinformation that the conservative coalition had fomented about the NWICO, meanwhile, revealed the distance that separated Heritage Foundation ideology from the realities of the national interest. Mass communications had indeed been a central issue in the campaign against UNESCO. Yet in a still secret government report of November 1984, the Third World position was seen as valid. According to Leonard and David Sussman, that report "by the Senior Interagency Group [SIG] for International Communications and Information Policy represents the first serious United States effort to produce a coordinated American policy for the telecommunications fields." The SIG investigation, the Sussmans asserted, "responded to a request from the National Security Council to consider U.S. options for assisting communications development in the Third World." The SIG reply, they concluded, "makes clear that American national interests as well as those of Third World countries are intertwined; further that North/South communication imbalances are real, and deserve to be addressed by the United States private and public sectors." Since this report remained classified, it, too, failed to influence the public debate over UNESCO and mass-communications problems.[82]

In December 1984 the denouement predicted by the long campaign against the U.N. system and focused on UNESCO finally came to pass.

Gregory Newell issued a statement regretting UNESCO's inability to correct the behavior that had outraged his conservative coalition. "The limits of toleration" in the United States had been reached. "Extraneous politicization," Newell claimed, continued as did "an endemic hostility toward the institutions of a free press, free markets, and, above all, individual human rights." While UNESCO's reform efforts "appear genuine," Newell said, "an unacceptable gap clearly remains" between those attempts and the U.S. demands for "concrete change." Secretary of State George Shultz reported the decision to Director-General M'Bow on December 19, 1984.[83]

There was a certain symmetry in the United States relationship with UNESCO in the forty years of their multilateral association. The loyalty-security testing that politicized UNESCO under U.S. leadership early on in their history represented a deep-seated suspicion that international organizations were un-American and had to be "Americanized." In the U.S. departure, that same ethnocentric, nativist obsession returned to dominance. Although UNESCO was not hauled before an Un-American Activities Committee as such, the Heritage Foundation and its right-wing administration allies played the same role. UNESCO, like the world at large, came to be viewed as a center of "subversive activities." J. Edgar Hoover had once sat in the U.N. headquarters in New York certifying acceptable standards of thought and behavior. Forty years later Gregory Newell resumed that screening process. One can hear him asking UNESCO, "Are you now or have you ever been a multilateral organization . . . ?" There was no possible defense.

NOTES

1. Shoup, pp. 53, 55, 103–4, 116–17; Cox and Jacobson, pp. 428, 436.

2. Franklin interview, May 1, 1987; interview with Barbara Newell, February 11, 1987; Esteban Torres statement on "U.S. Withdrawal from UNESCO," pp. 42–56; Shoup, p. 123; see also Farer, pp. 79–96.

3. Interview with Leonard Sussman, May 1, 1987; Sussman statement in "U.S. Withdrawal from UNESCO," pp. 213–14; Sussman statement in "World Forum," pp. 158–63.

4. Torres, *Texas Observer*; Torres statement, "U.S. Withdrawal from UNESCO," p. 47; Newell, pp. 1–5; Newell interview, February 11, 1987.

5. Coate, p. 32.

6. Finger, pp. 20–21; Hughes, "Twilight of Internationalism," pp. 30–33, 41–48; Hufner and Naumann, p. 10; see also *New Republic*, December 3, 1984.

7. Preston, "Information as Obscenity," pp. 1–5; Preston, "Executive Overkill," pp. 7–8; see also Ginsberg, *passim*.

8. Herbert Schiller's statement in "World Forum," pp. 126– 28; Hans N. Weiler, "UNESCO: Take it or Leave it," in "U.S. Withdrawal from UNESCO," p. 110; Massing, 1984, in House Subcommittee on Human Rights and International Operations, "Recent Developments," Appendix 12, p. 273; Hufner and Naumann, p. 5; Sussman interview, May 1, 1987.

9. See Cox and Jacobson, *passim.*

10. Nobbe interview, February 5, 1987.

11. "Recent Developments," p. 55.

12. Finger, p. 20.

13. Fobes interview, February 5, 1987; interview with Dr. James Holderman, New York City, April 9, 1987; interview with John Davidson (executive secretary of USNC under Holderman) Washington, D.C., May 12, 1987; Sussman interview, May 1, 1987, Coate, p. 33.

14. Executive Order 12048, March 27, 1978; Nobbe interview, February 5, 1987, interview with Dr. Max McCulloch, Washington, D.C., February 4, 1987.

15. House Foreign Affairs Committee, "U.S. Withdrawal from UNESCO," pp. 10–11.

16. Nordenstreng with Hannikainen, pp. 59–65; Coate, pp. 31– 32; Banks, pp. 85–89; Mowlana in "World Forum," p. 139 and fn 1.

17. Nordenstreng with Hannikainen, pp. 59–60.

18. *Ibid.*, pp. 60–61, 458–60.

19. *Ibid*, pp. 59–61; Mowlana in "World Forum," pp. 139–41.

20. Nordenstreng with Hannikainen, p. 61.

21. *Ibid.*, p. 62; Coate, p. 31; Banks, pp. 88–89.

22. Nordenstreng with Hannikainen, p. 63, especially note 157.

23. *Ibid.*, pp. 64–65, 67.

24. Ad Hoc Group on United States Policy toward the United Nations, "The United States and the United Nations," pp. 1–17; see also Finger, p. 20.

25. *Ibid.*; see also Wete, p. 5.

26. Fobes interview, February 5, 1987; Nobbe interview, February 5, 1987; Holderman interview, April 9, 1987; Sussman interview, May 1, 1987; Davidson interview, May 12, 1987.

27. Sussman interview, May 1, 1987; Coate, p. 34; United Nations Assessment Project Publications, January 8, 1987 (Heritage Foundation Price List, 4 pp.).

28. "A Critical Assessment," pp. 1–2 and *passim.*

29. *Ibid.*

30. Gerbner, p. 38 and *passim.*

31. "What are the Issues Concerning the Decision of the United States to Withdraw from UNESCO?: An Advisory from the U.S. National Commission for UNESCO" (privately funded and published, 1984), p. 5.

32. U.S. State Department, Reports to the Congress Requested in Sections 108 and 109 of Public Law 97-241 (mimeographed mss), February 24, 1983, pp. i–iii; see also "What are the Issues," p. 5.

33. State Department, Reports to the Congress, Part 1, pp. 2– 3; "What are the Issues," p. 21; Nobbe, "Annotated Bibliography," p. 5.

34. State Department, Reports to the Congress, Part I, pp. 4– 5; Part II, 6–7.

35. "What are the Issues," pp. 4–5.

36. Majid Tehranian statement in "World Forum," pp. 141–42; the M'Bow quote cited there is from "North-South Dialogue: Interview with Amadou Mahtar M'Bow," *Third World Quarterly*, April 1984.

37. Tehranian in "World Forum," pp. 148–50.

38. Hon. E. Gough Whitlam, "A Longer View" (address at the inaugural meeting of the South Australian Branch of the Australian Fabian Society, Adelaide, February 13, 1987), pp. 27–28.

39. Finger, p. 21.

40. Interview with Edmund P. Hennelly, New York City, March 17, 1987; Sussman interview, May 1, 1987.

41. U.S. Delegation Plenary Speech—UNESCO 22nd General Conference, Hon. Edmund P. Hennelly, Congressional Record, No. 160-Part II, Vol. 129, 98th Congress, 1st Session, November 17, 1983.

42. Hennelly interview, March 17, 1987; "Remarks of Edmund P. Hennelly before the 47th Annual Meeting of the U.S. National Commission for UNESCO, December 16, 1983"; Hennelly statement in "U.S. Withdrawal from UNESCO," pp. 12–18, 32.

43. Ibid.

44. Ibid.

45. "What are the Issues," p. 5.

46. James B. Holderman to Gregory Newell, November 8, 1983.

47. Confidential Memorandum, Gregory Newell to the Secretary through Mr. Eagleburger, December 13, 1987; see also Banks, pp. 132–261.

48. Confidential Memorandum, Newell to the Secretary through Mr. Eagleburger, December 13, 1987, pp. 2–3.

49. Ibid., pp. 4–6.

50. Ibid., pp. 6–8.

51. Confidential Memorandum, Lawrence S. Eagleburger to George Shultz, December 22, 1983.

52. "What are the Issues," p. 1; Holderman interview, April 9, 1987; "U.S. Withdrawal from UNESCO" (Staff Study Report), p. 26.

53. Holderman interview, April 9, 1987; Davidson interview, May 12, 1987; Tamas Szechsko statement in "World Forum," p. 102.

54. Ibid.; Nobbe interview, February 5, 1987; Herman: Part II, Sections III and IV; "U.S. Withdrawal from UNESCO" (Staff Study Report), p. 26.

55. George P. Shultz, "Memorandum for the President," December 22, 1983; Confidential Memorandum of Conversation in Under Secretary Eagleburger's office between U.S. and Canada, December 23, 1983; Robert C. McFarlane, "Memorandum for the Honorable George P. Shultz," December 23, 1983; George P. Shultz to Amadou-Mahtar M'Bow, December 28, 1983.

56. Shultz, "Memorandum for the President," December 22, 1983.

57. Ibid.; Holderman interview, April 9, 1987; Davidson interview, May 12, 1987.

58. McFarlane, "Memorandum for Shultz," December 23, 1983.

59. Coate, pp. 36–37; statement of Keith Geiger, Vice President, National Education Association in "U.S. Withdrawal from UNESCO," p. 123; House Foreign Affairs Committee, "Assessment of U.S.-UNESCO Relations, 1984," p. 5.

60. Joseph A. Mehan statement in "World Forum," pp. 123–24; Herman: Part II, Section III.

61. "What are the Issues," p. 6.

62. Mehan in "World Forum," p. 123.

63. The hearings were published as "U.S. Withdrawal From UNESCO"; "Recent Developments in UNESCO and their Implications for U.S. Policy"; and "Human Resources Impact of U.S. Membership in UNESCO." The two staff studies were published as "U.S. Withdrawal from UNESCO" and "Assessment of U.S.-UNESCO Relations, 1984." The GAO reports appear in the "Assessment," pp. 57–75.

64. Hearings cited in ibid., passim.

65. "U.S. Withdrawal from UNESCO" (Staff Study Report), pp. 1–4, 40–44; "Assessment of U.S.-UNESCO Relations," p. 207.

66. "U.S. Withdrawal from UNESCO" (Staff Study Report), pp. 24–31.

67. Ibid., pp. 32–35.

68. "Assessment of U.S.–UNESCO Relations," pp. 2-3.

69. Ibid., p. 4.

70. Ibid., Appendix 4, pp. 48–54.

71. Ibid.; Coate, pp. 27–29.

72. "Assessment of U.S.-UNESCO Relations," p. 5; Coate, p. 28.

73. Hoggart, pp. 17, 61–64, 72–75, 190.

74. *Ibid.*, pp. 136–59; Finklestein, "Political Role of the Director-General," *passim.*

75. Coate, pp. 29, 36–39.

76. "Assessment of U.S.-UNESCO Relations," Appendix 5, pp. 55–56.

77. "What are the Issues," *passim*; Herman: Part II, Section III.

78. "Assessment of U.S.-UNESCO Relations," pp. 5–7; Holderman interview, April 9, 1987; Davidson interview, May 12, 1987.

79. U.S., Department of State, Report of the Monitoring Panel of UNESCO for the Secretary of State, November 27, 1984; Davidson interview, May 12, 1987.

80. Herman: Part II, Section II, Subsection B. "What are the Issues," p. 21.

81. Comptroller general's Report to the Committee on Foreign Affairs and Committee on Science and Technology, House of Representatives, "Improvements Needed in UNESCO's Management, Personnel, Financial and Budgeting Practices," (GAO/NSIAD-85-32), November 30, 1984, passim; Hufner and Nauman, p. 6; Herman: Part II, Section II, Subsection E.

82. Sussman and Sussman, fn. 15, p. 359.

83. "Assistant Secretary Newell's December 1984 Statement" Appendix 7, "Assessment of U.S.-UNESCO Relations," p. 76; George P. Shultz to Amadou-Mahtar M'Bow, December 19, 1984, Appendix 8, *ibid.*, pp. 77–78.

X. EPILOGUE: A POST-MORTEM INTERPRETATION

In 1945 after the second of two vast international conflicts, the world took a utopian gamble and established the United Nations Educational, Scientific, and Cultural Organization. Recognizing the terrifying and damaging influence of the "hostile imagination" and "the war of words," the allied survivors of the latest holocaust committed themselves to building the defenses of peace in the minds of men on a universal and multilateral basis. They seemed determined to reverse the ravages of hate and the propaganda of intolerance by instilling the habits of cooperation and discovering the insights of mutual understanding. Through intellectual and scientific collaboration and by intercultural assimilation, an ideal of human solidarity might slowly become a precarious reality, and unity through diversity a definition of international community. In a very real sense UNESCO would be the essential foundation for the U.N. itself, making its resolution of potentially violent conflict that much more likely and easier to achieve. At least that was the dream that inspired UNESCO's founders.

However, this lofty abstract declaration of purpose left a void to be filled by the concrete programs the initial leadership and succeeding generations would devise. From the very start, a wide spectrum of priorities competed to decide the focus and direction UNESCO would take. A process of politicization thus emerged immediately, inherent in the very nature of the constitutional mandate. As George Sherry has argued, "the determination of action required to fulfill an abstractly stated purpose is in itself a political issue, since each of the actors . . . will inevitably define the required action in terms of its own interests."[1] The United States' desire for UNESCO to return to its original purposes and abandon politicization is thus a contradiction in terms, impossible, and incomprehensible. Politicization is not "a defect to be corrected" but a fact of multilateral, organizational life and part and parcel of the "planetary bargaining" over the proper means to achieve UNESCO's idealistic ends. The degree of political intrusion may vary as the nations achieve more or less consensus and issues with different degrees of salience are addressed, but depoliticization is nonsense as an aim. As a national foreign-policy goal, it is a fraud.[2]

In terms of evaluating UNESCO's performance, politicization is also a non-issue. Its presence in UNESCO has no more importance than as evidence that nations have different priorities and interests, not exactly an earth-shaking discovery. What role politicization does serve is as "an indicator to be understood," a barometer reflecting the goals that diverse constituencies may be seeking and the intensity of their feelings on the subject. When the United States politicized UNESCO on mass-media, information, and Cold War issues, therefore, other member states received this as a communication of a powerful foreign-policy agenda that the U.S. wished to achieve and did not accuse UNESCO of succumbing to some hideous vice. Since governments rather than individuals rapidly took charge of agenda-setting within UNESCO, reducing the influence that the intellectual communities and national commissions had in the organization, politics just as quickly intruded into the deliberations of the Executive Board and the General Conference. In the era of U.S. and Western dominance, politicization had less notoriety; it simply existed as a latent factor behind the "structure of influence" those powers maintained. When it became the weapon of the Third World, however, the U.S. reviled it as an instrument of contentious, irrelevant, and destructive division. Politicization thus became an illegitimate communication and the U.S. was unwilling to understand it or learn "adaptive behavior" from the messages it conveyed.[3]

A second spurious characterization of UNESCO portrayed it as a technical, functional agency that had abandoned noncontroversial activity for the pleasures of ideological muckraking. In this analysis of organizational life, only neutral, objective experts exist within it, and their international contacts as specialists performing narrowly professional tasks represent the definition of acceptable multilateral behavior. While UNESCO's founding obviously imagined unleashing such cooperative activity in education, science, and culture, even imagined UNESCO itself being run by these technocrats, their autonomy disappeared during the governmental takeover, which even denied their neutrality by loyalty-security evaluations of their supposedly nonexistent politics. Func-

tionalism obviously did not eliminate politics, although in certain arenas it could diminish, if not restrain, their influence. But as a weapon of
disinformation, the theory by inference condemned the concept of
UNESCO as a forum for ideas and a marketplace where ideologies freely
competed for effective influence in the world. Functionalism implied
that there was something unhealthy and abnormal about debates, resolutions, conventions, standard setting, rhetoric, all that collective noise
expressing a dialectical reaction against the very status quo of wealth
and power that UNESCO's mission had an obligation to measure and
criticize.[4] As the philosopher and conscience of the U.N. system,
UNESCO was bound to deal in values and, as Hoggart insisted, evaluate
"the ethical dimension and social and individual costs" of the solutions
proposed for the world's improvement. By questioning and "organizing
the hue and cry," UNESCO could slowly arrange a "collective legitimi-
zation" of better international conduct. And to do so required an active
forum for ideas, even those the United States opposed.[5]

Both politicization and ideological confrontation in the marketplace
of intellectual exchange had a necessary and proper place in UNESCO's
work. Neither was endemic nor deforming, yet they tended to attract
the greatest publicity and controversy because of their importance to the
national interests of the member states. While they represented a small
proportion of UNESCO's overall activity and spending, they often
seemed to represent the totality of it. In addition, they appeared to have
significant short-term consequences which always intensified the magnitude of their fame. The day-to-day programming and project development in education, science, and culture, consuming perhaps 95 percent
of UNESCO's energy and expenditures, never achieved a similar recognition or status. Those areas remained as remote and ill-noticed in
UNESCO as they did in the foreign cultural relations of the various governments, partly because of their very nonpolitical, noncontroversial
character, partly because they lacked a high priority in world politics,
and partly because their efforts were hard to measure and then mainly
in the long run. The U.S. attitude toward its National Commission,
UNESCO bureau, Paris mission, and General Conference delegation symbolized a more general disdain for and indifference to education, science,
and culture as vital aspects of its geopolitical policies. Which is why one
contentious resolution counted the same as hundreds of successful programs in the field when it came time to judge UNESCO's achievements.

Typifying the imbalance in estimation that forum activities attained as
opposed to those in the technical and professional fields was a similar
distortion of emphasis between education, science, and culture on the
one hand and mass communications on the other. Because of their supposed magnificent ability to transform attitudes and behavior, the latter
had been added to UNESCO's mandate on the insistence of the United
States. If minds were to be changed and the defenses of peace were to be

erected, then let it be done by massive injections of information immediately. If that seemed typical of the U.S. impatience to get things done, it also reflected the experience with radio propaganda and mass-circulation journalism, and the U.S. desire for supremacy in both arenas. The dangers of this development to UNESCO's mission were three-fold: it elevated the technology of information as the primary instrument of influence over the other three approaches; it emphasized short-term results and further diminished those that took place slowly over the long run; and it politicized the information/free-flow issue by attaching it to a self-serving national interest at the very start. Control over the means of changing "men's minds," the key to UNESCO's significance as an educating force in world affairs, thus remained largely beyond its grasp and in the hands of private and national entities. Sooner or later other less developed countries forming a new majority in UNESCO would attempt to redress that imbalance both for the good of the organization and for the sake of their own cultural autonomy. Having exercised a communications authority for so long, the U.S. and its media industry would resist any such challenge and blame UNESCO for letting it happen.

Condemned to be politicized, chastised for failing to be nothing but a functional agency, yet ignored for its functional achievements, and subverted by the impact of mass communications, UNESCO moved uncertainly ahead, a creation of governments that often gave it short shrift. No one, of course, had provided a timetable for bringing into existence the secular visions of utopia that the founders had imagined within reach, nor had any standards of achievement been established. Apart from its constitution and institutional shape, UNESCO had to define itself, and it set forth on its journey without much guidance. The governments that sustained it seemed in no hurry to get there, however, for they kept UNESCO's budget at levels that seemed inconsistent with the inflated expectations of what its impact might be. All of these considerations must be taken into account when assessing its significance, and judgments about UNESCO must not be distorted by false or misleading accounts of its character and performance. As has been seen, certain charges against UNESCO are either false or irrelevant and should play no role in any objective evaluation of it.

The world, of course, remained resistant to the programs and philosophy UNESCO dispensed, and numerous international developments complicated UNESCO's task. The pace of change was one such factor, not only in the economic and technological realm but in the political as well. As decolonization progressed and liberation into self-determination occurred, new nationalisms proliferated. Not only did they need UNESCO's assistance in every area of its responsibility, but they also swelled the ranks of its membership. The new Third World majority complicated UNESCO's internal governance and administration by the sheer increase in size and created new priorities for action as those nations sought their full cultural autonomy and rightful place in the international decision-making process. In the 40 years after the end of World War II, UNESCO grew from some 20 to 161 members, and the number of intergovernmental organizations increased from 800 to 3,000. This explosion of variety manifested itself in decentralization of authority, regionalization, new alignments of power, and a North-South axis of competition alongside the older Cold War division between East and West. Former Deputy Director-General Jack Fobes cites "Ashby's Law, the law of requisite variety" as one necessary response to this potential global chaos, for "only variety can control and manage increasing variety and promote stability and resilience."[6]

Neither violent conflict nor the war of words disappeared, for the hostile imagination seemed as active as ever on both the overt and covert level of rival operations and propaganda. Both the Cold War and the multiplication of nationalisms intensified these divisions as did the last remnants of colonialism and the continuing pervasive racism abroad in the world. UNESCO's efforts to monitor and improve the quality of international communications and diminish the circulation of defamatory, hostile, false, and misleading information met with little support. Building the defenses of peace, in fact, struck some nations as a subversive undertaking, as though peace and disarmament efforts were themselves enemy conspiracies that UNESCO was foolishly assisting.

Illiteracy, poverty, and underdevelopment, and the deterioration of the quality of life in two-thirds of the world also increasingly concerned UNESCO, not only because of the injustice and need, but also because the defenses of peace would not be erected on the sands of hopelessness and despair. Development thus became a second major theme during UNESCO's second generation of activity under Director-General René Maheu. And development linked itself naturally to the major scientific collaborations that the organization sponsored, since the former required the preservation of the world's ecology, environment, and resources so that they might still be available to the deprived communities now seeking access to them.

While development assistance, the struggle against illiteracy, and scientific projects in global analysis and conservation required the kind of technical expertise that UNESCO's functional operations represented, these problems necessarily raised issues of distributive justice, equality of opportunity, and democratic control. Less powerful latecomers and have-not nations emerging from the constraints of a colonial past believed that UNESCO was a natural ally in this process of change. By 1970, if not sooner, the organization had become a parliamentary forum for the expression of the Third World's desire to reformulate the terms of their relationship to the elite nations in control of global power and wealth. A dissatisfied peripheral majority challenged the status quo in UNESCO and other U.N. arenas, and suggested a new set of international arrangements more favorable to their own survival, growth, and independence. Neither the service nor the forum activities were in any way inconsistent with UNESCO's mission. They enhanced the quality of life by technical cooperation and extended the free flow of ideas about life's purposes and possibilities.

Two contradictory attitudes toward UNESCO had emerged by the 1970s, and they endangered its future stability and vitality. The Third World viewed the developmental approach as a liberation from neo-colonial dependence, leading naturally to greater equality and autonomy. Both the technical services and the discussion of ideas in the UNESCO forum were seen, therefore, as a challenge to the international status quo. The United States, on the other hand, viewed development and the debates over the existing distribution of power and wealth as a program of containment rather than liberation. UNESCO would moderate radical demands for change through increments of assistance that would alleviate the worst problems of economic deprivation and stagnation and bring the UNESCO majority into the constructive channels of modernization controlled by the U.S. and its industrialized allies. As the heated confrontation over mass communications demonstrated, the unstated premise behind the service functions and the forum resolutions in the information area was a struggle to define the future. And that was always a political issue of the first importance to all the contending parties.

The United States, meanwhile, had not prepared itself for the critical "planetary bargaining" that became a feature of multilateral life in the more pluralistic universe following decolonization. Having long regarded education, science, and culture as diplomatic back waters and largely irrelevant to the major issues of wealth and power, a steady depreciation of UNESCO's importance had accelerated after the 1960s. The United States had forgotten its own use of UNESCO as a significant political instrument in the Cold War struggle for "men's minds" and consigned UNESCO, so it thought, to narrowly mundane technical tasks of a noncontroversial nature. Assuming that the free flow of ideas had been forever secured by its own technological supremacy and vast cultural domination, the U.S. apparently did not imagine that other nations would dare to demand equal access to that global marketplace. Nor had it shifted the axis of its own geopolitical thinking from the accustomed anticommunist format to the new dimensions of North-South confrontation. Its traditional ethnocentric outlook also inhibited that shift of focus. A benign neglect, much like imperial Britain's attitude toward its American colonies before the revolution, had thus become characteristic of the U.S. management of its UNESCO affairs. Since no experienced and talented officials were in place to anticipate the new conditions of multilateral diplomacy, policy tended to be formulated on an ad hoc, reactive basis determined mainly by the political lobbies hostile to UNESCO and its Third World majority. The United States, in fact, treated the rise of this novel and unexpected aggregation of power as though it were a Southern community facing a civil-rights call for an end to segregation in the 1950s.

As in all such apparently abrupt discontinuities in the customary relationships of a social setting, emotional fervor and ideological outrage colored the perceptions of those who feared change in the established order. A certain hysteria could be expected, and it would be one that denied the historical realities and any responsibility for the crisis that had arisen. An indictment framed in such circumstances would, therefore, be more of a libel than a true bill and have the qualities of a legal lynching rather then a sober evaluation of the rights and wrongs of the relationship. The United States charges against UNESCO had that character and they cast much more light on the accuser than the accused. Any real understanding of the events must depend on a different and broader perspective than the one the Reagan administration disingenuously paraded as the truth. Politicization was not the issue, nor was deviation from UNESCO's original principles, nor was its combination of forum activities with those of a functional kind. Since UNESCO had been regularly assessed over the years and always received a positive rating even in the limited perspective of the U.S. national interest almost to the moment of the Reagan administration's announced departure, something else was obviously at stake. And that something had little to do with the forty-year record UNESCO had established.

By what standards should UNESCO be judged? How many achievements should it have attained and how valuable to humanity must they be deemed for UNESCO to pass muster before its critics? And how will those critics allot responsibility between UNESCO and the member states whose national interests allow it the only freedom to operate that it has? Historians have interpreted the success and failures of many organizations with less than consensus and from different perspectives, so there will always be controversy over any conclusion. Yet some semblance of agreement has been reached in most cases. It can be found in the UNESCO story as well.

Would it not be possible to single out the fight against illiteracy as a contribution that alone would justify UNESCO's existence? Some educators would certainly so argue and they would not be wrong. Even some U.S. presidential administrations have achieved historical recognition for one great contribution to the general welfare. But UNESCO has, of course, done much more than that and is still doing so. In his memoir of thirty years at UNESCO, Julian Behrstock listed fifteen such magnificent programs "fully consonant with the Organization's great objectives . . . [and] *ongoing to this day* [1987]." Behrstock concluded that all of them signaled "UNESCO's capacity to perform the valuable work foreseen for it in the constitution," and that "these accomplishments were not easily won."[7] Richard Hoggart's similar accounting of UNESCO made from his perspective as a top administrator during the 1970s assembled material on its "indisputable useful activities" in dozens of areas, all of them consistent with UNESCO's original principles.[8] The testimony of the United States' own professional experts in education, science, and culture came to an equally positive conclusion in numerous congressional hearings, State Department studies, and USNC evaluations. A summary of the "major benefits" accruing to the U.S. from its participation included the following items:

1. UNESCO is the preeminent vehicle for international cooperative work on global scientific problems, a forum for discussion of emerging ideas and forming cooperative research networks. Among its programs:

• The International Center for Theoretical Physics at Trieste is the world's only effective forum for cooperative research and training with broad involvement of underdeveloped countries, communist and industrial countries, and in which U.S. physicists cooperate.

• The International Geological Correlation Program cosponsored by UNESCO promotes research on the geologic structure and history of the Earth.

• The International Hydrological Program promotes rational management of water resources, an area of concern that transcends national boundaries.

• The Program in Informatics encourages research and training for improved understanding of computers and computer-based systems in science, technology, and economic development.

• The Intergovernmental Oceanographic Commission promotes research on the oceans and gives the U.S. access to the 60 percent of its data which are from foreign sources.

• The Man and the Biosphere program, involving 100 nations, fosters understanding and management of the world's ecosystems.

• MAB actively promotes the conservation of natural areas throughout the world and has established 226 biosphere reserves in 62 countries.

• The National Hazards Program develops means of assessing and predicting natural hazards such as earthquakes and floods, and works to mitigate the loss of life and physical damage from hazards.

• The Statistical Division is the only source about R & D [research and development] in many countries in the world.

2. UNESCO provides to the U.S. the opportunities to present U.S. technology to other nations, thus promoting sales of U.S. expertise, instruments and tools; and the opportunity to evaluate the level of technology available in other countries.

3. It provides access to important research localities, expertise, facilities and other resources; access to research data generated from international projects; sharing of costs and expensive instruments needed for large-scale, international scientific efforts, and scientific and technical assistance to LDCs.

4. The Education of All program is working to eliminate illiteracy among the nearly one billion people who are illiterate, nearly 250 million of whom are children under the age of 17.

5. In the cultural area, UNESCO supports translations into English of works that contribute to an understanding of the history, intellectual achievement and social development of other cultures from antiquity to the present.

6. UNESCO supports archaeological projects where sites are threatened by destruction or deterioration, such as the rescue of Egypt's Temples of Nubia and Philae (from the Aswan dam waters) and recovery of artifacts in Venice and Florence.

7. Trafficking in stolen art is curtailed by the UNESCO work on conventions on stolen cultural property.

8. In communications UNESCO is an important international forum for discussion of issues such as the freedom of the press where the U.S. can make its views known and mitigate against the development of restrictive covenants by other nations.[9]

One is tempted to ask why the United States has turned against an agency that has been so crucial as supporter of development, promoter of cultural diversity and tradition, saver of monuments, "world resource center," sponsor of "international dialogue among experts," as well as of East-West exchanges, provider of all sorts of training, and overall "a great market for the traffic of knowledge." Not only did UNESCO spend 40 percent of the U.S. contribution within the United States, but it never had the funds as a multilateral organization to do more, most nations, like the U.S., preferring to provide bilateral assistance whose expenditures they controlled.[10]

A list of outstanding achievements, however, does not exhaust the contributions UNESCO has made to international life. Although the Reagan administration has deplored "politicization" and the "endemic hostility" to Western values, those accusations misrepresent the reality of multilateral organizations and the role UNESCO has played in resolving the conflicts of interest that occasion the Reagan charges. Since U.N. agencies are not world government, but "networks and coalitions" of shifting alliances of member governments, they inevitably contain the full spectrum of systems and ideologies people have adopted throughout the world. And those differences and their combination with national interest structure contention into the U.N. system as a struggle to define agendas and set priorities. An organization such as UNESCO should also be evaluated on two further grounds: How successfully has it kept the controversial elements out of its functional programming, and how well has it managed the politicization that national rivalries have brought into the forum of discussion? It would be absurd, of course, to expect UNESCO to impose a censorship on the airing of views other than those of the United States, although that seemed to be the purpose of Gregory Newell's proposed reforms.

As has already been observed, UNESCO operated the vast majority of its most important projects without a trace of political contention or distortion, especially in the area of education, science, and culture and even to a great extent in mass communications. In addition, it created a number of procedures to maintain the integrity of those technical arenas such as "negotiating and drafting committees, consensus, and working groups," not to mention the skillful mediation of the director-general himself. To use the terminology applied to the United Nations' operations, UNESCO engaged in successful crisis management through the imposition of a cease fire on most divisiveness and the consequent achievement of peace keeping as the agreed state of affairs.[11]

UNESCO also performed ably in moderating the conflicts that member states brought into the organization. National and regional rivalries were, of course, heated and intense before the U.N. system was created. All of its agencies became centers where those quarrels could be aired and "globalized" as the parties sought to win adherents and international recognition for their claims. The United States had done no less during the long course of its obsession with Cold War issues. Having successfully accommodated the arrival of many new nations as decolonization progressed, UNESCO then faced their claims to a share in the formation of its agenda. As George Sherry has pointed out, when restlessness with the status quo occurs, "governments tend to act as if their worst fears might come true" which makes it "idle to expect issues involving vital interests to be negotiated out of existence."[12]

Two major disputes entered the UNESCO forum during the 1970s, one involving the Third World and the industrialized West and focusing on mass communications, the other concerning the Arab-Israeli hostility and diverted to symbolic behavior affecting Palestinian refugees, West Bank education, and archaeological preservation. Since "regional disputes tend to be extraordinarily intense, durable, and difficult to resolve," UNESCO, in a sense, became a "hostage" to the larger failure of the United States and others to resolve the Middle East crisis. Yet educational assistance and training to Palestinian refugees did not become contentious except in the eyes of the Heritage Foundation. The anti-Israeli resolutions dealing with excavations in Jerusalem and Israel's membership in a regional association festered and threatened but, after several years, dissolved as an issue when Israel joined the European group. If anything, UNESCO had achieved what George Sherry would call successful "impasse management" that recognized no "winner" in the conflict and did not solve the antagonism, but did leave it "in suspense" with the tension reduced as a destructive intrusion in the organization's affairs. When Israel urged the United States not to withdraw, it recognized this reality and the useful influence the U.S. could bring to bear should similar crises develop.[13]

Just as UNESCO had kept the anti-Israeli contention under control and achieved a grudging acceptance of a truce among the antagonists, so, too, did it move the seemingly irreconcilable interests over information issues toward successive accommodations that gave neither side what it wanted. And that in itself was no small achievement. The problem was not that UNESCO under M'Bow's leadership was irresponsible, quite the opposite. The fatal flaw in the process was that the United States refused to accept an impasse that favored negotiated settlements and instead sought an end to bargaining about the mass communications imbalances. Blaming the director-general for a conciliation that did not hand the United States a total victory was the same as condemning a labor arbitrator for successfully concluding a labor-management agreement when both sides in bitter division would have seemingly reached no solution at all. Since "few things are more permanent than temporary arrangements" as George Sherry has argued, the specter of endless controversy was more a figment of the Reagan administration's imagination than a reading of objective reality.[14] The United States had no reason to abandon multilateral bargaining given its experience in UNESCO. It pursued "depoliticization" in the "absence of a political strategy" of its own, in ignorance of history, and in thrall to the myths of an ideology a conservative coalition had imposed upon it.[15]

The ability to defuse volatile issues, while nowhere mentioned in UNESCO's constitution, represented, nevertheless, a significant management skill for which the U.S. gave it little credit. As notable as this was, it naturally did not encompass the entire range of UNESCO's administrative responsibilities. If there was one major problem area that needed attention, that field qualified as a subject for reform, but never called for a sanction as extreme as withdrawal, since member governments themselves were a large part of the problem. As Jack Fobes has described it, by the late 1970s all the U.N. agencies were undergoing "a crisis of administrative legitimacy," occasioned by their rapid growth, increased activities, and more complex and diverse constituencies. They were like small colleges that had become major research universities without a change of style or procedure. That the main UNESCO efforts in 1984 dealt with just such problems suggests their relevance as core issues and their susceptibility to improvement once recognized and addressed.[16]

Although the United States had dominated UNESCO's administrative areas for years in its belief in the management know-how its nationals possessed, the reconstruction and renaissance the organization needed involved a cooperative, sustained, and gradual restoration of procedures suited to the new conditions. That meant a combined effort by the national commissions, the NGOs, the universities, and the member states, most of whom had not paid close attention to the area and some of whom had atrophied for lack of governmental support. The director-general had naturally stepped into the vacuum of leadership that benign neglect elsewhere had created, but the renovation required a revival of the interest and enthusiasm for UNESCO that had marked its founding years. If Secretary of State Shultz wanted a return to the original scenario, his first priority should have been the commitment and rededication of his own country, not its withdrawal.

A prescription for the long-term, step-by-step redesigning of UNESCO that would have revitalized the role of multilateral diplomacy among all participants and enhanced the organization's capacity for more effective service to its global community would have been a wise, sane, and responsible reformation for the United States to have proposed. One can imagine the excitement of scholars and experts, the stimulation of historical studies and consultant evaluations, the resurgence of the national commissions, and the development of new networks of support. A UNESCO career might even have become a sought-after assignment for foreign-service officers in the United States and elsewhere. But no such agenda ever came forth from the officials in charge of State Department international organization affairs. Their one-year deadline (an effective five months) had no such project in mind. A strengthened and influential UNESCO capable of realizing its mission in ever more challenging ways was not the aim of Newell and his allied ideologues.[17]

Any rereading of history should discover new meaning in past events and give them an added dimension of perspective, thereby enriching contemporary understanding once again. Analyzing the U.S./UNESCO relationship from the point of view of the United States' own history provides that fresh vision and refocuses attention on the proper source of the U.S. withdrawal. That imprudent and impudent decision did not represent a rational response to the events that had transpired during UNESCO's first forty years of life. The U.S. indictment must be thrown out of History's court as invalid and prejudicial; its charges were of that sensational and spurious kind that characterize political propaganda and ideological disinformation. History cannot support or justify them, and is embarrassed that they should ever pass as History.

Dissenters in the United States and victims of political suppression there could have forewarned their Third World successors about the limits of acceptable protest at home and abroad. So could native populations experiencing the pressures of U.S. intervention on behalf of the Open Door empire of economic control established in the early twentieth century—and as pawns of U.S. covert international operations since World War II. The Populists, the Blacks, the radicals rounded up in the Palmer Raids of 1920, and the many individual and organizational suspects attacked by McCarthyism or disrupted and silenced by J. Edgar Hoover's FBI represented object lessons in surveillance and intimidation on behalf of the established order of being and believing. Overseas a similar pattern of influence characterized as missionary diplomacy and upheld by a variety of presidential doctrines insisted on support for U.S. objectives and values. The ideological banners justifying these policies included ethnocentric nativism, racism, anticommunism, and un-Americanism. All of the above constrained and constricted the free marketplace of ideas, an arena already narrowed by the media industry's concentration of control and its support for the system's authority. As Angela Gilliam has pointed out, the demand for "media justice" in the covering of oppressed and disinherited populations has been as consistently denied in the U.S. as it has been in the Third World.[18]

When the United States assumed its international role in UNESCO in 1945, therefore, numerous national cultural obsessions lay in wait, unconverted to the ideals of full and equal multilateral cooperation and extremely suspicious of it. The U.S. commitments to the U.N. agencies of action and debate were largely intellectual, a sort of latter-day gloss that failed to devise any internal social adjustments to the new realities, an almost schizoid dualism of purpose and philosophy. And isolationist and unilateral traditions also tempered the shift to collective decision-making. Both the postwar idealism and the U.S. pre-eminence in wealth and power, however, diminished the inroads of alternative patterns of international behavior and the Cold War drew influence into multilateral cooperation as one of the instruments of Soviet containment. The later enthusiasm for development serving U.S. national interests temporarily revived UNESCO's standing in the 1960s after the challenges to it in the Eisenhower years. As the postcolonial era hit its stride with an explosion of Third World reactions against the U.S. imperium or any suggestion of neo-colonial subordination, protest and power began to reach unacceptable limits in the eyes of the vested interests that U.S. policy represented.

Social disruption, rapid change, and confrontational attitudes on behalf of reform had always triggered a much harder line in response. Signs of this urge toward repression first emerged when the LDCs challenged the mass-communications/information supremacy that threatened their own autonomy. At the same time, new centers of conservative influence in the United States revived all the latent cultural anxieties and attached them to their agenda of economic deregulation and free-enterprise ideology. In spite of its many useful and successful achievements, UNESCO was becoming a target waiting to be shot down. Not as some have said as the Grenada of the U.N. system, but as the focal point of protest in a parliamentary democracy opposed to the right-wing doctrines of the U.S. administration about to take power. Because UNESCO cared about moral and social problems, human values, and shaping the world to its imaginative possibilities, it raised a "cri du coeur" against the fragmentation and Hobbesian future the Heritage Foundation desired to impose.

Created to pacify the hostile imagination and disarm the war of words, UNESCO found itself the unwitting victim of the very misinformation, hatred, and intolerance it had hoped to extinguish. Equally ironic was the abhorrence of the free market in ideas that the United States symbolized in its campaign against alternative definitions of the international order. The withdrawal itself, an ideological manipulation of the power to impose sanctions on sources of dissent, also violated the principles of free speech and fair play. Media McCarthyism one-sidedly set the parameters of interpretation, a false and distorted reading of history and contemporary realities that described UNESCO as the vile sewer of the U.N. system. Congressman Gerald Solomon uttered the unforgettable epitaph that marked this final U.S. disengagement from the intellectual commonwealth of good works it had once founded. He foresaw no problem for the United States should it leave UNESCO. "We will survive," he predicted, "we have more than 200 years of national experience. . . . The United States does not need UNESCO. UNESCO needs the United States. . . . Our scientific prominence is unchallenged, not to mention the cultural impact that our country has had wherever other countries have opened themselves to the free exchange of ideas and information."[19]

NOTES

1. Sherry, p. 756.
2. Lyons, Baldwin, and McNemar, pp. 83, 86–87.
3. *Ibid.*, pp. 86–92; Cox and Jacobson, pp. 13–35, 433–35.
4. See, for example, Cox and Jacobson, pp. 30, 33–34, 403–4.
5. Hoggart, pp. 164–65, 174–75.
6. Statement of Jack Fobes, "U.S. Withdrawal from UNESCO," pp. 58–60.
7. Behrstock, pp. 167–69 (emphasis added).
8. Hoggart, pp. 31–40.
9. "How UNESCO Participation Benefits the U.S." (two-page ms. based on documents submitted to the U.S. State Department by agencies of the U.S. government and by nongovernmental organizations, undated), pp. 1–2.
10. Hoggart, pp. 31–40.
11. See Lyons, Baldwin, and McNemar, pp. 81–92 for this and preceding paragraph.
12. Sherry, p. 757.
13. *Ibid.*, pp. 756–59; Lyons, Baldwin, and McNemar, p. 84.
14. Sherry, p. 759.
15. Lyons, Baldwin, and McNemar, p. 92.
16. Fobes statement, "U.S. Withdrawal from UNESCO," p. 67.
17. I am indebted to Fobes, *ibid.*, pp. 58–80, for his thoughtful analysis and many suggestions for reform. They seem to have had little or no impact on the U.S. decision.

18. Gilliam, p. 94.
19. Congressman Gerald Solomon in "U.S. Withdrawal from UNESCO," pp. 286–87.

Edward S. Herman

U.S. MASS MEDIA COVERAGE OF THE U.S. WITHDRAWAL FROM UNESCO

I. INTRODUCTION

A. Objective Coverage versus Propaganda

The central focus of the U.S. mass media in their treatment of the U.S. withdrawal from UNESCO—and in their attention to UNESCO more generally over the past decade—has been its alleged threat to a "free press." In mass-media discourse, a free press is implicitly or explicitly one in private hands, financed largely by advertising, and not subject to government controls or any other obligatory norm of social responsibility. It is postulated in this "mercantile conception of information"[1] that a press so organized will be fair and "objective," and that the commercial interests of the private owners, their advertising customers, governmental pressures and inducements, and patriotic bias do not seriously influence their news coverage.

In this perspective, only government-imposed rules systematically impair media fairness and objectivity. Where the government has taken upon itself rule-making authority for the media, it may insist that the media support national policies and assume that the leaders of their own state have beneficent objectives (in contrast with the motives of foreign leaders); it may restrict debate and require the media to rely heavily on government handouts and follow an official line, ignoring dissidents and excluding opposition views; it may put forth fabricated claims and compel the media to publish them and to suppress contrary evidence; and, finally, the government and its controlled media may rewrite history in accordance with present policy demands and push incompatible facts and alternative interpretations into a black hole.

The possibility that private, commercially based media might similarly abuse principles of fairness and objectivity is ruled out by Western media spokespersons on several grounds. One is that there is a multiplicity of private channels, not a single controlling monolith. Furthermore, entry into the media is free, i.e., not limited by government licensing (at least for the print media). It is also contended that ownership interests and viewpoints are not homogeneous, so that a single perspective will not prevail. Further, it is argued that owners do not impose their views on their journalist-editor underlings, who, in their turn, are devoted to and ruled by professional standards of fairness and objectivity that are beyond the reach of mundane interests.

An alternative view asserts that by virtue of their commercial nature, concentration, and integration into a corporate system, the Western mass media speak for dominant national interests and function as a *de facto* propaganda agency for such interests. The mass media comprise a small and relatively stable set of quite large, profit-making business firms,[2] frequently multinational in scope and integrated into the overall corporate community by interlocks and multiple business relationships. The dominant owners, in this view, may have varying viewpoints on some matters, but they have a number of common basic interests among themselves and with the rest of the business community. There are no mass-media firms in the United States whose owners could be said to represent or share basic interests with the working class, farmers, black and Hispanic communities, or the poor. Large-circulation media owned by and/or representing nonbusiness interests have largely disappeared in the West under the impact of the working of market forces.[3] Entry into the mass media is nominally free, but substantively extremely difficult even for those with large aggregations of capital. Thus the transmission to the public of the views and interests of noncorporate bodies and groups requires that they pass through the filters established by corporate gatekeepers.

In this alternative view, the commercial interests of owners and advertisers have an inevitable and systematic effect on news choices of the mass media, occasionally through direct intervention, more commonly and importantly through a stress on the criterion of profitability, through personnel selection, and through other methods of rewards and penalties. The lower echelons of the mass media must operate within the dominant frameworks imposed from above and adapt to the organizational priorities and reward systems. The "professional standards" widely applicable in the media are quite elastic in practice and provide little or no assurance of protection against outright propaganda. These standards do not establish which stories are to be selected in the first place, their relative prominence, the emphasis given the various themes within the story, the tone, and the weight given the various protagonists. It is well known that nominal objectivity can be spurious; that the preferred viewpoint can be transmitted by questioning someone who says what one wants said. The appearance is maintained that one avoids giving a personal opinion, when in fact this is done by proxy.

The mass-media coverage of the U.S. withdrawal from UNESCO provides an excellent test of the media claim that a "free press" is an objective and unbiased instrument of communicating news. It is an especially interesting test in that the mass media had a material stake in the outcome of the controversy. A New World Information and Communication Order (NWICO) and a New International Economic Order (NIEO) as conceived by their leading spokespersons would have encouraged rival media organizations in the Third World and might have constrained media (and other transnational corporate) advertising, ownership, sales, investment, and freedom to transmit messages at their own discretion in the Third World. Would the Western media acknowledge this clear conflict of economic interest—as would be required under U.S. Securities and Exchange Commission disclosure rules in a prospectus for a new security issue—or would they pretend that their concern was only with high principles? Would they be able to maintain a reasonable degree of fairness and objectivity in the face of the perceived threat to self-interest (or high principle)? They had an incentive to perform well because their basic claim for the unreasonableness of the proposals for a NWICO was that the *New* order threatened systematic bias: the existing *Old* order—the "free press"—provided unbiased news. In brief, the mass media's coverage of the U.S. withdrawal provides an important test of their claim of the fairness and impartiality of a concentrated, commercial press.

B. The Record of Earlier Studies of Mass-Media Treatment of UNESCO

Studies of both U.S. and Western European press treatment of UNESCO in the years before the U.S. withdrawal suggest the unlikelihood that the U.S. mass media will pass this test of impartiality. On the contrary, these studies consistently point to self-serving and biased presentations in mass-media coverage of news on UNESCO.

Associated Press's coverage of the 1976 Costa Rica Conference on Communications Policies. In a study of Associated Press (AP) coverage of the first Intergovernmental Conference on Communication Policies in Latin America and the Caribbean, sponsored by UNESCO and held in Costa Rica in July 1976, Raquel Salinas Bascur showed that AP's news was seriously biased at a number of different levels[4]: (1) It suppressed statements during the conference that called attention to the economic interests underlying opposition to the Costa Rica proceeding, which included those of AP itself.[5] (2) The basic frame used in AP reporting was the threat posed by the conference and its supporters to freedom of the press. The threats seen by the conference majority—unbalanced reporting of regional news, underdeveloped media resources, inundation and capture by the media of the developed countries—and the main proceedings and resolutions of the conference were largely ignored. (3) AP downplayed positive and consensus elements of the conference, entirely ignoring half of the resolutions. Of those mentioned, "the news agencies and the role of the private sector were given more than half the space, while issues such as the right of states to formulate communications policies, the need for a balanced flow of information and supplementary communications systems, were obviously minimized or even ignored . . . "[6] (4) AP elevated to prominence the Inter-American Press Association (IAPA), which, although not a participant in the conference, received far more coverage than any participating country. IAPA represents private media interests, and served as the vehicle for framing the issues in terms of private versus governmental control and expressing the private media view that the former is synonymous with freedom, the latter is a threat, and UNESCO's activities encouraged something menacing.[7] (5) "Although in accordance with the rules of 'objectivity' most criticism was voiced by an identifiable source—mainly IAPA—AP also found non-identifiable sources to stress the importance of issues that are in the interest of transnational news agencies and private interests in general."[8] (6) Many attacks quoted by AP were personal in nature; not more than 15 percent of the lines citing IAPA contained substantive information or argument.[9] (7) Not only did AP allocate more space to aggressive critics of the conference than to the participants, it ignored credible outsiders who represented positions contrary to that of the private media. "An example is the extensive quotations that AP made of declarations by the president of a national Association of Journalists while ignoring the support given the meeting by the Latin American Federation of Journalists."[10]

In sum, AP gave the conference a negative image by "(a) stressing IAPA's position and the criticisms of other biased commentators, (b) overemphasizing minor events that cast the meeting in a negative light and (c) minimizing or ignoring the background and actual context that might have explained better the meaning of the event."[11]

The 1980 Belgrade General Conference. An important examination of the U.S. media's coverage of the 1980 Belgrade General Conference was carried out by the National News Council, an independent U.S. monitoring agency sponsored by the media themselves. The News Council was concerned over whether the media's own "fears" were "expressed in a one-sidedness in news coverage" that might obstruct "public understanding of the depth of dissatisfaction with existing practice among developing countries and of the degree to which these Third World critics were not monolithic in their own concepts of what might constitute appropriate remedies."[12] The council's investigation showed that media bias in its coverage of the conference was blatant. It found, first, that newspaper opinion was in fact virtually homogeneous, representing a self-serving media and national viewpoint: "Without exception, the editorials expressed apprehension about UNESCO's involvement in attempts to establish policy in matters affecting the worldwide flow of information." And the great majority of editorials were "strongly hostile" to the perceived drift of UNESCO opinion on these matters.[13] Leonard Sussman of Freedom House referred to the "monolithic" quality of both the news stories and editorial opinion.[14]

The News Council found, second, that news priorities closely reflected editorial opinion: "The news events that got the widest press use and the greatest prominence tended to be those that reinforced the fears expressed on editorial pages."[15] Other matters were rarely discussed at all, even though they were important in the deliberations of the participants at Belgrade and in terms of UNESCO functions: "Not one story emanating from the six-week conference dealt with any of the reports, speeches, or resolutions on UNESCO's basic activities in combatting illiteracy, developing alternative energy sources, protecting historic monuments, . . . and scores of other fields. According to Leonard Sussman, 'I sat through much that was fascinating in the scientific and cultural realm. None of it was reported on.'[16] By contrast, there were 173 news and feature stories dealing with the debate over communications policy."[17]

The council found, third, that the press tended to focus only on the negative aspects of even those things that interested it. Thus, in a speech by Leonard Sussman lauding a program for technical assistance to Third World journalists, but warning UNESCO to shun press censorship, the only thing included in an AP account was his warning. And the fact that UNESCO adopted a modified version of a U.S.-proposed technology transfer plan to sharpen journalistic skills in the Third World "went almost unreported."[18]

A fourth finding was the media's tendency to focus on, and even create, conflict. Thus the News Council describes an AP story, which took one element from a report by U.S. delegate William Harley urging restoration of two features of an earlier consensus that did not appear in UNESCO Director-General Amadou-Mahtar M'Bow's proposals for a particular program, but AP put in Harley's mouth the language that M'Bow had "tampered with" the earlier language, and started its story with the statement that this devious action "brought closer an expected showdown between the West and Communist and Third World nations." Harley regarded M'Bow's proposals as generally "constructive," and he felt that his overall statement was supportive. The AP story, which Harley himself complained about, omitted mention of anything affirmative in the Harley report, while literally concocting its own negative stress and framework of conflict. A fifth finding was that media spot news was also highly selective, with attention closely geared to editorial concerns and biases. Thus, the greatest news coverage was given to a defecting Afghan delegate and his attacks on the Soviet Union; second most important was a speech by Yasser Arafat and an Arab bloc effort to expel Israel; and the third most important spot news was the re-election of M'Bow, with a focus on his role in the controversy over the NWICO.

Finally, the News Council found that alternative viewpoints were given little or no attention by the U.S. media. "Maximum attention was given to stories indicating that the West was being outmaneuvered on the freedom front and little space was given in most of these stories or in others reviewed in the survey to expositions of opposing viewpoints."[19] The News Council concluded that news coverage about UNESCO "was inconsistent with the spirit of detachment that is invariably set forth as the touchstone of sound news judgment. . . . The imbalance that characterized most of the Belgrade news coverage in the United States provided an inadequate foundation for independent judgment by U.S. readers of the correctness of the editorial positions their newspapers were taking on the UNESCO communications issue."[20] Significantly, and reinforcing these devastating findings, the News Council Report itself was almost entirely ignored in the press, and the National News Council soon died of financial attrition.[21]

The 1982 Paris Conference. A further study of U.S. press coverage of UNESCO proceedings was carried out by George Gerbner, dean of the Annenberg School of Communications of the University of Pennsylvania, in "The American Press Coverage of The Fourth Extraordinary Session of the UNESCO General Conference, Paris 1982."[22] The Gerbner study details quite similar lines of bias to those described in the report of the National News Council. Once again, there is an almost exclusive focus on communications issues, put into a simple-minded frame of conflict between the forces of freedom and those supporting "government control." Third World views were "glossed over" with very superficial and repetitive summary phrases, and the media gravitated quickly toward clashes and disagreements, while carrying any news of agreements less frequently and in "muted tones."[23] The conference was generally described as a "communications conference," and "no news story or editorial feature stressed any of the other 13 major programs that occupied much of the time and all but 5.3 percent of the final report."[24]

The tone of press editorials was not consistent with a fair and objective press. "As if in response to the press image of the meeting, a defensive, belligerent and often paranoid tone pervaded most editorials published about the conference. There was little recognition of American points of view other than that of the press and its trade associations and public relations spokespersons."[25] Gerbner stresses the extent to which the news coverage was independent of the actual events of the conference[26]:

> The press constructed a picture of the meetings more from selected speeches and prior information than from the actual resolutions and official actions of the conference. That construction showed a preoccupation with real and imagined threats to private control of the press to the virtual exclusion of other issues.

The Gerbner study explicitly notes the coincidence of the bias in news coverage and editorial opinion with the special interests of the press, which "selected, edited, and interpreted the news to fit their own interests which they presented as the national interest."[27]

The British press debate of 1980-1981. The bias shown by these earlier studies of U.S. press accounts of UNESCO activities is replicated in the press coverage of UNESCO in other Western countries. In a study of "British Press Reporting of the New World Information and Communication Order Debate 1980-1981,"[28] Y. Kondopolou, P. Schlesinger, and

C. Sparks found a pattern similar to that described by Raquel Salinas Bascur, the National News Council, and George Gerbner. Although this study was oriented specifically to press and communication issues, the authors note that this set of issues was the only thing involving UNESCO of any apparent interest to the British press. The framework for the British press, as was true in part in America, was the conflict between East and West, with the Third World a "pawn in the middle of the argument" (*London Times*, April 23, 1980); the West was regularly portrayed "as the object of hostile coalitions."[29] The struggle between East and West was allegedly about freedom of the press versus government control. Thus even in the preferred area of communication, the British press[30]

> gave attention only to a tiny range of the issues, and gave detailed and persistent attention to even fewer. The cluster of issues around news flows, press freedom, state control and censorship were the subject of frequent attention. Other issues . . . , for example the domination of world broadcast television production by industries located in a handful of developed countries, were not mentioned at all. Other issues of considerable importance, for example, cross-border data flows, satellite communications and radio spectrum allocation are mentioned infrequently.

The issues attended to by the British press were most closely related to "the sectional concerns of journalists," i.e., to press self-interest.[31]

Ideological bias entered British press coverage of UNESCO in other ways: most notably, in the use of code words to frame issues, what Kondopolou, Schlesinger, and Sparks call "opinion catalyzers," like "totalitarian," "Russians," "democratic values," and Seán MacBride's "Lenin Peace Prize," which "mobilize a more general body of beliefs and knowledge . . . precisely calculated to elicit a response within a definite and narrow range of political readings."[32] The authors point out that "it was rarely the case that arguments were spelled out with any degree of rigor or logic. Rather they were organized chiefly by means of these opinion catalyzers."[33]

The French press coverage of the Belgrade Conference. A study by Colleen Roach of "French Press Coverage of the Belgrade UNESCO Conference"[34] indicates that in France as well the biases of the Western media were blatant and inconsistent with their claims of fairness and objectivity. Roach shows that, once again, UNESCO is dealt with in a framework of East-West conflict, an alleged struggle between a free press and government control, and with non-Western views ignored or marginalized. Only one French news dispatch ever dealt with the work of UNESCO in a field other than communication. Those that did deal with communications were generally exceedingly superficial, with one-line definitions of the MacBride Report and a description of the International Program for the Development of Communications (IPDC) in which "the information provided was very limited."[35] On the MacBride Report, "Several dispatches and articles presented only the information that the Report 'had been severely criticized by much of the Western press . . . for being against free enterprise and in favor of government control of the press.' "[36]

Almost never did the French press actually quote from the MacBride Report in describing its contents. There was a heavy bias in favor of opinions of Western spokespersons on media issues, and a regular blackout of UNESCO official and especially Third World opinion, including some that "provided direct responses to certain points raised by Western spokespersons."[37] The dramatic defection of the head of the Afghan delegation and his denunciation of the Soviet Union was the subject of 28 articles. The French press stressed the alleged "politicization" of UNESCO, and unproductive ideological debates, but its own use of the Afghan defection was a premier illustration of self-serving politicization and "testifies to the East-West and basically anti-Soviet perspective adopted by much of the French press."[38] The defector was even given the floor to discuss his criticisms of the MacBride Report, precisely along Western-preferred lines. Roach summarizes her paper, as follows: "analysis of the French coverage of the UNESCO conference at Belgrade leads to the conclusion that only one side of the New International Information Order story is being told."[39]

NOTES

1. Rafael Roncagliolo, "New Information Order in Latin America: A Taxonomy for National Communication Policies," in Becker, Hedebro, and Paldan, p. 172.

2. In 1985, the median size of the two dozen largest mass-media firms in the United States was approximately $1.5 billion; median after-tax profits were in excess of $100 million. See Herman and Chomsky, chapter 1, Table 1. It may be noted that the Associated Press is not a profit-making company, but is cooperatively owned by a large number of media firms that it services, who *are* profit-seeking companies.

3. For the British experience, see Curran and Seaton, especially Part I; and Curran. On the United States, see Bagdikian; Barnouw.

4. Bascur, "News Agencies and the New Information Order," in Varis, Bascur, and Jokelin.

5. One recommendation of the conference was that the countries of Latin America try to develop a joint news agency, which would compete directly with AP. *Ibid.*, pp. 49, 53.

6. *Ibid.*, p. 72.

7. *Ibid.*, pp. 68–69.

8. *Ibid.*, p. 72. See also Landis.

9. Bascur, p. 71.

10. *Ibid.*

11. *Ibid.*

12. Raskin, p. 165. Raskin was the associate director of the National News Council, and his article quotes generously from the council's report, which he wrote.

13. *Ibid.*, p. 166.

14. Quoted in the original National News Council "Report on News Coverage of Belgrade UNESCO Conference," March 6, 1981, p. 4.

15. *Ibid.*

16. Quoted in National News Council Report, p. 4.

17. *Ibid.*

18. Raskin, p. 167.

19. National News Council Report, p. 15.

20. Raskin, pp. 173–74.

21. Leonard Sussman and his organization, Freedom House, were also penalized for Sussman's harsh criticism of the media's handling of UNESCO issues [see below, under Sources]. Usually a staunch supporter of U.S. policy, Sussman deviated markedly in this one case. Freedom House's contributions fell off sharply as a result, and the organization was obliged to move to smaller and cheaper quarters.

22. This work, sponsored by UNESCO, was reproduced in mimeographed form in August 1983, but has not yet been published.

23. *Ibid.*, pp. 21–22.

24. *Ibid.*, pp. 23–24.

25. *Ibid.*, p. 39.

26. *Ibid.*, p. 38.

27. *Ibid.*, p. 39.

28. Mimeographed, June 1985. This is an unpublished report to UNESCO.

29. *Ibid.*, p. 17.

30. *Ibid.*, pp. 17–18.

31. *Ibid.*, p. 20.

32. *Ibid.*, p. 25.

33. *Ibid.*, p. 26.

34. *Journal of Communication*, Autumn 1981, pp. 175–87.

35. *Ibid.*, p. 179.

36. *Ibid.*, p. 177.

37. *Ibid.*, pp. 183–84.

38. *Ibid.*, p. 186.

39. *Ibid.*, p. 187.

II. AN ANALYSIS OF U.S. MASS-MEDIA TREATMENT OF THE U.S. WITHDRAWAL FROM UNESCO

This study of the media's coverage of the U.S. withdrawal from UNESCO is based directly on two sets of data: One is a sizable sample of news articles from the print media; the other is a fairly comprehensive collection of transcripts and videotapes of network television coverage of the withdrawal. Included in the sample of print media are 215 articles that comprise the entire published news coverage of the withdrawal by *The New York Times*, *The Washington Post*, Associated Press,[1] *Time*, *Newsweek*, and *U.S. News & World Report*, for the period extending from

June 1, 1983 to January 31, 1985. I also use on occasion in this study the opinion and commentary items published by *The New York Times* and *The Washington Post*, including editorials, letters, and opinion columns, although the primary focus here is on "news." There were fifteen news items on the withdrawal during our time period on the various network evening news programs, including a UNESCO segment on the CBS-TV News program "60 Minutes" on April 22, 1984, which was the most extended treatment of the subject on network TV.[2]

Also examined for background was the coverage of the withdrawal in the nonestablishment press of the United States,[3] and assorted foreign newspapers and news magazines, which gave a sense of what kinds of alternative sources, frames, and facts the U.S. mass media might be neglecting. Even more important for purposes of this study was an examination of the underlying documentation in journals, books, theses, and government hearings, and reports that provided the material potentially available to the media as sources and for background and story context. From either the foreign press or a volume of hearings, for example, one would have been able to read the testimony of the one strong dissident in the 1981 House Foreign Affairs joint hearing to review U.S. participation in UNESCO, Dr. Hamid Mowlana, a professor of international relations at American University.[4] In the *Journal of Communication* Mowlana himself states:

> Most interesting was the fact that the major U.S. media covering the hearings, including the *Washington Post*, the *Washington Star*, and the *New York Times*, ignored my testimony. Ironically, I had to read the coverage of my own statement not in the local newspapers but in the *Times* of London. The *Times*'s story from Washington by its correspondent, Nicholas Ashford, varied so drastically from American coverage that he appeared to be covering an entirely different hearing.[5]

This points up important features of media coverage that are examined in detail below. The media pick and chose their sources in ways that fit their preconceived ideas of what is important and relevant. These choices, their bases of selection, and their consequences are amenable to scientific inquiry. In the sections that follow these matters are treated under the following rubrics: A. Sourcing. B. Premises, Frames of Reference, and Agendas. C. Ideological Language and Tone. D. Rewriting History. E. Programmatic and Management Deficiencies: Misrepresentations and Suppressions. F. Portrayal of the New World Information Order and Threat to a "Free Press." G. The Non-Correctability of Error. H. Non-Disclosure of Corporate Interest.

A. Sourcing

It is a common observation among media analysts that bias may be struc-

TABLE 1. Sources Used in Print Mass Media* News Coverage of the U.S. Withdrawal from UNESCO

Sources	(1) New York Times and Washington Post		(2) Associated Press		(3) (1) + (2)		(4) Three National News Magazines**		(5) (3) + (4)	
	#†	%	#	%	#	%	#	%	#	%
U.S. government	110	38.7	107	43.1	217	40.8	15	45.5	232	41.1
Support withdrawal	(105)	(36.9)	(100)	(40.3)	(205)	(38.5)	(14)	(42.4)	(219)	(38.8)
Oppose withdrawal	3	(1.1)	5	(2.0)	8	(1.5)	(1)	(3.0)	9	(1.6)
Unknown	2	(0.7)	2	(0.8)	4	(0.8)	–	–	4	(0.7)
Other Western officials	64	22.5	45	18.1	109	20.5	8	24.2	117	20.5
Support withdrawal	(33)	(11.6)	(22)	(8.9)	(55)	(10.3)	(4)	(12.1)	(59)	(10.4)
Oppose withdrawal	(13)	(4.6)	(15)	(6.0)	(28)	(5.3)	(4)	(12.1)	(32)	(5.7)
Unknown	(18)	(6.3)	(8)	(3.2)	(26)	(4.9)	–	–	(26)	(4.6)
Heritage Foundation	8	2.8	3	1.2	11	2.1	1	3.0	12	2.1
Freedom House	1	0.4	1	0.4	2	0.4	–	–	2	0.4
Soviet Union	5	1.8	10	4.0	15	2.8	–	–	15	2.7
Third World	14	4.9	9	3.6	23	4.3	–	–	23	4.1
Support withdrawal	(6)	(2.1)	(2)	(0.8)	(8)	(1.5)	–	–	(8)	(1.4)
Oppose withdrawal	(4)	(1.4)	(4)	(1.6)	(8)	(1.5)	–	–	(8)	(1.4)
Unknown	(4)	(1.4)	(3)	(1.2)	(7)	(1.3)	–	–	(7)	(1.2)
UNESCO officials	59	20.8	55	22.2	114	21.4	5	15.2	119	21.1
Other	23	8.1	18	7.3	41	7.7	4	12.1	45	8.0
Support withdrawal	(4)	(1.4)	(6)	(2.4)	(10)	(1.9)	(3)	(9.1)	(13)	(2.3)
Oppose withdrawal	(13)	(4.6)	(7)	(2.8)	(20)	(3.8)	(1)	(3.0)	(21)	(3.7)
Unknown	(6)	(2.1)	(5)	(2.0)	(11)	(2.1)	–	–	(11)	(1.9)
Totals	284	100	248	100	532	100	33	100	565	100

*The mass media used here, as shown at the column heads, are *The New York Times, Washington Post,* Associated Press, *Time, Newsweek,* and *U.S. News & World Report.*

**Time, Newsweek,* and *U.S. News & World Report.*

†For purposes of this table, sources are counted only once per article, even if used in several different paragraphs. For a different way of counting, see Table 2.

tured, or "built-in," by the media's choice of and relationships with their primary sources of information.[6] Because the mass media need a steady flow of credible information they tend to attach themselves to govern-mental and corporate agencies that provide a large volume of official "news." This "law of bureaucratic affinity"[7] gives powerful sources a special edge in supplying information, and allows them to "manage" the media, by the careful timing of releases to maximize exposure and minimize time for checking claims, and by providing a steady flow of documents and allegations that make good copy. "News management" is especially effective where the media are in agreement with the government's line, in which case the government can carry out a full-fledged propaganda campaign, with the media serving as conduits and supporters.

Alert, independent, and unbiased media would not allow themselves to be "managed" and would not play a supportive role in a propaganda campaign. They would check out claims carefully, would explore the *real* bases of actions and not accept nominal reasons at face value, and would search out contending sources and documents and give them full value. When they found that they had been misled, they would disclose this fact, make amends, and learn a lesson from the experience.

That the U.S. mass media did not engage in such enterprising and unbiased inquiry in connection with the U.S. withdrawal from UNESCO is clearly evident in their use of sources. To demonstrate this I will describe first the overall pattern of sourcing and then show how bias in sourcing manifested itself in several important illustrative cases.

Overall picture of biased sourcing. The sources relied on by the media may be counted in several ways. If a source is cited several times in a single article, we can count it once per article, once per theme per article, or as many times as the source is used, paragraph after paragraph. The same possibilities exist for tracing sources used in a radio or television broadcast, or transcript.

In Table 1, the sources are counted only on a conservative once-per-article basis, for all 215 news articles on the UNESCO withdrawal which appeared in six important mass-media outlets—*The New York Times*, *The Washington Post*, Associated Press,[8] *Time*, *Newsweek*, and *U.S. News & World Report*—between June 1, 1983 and January 31, 1985. The sources are divided into seven important categories, and two are shown with subdivisions to distinguish between sources that supported or opposed the U.S. withdrawal. On this basis, it may be seen that Western officials were the dominant sources for the mass media, accounting for 61.8 percent of the source totals, and even more (69.7 percent) in the case of the three national news weeklies. If we break down these numbers according to whether the sources supported or opposed the U.S. withdrawal, 57.2 percent were pro-withdrawal, 35 percent were op-

TABLE 2. **Sources Used in Twenty-Two Articles on the U.S. Withdrawal from UNESCO by Paul Lewis in** *The New York Times*, **1983-85**[*]

Sources	Number of Times Cited	Percentage
U.S. officials	75	26.1
British officials	13	4.5
French officials	3	1.1
German officials	2	0.7
Anonymous Western officials	100	34.8
Other anonymous critics of UNESCO	6	2.1
Western documents critical of UNESCO	15	5.2
Mr. Amadou M'Bow	32	11.2
Other UNESCO sources	30	10.5
Soviet officials	8	2.8
Other	3	1.0
Total	287	100.0

[*]An identified source is counted once for each paragraph in which the source is cited.

posed, and the remainder were not classifiable one way or the other.[9] This might appear to be only moderately unbalanced, with substantial representation to opposing sources. But this ignores the question of attention and prominence within articles, the role of UNESCO and Soviet sources in the pat-tern of coverage, and the almost total exclusion of sources representing fundamental criticism and major alternative views.

Table 2 shows the distribution of source citations in twenty-two articles on the UNESCO withdrawal written by Paul Lewis, *The New York Times*'s main reporter dealing with this topic, giving value in this case to each repetition in the use of a source within the articles.[10] Lewis tends to use his favored sources intensively and his less favored ones in brief counterpoints to his main themes; this is the general pattern in our media sample. The table shows the great dependence of this *Times* reporter on official Western sources, which account for 70.5 percent of his citations.[11] It can also be seen that anonymous and therefore unverifiable sources—all supportive of the U.S. charges and line of attack—account for 35.9 percent of the aggregate citations. We will see in the next section that Lewis (and the mass media in our sample in general) works within a set of premises and frames that are coordinate with his source selection.

Table 3 describes the sources used in fifteen network TV news broadcasts on the withdrawal, with sources used more than once in a program counted for each separate sequence of use or separate theme developed. It can be seen that the huge dependence on Western official sources in TV coverage is almost identical with that for the Lewis articles in Table 2. The TV programs rely more openly on U.S. officials and less fre-

TABLE 3. **Sources Used in Fifteen Network Television News Stories on the U.S. Withdrawal from UNESCO**

Sources	Number of Times Used[*]	Percentage
U.S. officials	33	53.2
Anonymous Western critics of UNESCO	9	14.5
Soviet defector	1	1.6
Soviet official	1	1.6
UNESCO-U.N. officials	9	14.5
U.S. Commission for UNESCO members	2	3.2
Other defenders of UNESCO	7	11.3
Total	62	100.0

[*]A source is counted once for each sequence of remarks that pursue a single question or theme.

quently than Paul Lewis on anonymous sources, although these are still significant in number and more frequently vague ("some say," "some observers say," "has been charged," "questions have been raised," "its critics say"), whereas Lewis more reliably cites "western diplomatic sources."

The substantial UNESCO and (to a lesser degree) Soviet representation as sources in these tables is misleading and exaggerates the balance that might be read from the raw numbers. UNESCO sources are rarely used to expound new ideas or to explore issues of their own choice. In a great majority of cases the citations to UNESCO personnel are terse, and they are placed in a defensive mode in which they are corroborating or denying allegations of Western critics. Typical citations are: "In the interview, Mr. M'Bow denied United States assertions that 70 percent of UNESCO's total budget of $188 million is spent in administrative expenses, although he did not provide an alternative figure" (Lewis, *New York Times*, December 31, 1984); "Some African and other third world nations also appear to be distancing themselves from Mr. M'Bow, who has said repeatedly he will not resign before the end of his term in 1987" (Lewis, December 1, 1984); "At a news conference today, the agency's Deputy Director, Gerard Bolla, said UNESCO 'intends to repay' the money, which has accumulated in a special fund." (Lewis, September 13, 1984).[12] In two of the nine network TV encounters with Director-General M'Bow, he was asked whether he might not resign, and in every other reference to a UNESCO official as a source, the questions were directed to allegations of malpractice (see the process in blatant form in the appendix analysis of the "60 Minutes" program on UNESCO).

The representation of Soviet sources is also misleading as evidence of media balance. Because Soviet officials are not credible to the U.S. public, their regular deployment as spokespersons by the U.S. press is often a tactic of trying to discredit a disfavored person, institution, or idea by negative association. Instead of having the NWICO defended by one of its many Third World spokespersons, or by a Western media analyst, the U.S. press prefers having a Soviet official give it his approval. This helps put it in an East versus West or Cold War symbolic framework, which substitutes for any discussion of substance. This is facilitated by the fact that media accounts of what the Soviets have to say are usually caricatures and involve distortion in one way or another.[13]

Although, according to U.S officials and press leaders, the threat of a NWICO was the greatest evil posed by UNESCO, people who supported it were frozen out of the mass media during the period of withdrawal. It can be seen on Table 1 that Third World opponents of the U.S. withdrawal comprised a negligible 1.4 percent of media sources. And they do not show up at all in the Table 2 and 3 listing of sources used by Paul Lewis of *The New York Times* and network TV news. Apart from UNESCO and Soviet officials, most of the opponents of the withdrawal used as media sources were present or former Western officials and scientists and educators involved with UNESCO. The general view of these opponents of the withdrawal was that while the U.S. charges had much merit, UNESCO had value and the United States should fight for reform from within.[14]

Whatever debate over the withdrawal occurred in the mass media— and I will show that it was extremely thin even within its own constrained orbit of tolerable opinion—the Third World opposition that supported the demands of the UNESCO majority was not allowed to participate.[15] When David Shribman of *The New York Times* asserted that "Both sides [sic] on the issue agree that UNESCO has become increasingly political in the last decade" (December 17, 1983), his concept of "both sides" was confined to Reaganites and "reformers"—spokespersons for the NWICO and their sympathizers were not a "side," they were invisible.

Lack of investigatory zeal: the State Department "action memo" and U.S./UNESCO policy review. Despite the pattern of dominance of official sources, and the exclusion of basic critics of the official line, it might still be hoped that the press would at least look carefully at government claims and maintain a modicum of alertness to the possibility of government manipulation of evidence. The mass media did not serve as watchdogs in the case of government management of the exit from UNESCO; on the contrary, they gave every appearance of being quite lazy lapdogs.

At the time of the initial announcement of U.S. withdrawal in December 1983, it was stated by top administration officials that the decision had been based on an extensive State Department review, which showed that membership in UNESCO "damaged" U.S. interests, that UNESCO could not be changed by U.S. policy, and that the United States "receives few benefits" from membership.[16] All of the major U.S. media repeated the State Department line of accusations, as well as the claim that the withdrawal was based on what *Time* referred to as "a six months intensive review" (January 4, 1984), but they were all satisfied to accept the State Department handouts without insisting on a copy of the report for their own inspection.

On January 23, 1984, the London *Guardian* published a story by Harold Jackson, which quoted from an "action memo" put up by the State Department's Gregory Newell, describing a coordinated plan for managing the media to build support for the withdrawal, which included extensive off-the-record briefings of governments, politicians, and press, and an effort to obtain the private placement of pro-withdrawal articles and letters in the press. On February 4, *Editor & Publisher* ran an editorial "Pressure by State Department" and a lengthy article entitled "Government wages UNESCO campaign," which contained extensive quotes from the "action memo." The editorial castigated this effort as "worthy of the commercial efforts of the lowliest huckster for a product or politician," and it went on to state that

> It indicates complete lack of faith in justification of an executive decision and the necessity, therefore, to drum up public support for the position. In order to do this, of course, articles must be planted and newspapers must be used to give the appearance of a spontaneous reaction, albeit phony.

A British paper first broke the news about this manipulative campaign, and *Editor & Publisher* discussed and criticized it, but the U.S. mass media did not see fit to discuss this matter in print at any time. When asked by *Editor & Publisher* whether the State Department had approached *The Washington Post* about placing an article on the withdrawal, and about the government media strategy, Meg Greenfield, the Op-Ed editor of the *Post*, stated that "The fact that they would be doing this is not a surprise. It's standard operating procedure for government these days."[17] But the failure of the mass media to uncover, report, and comment on this press campaign deserves several comments. First, the media's concern over UNESCO stressed the threat of "government control." If government manipulation is "standard operating procedure these days," isn't this a manifestation of the kind of evil the press claims to be interested in and that a free press is supposed to be protecting the public against? Second, when UNESCO itself hired a public relations firm in 1984 to present its side of the case, *The Washington Post* devoted two entire news articles to this subject. Their reporter, Lena Sun, even quoted State Department spokesman John Hughes: "We find it an interesting commentary on UNESCO's performance that an organization under criticism from so many quarters is taking this approach to winning public support."[18] Why was UNESCO's PR effort newsworthy and that of the State Department not? Could it be that because the *Post* supported the withdrawal it suppressed derogatory information about a PR campaign supporting withdrawal, and publicized the one opposing it?[19]

Equally important as their revelation of the "action memo" was the disclosure of the London *Guardian* article of January 23, 1984 and the *Editor & Publisher* article of February 4, 1984 that in their announcement of the U.S. withdrawal, Reagan administration officials had lied about the findings of the "six months intensive review" and the *contents* of the State Department report. In fact, the original report, which the media had never seen, stated that the findings "do not provide a clear, unequivocal answer" to the question of the desirability of withdrawal, which "must be based on several key political judgments." An article in *Newsday* by Roy Gutman on January 27, 1984, entitled "Pro-UNESCO Report Failed to Sway U.S.," noted that the internal study pointed to positive political trends in UNESCO, including the finding that controversy over communications issues had "receded," and to the fact that "the great majority" of UNESCO programs "promote general U.S. policy values." Gutman pointed out that "none of [Newell's] conclusions [as set forth in his "action memo"] appears to be drawn from the internal review."

Here again, the mass media failed to uncover the facts for themselves, and when they were disclosed by others, the dominant media did not even report the story, even though they had transmitted the false claim that the withdrawal had been "based on" an intensive six-month internal review. Their failure to develop the story in the first place shows a remarkable lack of enterprise, since the claims about the report had been made under suspicious circumstances that should have aroused a live watchdog. For example, at a December 16, 1983 meeting of the U.S. National Commission for UNESCO, Under-Secretary of State Lawrence Eagleburger was asked whether the members couldn't see a copy of the document on the basis of which a decision was allegedly being made. Eagleburger demurred on the ground that the report was moving through the decision-making process and "the decision-makers ought to be able to deal with that report on its merits," independent of "external pressures."[20] This was misleading and dubious in principle. Newell's memorandum to Shultz urging withdrawal had actually been finalized two days earlier, and as *Newsday*, the London *Guardian*, and *Editor & Publisher* pointed out, the administration's problem was that they had made a decision independent of and unsupported by the "merits" as developed by their own review. Furthermore, that the government should exclude the press and public from consideration of a report till *after* a decision had been made should have aroused the ire and curiosity of a press devoted to the free flow of information. But the mass media not only lacked initiative, they didn't even feel obliged, after the material was dug up by others, to correct misinformation which they had earlier provided the public as "news."

Again, the contrast with the media's aggressiveness in pursuing documents at UNESCO is striking. In September 1984 an internal report critical of UNESCO's operations was leaked to the media, who not only wrote it up in considerable detail, but gave prominence to the fact that UNESCO was not making the leaked document public. UNESCO officials were pressed on the subject, with ironical quotes attributed to Director-General M'Bow that making the document public "only gets in the way of finding a solution" to problems.[21]

When the State Department finally released its internal report on February 27, 1984, the mass media, now apprised by their smaller rivals that they had been misled and had transmitted false information to the public, failed even then to use the release to shed new light on State Department tactics and the substantive issues involved in the U.S. withdrawal. The release passed unnoticed; the free flow of information was constrained by a combination of bias and self-censorship.

Source selectivity: Harries versus Whitlam. Two Australians, Owen Harries and E. Gough Whitlam, spoke and wrote a great deal on UNESCO and the withdrawal issue. Whitlam was the Australian ambassador to UNESCO in 1984 and a former prime minister of Australia. Harries, a former Australian academic of no great distinction, who had served earlier as a member of the Australian delegation to UNESCO, became affiliated with the Heritage Foundation during the period of the withdrawal controversy. Whitlam was a critic of the U.S. (and British) withdrawal; Harries was a strong supporter. Harries, with far fewer qualifications than Whitlam, and whose commentary on UNESCO consisted largely of confident assertions and invective, was the non-official authority on UNESCO most frequently cited by the U.S. mass media. He was helped along by the fact that his views were pushed by Heritage, which had money, media contacts, and close ties to the Reagan administration. But the mass media were still, in principle, free to choose, and, in principle, adherents to objective and impartial news-making. But by another strange coincidence they latched on to the man whose views coincided with the official, and their own editorial, position on UNESCO.

Harries was given Op-Ed column space in *The New York Times* and was cited as a credible authority on at least ten separate occasions in *Times* news articles and commentaries; Whitlam was mentioned once, as follows:[22]

A former Australian Prime Minister, Gough Whitlam, accused the United States Ambassador to Unesco today of helping a "destabilization and disinformation campaign" to persuade Britain to withdraw from the agency.

An American spokesman, Franklin Tonini, asked for reaction to Mr. Whitlam's criticism of Ambassador Jean Gerard, said, "I am not going to dignify his absurd remarks with any comment." Mr. Whitlam is Australia's permanent delegate to Unesco.

The article is, of course, lacking in substance, confining itself to a general accusation by Whitlam and an indignant response by the other side. In a number of speeches in Europe and Australia, unreported in the U.S. mass media, Whitlam gave significant details that would have made his general accusations credible and worthy of discussion. He pointed out that during the very week she was participating in Executive Board discussions in Paris on "reforming" UNESCO, U.S. Ambassador Jean Gerard made a series of secret trips to London to join Owen Harries in lobbying the British press and political elite in support of British withdrawal from UNESCO. This was done unbeknownst to the Western officials with whom she was working in Paris. Whitlam gave details on the meetings, described the intensive campaign that followed in the British press, and showed how closely its arguments and formulas followed those which had appeared in the U.S. press during the previous year.[23] These details, plus the many other important observations that Whitlam made in his speeches, were blacked out by the *Times*.

An article by Michael Dobbs in *The Washington Post* of January 1, 1984 ("U.S. Quits UNESCO"), gave Whitlam somewhat more attention, with three short paragraphs toward the end of a long article, followed by two paragraphs of defense by Jean Gerard that completely evade the issue. At least Dobbs mentions the fact that Gerard left the Executive Board meetings in Paris to lobby in London, and that a press campaign followed. But Whitlam is only paraphrased, the many telling details that give life and substance to his claims are missing, and no inferences are drawn directly or by asking questions. Gerard's reply is given in two direct but unresponsive quotations (in one, Gerard says that Mrs. Thatcher was "perfectly capable of pursuing an independent policy toward UNESCO" without being influenced by the United States). In any case, the three short paragraphs exhaust the *Post*'s mention and use of Whitlam as a source. Harries was used at least half a dozen times, featured more prominently, and without the juxtaposition of somebody's contesting views.

The U.S. National Commission for UNESCO's press conference of August 8, 1984: The media refuse to discuss the issues. As suggested by the media's handling of Whitlam, it is possible for the press to give nominal value to a source but effectively to suppress it. This is most likely to happen when the source expresses opinions or raises issues that conflict with the premises and frames which the media bring to a subject. One of the most important features of media coverage of UNESCO was its consistent superficiality, which was notable even when the media were dealing with congenial sources and topics.[24] When faced with threatening sources and issues, superficiality attained new heights, based on a lack of understanding of the novel thoughts being expressed and perhaps also a deliberate desire to obfuscate and suppress.

The U.S. National Commission for UNESCO's press conference of August 8, 1984 provides an outstanding example of how the media used a source with impeccable establishment credentials,[25] which offered the media fresh data, and discussed the central issues involved in the withdrawal in a compelling and provocative way, but which disagreed strongly with the State Department (and media editorial) line. The media treatment of this press conference was so superficial and trivializing as to amount to *de facto* suppression. The commission went to great pains to make its voice heard. It held press conferences in both New York City and Washington, D.C., and made a strong effort to get the major media to attend (and 25-30 persons attended the New York meeting). Leonard Sussman of Freedom House and Edmund J. Hennelly, a Mobil Oil executive and head of the U.S. Delegation to the 1983 UNESCO General Conference, were among the leaders of the New York press conference who spoke and answered media queries. The commission also distributed at the press conference its own 30-page paper entitled "What Are the Issues Concerning the Decision of the United States To Withdraw from UNESCO?," which raised a series of major questions that were discussed in detail with argument and evidence.

The press conference was made even more newsworthy by the fact that Leonard Sussman made a dramatic attack on the State Department withdrawal campaign and on the qualifications of its leadership. Among the points Sussman made at the press conference were the following (an asterisk means that the point summarized here never made it into the mass media)[26]: (1)* The campaign against UNESCO did not begin in June 1983, as the administration has claimed, "but when David Stockman, just before the administration assumed power, struck UNESCO from the U.S. budget," and continued in 1982 when the administration, "without consultation and explanation, completely removed from the Federal budget all funds for the U.S. National Commission for UNESCO." (2)* The anti-UNESCO program is only part of a larger anti-U.N. campaign. (3)* Newell was not a provider of information on the issues but "manager of an ideological program." (4) The irrelevance of substantive issues in the decision to withdraw is indicated by the fact that not one of 83 State Department missions abroad or 13 nongovernmental organizations responding to the State Department supported withdrawal. (5)*U.S. performance at UNESCO has been apathetic and uninformed. (6)* Newell, the manager of the withdrawal operation, never finished college, spent two years overseas as a Mormon missionary, and subsequently was active in Mr. Reagan's political campaign. (7)* The United States will pay only some $25.8 million to UNESCO this year (1984) because of a currency readjustment, and 40 cents of every dollar paid to UNESCO returns to the United States. (8) The U.S. National Commission was informed only four days before a deadline of a request from the director-general of UNESCO for U.S. suggestions for new programs and budget. (9)* The Secretariat of UNESCO was "actually lobbying on behalf of U.S. proposals" in the last UNESCO General Conference.[27] (10)* No UNESCO document contains support for censorship or the licensing of journalists. (11)* The Israeli government is worried about the effect of a U.S. withdrawal, and Israeli delegates came up to Sussman and other U.S. delegates at the last General Conference and said "please do not withdraw."

The Washington Post gave the press conference and paper on "What Are The Issues . . . " far less attention than it did UNESCO's hiring of a public-relations firm to present its case to the U.S. public. The single, back-page article by Lena H. Sun noted that the 30-page report by the commission "challenges in detail the U.S. basis for withdrawal," but of her eleven paragraphs only a single one specifies any detail provided in the report. Sun notes the commission members' finding that UNESCO is no more politicized than are other international organizations, and she gives one fact: that disarmament studies make up less than 1 percent of UNESCO's education outlays. That's it. Meanwhile, four substantial paragraphs are used to give a rehash of the usual administration formulas of "unacceptable politicization," monitoring panels being established,[28] and the fact that the GAO is investigating UNESCO spending. Thus a great deal of new information never reported in *The Washington Post* is bypassed in favor of official "background" that is repeated in article after article.

The New York Times did almost as poorly in a background article on the back pages by Richard Bernstein (" 'Distortion' Laid to U.S. On Unesco," August 9, 1984). Bernstein manages to repeat in three separate paragraphs that UNESCO needs reforming, and he gives the full litany of the administration's position spread over two paragraphs that absorbs a quarter of the article's space. An additional two paragraphs at the end give the State Department's reply to the press conference and extensive report whose contents are summarized in six short and sketchy paragraphs. Bernstein does get in some of the Sussman-commission criticisms on misleading tactics, distortion of facts, the administration's disregarding of recommendations from 83 missions and 13 government departments, and administration bad faith in failing to consult with the commission before the withdrawal. This is done in very general terms, however, and only the figures on the ignored recommendations are put forward from among the scores of hard facts that Sussman and the commission's report offer.

Not *Time, Newsweek, U.S. News & World Report,* or network TV news ever mentioned the press conference or commission report. Associated Press put out a report on this event as superficial as those of the *Post* and *Times,* with the same proportionate allotment of space to a rehash of the official position and the State Department's reply to the report.[29] In short, the opportunity for debate on the issues provided by a highly respectable establishment source was not taken advantage of by the mainstream press. A great majority of the issues raised and new facts provided were ignored, and were not allowed to be made available for public consideration. The commission's valiant effort made no dent in the established, and continuously repeated, propaganda line offered.[30]

NOTES

1. The Associated Press does not "publish" articles, but the 86 AP releases in our set, published by various newspapers, represent virtually all AP output covering the withdrawal in our time frame.

2. This program is analyzed at some length in Appendix III.

3. Included here are *The Nation* (New York), *The Texas Observer* (Austin), the *Guardian* (New York), and *In These Times* (Chicago). See Table 4 and the associated text for some illustrations of their differences in coverage from the mainstream press on UNESCO-related issues.

4. Ashford; *Review of U.S. Participation in UNESCO*, in House Foreign Affairs Committee Subcommittee on International Organizations Hearings, July 19, 1981.

5. Mowlana, p. 139.

6. See Sigal; Tuchman; and Fishman.

7. Fishman, p. 143.

8. As noted earlier, AP is a wholesaler of news to retail outlets.

9. This count includes as "pro-withdrawal" all the subtotals so designated, plus Heritage. "Anti-withdrawal" includes the anti-withdrawal subtotals, plus Freedom House, the Soviet Union, and UNESCO officials.

10. Source repetition is counted on a paragraph-by-paragraph basis.

11. While Lewis is a remarkably biased reporter, as will be made clear below, I do not think this tabulation would be substantially different if applied to the Associated Press or the other media included in our sample.

12. In the section below on Noncorrectability of Error we will see that this was a contrived propaganda ploy engineered by the State Department and carried out by Paul Lewis and *The New York Times*.

13. As an example, an article by Paul Lewis in *The New York Times* of September 27, 1984 is headlined "Soviet to Fight Any Changes in Unesco," but within the article itself it is noted that "the Soviet Union said it favored making Unesco more efficient and had 'a number of wishes and views regarding improvements in Unesco's work.'" Thus it is admitted that the Soviet Union favored changes, but not "in association with crude pressure," and not those particular ones favored by the United States. The headline transmutes this into Soviet opposition to "any" change!

14. The typical opponent of withdrawal would begin with "we're not happy with UNESCO either" (James Holderman, of the U.S. National Commission on UNESCO, on NBC Nightly News, December 26, 1983), before giving the pragmatic grounds for remaining.

One exception was former U.N. Ambassador Donald McHenry, interviewed by Connie Chung on the "Today Show" on December 30, 1983. Chung asked McHenry a series of questions that accepted every Reaganite premise, but McHenry refused to give a single response that fit Chung's formulas. For McHenry, the withdrawal was wrong, the message conveyed by Reagan was of a refusal to accept diversity and multilateral institutions, the UN is not ineffective and its debates are not without value, and the inefficiency of UNESCO is a red herring. McHenry was the only person in our sizable mass-media sample who suggested comparing the Pentagon's and UNESCO's waste. The cognitive dissonance between McHenry and Connie Chung was complete.

15. This applied to opinion and commentary as well as to "news."

16. According to Gregory Newell, the assistant secretary of state for international organizations, "A summary of our assessment of the proposed action, following upon the review described earlier [i.e., the U.S./UNESCO Policy Review], is . . . Membership in UNESCO damages . . . interests of the United States . . . cannot change [UNESCO] . . . . [The United States] receives few benefits. . . . " Quoted in Roy Gutman, "Pro-UNESCO Report Failed to Sway U.S.," Newsday, January 27, 1984.

17. Quoted in the Editor & Publisher article cited in the text.

18. "UNESCO Hires Public Relations Firm to Fight Withdrawal Plan," August 17, 1984.

19. The New York Times also suppressed information on the "action memo," and published an Associated Press report describing the UNESCO PR effort, with a denunciation of this nefarious UNESCO action by Edwin Feulner, head of the Heritage Foundation. ("Unesco Foe Seeks Money," New York Times, October 20, 1984.)

20. "Policymaking Process: The Case of the Revolving Report, or Who Peeped at the Purloined Pages," Chronicle of International Communication, January-February 1984, p. 46640.

21. Richard Bernstein, "Staff Report Criticizes the Way Unesco is Run," New York Times, September 7, 1984; "UNESCO report not made public," an AP report, published, among other places, in the Register, Mobile, Alabama, on September 28, 1984.

22. "Australian Accuses U.S. Envoy," New York Times, November 27, 1984 (Reuters).

23. Extensive details were given by Whitlam in a London speech April 13, 1985, before the General Council of the United Nations Association of Great Britain and Northern Ireland. This speech is set forth in Appendix IV.

24. For a telling case and illustration, see the analysis of Ed Bradley's "60 Minutes" program on UNESCO in Appendix III.

25. The U.S. National Commission for UNESCO was established by law to serve as a liaison between UNESCO and its programs and the major U.S. organizations "interested in educational, scientific, and cultural matters," and it was also designed to advise the secretary of state on issues pertaining to UNESCO. Its 60 organizational members run the gamut from the National Academy of Sciences to the Young Women's Christian Association. Its members are prestigious, and many are exceptionally familiar with UNESCO's activities.

26. The quotations are from the commission's report on the press conference.

27. This point was made at the press conference by Ambassador Edmund Hennelly.

28. Neither Lena Sun nor any other mass-media commentator ever bothered to explain why a monitoring panel was established by the Reagan administration in 1984 to follow changes implemented in UNESCO, given the fact that a U.S. National Commission for UNESCO was already in existence and well suited to serve this function.

29. The AP report ended with a quote from Alan Romberg of the State Department, regretting that the commission focused on disputing the withdrawal instead of discussing "how to eliminate the serious faults in UNESCO which all of us agree need correction." Tribune, South Bend, Indiana, Aug. 9, 1984. This statement implies that the withdrawal was a constructive effort to remedy UNESCO's defects and that the State Department was really interested in reform proposals. The fact that the commission was never consulted in time to *advance* reform proposals—a point made in the commission press conference and report—contradicts this hypocritical statement. AP's coverage of the press conference was so poor, however, that such State Depart-

ment propaganda could be given without embarrassment in an article reporting on the press conference—a testimony to truly atrocious newsmaking.

30. *The New York Times* did allow some modest letter and Op Ed column space to Sussman, Hennelly, and other establishment opponents of the withdrawal, and to UNESCO officials. (See, however, The Noncorrectability of Error, below.) *The Washington Post* did less well in allowing opinions differing from the editorial-news slant to reach its readers. These ten to a dozen Op-Ed and letter rebuttals in these two papers taken together, often specialized replies to specific allegations, were overwhelmed by the greater number of strident, pro-withdrawal editorials and Op-Ed columns, plus the vast outpouring of "news." An excellent discussion of the overall huge bias of syndicated columnists on the withdrawal issue is provided in C. Anthony Giffard, *Through a Lens Darkly: Press Coverage of the U.S. Withdrawal from UNESCO*, Longman-Annenberg, forthcoming, chapter 8.

B. Premises, Frames of Reference, and Agendas

Media objectivity may be compromised not only by biased sourcing, but also by the uncritical use of patriotic and self-serving premises and frames of reference. The latter determine the questions that the media deem relevant and the facts they seek and use. There is a close connection between sourcing, on the one hand, and premises and frames of reference, on the other. Dominant sources have their own preferred frames and agenda, which they try to impose on the media, and the media themselves seek out sources that fit their own conceptions of relevance.

In the case of the U.S. withdrawal from UNESCO, the primary source of information, the U.S. government, and the mass media had no serious disagreements, and, accordingly, the premises, frames, and agenda of the government and media were substantially identical.

The premises: U.S. benevolence, the free press as an unequivocal good. One set of assumptions by U.S. officials and the mass media we may designate "the patriotic premises." These are that the United States and its leaders are benevolent, rational, and honest. On these assumptions, when U.S. leaders speak, their words can be taken at face value as reflecting real motives and intentions—there are no hidden agendas and deceptions to which one has to be alert. It is sometimes acknowledged that U.S. policy is not always disinterested, but when this is so it is generally assumed that U.S. interests coincide with world interests. What's good for the United States is good for the world.

This identity of interest is illustrated by the government-media formulation and treatment of the other major premise relevant to the discussion of the U.S. withdrawal—namely, that a "free press" is an unequivocal good. Essentially, a "free press" in this perspective is a commercial press not subject to government constraint. It was postulated without discussion that a free press so defined was good for everybody, and "government control" was bad. Thus an open door to U.S. advertising and media investment and sales was coincident with "everybody's" interest, and not just that of the U.S. media and corporate system. This constitutes a blatantly ideological and self-interested set of definitions and premises, but the mass media rarely departed from it in discussing the issues connected with the U.S. exit from UNESCO.

The government-media frames of reference. Two frames of reference can be observed in media portrayals of the issues in the withdrawal, derived from these premises and from traditional Cold War ideology. The dominant frame is the litany of charges against UNESCO leveled by the State Department. The second frame is that of the Cold War struggle between the United States and its allies and the Soviet bloc, with the latter engaging in divisive political activities and trying to manipulate the Third World, while the United States is benevolent and constructive. As Paul Lewis expresses it, the West "had hoped to eliminate divisive political programs . . . and to concentrate Unesco's remaining funds on practical measures to help poor countries."[1]

The dominant frame was fixed by the initial U.S. charges made at the time the withdrawal was announced. In the words of State Department spokesman Alan Romberg, the decision had been made because "Unesco has extraneously politicized virtually every subject it deals with, has exhibited hostility toward the basic institutions of a free society, especially a free market and free press, and has demonstrated unrestrained budgetary expansion." The key words in the usual formulations were politicization, mismanagement, and threat to a free press. This is obviously an accusatory frame in which those doing the accusing are implicitly pursuing a just course against perpetrators of bad things. Nevertheless, the frame was appropriated by the mass media without the slightest qualm of doubt and immediately fixed their agenda. In 175 of the 215 news articles in our sample (81.4 percent), one or more of these three charges was featured, frequently all three together, and the charges were featured in 12 (86.7 percent) of the 15 network TV news programs on the subject. They are almost always introduced in a rote repetition of the State Department claims. Typical language is that used by Romberg above, which was repeated intact in six different *New York Times* articles. A briefer format is that "the United States has asserted that the organization had become too politicized, had repeatedly demonstrated its hostility to market economies and press freedom, that its budget was excessive and that the organization was top-heavy with bureaucrats."[2] The charges are often dragged in even where they are irrelevant to the story. In a December 9, 1984 article addressed to the GAO report on UNESCO management, the *Times* provides a long quote which presents the entire gamut of U.S. charges, although only the question of mismanagement is addressed in the GAO report itself. Similarly, in a rare article describing scientists' claims of the value of UNESCO programs, Walter Sullivan interrupts to throw in a long paragraph explaining why the United States is leaving UNESCO, quoting once again the rhetorical language of Romberg.[3]

The essence of propaganda is repetition, and the formulaic reiteration of the U.S. charges allegedly underlying the U.S. withdrawal fits this essence perfectly. Figure 1 shows the formula actually pinned under a photo in *Time* magazine to reinforce the propaganda image.

All ten of the articles on the U.S. withdrawal published in the national weekly newsmagazines centered on the trilogy of charges, and the words do not vary much or depart from the official formulation. In eight of his twenty-two articles in *The New York Times*, Paul Lewis used approximately the same language to reiterate his ideological expression of the NWICO: "This is a code inimical to Western concepts of a free press that would acknowledge governments' right to control the press and set up an international licensing system for journalists as well as a code of press conduct, both administered by the Unesco Secretariat."[4]

The third important feature of the media's formulaic repetition of the U.S. charges is that they are presented as if true, not as assertions by an interested and biased source. The media do not feel obligated to treat them as unproven claims; on the contrary, they are often put forward directly as truths—thus "the United States is withdrawing to protest budget mismanagement and the politicization of its programs," not "alleged" mismanagement and politicization.[5] When expressed through conduited quotes from the State Department, the media defense is that the U.S. withdrawal, and charges levied as the basis of the withdrawal, are themselves important news; reporting them without comment is therefore "objective." This is not a tenable defense where the uncritical repetition of serious charges implies their veracity and will instill that belief. Such practice is never followed in reference to allegations critical of the powerful. As was pointed out in the previous section, Whitlam's criticisms, in addition to being buried and emasculated, were immediately rebutted by establishment sources; and the same process was applied to the U.S. National Commission's attempt to raise issues. Furthermore, the formulas used in the repetitive charges are loaded with negative symbolism and ideologically biased. Paul Lewis's portrayal of the NWICO is an almost comic illustration of ideological loading,[6] but he repeats it without challenge as fact.

The uncritical reiteration of the frame of U.S. charges did three things: (1) it established the truth of the allegations in advance; (2) it put UNESCO on the defensive, having to respond to the assertions of the presumed benevolent and apolitical Reagan administration; and (3) it fixed the agenda of issues.

The second frame used by the media placed the withdrawal issue into the context of the Cold War conflict. As was noted in the previous section, the press uses the Soviet Union as a source far more than Third World spokespersons for a NWICO. This is partly a function of the press

Paper Torch

Suspicious fires at UNESCO

If timing is truly everything, a series of fires at the Paris headquarters of the United Nations Educational, Scientific and Cultural Organization (UNESCO) last week was right on schedule. Relations between the U.N. agency and the U.S. have deteriorated steadily over what the U.S. has felt to be a consistent anti-Western bias on UNESCO's part. Citing waste, mismanagement and abuse of UNESCO's $374.4 million budget, 25% of which the U.S. provides, President Reagan announced in December that the U.S. would pull out of the agency by the end of this year unless UNESCO's performance changed substantially. To help make a final determination, Congress asked a team of investigators from the General Accounting Office to examine UNESCO's internal operations.

The first blaze started in the archives area of the concrete-and-glass building and spread quickly through dozens of offices on seven floors, destroying tons of documents and causing some $640 million in damage. Even as it was being brought under control, several smaller fires broke out in other parts of the building. Those blazes were contained, and there were no injuries. After determining that large quantities of a flammable liquid had been splashed on walls throughout the building and finding several unused crude paper torches, investigators quickly blamed the fires on arsonists. UNESCO Director-General Amadou Mahtar M'Bow of Senegal called for a full investigation of what he termed "a criminal act." Said he: "I am asking everyone to do all they can so that we can find out the reasons for the fire and the identities of the person or persons at the root of this."

Although the authorities had no firm leads, suspicion spread just as quickly as the blazes. Many UNESCO staff members thought that someone inside the organization had hoped to destroy potentially embarrassing documents. Precisely what sort of records was hard to say, given the long list of complaints against the agency. Many Western nations have strenuously objected to its politicization under M'Bow. In 1975 Soviet bloc and Third World nations provoked a walkout by the U.S., Israel and ten other Western nations when they voted to equate Zionism with racism. The same majority has been trying to use UNESCO to muzzle the press through proposed programs such as the licensing of reporters and the establishing of a code of conduct for journalists. Western nations have also accused UNESCO's bloated bureaucracy of preferring the comforts and generous tax-free salaries of Paris to the rigors of the underdeveloped nations they profess to serve.

Yet if last week's fires were designed to eliminate troublesome records, the arsonists apparently failed. According to UNESCO officials, most documents of interest to the GAO investigators and to a separate team of British auditors who were to do a routine check of the agency's books were stored in areas untouched by the flames. Moreover, copies of documents that were destroyed are readily available in departmental offices. ∎

A policeman inspecting damaged archives

Politicization, waste and mismanagement.

Figure 1. *Time* magazine article from April 2, 1984.

interest in drama and conflict, but it is also a way of scoring cheap political points for the side the media favors. By quoting Soviet Prime Minister Yuri Andropov in favor of M'Bow, the Soviet Union in support of a NWICO, and Soviet accusations against the withdrawal as a political maneuver, the press uses the established symbolism of good and evil to denigrate individuals and positions that it opposes, without having to address substantive issues.

The propagandistic quality and application of this tactic is well illustrated by Paul Lewis's article "Soviet, at Unesco Conference, Urges Press Curbs" (October 26, 1983). According to Lewis's anonymous Western sources, the proposals in the form of draft resolutions constituted a "major drive" by the Soviet Union, and "it now appeared that there would be a major confrontation over the issue." Without going into the biased description of the substance of the Soviet resolution and the issues as portrayed by Lewis, we may note three facts. One is that there were hundreds of resolutions introduced at this conference, of which Lewis and *The New York Times* picked out the one fitting the framework of Cold War conflict (and the U.S. charges). Second, Lewis and the *Times* suppressed the fact in this article and subsequently that when the Soviet resolution was circulated, Director-General M'Bow attached to it a critical comment that amounted to a repudiation. This doomed the resolution and contradicts Lewis's dire prediction of an imminent major conflict (which never ensued). The *Times* was regularly critical of M'Bow, and to have noted his role in defeating the Soviet resolution would have weakened the image of Soviet dominance, a "Third World-Soviet collective" dear to the heart of the right wing, and the desired negative view of M'Bow. The suppression is thus understandable, though obviously inconsistent with objective news coverage. A third point of interest is that after the Soviet draft resolution was killed, the fact was never reported to readers of *The New York Times*.

Alternative frames. If the mass media had used different frames, other issues would have surfaced and facts that the media ignored would have become relevant. It would have been possible, for example, for the media to have focused on the U.S. withdrawal as a right-wing ideological and political project, fostered by the extremist Heritage Foundation and reflecting the anti-humanistic, aggressive, and unilateralist tendencies of Reaganism more generally. In this frame, the media would have addressed different topics. Among others: (1) they would have been skeptical of the administration's alleged interest in "reforming" UNESCO and looked closely at the Heritage Foundation's (and right-wing's) more generalized attack on the United Nations system; (2) they would have explored the connection between the UNESCO exit and the repudiation of the Law of the Sea treaty, the administration's refusal to be bound by the decision of the International Court of Justice on its covert operations against Nicaragua, and its arms buildup; (3) they would have drawn the analogy between the exit and reduction in funding of UNESCO programs, generally addressed to the needs of the world's poor, and the drastic cutbacks in programs for the less affluent within the United States; (4) they would not have repeated with patriotic naïveté the administration's statements that they were going to "redouble" their efforts in other international organizations to compensate for the withdrawal from UNESCO,[7] and they would have followed up on these claims, which were not realized (unbeknownst to the public)[8]; (5) they would have raised questions about the contradiction between the administration's and Heritage Foundation's alleged concern over the free flow of information abroad and their actions and plans for closing down the free flow of information within the United States[9]; and (6) they would have been alert to the manipulative aspects of the withdrawal. The media never used this alternative frame, and as shown throughout this chapter, the issues and agenda that it suggests as relevant were largely ignored.

Another alternative frame would have been a critical Third World view of the issues involved in the NWICO. The communications literature is replete with portrayals of the NWICO as a phase of decolonization, activated in the 1970s by the Third World's majority status and temporary relative prosperity, along with recognition of the difficulty of carrying out development programs—and even achieving or maintaining independence—without an independent communications system. A country that is trying to mobilize its population to sacrifices, including restrained consumption and high rates of saving, while maintaining its cultural and political integrity, would be greatly impeded in that effort by the free flow of consumerist messages and the integration of its elites into the world market.[10] Awareness of these problems was heightened by the development of satellite communications, the rapid occupation of satellite space by the developed countries, and the possibilities of direct beaming of satellite messages to local populations from foreign agents, independent of local institutions and authorities.

In the alternative models reflecting Third World positions, there is a serious conflict of interest between the developed countries and their transnational corporations and Third World countries striving for independent growth. In fact, looked at from the standpoint of the developed countries, independence and autonomous development in the LDCs are *threats* to the transnational corporations, who want to invest, advertise, and sell goods, and move corporate messages across borders without constraint. Their "transnational project" supporting free flow is in serious conflict with real "decolonization," which requires some degree of distance and protection from economic-political domination by technically advanced great powers.[11]

Frames reflecting such alternative models were entirely avoided by the U.S. mass media, although coherent, readily available from numerous sources, and in the case of the "decolonization" models representing the underlying position of numerous supporters of the NWICO. The use of some version of a "decolonization-transnational project" model would have raised a number of questions that the mass media ignored. For example, such frames would have made it difficult to avoid discussing the considerable U.S. corporate and media interest in an open door, whereas the patriotic frame allowed the media to portray the struggle as one between high principle and "government control."

Premises, frames, and agendas. The choice of premises and frames has an enormous impact on what is selected as news. For example, the patriotic premises of the benevolence and honesty of the U.S. leadership immediately pushed important questions *off* the media agenda. We saw in the previous section that the media did not see fit to look closely at the State Department's U.S./UNESCO Review, or examine its manipulative strategies in "selling" its plan to exit from UNESCO. The public-relations effort of UNESCO was newsworthy, but not that of the State Department. Similarly, the motives and qualities of UNESCO officials were subject to frequent mention and disparagement, but the qualities and qualifications of the State Department officials managing the withdrawal were not newsworthy.[12]

Many qualified commentators, including the authors of the GAO reports of 1979 and 1984 on UNESCO, stressed the heavily "political" character of U.S. appointments to UNESCO, and the short tenure and other weaknesses of the U.S. delegation, as important reasons for U.S. frustrations and ineffectiveness. There is much evidence of incompetence and mismanagement in the withdrawal effort as well.[13] In his press conference of December 29, 1983, Gregory Newell, assistant secretary of state in charge of international organizations, and the man shepherding the withdrawal, showed that he was not even aware of the fact that UNESCO's budget was on a biennial rather than annual basis.[14] Jean Gerard, whose main qualification for the UNESCO ambassadorship appears to have been her important role in "Women for Reagan" in the 1980 political campaign, distinguished herself on the job by the absence of a germ of constructive effort and by a steady stream of ideological and petty jabs at UNESCO and its officials. For the press, however, since U.S. officials are presumed to be honest and competent professionals, the qualifications and performance of Newell and Gerard were off the agenda.

According to William Safire, "the professionals at the State Department have sent a tough withdrawal recommendation to the President."[15] This referred to Newell and the other political appointees with links to the Heritage Foundation—ideologues who actually pushed the "professionals" in the State Department into the background, over-riding the remarkably favorable consensus of opinion on UNESCO from the embassies and consulates. The Safire reference to "professionals" stood uncontested, however, and conflict within the administration on the withdrawal as well as the manipulative tactics used in its implementation remained unmentioned, given the premises of benevolence, rationality, and honesty.

Similarly, if the U.S. official position was that the administration was interested in the "reform" of UNESCO, the media were not about to suggest that this might be a misrepresentation of actual intent (which would imply dishonesty and a hidden agenda). As Francis Clines says, "The question Mr. Reagan is considering is how best to seek policy changes in Unesco: by continuing as a major participant, or by applying greater pressure on the agency with notice of withdrawal."[16] If the administration says that this is the question Reagan is considering, that claim is taken as a truth. The alternative, that Reagan is using a nominal interest in reform to make an exit based on ideological and political considerations more palatable, does not arise for the press, except as a suggestion by hostile and untrustworthy forces. Michael Dobbs says that "M'Bow's attempts to depict Washington's move as motivated by frustration with the loss of political power rather than by real concern for the way UNESCO is run have met with some success in Third World circles."[17]

Dobbs never discusses whether or not M'Bow's alleged charges have substance, and he misleads his readers by implying that the view attributed to M'Bow is not also held by respectable sources in the West—for example, Leonard Sussman of Freedom House charged that the exit was based on ideology, not a zeal for reform. In fact, both the U.S. National Commission for UNESCO and the House Foreign Affairs Committee Staff Report of January 1985, among others, pointed out that the administration never did anything helpful to reforming UNESCO either before or after the announcement of withdrawal: it didn't circulate an agenda of reform to its allies before its announcement, it failed to ask the U.S. National Commission to help formulate a reform program, and it never put up reform proposals in time to have affected UNESCO actions during the year of exit.[18] These points were very rarely allowed to surface in the mass media, and they were never drawn together into an intelligible package, because this would have suggested bad faith, systematic deception, and a hidden agenda on the part of the administration.

The frames used by the media dominated their news selections more comprehensively. I have shown this already in describing the mass media's overwhelming use of the dominant frames, but it can be seen in another striking way and with more detail in Table 4, which is organized according to topics that "fit" the dominant frames and those that do not.

Those that fit are shown on lines 1-8, as "on the agenda," whereas topics that are off the agenda for the U.S. government, but which are impor-

TABLE 4. **Mass Media and Dissident Press Coverage of Issues On and Off the Government Agenda in the U.S. Withdrawal from Unesco**

Agenda Status	Coverage in 215 News Articles in Mainstream Press[*]		Coverage in 15 TV Network Programs		Coverage in 7 Articles in Dissident Media[2]	
	#	%	#	%	#	%
On the Agenda						
1. Politicization	87	40.5	10	66.7	1	14.3
2. Deviation from original purpose	21	9.8	3	20.0	2	28.6
3. Mismanagement	133	61.9	12	80.0	—	—
4. Threat to free press	88	40.9	6	40.0	2	28.6
5. Licensing of journalists	25	11.6	1	6.7	2	28.6
6. New World Information Order	28	13.0	1	6.7	4	57.1
7. Communist and Third World Domination of UNESCO	46	21.4	3	20.0	—	—
8. U.S. Monetary Contribution to UNESCO	95	44.2	13	86.7	—	—
Off the Agenda						
9. Explanations of meaning of "politicization"	—	—	—	—	2	28.6
10. Previous U.S. use of UNESCO for political purposes	4	1.9	1	6.7	2	28.6
11. Withdrawal as refusal to accept majority rule	2	1.0	1	6.7	2	42.9
12. The Reagan administration's rejection of the Treaty of the Sea	2	1.0	—	—	2	28.6
13. Withdrawal as a project of and sop to the U.S. right wing	1	0.5	—	—	3	42.9
14. Withdrawal from UNESCO as the Grenada of multinational organizations	1	0.5	1	6.7	2	28.6
15. The manipulative withdrawal campaign of the State Department	—	—	—	—	1	14.3
16. Corporate and media self-interest in NWIO issues	3	1.4	—	—	2	28.6
17. Criticisms of media record in covering UNESCO	—	—	—	—	3	42.9
18. U.S. neglect of UNESCO and appointment of political hacks as a cause of difficulties	1	0.5	—	—	1	14.3
19. Reagan-Thatcher restraints on the free flow of information	—	—	—	—	2	28.6

TABLE 4. **Continued**

Agenda Status	Coverage in 215 News Articles in Mainstream Press[*]		Coverage in 15 TV Network Programs		Coverage in 7 Articles in Dissident Media[2]	
	#	%	#	%	#	%
20. Substantive discussion of NWIO issues	4	1.9	1	6.7	4	57.1
21. Quantitative data on actual UNESCO programs	5	2.3	—	—	2	28.6
22. Comparisons of UNESCO budget with needs	—	—	—	—	1	14.3
23. Comparison of UNESCO budget with that of Pentagon	—	—	1	6.7	1	14.3
24. Distinction between UNESCO debates and proposals actually passed	—	—	—	—	2	28.6
25. Limits on UNESCO powers to implement proposals	—	—	—	—	1	14.3
26. UNESCO criticisms of Soviet Union on human-rights issues	—	—	—	—	1	14.3
27. Systematic murder of journalists in U.S. sphere of influence	—	—	—	—	1	14.3

[*]See text for inclusions.
[2]The articles were distributed as follows: *The Nation,* 3; *In These Times,* 1; *The Guardian* (New York), 2; *The Texas Observer,* 1.

tant from the standpoint of the alternative frames referred to earlier, are listed on lines 9–27. The columns provide a basis for comparison of the coverage of these items by the mass media in our sample of 215 news items and 15 network TV news broadcasts, and by 4 nonestablishment publications in the United States that addressed the issues involved in the U.S. withdrawal from UNESCO.

The table displays clearly the huge preoccupation of the establishment media with the government charges, and their incessant repetition of the formulas and symbols associated with the government's (and media's) frames and agenda. If we look down to the off-the-agenda items, we can also quickly see not only the extent to which the media screened out context and alternative perspectives, but also how superficially they dealt with issues. For example, while "politicization" was heavily featured by the media (line 1), we can see on line 9 that not a single media article explained the meaning of the word, and only a handful referred in any way to the fact that the United States had used UNESCO for political purposes in prior years (line 10).[19] From the standpoint of a more critical frame, in which the withdrawal was part of a conservative political project of wider ramifications, other administration actions such as the rejection of the Treaty of the Sea, the express hostility to majority rule where the votes were going the wrong way, and the administration's manipulative propaganda campaign would be highly newsworthy. Arguably these and related matters provide important context to the withdrawal from any but a strictly propagandistic perspective. We can see, however, that for the U.S. mass media these topics were almost entirely suppressed (lines 11–15).

We may note also that while the press focused heavily on alleged UNESCO mismanagement and waste (line 3), and on the size of the U.S. contribution to UNESCO, it presented minimal comparative information that might have made these assertions and numbers meaningful. Discussions of the costs of actual UNESCO programs appeared in only 5 of 215 articles and none of the TV programs, so that media audiences would have had no basis for evaluating either the absolute or relative importance of major and disputed UNESCO activities.[20] If the United States gave UNESCO $50 million a year, how did this compare with the needs serviced by that organization's programs, and how did it compare with the Pentagon budget (which *increased* by 1,840 times the aggregate U.S. contribution during the first four Reagan years)? It can be seen in lines 21 and 22 that these issues were muted or suppressed in the mass media, but not in the non-establishment press.

Similarly, when discussing the NWICO and the alleged threat to a free press, the mass media almost never mentioned their own conflict of interest in dealing with the issue (line 16, and section H below), and they never once mentioned past criticism of their own reporting on UNESCO (line 17). The irony of exits from UNESCO carried out by Reagan and Thatcher on the grounds of hypothetical threats to the free flow of information, when those two leaders seemed to be aggressively constraining the free flow of information in their own countries, was never mentioned in our establishment media sample (line 19 and section F). Nor did this media sample ever address the murder of large numbers of journalists in the Western sphere of influence, or attempt to explain the exceptionally low-key and non-indignant treatment of this phenomenon by the Western press (line 27 and F), in contrast with their preoccupation with and indignation over the threats posed by the NWICO.

One non-establishment publication had a discussion of the sometimes sharp criticisms of Soviet human-rights violations in UNESCO (line 26),[21] a point never made in our mass-media sample, in which Soviet attempts to constrain the growth of UNESCO's budget were also rarely mentioned. These facts would interfere with the mass media's attempt to portray the issues in terms of an East/West conflict or a Soviet-Third World alliance against the West. We should note also how the media places off the agenda the distinction between debates in UNESCO and proposals actually passed by that organization (line 24 and section F).

They also never discuss the extremely limited powers of UNESCO to implement resolutions actually passed (line 25 and section F). Ignoring these matters allows the press to inflate the "threat" to the "free press," and makes their disregard of the actual killing of journalists even more anomalous.

The anti-UNESCO, anti-M'Bow propaganda campaign of 1984. Throughout the year that followed the U.S. announcement of withdrawal in December 1983, the mass media carried a steady stream of critical reports on alleged UNESCO mismanagement and corruption. The media's performance in this year of exit fits well a model of a propaganda system. For one thing, the reporting focused almost exclusively on one of the central U.S. charges justifying the withdrawal. UNESCO had been of little interest to the media before December 1983, and after the U.S. and British withdrawals were consummated the media returned to their almost total unconcern with that organization. But during the year of exit the media focused on UNESCO's failings, and precisely in the terms desired by the government managers and other proponents of withdrawal.

Second, a large fraction of the charges reported by the press were leaked by U.S. government officials or were based on documents or actions of the government.[22] The stream of government releases, press conferences, and leaks never suggested to the establishment media that these were being orchestrated as part of a propaganda campaign. The claims and speculation about "corruption" just "surfaced," inexplicably for the media. Nor did they ever suggest the possibility that the purpose of the stream of charges of mismanagement and corruption might be to justify an action decided on entirely different grounds.

Third, just as it never seemed suspicious to the media that the "smoke" was being produced by the party making the charges, they also tended to interpret the steady flow of probes and allegations against UNESCO and its officials as indicating that the charges were valid. James Bitterman of NBC-TV News was so aggressive in suggesting that "there must be pretty good proof that these charges [of corruption] are real," that even Congressman James Scheuer, a leader in the attack on UNESCO, was pushed into pointing out that the charges he and others had been making "would not hold up in a court of law," and that it was inappropriate to make any "prejudgments" before the forthcoming GAO inquiry.[23]

Fourth, an important mechanism for creating smoke is the aggressive hunt for people who are dissatisfied with an individual or organization. With over 3,000 employees at UNESCO, an aggressive and wealthy "free press," and powerful governments trying to make a case that there was abuse, there should have been no trouble in finding individuals with supportive tales. In 1984 the search was on, and the media produced a steady stream of complaints (despite an alleged "climate of fear") supporting the official charges. The media gave the floor to numerous Western officials and to named and anonymous Western critics of UNESCO, a large fraction of whose stories and charges were speculative and based on unidentified sources, and who did not hesitate to use extremely strong language denouncing UNESCO and its leadership, much of it in anticipation of the results of investigations not yet completed. Most of the anti-UNESCO charges were petty, and a great number were untrue.[24]

Finally, the media failed to follow up on their speculations and name-calling. The word "corruption" was bandied about frequently before the issuance of the GAO report of 1984, with strong hints that that investigation would yield a bonanza on the subject, and there was much speculation on what would happen *if* corruption were uncovered. But when the GAO report failed to sustain any such claims, and the charges of M'Bow's financial irregularities were never confirmed, the media never offered a final assessment or apologies. Neither did Congressman James Scheuer, who had stated on national television on March 2, 1984 that "one thing I can assure you is that all the facts will come out" in the GAO investigation, and that "all allegations should be put to rest." The allegations were never "put to rest." Scheuer and the media had scored their propaganda points, and left it at that.

In an early phase of the propaganda campaign, Scheuer, then head of a House Subcommittee on Science and Technology, arranged with UNESCO Director-General M'Bow to cooperate with a GAO inquiry into UNESCO finances. Although Scheuer had previously displayed considerable hostility toward UNESCO, he, Newell, and Gerard were the primary sources used by the mass media, and their judgment that UNESCO was irretrievably corrupt was reported often. The media were pleased to discuss at length the motives of UNESCO officials in relation to the proposed investigation, although their only material was derogatory speculations. An example is Michael Dobbs's article in *The Washington Post* of March 2, 1984, which, in citing the UNESCO agreement to allow the GAO to investigate, refers to Scheuer having a "commitment in writing" (implication: we have to nail down these wily foreigners), and quotes unnamed "diplomatic observers" who see M'Bow's agreement to a congressional investigation as "a calculated gamble to defuse growing criticism" (derogatory speculation, and as usual no hint that the "growing criticism" could be part of a propaganda effort of a powerful government, with the aid of *The Washington Post*).

Apparently reacting to the overt hostility by Scheuer and the U.S. media, UNESCO officials insisted that they would cooperate in the GAO inquiry only if the U.S. executive branch requested this. This amounted to "going formal" and requiring that the United States proceed through the established channels. This led Walter Pincus of *The Washington Post* to cite other anonymous officials to the effect that this was "a deliberate delaying tactic by M'Bow, who is seeking to defend himself against charges of political bias and misappropriation of funds."[25] Not once did Dobbs or Pincus suggest that the attacks on M'Bow could have been based on motives other than the search for truth, whereas M'Bow's motives were subjected to repeated derogatory speculation.

In this period of negotiations and dispute over the GAO investigation there were also a series of unattributed claims of "financial irregularities" on the part of the "controversial," "wily," "autocratic" M'Bow. He was alleged to have hired his brother-in-law as personnel director of UNESCO, to have fixed himself up with a 28 percent salary increase in a time of financial stringency, of arranging for a rent-free penthouse apartment, and for having "sought reimbursement from UNESCO for thousands of dollars in food, hotel and travel expenses already paid for by other organizations,"[26] and assorted other charges.[27] The allegations regarding the brother-in-law and the 28 percent salary increase were outright falsehoods, but the reader of the press would have had to be extremely acute to note the admissions of error.[28] The apartment arrangement dated back to M'Bow's appointment a decade earlier and was defended by the UNESCO official then in charge of administration as follows: "The personal installation of the director-general at the UNESCO headquarters was justified by obvious security reasons. The problem was discussed in a perfectly transparent way in front of the headquarters committee without any objections."[29] The charge about thousands of dollars of reimbursement "sought" by M'Bow was made, denied, and the point was never again referred to in the media. When the GAO investigation was arranged, Paul Lewis (March 1, 1984) quoted "western diplomats" as saying that the inquiry would seek to find out about "corruption." When the report was completed, Lewis says (September 21, 1984) that "although the report does not list any instances of corruption, it depicts a top-heavy, inefficient organization with no effective spending controls." This is a rather back-handed way of acknowledging that a serious charge was not validated; Lewis can't even wait for another sentence to continue his critical barrage. In *The Washington Post*, Walter Pincus had used the unproven corruption charge to raise the question of what would happen *if* the charges were validated in the GAO report. He cites Scheuer asking U.S. Ambassador Gerard "if she believed that a majority of the organization's members would want 'a change at the top' if allegations of corruption were proved by the GAO investigators. 'It's possible,' Gerard replied, 'and I hope that would be the case.' "[30] This is a rather full exploitation of unproven charges, and contrasts revealingly with Pincus's and *The Washington Post*'s later failure to mention, let alone apologize for, their full play on "corruption" without evidence, when the GAO report finally became available. This is "hit-and-run" as well as propagandistic journalism.

Scheuer heard a "rumor" that documents were being shredded at UNESCO. These rumors were highly newsworthy in the mass media. On March 21, 1984 there was a fire at UNESCO headquarters in Paris. This provided a new spate of rumors that fed nicely into the propaganda framework. All the media covered the fire, reiterated the usual propaganda formulas about the "problems" with UNESCO, and hinted that perhaps the fire had something to do with the forthcoming GAO investigation.[31] *Time* magazine headed its April 2 article "Paper torch: Suspicious fires at Unesco," waiting till the last sentence to note that "moreover, copies of documents that were destroyed are readily available in departmental offices."

Later in the year, other documents that provided a basis for attacks on UNESCO were produced, leaked, and given prominent attention by the mass media; others that were more critical of the withdrawal position were given short shrift, including a Staff Report of the House Foreign Affairs Committee (unmentioned in the press), and the U.S. Commission study of "What are the Issues . . . ," whose treatment was described in the previous section. The mass media did not provide a debate on the issues; their incessant focus on and uncritical support of the administration charges against UNESCO during 1984 was a propaganda campaign, not objective newsmaking.

NOTES

1. "Soviet to Fight Any Changes in Unesco," *New York Times*, December 27, 1984.

2. E. J. Dionne, Jr., "Soviet Assails U.S. Decision to Pull Out of Unesco," *New York Times*, May 5, 1984.

3. "Some Scientists Protest Plan to Leave Unesco," May 29, 1984. Although the heading stresses "some" scientists protesting the exit, implying perhaps a significant division among the scientists, the text says that "the only speaker" at the meeting to support the U.S. withdrawal was Jean Bergaust, the deputy assistant secretary of state.

4. "Unesco Receives U.S. Pullout Notice," December 29, 1984. The NWICO is not a "code," and its administration was not to be located in the UNESCO Secretariat, except in the ideological constructions of Paul Lewis and the Western press. As William H. Melody and Rohan Samarajiwa point out, the NWICO came into existence "as a general manifesto or petition of complaint on international communication issues formulated by Third World countries. There is no firm, accepted definition of the NIIO, not even agreement on what it is to be called." "Canada's Contradictions on the New International Information Order," in Becker, Hedebro, and Paldan, pp. 160–61.

5. "Andropov assails U.S. on Unesco," February 1, 1984 (no byline). We may note also the typical assumption that the claimed reasons for withdrawal were the real reasons.

6. See footnote 4, and the sections below on Language and the NWICO.

7. Bernard Gwertzman quotes Newell on our "redoubling" of effort (*New York Times*, December 30, 1983), and Jonathan Friendly cites Newell uncritically and to the same effect in the *Times* under the heading "U.S. Says Unesco Withdrawal Will Not Cause Aid Reduction," May 9, 1984. The press never looked at the trend of education aid outlays, never mentioned the reduction in money to IDA, an "efficient" organization under U.S. control, which as Klaus Hufner and Jens Naumann point out "clearly reveals the ideological core of the confrontation." "Unesco: Only the Crisis of a 'politicized' UN Specialized Agency?," p. 10.

8. The House Foreign Relations staff report of January 1985 pointed out that "to date, the administration has not provided Congress with a plan of alternatives for UNESCO to promote international cooperation in education, science, culture and communications. The committee has received no supplemental request for alternatives to UNESCO for 1985." *Assessment of U.S.-UNESCO Relations, 1984*, p. 6. Leonard Sussman reacted to the Reagan administration claims of new inputs that would replace those lost by withdrawal as follows:

> I am reminded of the pledges the U.S. has made repeatedly in the field of communications. In 1976 at UNESCO we promised $25 million—never given. Repeated $25 million in 1978—never given. Pledged $150,000, then $300,000— not a dollar ever given. And now we pledge $850,000 but fulfillment remains to be seen. (Speech on the U.S. withdrawal before the International Committee of the Public Relations Society of America, April 12, 1984.)

This speech and the facts related here were ignored by the press. Subsequently, a senior Foreign Service officer, Allen Greenberg, stated that "the administration zeroed out the entire post-UNESCO exercise in its fiscal year 1986 budget submission." "Impasse? The U.S. Stake in Third World Telecommunications Development," *Journal of Communication*, Spring 1985, p. 46. An informal memo from William Harley, a State Department communications consultant, dated July 1, 1986, notes that administration "good intentions" were "dashed by the overriding concern with the budget deficit," and that the administration's fiscal 1987 request for UNESCO-related items was $2.3 million. As far as the American public knew, however, the Reagan administration had "redoubled its effort."

9. See Section G below.

10. See Felix, "Economic Development: Takeoffs into Unsustained Growth"; Felix, "Interrelations Between Consumption, Economic Growth and Income Distribution in Latin America Since 1800: A Comparative Perspective."

11. See the two papers by Felix cited in the previous footnote; also, Argumedo, pp. 179–88.

12. See the section on Ideological Language and Tone, and Tables 5 and 6 below, for contrasting designations of U.S. and "hostile" officials.

13. This is discussed in the previously cited House Foreign Affairs staff report, which says, among other things:

> In advancing several proposals at the September Board, the United States appears not to have adequately consulted its friends. . . . The U.S. Ambassador surprised the Board by saying it intended to call for an Extraordinary Session of the Executive Board to begin on November 8, to discuss the draft GAO Report on UNESCO. The U.S. delegation appears to have conducted little or no prior consultations . . . in Washington or with our Western allies on the timing, agenda or cost of an Extraordinary Session. The United States did not follow the UNESCO procedure to request a special session that provides for sending a letter with six signatures to the Chairman of the Executive Board to request an Extraordinary Session. The Belgian Representative "saw no point in discussing a Report that did not exist." . . . the GAO Report was still in draft. . . . Customarily international meetings do not consider national reports. Such reports are circulated for information purposes.

This critique goes on to point out that the Executive Board had already discussed many of the GAO points, also made by the temporary committee, and that the director-general had announced various reforms he planned to initiate. "Thus, it was unclear why the United States wanted to call an extraordinary session to discuss the GAO Report exclusively, particularly since the GAO Report made no observations on politicization of program content, a principal U.S. concern." *Assessment*, op. cit., pp. 20–21.

14. Off-the-Record Briefing, December 29, 1983, p. 8. For other aspects of Newell's record that suggest a political-ideological appointment based on no qualifications, see Sussman's remarks, above.

15. "The New Order Changeth," *New York Times*, December 25, 1983.

16. "State Department Bids Reagan Act To Leave Unesco," *New York Times*, December 24, 1983.

17. "U.S. Quits UNESCO," *Washington Post*, January 1, 1985.

18. As the staff report notes, the proposals finally put forward by the State Department focused heavily on "reform" of voting procedures, which would weight voting according to financial contribution. This proposal was radical, was a reform of power relations only, and was politically unrealistic. See *Assessment*, pp. 19–22.

19. U.S. "politicization" of UNESCO is described below under Rewriting History, and more fully in William Preston's historical account above.

20. This is discussed further under Programmatic and Management Deficiencies in the text below.

21. Garcia, *The Texas Observer*, February 10, 1984 (an interview with Estéban Torres, a former U.S. Ambassador to UNESCO).

22. Another significant contributor to the supply of charges was the Heritage Foundation, which was in a close alliance with the Reagan administration in propagandizing the case for withdrawal.

23. "Today Show," March 2, 1984.

24. See further, sections E and G below, and Appendix III.

25. "Administration Expected to Back UNESCO Probe," *Washington Post*, March 15, 1984.

26. *Ibid.*

27. Most of these were about allegedly questionable uses of funds from particular accounts or in violation of rules in allocating funds, not personal aggrandizement. Some of these allegations are discussed in E and in Appendix III.

28. See the section below on Non-Correctability of Error.

29. Jacques Rigaud, Letter to the *Wall Street Journal*, May 8, 1984. Rigaud notes that the United States had no management complaints whatsoever during his tenure as administrator, including any about M'Bow's quarters.

30. "GAO Probes UNESCO Corruption Charges," March 9, 1984.

31. No mass-media organization suggested the possibility that the fire, which had no effect on documents relevant to the investigation, might have been started by somebody who would recognize that the Western media would treat it as a likely attempt at a UNESCO coverup.

C. Ideological Language and Tone

Although the U.S. mass media frequently repeated the official view that ideological considerations and rhetoric had taken over at UNESCO, not only was the basic frame used by the media highly ideological, so was their language and tone. Beyond this, the mass media indulged in a remarkable degree of vituperation and innuendo.

Many of the words embodied in the original U.S. charges are vague and have ideological overtones, but the media used them freely and never analyzed their meaning. In effect, these words served as emotive symbols rather than instruments for the communication of information. On television, the words were reinforced by visual symbols. As Dan

Rather or Marvin Kalb solemnly intoned the charges, a map of the world or a bank of flags would be seen in the background, lending the authority of both the personalities and symbols to the official position. On three television reports on UNESCO, the list of U.S. grievances was written out in authoritative graphics — politicization, mismanagement, etc. — words brought down by Marvin Kalb from Mount Sinai.[1]

"Politicize" is the most important example of a word used as an ideological symbol. U.S. officials employed it mainly to designate both polemics and programs to which they objected. In his original letter to M'Bow announcing the U.S. withdrawal, U.S. Secretary of State Shultz seemed to identify politicization with a departure from original principles.[2] Presumably, adhering to original principles is nonpolitical. Shultz also mentioned "serving the political purposes of member states" and "becoming a servant of one or more national policy" as manifestations of politicization. This is partly rhetorical nonsense, because UNESCO is structured to give states domination over policy, and it is partly bad history (see the next section and William Preston's review above).

U.S. officials also used words closely related to politicization like "statist" and "collective" (as opposed to individual) rights and actions in a derogatory sense. In his memorandum of February 1984 explaining the U.S. position on the withdrawal, William Harley, a State Department consultant on communications, stated that UNESCO "has taken on an anti-Western tone . . . [and] has become a comfortable home for statist, collectivist solutions to world problems and for ideological polemics." While conceding the merits of UNESCO's educational services, he stated that "it increasingly orients its educational activities toward such purposes as 'peace and disarmament,' not as they are legitimately sought after by many peoples, but as they are promoted and distorted in Soviet propaganda." Harley also claimed that despite its value to the United States in the field of science, "politics has also begun to make itself felt here, with the injection of such concepts as 'scientists for peace' and 'scientists for disarmament.' "[3]

Harley and company imply that "statist" solutions are unnatural, illicit, and "political," whereas private-enterprise initiatives are natural and apolitical. This is completely arbitrary and an expression of a *political* preference, a preference that is not even consistently maintained by U.S. officials. They do not insist that "statist" illiteracy programs are illicit, and even in the communications field they do not maintain that government underwriting of satellite technology for the private sector produced an unfair, "statist" basis for the technological edge of the private U.S. communications industry. "Statist" means government intervention in those selected areas where the government does not intrude in the United States, and/or where it is U.S. policy to support private sector initiatives. This is a politicization of language that the U.S. mass media never addresses.

In the official and mass-media view, UNESCO became hopelessly politicized in the 1970s and 1980s. This is the period during which majority control passed from the Western powers, which suggests the strong possibility that "politicize" is a "snarl" word used to denigrate the raising of issues and support for proposals that the user of the word dislikes. This is supported by the frequency with which U.S. officials refer to the lack of respect for, or "suppression" of, minority views—meaning that they are outvoted![4] The mass media in our sample never once discussed the meaning of the word or hinted at the possibility of its manipulative use to express dissatisfaction with outcomes. Nor was it noted that, before the shift in the balance, the United States never objected to majority rule (as described by William Preston, above). In fact, the press added its own convolutions to the standard semi-Orwellian usage: R. W. Apple, Jr. in *The New York Times* (November 23, 1984) states that "critics have asserted that Unesco has succumbed to political pressures from the developing countries." A democratic vote is "succumbing to political pressure"! And for press commentators like George Will, it is in *UNESCO* that "we are studying the steady inoculation of the world with degraded political language manipulated by America's enemies [*sic*!]."[5]

Another important display of ideological language was the press's use of the concept of a NWICO. In almost all cases, this was identified simply with censorship, licensing, and "government control" of the press. For the right-wing ideologue William Safire, the NWICO is simply "a power play to bring all foreign correspondents under the control of local dictators."[6] A *New York Times* editorial describes the NWICO as "an effort to legitimize state manipulation of international news," and in its news columns, the NWICO "would endorse political control of the press."[7] These are ideological caricatures that define the phrase in terms of the Western press's own narrow, negative, and self-serving perception and entirely ignore the perspective of the proponents of the NWICO.[8] The most famous statement of the philosophy of a NWICO, by Mustapha Masmoundi,[9] was never cited in our mass-media sample or associated commentaries, possibly because he never mentions or advocates licensing or censorship. Better to put up one's own, more convenient, definition. The U.S. press would perhaps consider somewhat ideological a definition of "capitalism" as a system that "gives free play to human greed and allows private monopoly to dominate the economy." Their capacity to see beams in their own eyes is remarkably limited.[10]

Not only did the media use (and allow the government to get away with using) vague and ideological words and frames, they also resorted frequently to emotional and violent language that was a far cry from the standards of objective journalism. Feelings ran high in the press as the government and press in tandem mobilized a fearsome set of negative symbols: domination by a Soviet and Third World collective, anti-Western, anti-Israel, pro-PLO, Soviet-sponsored "peace" and "disarmament" studies, Third World bureaucrats living riotously in Paris at the expense of the American taxpayer, etc. In an Associated Press report in May 1984, John-Thor Dahlberg notes that "criticism against M'Bow has become personal," and Dahlberg joins in the assault: "the world's most controversial civil servant," "an insecure, short-fused bureaucrat" ("to many in the West," though unnamed), who "hates not just the United States, but the West and all white people" (an anonymous "European diplomat"). Apparently personal attacks are legitimate when dealing with an M'Bow, even if in bad taste and not permissible for describing Western officials.

The double standard applied by the mass media in its use of descriptive adjectives and derogatory language is partially captured in Tables 5 and 6, which juxtapose the words used in four major print media to describe UNESCO and its officials, on the one hand, and those applied to the United States, its institutions and officials, and others expounding the preferred viewpoint (e.g., Owen Harries), on the other.

Table 5 lists the descriptive adjectives and phrases applied to these various parties in *Time, Newsweek,* and *U.S. News & World Report* in their ten articles dealing with UNESCO during the withdrawal period. It will be noted that the descriptive adjectives and phrases applied to Newell, Gerard, Shultz, and Harries are entirely neutral—they do not deal with anything personal, do not suggest questionable motives, or transmit derogatory information or rumors. M'Bow, by contrast, was subjected to a barrage of vituperative language and adjectives obviously intended to denigrate (even, "former school teacher," presumably a lowly occupation for a person heading an international agency). As was noted earlier, Newell's qualifications to serve as a high State Department official in charge of relations to U.N. agencies were eminently challengeable, and Gerard's and Harries's backgrounds and performance could also raise questions. But the mass media never referred to Newell as a "college dropout" and "former Mormon missionary," or to Gerard as a wealthy Reagan loyalist, or to Harries as an embittered hatchet man for the right-wing Heritage Foundation.

In a propaganda frame, "we" and spokespersons for the positions we espouse are clearly treated rather differently from "they." It can be seen in Table 5 that the United States itself is also postulated as a benevolent parent whose patience has run out. UNESCO, on the other hand, like M'Bow, is treated with no holds barred in derogatory epithets.

Despite the flood of invective leveled at M'Bow in the establishment press, on the single occasion when the mass media accused anybody of an "insult," M'Bow was the villain! M'Bow allegedly referred to U.S. Ambassador to UNESCO Jean Gerard as "that woman," and "a politician" who had "no idea how UNESCO works." Paul Lewis of *The New*

TABLE 5. **Biased Word Usage in Articles on the U.S. Withdrawal from UNESCO in** *Time, Newsweek* **and** *U.S. News & World Report,* **1983-1985**

Words and Phrases Applied to:

UNESCO Director-General Amadou M'Bow	U.S. Officials	Owen Harries	UNESCO	The United States
He does right well	**Gregory Newell** Asst. Sec. for International Organization Affairs oversees work of UN agencies	an Australian foreign-affairs expert	wasteful	took a long-discussed step
"Third World is being ripped off by him"		a former Australian ambassador to UNESCO	politicized	formally withdrew
"inclined to give jobs to his family and friends. This is normal in Africa."	**Jean Gerard** the U.S. Ambassador U.S. Ambassador to the Agency		debased	patience had finally run out
Staff "atomized by suspicion and fear"			mismanaged	irked
A man of towering rages	**George Shultz** Secretary of State		statist	goaded beyond endurance
Ex-school teacher			antidemocratic	
Senegalese director			bloated bureaucracy	
autocratic			collectivist outlook	
"an extraordinarily biased man"			relentless hostility to Israel	
"temperamentally confrontationist and combative"			pro-Third World, anti-Western bias	
pandered to Third World interests			ideological posturing	
portrays himself as a champion of the have-nots			partly corrupt organization	
"uncommonly subdued" (after the U.S. exit)			plans for restricting press freedom	
			dedicated to spreading leftist ideology	
			Iron Curtain spy base	

York Times was shaken by the violence of this attack and allowed Mrs. Gerard an indignant reply that such language was "unacceptable for an international civil servant." Lewis himself notes that his anonymous "western diplomats" believed that M'Bow had "weakened his position inside the organization . . . by publicly insulting Mrs. Gerard."[11] Thus, paralleling the use of invective, the press maintains a double standard in denouncing its use. M'Bow can be insulted on a massive scale and highly personal basis without critical comment, but M'Bow's own attacks (which are extremely mild in comparison with those leveled at him) can elicit indignant ripostes about "insults."

The dichotomous application of words can also be seen in Table 6, which compares *The New York Times*'s usage in discussing "mismanagement" in UNESCO and in the Pentagon. Pentagon waste and mismanagement have not only been substantial, they have also involved sums that make the UNESCO budget look quite insignificant. However, the *Times* has supported the Reagan military buildup and the Pentagon's claims to an enlarging share of the national product, and has been a patriotic defender of national foreign policy. By contrast, it has been hostile to UNESCO and gave support to the U.S. withdrawal. The majority of words in the table applied to UNESCO and M'Bow are taken from three "news" articles by Flora Lewis, the rest from three *Times* editorials on UNESCO. The words applied to Pentagon waste, and the leaders of the Pentagon, were drawn from five *Times* editorials on that subject. It may be seen, as in the previous table, that the words applied to M'Bow are personal and insulting, those applied to the Pentagon leaders are not personal and, in fact, exonerate them—they are "unlucky," and dreamers with noble ideals, not wily and evasive manipulators of patronage. We may note that although Weinberger is said to have "stapled together the wish lists of the respective services"—a wildly irresponsible and wasteful procedure—no negative adjective is applied to him as a manager. M'Bow doesn't have bad luck and admirable dreams. Looking further down the list at the words applied to UNESCO versus the Pentagon, the latter has "too little to show" for its trillion dollars, and relatively benign words and phrases like "unwisely," "indifferent," "unfortunate," and "lack of reform" are prevalent, with a minimum of strong adjectives and venom. The Pentagon "never developed a coherent strategy," it wasn't "abominably" or "woefully" managed, a "boondoggling organization," and "thoroughly deformed." Although the Defense Department's spend-thrift qualities are on a vastly larger scale, and with less effective constraints than those of a highly exposed and dependent international organization like UNESCO, words like "spendthrift," "profligate," "dishonesty" and "scandalous" are reserved for the smaller, weaker instrument of "them."

This word selectivity is blatant and is indicative of blatant bias. One *New York Times* editorial was sufficiently distorted by sheer error of

TABLE 6. **The Dichotomous Use of Language by the *New York Times* in Discussing Waste in the Pentagon and in UNESCO**[*]

		Words and Phrases Applied to:	
UNESCO	*Pentagon*	*UNESCO's M'Bow*	*Pentagon Leaders*
abominably managed	unfortunate	evasive	**President Reagan**
woefully managed	indifferent	wily	has a wish
boondoggling organization	confused	ambitious	offered one noble rationale
irritating international problem	provocative	cultivated back-scratching to a fine art	The President recognized vanity
demoralized	blunders	wields patronage and job assignments like a truncheon	Mr. Reagan now understood
scandals	buying weapons unwisely		the President's dream
Yugoslav mafia of bureaucrats	never developed a coherent strategy		**Sec. of Defense Weinberger**
totally politicized	remarkably poor [record of innovation]		had poor luck
totally deformed	least forgivable		stapled together the wish lists of the respective services
worst	tragedy		
scandalous	trillion-dollar roller coaster		
political hackery	not nearly enough [to throw money after a problem]		
muddiness	far-fetched		
dishonesty	highly dangerous		
wooliness	"corruption of purpose"[**]		
equivocal mumbling			
shriller			
sloppier			
windy			
profligate			
spendthrift			

[*]This table is based on words and phrases taken from the following: on UNESCO and M'Bow, the three *New York Times* editorials on UNESCO, "Little Education, Science or Culture," Dec. 16, 1983; "Defogging Unesco," Feb. 25, 1984; and "Keeping the Pressure on UNESCO," Dec. 6, 1984, and three articles by Flora Lewis, "UNESCO: U.N.'s Worst Failure," Dec. 23, 1983; "Airing Unesco's Closets," March 1, 1984, and "A Shoddy Trick," May 10, 1984. On the Pentagon and its leaders, the following editorials in *The New York Times*: "It's Still Star Wars," Feb. 24, 1985; "The Pentagon's Misuse of Technology," April 5, 1985; "What a Trillion Bought," May 11, 1985; "Star Wars: Vanity and Reality," Sept. 19, 1985; "Attacking Arms Control, and Arms," Feb. 6, 1987.
[**]This is quoted from an outside source.

fact and illogic that Edmund Hennelly, the Mobil Oil executive who headed the U.S. Mission to the UNESCO General Conference of 1983, was impelled to write that "these inaccuracies suggest a conclusion to which I come reluctantly: that you have been pursuing a policy of criticizing Unesco with such tenacity and passion that you have allowed it to override your concern for accuracy and logic."[12]

Network television used and abused language with the same bias as the print mass media. M'Bow was denounced in strong language and his motives called into question; U.S. officials always spoke from Mount Sinai, and none was ever described with an invidious adjective. Dan Rather could repeat that UNESCO is "charged" with being "antiwestern" and "antidemocratic," but he did not stop to explain what these words meant, whether the charges were valid, and whether there was a hidden agenda underlying this rhetoric. In two of his three brief encounters with UNESCO on the "CBS Evening News," Rather referred to charges of "corruption," but again, he failed to explain and never subsequently discussed whether his hit-and-run accusations were verified in later investigations. We saw earlier that Jim Bitterman of NBC News could hardly contain himself in trying to get Congressman James Scheuer to elaborate on corruption charges, even driving Scheuer to ask for a bit of restraint on unproved claims.

TV has greater symbolic power than the press because of its use of visual images. I noted earlier how the symbolism of authority (maps, flags, the White House, graphics listing truths) are used to reinforce favored messages, in this case the official position in favor of withdrawal. UNESCO is designated by a building, women answering telephones, employees shuffling papers, or delegates (frequently black, or Arabic-looking, or labeled Czechoslovakia), sitting in a large room and looking bored or boring. M'Bow is shown in his office with an interrogator, or in his office at a desk with an African primitive statue in the foreground, or in a primitive African setting. He and the NWICO do not get graphics listing their complaints and positions.

TV as used by the networks in dealing with UNESCO fails entirely to capture process or to elucidate complex issues like the NWICO or politicization. It shows a series of pictures that are static and frequently not connected with or helpful in clarifying the oral text. This static quality and fragmentation obscure understanding, so that the viewer is left even more firmly in the grip of the chosen frame and the symbolic support given that frame. CBS-TV newsmen Dan Rather and David Andelman focus on UNESCO as a Soviet espionage base, which they assure viewers is supported by "a considerable body of evidence." But they do not give any of that considerable body of evidence, except the fact that France expelled 47 Soviet citizens as alleged spies, of whom 12 worked for UNESCO.[13] They do, however, use a great deal of symbolism: a hammer and sickle in the corner of a graphic is repositioned onto the UNESCO building, with an arrow then running to Paris showing the flow of Soviet espionage activity. With a minimum of fact, a Cold War identification of UNESCO with the Soviet Union and subversion is made. This was Rather's longest venture into a discussion of UNESCO, and along with a reiteration of the Reagan administration's charges, exhausts his analysis of the issues involved in the withdrawal.[14]

Beyond derogation, the language of the mass media in treating UNESCO and its officials was notable for its innuendo. We have seen that U.S. government officials were consistently described either neutrally or in terms suggestive of benevolent intent and innocent (nonmanipulative) behavior. By contrast, M'Bow and his allies conspire, pursue questionable objectives deviously, and insult honorable civil servants doing their duty (who are allowed to get in the last word).[15] What is more, anonymous informers can claim anything derogatory—shredding of documents, a climate of fear, the intentional obfuscation of budgets, an intent not to pay off obligations, corruption—and the media will rush it into the public domain without corroboration, for "them." This is the language of a propaganda system, not an objective press.

NOTES

1. For a more detailed examination of the use and abuse of symbols on a television program dealing with UNESCO, see Appendix III.

2. Shultz asserted that the "trend in policy, ideological emphasis, budget mismanagement . . . have led UNESCO away from the original principles of its constitution." Letter reprinted in "World Forum," pp. 82, 84.

3. Harley's memorandum is also reproduced in the Winter 1984 issue of the *Journal of Communication*, pp. 89–92.

4. An NSC Memo of December 23, 1983 from Robert McFarlane to Secretary of State George Shultz says that "The President wishes us to continue to expend every effort to effect meaningful changes over the next year to eliminate *the suppression of minority views* [my emphasis]" in UNESCO. See *Assessment*, p. 33. Shultz and other administration spokesmen repeated this language.

5. "Farewell, UNESCO?," *Washington Post*, December 22, 1983.

6. "The New Order Changeth," *New York Times*, December 25, 1983.

7. Paul Lewis, "Unesco Budget Hits $374 Million," *New York Times*, November 17, 1983.

8. It is interesting that a distinguished work on political science refers specifically to "government control" as a phrase that "is in no sense descriptive, but only evocative," and from which we learn nothing of reality but "something important about the group values with which each identifies." Edelman, p. 125.

9. "The New World Information Order," Document 31, UNESCO's International Commission for the Study of Communication Problems, Paris, 1978, reprinted in *Journal of Communication*, Spring 1979, pp. 172–85.

10. Media treatment of the NWICO is discussed further below under that heading.

11. "Unesco Head Denounces U.S. Delegate," December 31, 1984.

12. Letter to the Editor, *New York Times*, December 14, 1984.

13. In none of the mass-media programs that bring in this expulsion is the slightest doubt ever expressed about the value of the French accusations as proof of espionage.

14. See the appendix for a discussion of the longest CBS segment on UNESCO.

15. As we saw under Sourcing, Whitlam's charges were dismissed by *The New York Times* by allowing a representative of Mrs. Gerard to brush them aside as beneath her dignity to answer; Michael Dobbs in *The Washington Post* allowed her the last (though irrelevant) word and direct quotations in rebutting Whitlam. We saw earlier in this section Mrs. Gerard getting in the last word at charges leveled by Mr. M'Bow, and *U.S. News & World Report* gives her the final riposte of walking out on him: "When the United States Ambassador to UNESCO, Jean Gerard, challenged M'Bow's budget figures, he accused her of treating him like 'an American black who has no rights.' Gerard walked out on M'Bow." ("Amadou Mahtar M'Bow: Man Who Pulls the Strings at UNESCO," December 24, 1984.)

D. Rewriting History

The official version of the reasons for the U.S. exit from UNESCO invokes a Golden Age when the organization adhered to "its founding purposes," which were nonpolitical and involved friendly cooperation in the fields of education, science, culture, and communications. Subsequently, with the entry of the Soviet bloc and Third World countries into UNESCO, its basic orientation changed: there were controversies over Israel's participation in UNESCO affairs, arguments became more contentious, and programs took on a new political coloring.[1]

With only minor exceptions, the media transmitted without question or debate the official version of the historical Golden Age of a nonpolitical UNESCO, followed by the "politicization" of the organization in the 1970s and 1980s.

> When UNESCO was founded in 1945, the agency's goals were high-minded enough: fostering literacy and education, preserving mankind's cultural heritage, promoting the exchange of scientific ideas. But as Third World nations became a more potent force in the U.N., the organization took a leftward turn. The first real scuffle came in 1974, when UNESCO voted to exclude Israel from a regional working group.[2]

The Golden Age view involves a number of falsifications of history. First is the conception of original purpose. *Time* excludes the goal of "peace" and limits "communications" to an exchange of scientific ideas. Both peace and communications were high on the list of areas under UNESCO jurisdiction. The preamble to the UNESCO constitution speaks of peace depending on the "minds of men," and in its earliest years UNESCO sponsored a number of conferences and studies concerned with education for peace. When U.S. officials state that questions of peace and disarmament are contrary to UNESCO's mandate, and should be left to the General Assembly, they are confusing *education* for peace (UNESCO's mandate) with state actions to be taken to bring about peace (the jurisdiction of the General Assembly). They are also misrepresenting history.[3] Although the media could have called attention to these misrepresentations by quoting from the UNESCO charter and asking the right questions, they never did this.

Similarly, the idea that UNESCO was once nonpolitical and carried out nonpolitical programs involves both word manipulation (as described in the previous section) and a perversion of history. In his initial reply to Shultz's letter announcing the U.S. withdrawal, Director-General M'Bow noted that UNESCO is an organization of states by choice of its founding members, led by the United States. Representatives of member states make up the General Conference and have the power to decide on activities according to the founding constitution. The board, however, was not initially made up of representatives of states, but "the Government of the United States was one of those on whose initiative it was decided in 1954 that the members of the Board should thereafter each represent the government of the State of which he or she was a national."[4] Thus the "politicization" of UNESCO, in the sense of making it an instrument of member states, was part of the initial U.S. plan for the organization, and was strengthened by U.S. choice in 1954 when the board was made more politically responsive to member states.

Flora Lewis states in one of her reports that "countries once sent their most eminent writers and scientists as delegates" to UNESCO,[5] but she fails to observe that this ended by U.S. initiative. This act of suppression allows her to maintain intact her vision of a Golden Age, without having to acknowledge a U.S. role in "politicization."

In his original letter to M'Bow announcing the U.S. decision to withdraw, Shultz refers not only to original principles abandoned, but also to the threat of UNESCO becoming a servant of some national policy. The implication is that if UNESCO was in fact the servant of a national policy this would constitute a form of "politicization." In principle, this should apply to the United States if it could dictate UNESCO policy, although Shultz would never suggest this, nor have the media ever acknowledged this as a theoretical possibility! Serious historical analyses of UNESCO (see Preston above) show that the United States dominated UNESCO in its early years, and that the "original principles" were mainly U.S. formulations that reflected its power and "automatic majority." The appeal to original principles thus says, in effect, a national policy that I imposed on an international organization does not reflect politicization; that occurs only when others wish to alter my chosen policy, even by majority vote.

The U.S. media never discuss U.S. domination and politicization in the early years of UNESCO.[6] The statement by *Time* that political conflict began with the Israeli scuffle of 1974 is a falsification of history, as can be seen in William Preston's account earlier. The Israeli-Arab squabble in 1974 was certainly a case of political conflict, but this episode pales into insignificance beside the long and successful campaign of the

U.S. government to keep the government of mainland China out of the United Nations system, which it succeeded in doing from 1949 until 1971, purely on the grounds of political preference.[7] Similarly, as described by Preston, the United States strove mightily to mobilize the U.N. and UNESCO in Cold War controversies and in statements and positions on the Korean War.

A more recent case of blatant politicization took place at Tashkent in September 1983, where, at a conference concerned with communications and the developing countries, the U.S. delegation insisted on placing in the final document a condemnation of the host country (the Soviet Union) for the shooting down of the South Korean 007 airliner. According to Tomo Martelanc:

> This demand threatened that the final report would not be adopted, that more than a week of work by the Intergovernmental Council would be futile, and that the whole activity of the IPDC, with many ongoing projects in developing countries, would be blocked. . . . Everybody deplored the human tragedy involved in the plane incident, but it was certainly not for the IPDC, which promotes aid in communication to developing countries, to deal with such a hot political issue, which is clearly within the competence of the U.N. Security Council.[8]

The problem was finally worked out by intensive negotiations, but the injection of an "extraneous political issue" by the U.S. representatives was clear, although ignored by the U.S. mass media when discussing "politicization."

The mass media offer one last nugget of special (or patriotic) history that is worthy of note. In 1977 the United States withdrew from the International Labor Organization (ILO), notice having been given by Secretary of State Henry Kissinger in 1975, on the basis of charges paralleling those leveled against UNESCO in 1983-84. The United States then rejoined the ILO in 1980, claiming that changes had been made in response to the U.S. criticisms which justified the return. This episode is cited by Gregory Newell as a "model" that shows the political contructiveness of withdrawal from a U.N. organization, and six news articles in our print media sample referred to this case. As explained by *U.S. News & World Report*, on January 9, l984:

> In 1977, the U.S. withdrew from another agency, the International Labor Organization, claiming it had become too political. After sharply cutting its programs and staff, the ILO adopted more evenhanded policies. The U.S. then returned as a member.

All six of these news articles say approximately the same thing, and each repeats the version provided by Newell in justification of the 1983-84 withdrawal.

The reality is more complex than the Newell-media account. As in the case of UNESCO, the United States had lost its dominance of the ILO and was having a difficult time adjusting to minority status. A non-establishment publication quotes a French delegate to the ILO in 1977: "What has changed . . . is that since the late 1960s the United States has increasingly been the target."[9] Majority rule had become unbearable. Richard Lesher, of the Chamber of Commerce of the United States, and an ILO delegate, stated that ILO was unreformable precisely because of majority rule.[10] Ideological considerations also influenced the U.S. exit. George Meany, the head of the AFL-CIO, had never adjusted to a Soviet bloc presence in the ILO and was influential in the exit; his death in 1980 was a factor in the return. Whether the ILO improved between 1977 and 1980, and whether, if it did, this was a result of the U.S. exit, are disputed points. A Congressional Reference Service study by Lois McHugh on the "U.S. Withdrawal from the International Labor Organization: Successful Precedent for UNESCO?," comes to no definite conclusion, but shows that strong doubts about any net benefits from withdrawal were held by credible participants and cannot be dismissed out of hand.[11]

Leonard Sussman, testifying on this issue, contended that there were some favorable and some detrimental changes in the interim — but that some of the favorable changes, such as the use of a secret ballot, "were the result of the normal development of the organization."[12] The most important force for improvement, according to Sussman, was that when the United States returned, it made a serious investment in personnel and oversight arrangements, so that "it seems clear that the lesson of the ILO withdrawal is more a record of what the United States itself did to improve its performance at ILO than the description of basic changes in ILO that induced the United States to return."[13]

In the dissident press the lesson was a little different: the precedent of a walkout and boycott of international organizations "has now been set as an instrument of American foreign policy."[14] It is interesting to note, however, that neither the reservations of the Congressional Reference Service, nor Leonard Sussman's "lesson," let alone the dissident views, could make a dent in the patriotic formulation uniformly presented in the U.S. mass media.

NOTES

1. See the quotation from Harley's memo in the previous section, at n. 3.

2. "Waving Goodbye to UNESCO," *Time*, January 9, 1984.

3. They are also displaying remarkable hypocrisy: In the General Assembly, U.S. representatives argue that disarmament talks are appropriately left to *bilateral negotiations*! ("One reason for U.N. impotence is the U.S. view that disarmament progress is possible only in bilateral or regional talks involving the countries who control the arms and away from what it believes is irrelevant rhetoric at the Assembly." Nick Lu-

dington, "United Nations returns to face same old issues," an AP dispatch in the *Great Falls Tribune*, September 16, 1984.) Mary Beth Reissen pointed out in the *National Catholic Reporter*, January 13, 1984, that the same hypocritical process was at work as regards disarmament education:

> The U.S. has been particularly disturbed with a UNESCO disarmament education program, claiming the project should be considered in other parts of the UN system. Yet the U.S. has not yet given financial support to the UN world disarmament campaign launched at the Second Special Session on Disarmament.

When the mass media quote Newell making the point that disarmament talks should be left to the General Assembly, the media never point out these facts suggestive of hypocrisy.

4. Before this decision, M'Bow notes, the board had been made up of "independent personalities of the intellectual world on whom the founders of UNESCO had wished to confer the greatest possible freedom of opinion and action vis-à-vis their governments." M'Bow's reply is reprinted in the Autumn 1984 issue of the *Journal of Communication*.

5. "Airing Unesco's Closets," *New York Times*, March 1, 1984.

6. In a partial exception to this generalization, an article by Paul Lewis in *The New York Times* of December 30, 1983, "Since '45, Unesco Has Been a Political Battlefield," provides a brief summary of Richard Hoggart's short history of UNESCO, *An Idea and Its Servants: UNESCO from Within*. It will hardly come as a surprise to readers of this study that Lewis twists Hoggart's history into conformity with the *Times*'s editorial position on UNESCO. According to Lewis, Hoggart says that in the postwar years before the Soviet Union and its allies joined UNESCO, it "concentrated on promoting intellectual exchanges between Europe and North America." In the actual book, Hoggart says that "UNESCO's intellectual non-political honeymoon was short. As the Cold War began in earnest, the USA chose to push the new Agency and other parts of the system, ostensibly on the highest intellectual and ethical grounds, into support for her side. Aid to her Korean war effort was put on the agenda of the Executive Board and approved" (p. 66). Hoggart also stresses the "clearance system" for UNESCO employees as the "greatest obstacle to the emergence of a secure and true international civil service," and says that "within that system the most inglorious procedure is that practiced by the USA," which requires that even a temporary UN worker be cleared by the U.S. government, a process he dates back to the McCarthy era (pp. 49–50). All of this, along with every one of Hoggart's numerous positive statements about UNESCO and critical remarks about Western mistreatment of UNESCO and the Third World, is blacked out by Paul Lewis, who is obliged in the end to resort to Owen Harries and various anonymous critics for his final touches of patriotic history.

7. "For the better part of 20 years, the United States and its political allies were actively 'politicizing' the entire U.N. system in an effort to keep Mainland China out of it. For almost as long, West Germany was successful, with help from its friends, in using its 'Hallstein Doctrine' as a tool to isolate East Germany from the rest of the international system, including the United Nations. It is hard to argue that there has been a quantum leap in the degree and intensity of politicization of the U.N. system between then and now." Weiler, p. 2.

8. Autumn, 1984, *Journal of Communication*, pp. 119–20.

9. Quoted in Koeppel.

10. Quoted in *ibid*.

11. This report is reproduced in *Human Resources Impact of U.S. Membership in UNESCO*, Hearings Before the Senate Committee on Labor and Human Resources, 98th Cong., 2nd Sess., December 10, 1984.

12. *Ibid*., p. 103.

13. *Ibid.*, p. 102.

14. McShane; also Koeppel.

E. Programmatic and Management Deficiencies: Misrepresentations and Suppressions

Mismanagement was one of the three core U.S. charges used to justify the withdrawal from UNESCO, and, correspondingly, almost two-thirds (61.9 percent) of the news articles in our mass media sample mentioned and discussed some aspect of this subject. As we saw earlier, the media followed in the wake of the government's charges, repeating the government's claims and using them to frame any further inquiries. Very frequently there is internal evidence from the media reports that their attention was directed to new claims of scandal by government officials. The internally generated enterprise of the media seems to have been exceedingly modest, and so was their willingness to examine and cite sources that challenged the official line.

In this section I will discuss briefly some of the issues raised by the government regarding UNESCO's growth, programs, and efficiency, noting particularly some of the counterclaims made in response to the official charges and the mass media's handling of these matters.

Budget growth and size. A primary claim of the State Department was that the UNESCO budget was growing too rapidly and was essentially out of control.[1] The Reagan administration tried to impose a "zero-growth" budget on UNESCO and all other U.N. specialized agencies as well in the early 1980s. There is no evidence that this rule was based on any kind of cost-benefit analysis, or any consideration of the needs serviced by UNESCO (and other U.N. organizations) and the extent to which the resources available to them were adequate to service these needs. The total U.S. allotment to UNESCO in 1984 for all of its global educational, scientific, and other responsibilities was $50 million,[2] and UNESCO's total regular budget was under $200 million per year. Several commentators, trying to put the UNESCO budget into perspective, have pointed out that it is substantially smaller than that of dozens of Western universities.[3]

The zero-growth rate sought by the Reagan administration may also be juxtaposed with the *increase* in the U.S. defense budget between 1981 and 1984, which amounted to $92 billion, or growth at the rate of 16 percent per year, after adjustment for inflation. The total U.S. allocation to UNESCO in 1984 was 1/1840 (.05%) of the 1981-84 *increase* in U.S. defense expenditures. In other words, a *doubling* of the U.S. contribution to UNESCO could have been traded off for a reduction in the defense budget of 1/1840th of the 1981–84 increment (or the elimination of an overrun on one of the Pentagon's smaller contracts).

Although U.S. officials characterized UNESCO's budget as wildly out of control, the United States National Commission for UNESCO found its budget growth "not far out of line with other UN agencies" and recently actually lower than the projected increases of the ILO, WHO, and the FAO.[4] For the 1984–85 biennial budget, which was passed during the year in which the administration was presumably deciding whether to go through with its plan to exit, UNESCO's approved budget of $187.2 million a year represented a real increase of somewhere between 2.5 and 5 percent.[5]

The U.S. mass media repeated incessantly that the U.S. contribution was $50 million a year and 25 percent of the UNESCO budget (see Table 3 above), but not once did they put this contribution in any context by discussing it in terms of (1) the needs serviced by UNESCO, (2) a comparison with American university budgets or (3) with internal U.S. budget allocations such as those to the Pentagon. The mass media also never mustered up the enterprise to make an independent computation of the UNESCO budgetary growth rate, or to cite or tap independent authorities such as the U.S. National Commission for UNESCO.[6] Paul Lewis of the *Times* did assert that "the organization's budget is so obscure that western experts [*sic*: unnamed] said they could not agree this year whether Mr. M'Bow was asking for an increase of 6 percent, 10 percent or 30 percent."[7] But this bit of anonymous obscurantism exhausted Lewis's and the *Times*'s effort to understand these facts.

In short, media discussions of the UNESCO budget involved a narrow-minded parroting of official claims and opinion. The U.S. National Commission, which did not find the data as obscure as Lewis's anonymous experts, explicitly repudiated the State Department charge that the UNESCO budget was out of control or growing faster than other U.N. agency budgets, but this source was not cited by the media. The media also failed to independently investigate the government claims, preferring to reiterate the official line.

UNESCO programs and budget allocations. UNESCO carries out a wide array of activities, of which those in the field of communications are of relatively modest importance. In terms of dollar distribution by function in the year of the U.S. withdrawal, UNESCO allocated its income as follows: education, 40%; natural science, 28%; social science, 6%; culture, 13%; communication, 8%; other, 5%.[8]

In its internal assessment of UNESCO in 1983, the State Department requested information on the value and demerits of these programs from its embassies and consulates and from governmental and nongovernmental organizations involved in fields in which UNESCO worked. Not one of the 83 U.S. embassies and consulates recommended withdrawal, and the 13 government departments and agencies consulted were generally quite favorable to UNESCO's performance. In field after field, the

State Department's own summary of the responses tends to be strongly positive. In the field of education, for example, the report notes that "UNESCO leads the international effort to eradicate illiteracy," that its educational activities "parallel, for the most part, U.S. foreign policy interests and provide services beyond the scope of present American bilateral technical assistance"; and that some of its important services "are unlikely to be duplicated by any other source."[9] The U.S. Department of Education concluded that "UNESCO is increasingly at the center of world educational concerns. . . . [and] AID could in no way make up for the UNESCO educational development."[10] The National Science Foundation, coordinating the responses of seven scientific and technical agencies, found that "the weight of tangible benefits over certain impediments clearly justifies continued U.S. participation in UNESCO."[11]

Interestingly, the State Department report even notes that UNESCO plays a positive role in the field of communications: "The U.S. has few problems with the work of the Division for the Development of Communications. Its study programs to improve communications planning, training, managerial capabilities, and technical capacities address critical member state concerns. Moreover, this division's pragmatic approach is consonant with U.S. objectives; for example, the Division effectively backstops the work of the IPDC."[12] It also notes that "UNESCO's activities in communications and information are wide-ranging, and UNESCO projects in communication are generally well received by developing countries."[13]

As was described earlier, these positive statements were suppressed by the State Department in its public-relations handouts that accompanied the announcement of an intention to withdraw. The underlying document was made available to the media in late February 1984, and a summary of these suppressed findings was provided by the U.S. Commission in its press conference of August 8, 1984 and in its small volume "What Are the Issues . . . ?" But the media did not take advantage of these sources and failed to provide their readers with essential information. The government had charged, and the media had repeated, that UNESCO had abandoned its original purposes. A close examination of actual UNESCO program allocations was essential for evaluating this claim. The mass media never once tested this charge by a detailed look at the evolution of UNESCO program composition and expenditures. Not a single news article in our media sample even broke down current UNESCO budgetary outlays into their main components, and only a handful made general reference to the major programs and their character. When the State Department review, with its considerable documentation on the internal assessment of the various UNESCO programs, was finally made available in February 1984, even this official document was ignored.

These suppressions of information on actual programs and their evaluation both within the government and without allowed the State Department and media to maintain a negative image of UNESCO's work and also to suggest that UNESCO was mainly concerned with communications issues. It also allowed the government-Heritage Foundation-media propaganda machine to inflate the importance of UNESCO involvement in peace and disarmament issues and aid to national liberation movements.

The Heritage Foundation and U.S. officials made much of UNESCO's funding of groups and issues that they found objectionable, and that could be used as symbols of evil in the U.S. political environment. Several points have been made in rebuttal to this focus. One is that these allocations came about by majority vote of the UNESCO General Conference and reflected large U.N. majorities in general. The PLO, ANC, and SWAPO were accorded nonvoter observer status in UNESCO and other U.N. bodies in the 1970s, and both ANC and SWAPO are recognized by the Organization of African Unity as the official representatives of the African people of South Africa and Namibia. Second, the bulk of UNESCO outlays for these movements is for education. The U.S Commission notes that "the U.N., which administers the relief program for Palestinian refugee camps, has designated UNESCO to provide educational services for the camps. Few would contend that helping to educate Palestinian children contributes to terrorism."[14] Third, the sums involved have been exceedingly small. As the U.S. Commission points out:

> The total allotted to all these movements from assessed budgetary funds for teacher training, fellowships, educational equipment and materials, teacher salaries, travel funds, and tuition and fees have averaged approximately $200,000 per year in the three years 1981, 1982, and 1983.[15]

As regards peace and disarmament studies, their funding would appear to be entirely within the province of UNESCO's original purposes, as was discussed earlier. It is also interesting to note the readiness with which U.S. spokesmen conclude that peace and disarmament education must necessarily hurt U.S. interests. This may be a realistic assessment of the true position of the militarizing United States in the world, but its spokespersons usually also proclaim a U.S. devotion to peace and interest in disarmament. We should also note, finally, that the sums allocated to disarmament studies have been under $1 million per year. The House Foreign Affairs Committee staff asked: "In what sense are educational programs politicized when disarmament studies cost only $1 million or less than one percent of the entire program?"[16] We may also ask whether, given the UNESCO mandate, the sum of $1 million is not much too small.

The mass media's handling of these touchy subjects was, at best, an uncritical reiteration of the government charges. A typical example is by Walter Pincus of *The Washington Post*: "UNESCO plans to spend more than $1 million over the next two years on peace and disarmament activities, Gerard said, calling them matters 'more properly dealt with' at the United Nations in New York or the Conference on Disarmament in Geneva."[17] In a slightly more frenetic vein, *Time* states that the "organization has spent some $750,000 [no time frame is given] for East-bloc 'peace and disarmament' initiatives, which the U.S. considers little more than a subsidy for Soviet propaganda." Both these articles involve what we might call "conduit reporting," where the reporters simply transmit a claim by an "authority," without raising any question about its veracity, without providing context that would make the claims meaningful, and in these particular cases violating the rule of "balance." Nobody is brought on in these instances to argue another side, or to provide the context that these accounts fail to offer.

Centralization in Paris. Frequent reference is made in official U.S. and other critical statements on UNESCO to its excessive concentration of resources in Paris.[18] The inference, drawn directly or implied, is that the organization is top-heavy with bureaucrats, congregated in a lush place to reside, with a corresponding neglect of real programs, which would involve more expenditures in projects outside of Paris.

These critical statements ignore important counterfacts. One is that the 80 percent figure for resources spent in Paris is an exaggeration based on accounting conventions. UNESCO spends a great deal of money on conferences and meetings held all over the world, and books distributed worldwide, all of which are allocated to the headquarters budget, as are fellowships, advisory services for member states, and other outlays not truly used in Paris. A further qualification rests on the fact that the 80 percent figure is confined to the regular budget. UNESCO has for a long time served as a planning and administrative agency for educational and other programs funded by the World Bank and the United Nations Development Fund. These funds, under special budgets, and which accounted for some 38 percent of the total UNESCO budget in 1984, are allotted very largely to field activities.

A third and closely related point is that the centralization of UNESCO activities in Paris has been a result of Western choices. Not wanting to allocate large sums for development aid—especially not to an organization whose budget was not under tight Western control—the Western powers themselves chose to make UNESCO into a planning and coordinating body, with the field resources to be fed in with voluntary contributions and through agencies under closer control.[19] Under these circumstances, there is a substantial element of hypocrisy in the Western focus on the centralization in Paris, with the West itself confining UNESCO to control functions, and then accusing it of failing to do more work in the field.

Once again, the mass-media treatment of the issue was a reiteration of official charges and disregard of counterfacts. The typical statement in the press was: "As an example of mismanagement, it [the U.S. State Department] said 80 percent of UNESCO's expenditures occurred in Paris rather than in the field. M'Bow denied this in a television interview but did not offer another figure."[20] That was it. No article in our press sample, or network TV broadcast on UNESCO, mentioned the view that centralization was a product of Western choice, nor did they ever discuss the role of UNESCO in planning and administering operations off-the-budget and funded through the World Bank and IDF.

Inefficiency and poor planning and coordination: The GAO reports of 1979 and 1984. That UNESCO was inefficient and poorly managed was a major official claim and media focus in 1983 and 1984. How did it happen that UNESCO mismanagement suddenly became an acute concern and newsworthy? Was it new to UNESCO? Was it worse in UNESCO than in other U.N. organizations? Was it as bad as in the Pentagon, Congress, or the Department of Agriculture? Is it possible that the alleged concern over UNESCO mismanagement was a cover being used to discredit an organization objected to for entirely different reasons? These questions were never raised in our mass-media news sample.

In early 1984 Representative James Scheuer and other congressmen asked the GAO to make a study of UNESCO operations, which was then arranged. We saw earlier that the negotiations, the statements by Scheuer, and many follow-up events, provided the media with a cornucopia of opportunities to press the government agenda, which they did in a highly biased and superficial fashion. The GAO report was "leaked" before publication and was used to suggest that the administration's claims of management deficiencies were justified. An Associated Press report says that the GAO study "supports the Reagan administration's argument" that UNESCO "wastes money because of sloppy management practices."[21] This AP report goes on to list fifteen separate criticisms dredged from the GAO report, with no indication of their importance; and it suppresses completely the numerous positive remarks in the GAO report. Paul Lewis does the same thing in *The New York Times*, selecting out only critical statements, paraphrasing others to allow him to use stronger language, and getting James Scheuer to conclude that things are "disastrous."[22]

The report is, in fact, quite mild, partly complimentary, and actually gives *de facto* clearance to UNESCO on a number of charges that had been levied against it. None of these is mentioned by Lewis[23] or the AP, nor do they ever point to incidental findings that might be regarded as favorable to UNESCO on their own narrow criteria, such as the fact that employment at UNESCO did not increase at all between 1970 and 1984. I noted earlier how Lewis handles the finding on corruption, which is a small masterpiece of bias: "Although the report does not list any in-

stances of corruption, it depicts a top-heavy, inefficient organization."
Notice that he starts the sentence with an "although," instead of making
a straightforward admission of a fact that he obviously doesn't like to
acknowledge in the first place. Note also that he expresses the point in
such a way as to suggest that although the GAO "does not list" instances
of corruption, maybe they're still there. Given the fact that Lewis and
Scheuer had put a lot of stress on the GAO investigation as an exhaustive inquiry that would settle the corruption issue, honest newswork
would have presented it straightforwardly and even featured it. But Paul
Lewis does not do this. I will return below to some of his other omissions.

In the case of the GAO report, once again the biased selectivity and
sheer superficiality of the mass-media's treatment of a topic are striking.
Measuring the efficiency of UNESCO is not easy, partly because some
program outcomes "are not quantifiable, and hence [are] not readily
identifiable."[24] It was also recognized by the GAO that UNESCO planning is rendered difficult because a plan "must try to reconcile the diverse and often conflicting comments of 161 member states."[25] The
mass media never mentioned these qualifications.

Both the GAO reports of 1979 and 1984 established that UNESCO programming involved significant duplication, lacked adequate controls
over the actual use of program funds, and needed improved systems for
program evaluation. Nowhere do they suggest, however, that UNESCO's
inefficiency is greater than that of any other U.N. organizations (or U.S.
domestic entities such as the Department of Defense or State Department), or so serious as to call into question the value of the organization.
Jens N. Hufner and Klaus H. Nauman state, accurately, that the GAO review "resulted in a series of minor objections, as is normally and rou-
tinely the case in any national inspection of national administrations."[26]

Both GAO reports note that UNESCO has long had as its external auditor the United Kingdom's National Audit Office, and the 1984 report
states that except for "minor technical exceptions in 1976 and 1977, it
has concluded that the financial reports accurately reflect the results of
UNESCO's operation."[27] The 1984 report also states that "UNESCO's financial rules, regulations, and detailed procedures include a variety of
internal controls which generally appear to provide a reasonable framework for UNESCO's financial control system."[28] The 1979 report was
more complimentary, stating that while UNESCO activities were not
studied in detail in a 1977 review, "we regarded the management procedures to be unique and forward looking compared to the other U.N.
agencies examined; and further, as having the potential for improving
the effectiveness of U.S. participation in UNESCO and in other international organizations as well."[29] None of these positive statements was
reported in any news article in our sample.[30]

Both the 1979 and 1984 GAO reports, especially the former, stressed
the lack of U.S. interest, competence, and planning as an important

source of UNESCO's failings. The 1979 report notes that "officials responsible for representing U.S. interest in UNESCO were handicapped by an overriding concern with political matters [U.S "politicization"!], by an inadequate system for identifying program goals and priorities, and a shortage of qualified staff to analyze the budget and emerging new issue areas."[31] It pointed out that U.S. priorities were never even spelled out to its own staff, that its policies were "reactive rather than innovative," and it states that "according to one observer, a major cause of the delegation's reduced effectiveness is that delegation membership is awarded too frequently for political reasons. As a result, some public members are insufficiently informed or interested in the proceedings."[32] The 1984 GAO report also points out that the U.S. would better restrain budgets if it improved its participation in the budget process—that it engages in broad pronouncements on the budget, but says little that is specific. It contends that "program and budget decisions may have a better chance of success if specific proposals and suggestions are made informally to the Director-General and Secretariat officials early—before and during formulation of the program and budget."[33]

In short, an alternative frame using the GAO documents could make a quite different case from the one made by the U.S. media. Although UNESCO was found to be in need of improvement, as is true of every large bureaucratic organization, corruption charges were not supported by the GAO investigation, and the GAO itself stressed the fact that a first-class external auditor had no major criticisms of UNESCO's system of controls. The GAO reports suggest that the United States has been too politically focused and inattentive to matters bearing on efficiency, that its personnel have been second rate and politically chosen, and that it has failed to specify or press for reform. The *U.S.* inadequacies extended through the year of withdrawal.[34]

This is consistent with the hypothesis that improved efficiency was not a serious U.S. objective, and that mismanagement was a red herring used to justify an exit desired on political grounds. This line of thought was never suggested in our mass-media sample, and not the Whitlam, nor the House Foreign Affairs Committee statements, nor those in the GAO reports that suggested U.S. politicization and failure to do anything useful about reform were allowed to see the light of day.

NOTES

1. See Gregory Newell's On-the-Record Briefing, December 29, 1983, pp. 6–8.

2. Actually, because of a refund based on a currency revaluation, the U.S. contribution was only $23 million. This point was never mentioned in our mass-media sample.

3. Hufner and Naumann point out that the UNESCO budget "comes to about two-thirds the current annual expenditures of the Free University of Berlin or two-fifths of the annual budget of Stanford university." Hufner and Nauman, p. 5. Dr. Seth Spaulding noted that the "total budget of UNESCO is far less than that of a medium-sized U.S. research university, such as my own University of Pittsburgh." Americans for the Universality of UNESCO, *Newsletter*, May 1986, p. 4.

4. "What Are the Issues Concerning the Decision of the United States To Withdraw from UNESCO?," 1984, p. 20.

5. *Ibid.*, p. 19. UNESCO officials estimated the increase at 2.5 percent, the U.S. State Department somewhere between 3 and 5 percent. It is difficult to give an exact figure because the UNESCO budget is fixed in dollars, but is based on an assumed exchange rate between the franc and dollar that may not correspond to the market rate.

6. As noted above, they suppressed the fact that the United States got a refund that made its contribution under $25 million.

7. "Since '45, Unesco Has Been a Political Battlefield," December 30, 1984.

8. This is taken from a State Department memo of 1984, " 'Balance Sheet' of Benefits From Unesco Membership."

9. U.S. State Department, "U.S./UNESCO Policy Review," 1984, p. 5.

10. U.S. Commission, p. 7.

11. *Ibid.*, p. 6.

12. State Department Report, p. 31.

13. *Ibid.*, p. 32.

14. U.S. Commission, p. 16.

15. *Ibid.*

16. Quoted in U.S. Commission, p. 14.

17. "GAO Probes UNESCO Corruption Charges," March 9, 1984.

18. In 17 of our 215 news-article sample centralization was specifically mentioned. For an illustration and comment, see Appendix III.

19. As noted by Hufner and Naumann, "The industrial countries have been trying for more than 20 years to prevent growth in the 'field work' (i.e., the practical development aid activities) of the United Nations specialized agencies, because this would entail higher compulsory contributions, rather like income tax or property tax, for the rich countries." Hufner and Nauman, p. 2.

20. Michael Dobbs, "U.S. Quits UNESCO," *Washington Post*, January 1, 1985.

21. "Study supports Reagan view of sloppy UNESCO practices," *News Leader*, Richmond, Virginia, September 21, 1984.

22. "Study by Congress Faults Unesco and Places Blame on Its Director," September 21, 1984.

23. Lewis does mention the corruption question, in the dishonest manner discussed in the text below.

24. GAO, Report to the House Committee on Foreign Affairs on Improvements Needed in UNESCO's Management, Personnel, Financial, and Budgeting Practices, November 30, 1984, p. 51.

25. *Ibid.*, p. 46.

26. Hufner and Naumann, p. 6.

27. GAO Report, 1984, p. 78.

28. *Ibid.*, p. 89.

29. GAO Report to the Congress on UNESCO Programming and Budgeting Need Greater U.S. Attention, September 14, 1979, p. 14.

30. Paul Lewis did mention the fact that UNESCO was audited by the U.K. National Audit Office, but he did this in such a way as to cause a reader to miss entirely its positive significance. That is, he failed to mention that this was a high-powered and quite independent auditor who might be expected to uncover whatever shenani-

gans an auditor might locate; and he overlooked mentioning that this auditor gave UNESCO good marks. See his article "Congress to Send Team to Study UNESCO," *New York Times*, March 1, 1984.

31. GAO Report, 1979, p. iv.

32. *Ibid.*, pp. 8, 10, 11.

33. GAO Report, 1984, p. 7l.

34. These points were made with considerable force by Whitlam, Sussman, Hennelly, the U.S. Commission for UNESCO, and the staff of the House Foreign Affairs Committee during the exit year, but as we have seen their penetration of the mass media was slight.

F. Misrepresentation of the NWICO and Threat to a "Free Press"

The alleged threat to a free press posed by UNESCO and the NWICO was probably the most compelling issue influencing media attitudes toward UNESCO (although "mismanagement" was discussed more frequently). Eighty-eight (43.3 percent) of the news articles in our mass-media sample mentioned and discussed (however superficially) the issue of "freedom of the press," and 44 (21.6 percent) mentioned the threat of censorship or the licensing of journalists. These adverse developments were alleged to arise from the pressing of a NWICO by the Soviet-Third World collective.

I showed earlier (in the subsection on Language) that the mass media used "free press" and "NWICO" as ideological expressions, couched in a self-serving frame of reference. The mass-media usage and discussions were also extremely superficial and may be described as "news by formula." In Paul Lewis's imitable language: "Communist and radical third world countries have pressed for Unesco to draw up an information order, which would endorse governments' rights to control the news outlets for their own ends, define 'responsible' reporting standards and set up a licensing system for journalists."[1] Lewis and his colleagues at the *Times, Washington Post*, AP, and the newsweeklies repeat this formula dozens of times with only slight variations. Only once in twenty-two articles does Paul Lewis let slip in a Third World perspective on the NWICO, when he says that "the goal of the information order is to end the dominance of the western press, which is presented as a threat to the 'cultural identity' of third-world nations and their citizens, who are described as 'mere passive receivers.' " This statement is surrounded by several paragraphs that reiterate the Western view, and which include some patently false assertions.[2] It is interesting to note that although dominance of the Western press and a threat to cultural integrity would seem like major issues, this is the only time such matters were ever mentioned by Lewis, and this is as far as the substance of the NWICO and its "goal" is elaborated upon in his numerous discussions of the subject. We may note also how Lewis carefully avoids any implication that these Third World claims are true—they are "presented as" a threat, and "described as" passive receivers. This is in sharp contrast with his exposition of the Western position, where qualifying phrases are not used. "Unesco is seeking to draw up an international 'code of conduct,' "— not "Unesco *is alleged* to be seeking . . . "

The Lewis paragraph just discussed is one of only three instances in 215 news articles (1.4 percent) in which a Third World perspective on the NWICO is even hinted at, and it is only one of two in which any possible threat of free flow to cultural integrity and national sovereignty is suggested, however grudgingly. Not a single article mentioned the issue of satellite technology, transborder data flows, or the possible incompatibility of externally stimulated consumerism with cultural autonomy or national development plans. The word "dependency" was never used. In short, the views of serious spokespersons for a NWICO order were not allowed into the discussion. And, in fact, there was no *discussion* of these issues, only the repetition of a formula.

The U.S. official position, followed consistently in our media sample, was that the only issues raised by a NWICO were "freedom of the press" versus "government control." Freedom of the press meant a commercial press funded by advertising. Could an advertising-based press reflect a systematic bias based on its restricted revenue source? Could it be affected by proprietary wealth and interest? Could it reflect the national and corporate interests of the home country and its leading multinational organizations? How concentrated could the media become before it was regarded as "unfree"? These questions were not raised once in 215 news articles, or on any network TV discussion of the withdrawal.[3]

Spokespersons for a NWICO have long been concerned over the concentration of international news provision, with the Big Four Western news agencies (AP, UPI, Reuters, and AFP) accounting for over 80 percent of international news and controling much of the news to the Third World about itself. Only a very few news articles even mention the Third World concern over news concentration, and none give numbers or discuss the subject even superficially. It has been pointed out in the critical literature that the former head of Associated Press, Kent Cooper, in his book *Barriers Down*, claimed that AP was needed because of the nationalistic bias of the other international news agencies, Reuters and Havas (a predecessor of AFP). According to Cooper, these agencies "present[ed] American news disparagingly to the United States if they presented it at all; [and] . . . they could present news of their own countries most favorably and without it being contradicted."[4] Cooper's views on this subject were cited in one of our small sample of non-establishment articles, but not once in our mass-media sample.

The model of the NWICO that the media prefer to work with is that of a tyrant who justifies his desire to clamp down on the press by proclaiming his devotion to a NWICO. In his press conference of December 29, 1983, Gregory Newell strongly recommended that the press corps read an article in *The New York Times* by James LeMoyne, entitled "Suriname's New Press: Unesco's Disciple," as a fine illustration of what the NWICO is all about. In the article, LeMoyne describes how a formerly "thriving independent press" had been crushed when Lt. Col Desi Bouterse seized power in a military coup, and set up a government news agency whose leaders say they are following UNESCO's NWICO. By the use of selective quotations, LeMoyne suggests that the former "opinionated" old press was more informative than the new. He shows how constraining the new press is by the fact that a strike in a bauxite works, "the most important political development of the year," was unreported by the Suriname News Agency for two days, and its belated published account said that taxes were not excessive.[5]

The LeMoyne article arouses suspicions by its superficiality and not very subtle attempts to make a case fitting the paper's editorial line. We may note the article's title, which makes the NWICO a UNESCO product—the kind of misrepresentation characteristic of *The New York Times* news-editorializing on the subject. This news-editorial line always identified the NWICO with censorship and licensing, and here, *mirabile dictu*, the *Times* finds that the NWICO "disciple" in Suriname behaves exactly according to the editorial model, using the NWICO as a cover for censorship and licensing. Consider, however, that both Generals Pinochet in Chile and Evren in Turkey have stated that they are believers in "true democracy." Is it likely that *The New York Times* would publish a "news" article that spelled out the conditions of "democracy" in Chile and Turkey as exemplifying the real meaning of democracy in the Third World?

A press worried about the effects of a NWICO on the free flow of information should also be deeply concerned about constraints on the free flow of information on its own Western turf, if their worry is based on principle rather than an undisclosed interest. It is one of the ironies of the U.S.-British withdrawals from UNESCO, however, that they were engineered by administrations notable for secrecy and the curtailment of information access, covert actions, deception, and the manipulation of the press. Under Reagan there was a steady attrition of Freedom of Information Act rights,[6] the pursuit of whistle-blowers in government, and the strengthening of the informational and suppressive rights of government relative to the individual.[7] Constraints were also placed on the flow of information across borders, with restrictions on the movement of dissident journalists and publications from disfavored countries to the labeling of Canadian documentaries on acid rain as "propaganda." This was in accord with the Heritage Foundation's 1980 agenda for Reagan, which "recommended weakening the Freedom of Information Act, strengthening the capacity of the Central Intelligence Agency for covert action, and monitoring leftist political organizations, all in the interests of protecting the national security."[8]

The Thatcher government was equally or more aggressive in attacking dissident media and whistle-blowers. Her government's attitude toward the free flow of information within Britain was suggested by an off-the-record briefing to U.S. correspondents on December 3, 1986, by Bernard Ingham, the prime minister's press spokesman[9]: "There is no freedom of information in this country; there's no public right to know. There's a commonsense idea of how to run a country and Britain is full of commonsense people. . . . Bugger the public's right to know. The game is the security of the state—not the public's right to know."

In short, the Reagan and Thatcher governments have displayed an open contempt for freedom of information at home, and have done a great deal to increase government control and restrict the public's rights to know. How could governments so restrictive of free flow at home be so concerned about hypothetical restrictions abroad? Why would a mass media devoted to free-flow principles not raise an outcry over Reagan-Thatcher policies as a matter of free-flow principle? Could it be that free flow is a euphemism for private control of the media and private access, and that the reconciliation of the seeming paradox is that Reagan-Thatcher have not threatened private control (in fact, have allowed greatly increased media concentration) and support "free flow" (i.e., private control and access) abroad? As can be seen on Table 4, no media news article raised even an ironical question about Reagan-Thatcher domestic policies curbing the free flow of information.

Another oddity that may strike an observer not operating within the establishment frames is the rise of authoritarianism in the U.S. sphere of influence over the past several decades, resultant attacks on the press that go well beyond "licensing" and other alleged evils of the NWICO, and mass-media silence. Thirty or more journalists were murdered in El Salvador between 1979 and 1986 by the forces supported by the U.S. government, and 48 were killed in Guatemala between 1978 and 1982.[10] Numerous papers were closed in these countries, and those that remained open learned a lesson from the murders. "In a number of Latin American countries it has become almost axiomatic that to report faithfully government-sanctioned atrocities is to invite similar treatment against conveyers of the information."[11] Journalist Allen Nairn notes that "the main method of censorship employed by the Guatemalan army is murder, directed primarily at the local press."[12] Such processes were also at work in Argentina, Brazil, Chile, Uruguay, Paraguay, and other states in Latin America in the period coincident with the rising media concern over a NWICO (1973–84).

James LeMoyne, in his article on Suriname, mentions that one consequence of the Bouterse coup in 1980 was the shooting to death of four journalists and the destruction of two radio stations and a paper. But of 48 journalists murdered in Guatemala in 1978–82, only four were mentioned at all in *The New York Times*, and these only very briefly on the back pages. The journalist holocaust has been treated by the establishment press in a remarkably restrained manner, with references mainly to events in places like Suriname, where useful lessons can be drawn about the threat of a NWICO.

It is hard to explain why the media would be passionately concerned over "licensing" in a NWICO that does not yet exist, and engage in a *de facto* blackout of the murder of journalists in Argentina, Chile, El Salvador, and Guatemala, on the basis of principled concern over the freedom of the press and the free flow of information. A "transnational project" model explains this dichotomy very well. Argumedo points out that when there is strong popular resistance to transnational corporate penetration "the transnational development model has been forced upon populations by means of profoundly repressive governments."[13] If repressive governments in Brazil, Chile, and Guatemala serve a larger transnational corporate interest, perhaps the national media will look the other way when free flow is being impeded by the murder of journalists. And the U.S. government and corporate business were pleased with the coming of repressive governments in those countries.[14] Thus, what appears to be an unaccountable dichotomization and hypocrisy can be explained, but the relevant principle would seem to be corporate access and profit, not freedom of information.

One of the most spectacular forms of bias in our media news sample was the consistent implication that *UNESCO* was proposing the licensing of journalists and censorship. U.S. officials regularly referred to the NWICO as a UNESCO project, virtually synonymous with licensing, and they never voluntarily acknowledged that licensing had not even reached the status of a formal proposal before the Executive Board or General Conference. In his December 29, 1983 press conference, Gregory Newell was confronted with a direct question: "What specific proposals have been brought before UNESCO and by the UNESCO Secretariat for the licensing of journalists?" Newell replied: "There have, to my knowledge, been no specific concrete proposals to begin that. Most of it is all under study, that goes from conference to conference." This question and answer was never reported in the press, and in general the media rarely if ever stated that no such licensing or censorship has gone beyond debate to the level of a proposal to be acted upon. In the 215 news articles in my sample, 30 imply that licensing-censorship are UNESCO proposals (and often imply that they are being pushed by UNESCO officials). A few state explicitly that licensing-censorship plans have never been enacted, but none pointed out that no such plan has even reached the floor to be voted upon.[15]

Because of the divisiveness of the NWICO debate, and the strong opposition of the West, UNESCO Director-General M'Bow insisted on a consensus vote on such issues in the Executive Board and General Conference. This means that the West has had a *de facto* veto power that would prevent the acceptance of any deeply objectionable media proposal, even on the assumption that it became a formal proposal. In the press conference of August 9, 1984, former U.S. UNESCO official Edmund Hennelly noted that Director-General M'Bow had been extremely active in "derailing" proposals strongly objectionable to the United States, and Hennelly saw "Secretariat members actively lobbying on behalf of U.S. proposals."[16] None of these points were transmitted to the American public in our sample of news articles. My explanation is as follows: To have mentioned them would suggest that the threat of "licensing," etc., was enormously exaggerated, whereas the official U.S. and the mass-media editorial position was that the threat of a NWICO was dire; and in the same frame, Director-General M'Bow was seen as a wicked instrument of a Soviet-Third World collective, so that evidence of his role in literally backing U.S. positions would be disturbing. The editorial positions and biased frames of the media thus filtered out uncongenial facts in what was purportedly news.[17]

NOTES

1. "Unesco's Budget Hits $374 Million," November 17, 1983.

2. For example, Lewis says that "Unesco is seeking to draw up an international 'code of conduct' . . . [and] wants to issue identification cards for journalists." "Since '45 Unesco Has Been a Political Battleground," *New York Times*, December 30, 1983. This personification of an organization and attributing to it a will is incompetent newspaper work. Does he mean Director-General M'Bow and the Secretariat, or some member states, or both? M'Bow and members of the Secretariat deny that they have been seeking these things, stressing their attempts to maintain neutrality and M'Bow's efforts to seek consensus, and claiming that there are divisions of opinion within the Secretariat.

3. As we shall see in H below, at the famous Talloires conference in 1981, the assembled mass-media spokespersons hinted in their final Declaration that advertising might theoretically influence editorial policy, but they pronounced that—by some unstated process—this must not be: Editorial policy "must be free" of advertiser influence!

4. Cooper argued, of course, that these other agencies were biased because they were subject to outside influences, whereas AP was owned solely by newspapers and was therefore objective. This point is not compelling.

5. One wonders what LeMoyne would think of a news agency that was given a misleading government handout, which it published without question, and then, when the full document was made available, refused to look at it and report the facts therein, indefinitely. See Sourcing, above, and the discussion of the mass media's handling of the State Department's U.S./UNESCO Review.

6. "The Reagan administration lost no time taking aim at FOIA. On May 4, 1981, Attorney General William French Smith sent a memo to all government agencies, instructing them that the Justice Department would defend all denials of FOIA requests based on legal technicalities." Pell, p. 51. And see Preston, "Information as Obscenity," and Walter Karp, "Liberty Under Seige," *Harper's*, November 1985, p. 53.

7. Pell, *passim*; see also Demac.

8. Pell, p. 3.

9. Quoted in John Lloyd, "The Ferret," *The New Statesman*, January 30, 1987.

10. Committee to Protect Journalists, "Journalists Killed or Disappeared Since 1976," December 1986.

11. Council on Hemispheric Affairs and The Newspaper Guild, "A Survey of Press Freedom in Latin America," June 1983, p. 1.

12. "Press Censorship," *CPJ Update*, October-November 1986.

13. Argumedo, p. 187.

14. See Herman, *The Real Terror Network*, chap. 3.

15. As noted in the introduction, a very senior editor at a major newspaper said he most opposed the NWICO because it called for the licensing of journalists. Although he had not read the MacBride Report, he had read dozens of articles *about* it, and since they all said it called for the licensing of journalists, he refused to believe that, contrary to those articles, the report nowhere calls for the licensing of journalists.

16. U.S. National Commission for UNESCO, Report of the Press Conference of August 9, 1984, p. 3.

17. The media also showed great hostility to any *discussion* of these issues, a strange pattern of behavior for spokespersons for free flow, but consistent with my analysis of the roots of mass-media devotion to this subject. On the media's hostility to open debate on these issues, see further the Summary and Conclusions below.

G. The Non-Correctability of Error

One of the charges against the Western press by advocates of a NWICO has been its unwillingness to acknowledge and correct error. Most of the deficiencies of the U.S. media in treating the U.S. withdrawal from UNESCO, as described above, such as systematic bias in the use of sources and in framing issues, and the patriotic rewriting of history, are more serious than the refusal to admit and correct specific errors of fact. The former are the big errors that reflect fundamental bias; the latter are relatively petty errors of detail. Nevertheless, it is still of some interest to see that here also mass-media performance has been flawed and has failed to meet the media's own proclaimed standard of objectivity.

UNESCO officials were greatly aggravated by the fact that throughout the withdrawal period the media kept repeating that *UNESCO* was pushing for a NWICO (which was identified in the distorted fashion already described, as equivalent simply to "licensing" and "government control"). Their point was that claims and resolutions of member states were not those of "UNESCO," which should be institutionally identified only with proposals actually passed by a properly constituted vote. UNESCO officials, accordingly, sent a barrage of letters to the press asking for corrections on this point. Only very rarely were their letters published or corrections made, on this or other matters, usually in tiny back-page boxes.

On February 14, 1985, for example, Paul Lewis wrote in *The New York Times* that a French government gift to UNESCO of $2 million was given on the understanding that it was "not for such politically controversial programs as *Unesco's efforts to restrict press freedom and promote the rights of the state over those of the individual* [emphasis added]." A UNESCO letter to the *Times* protested that "it simply is not factually correct for Lewis to keep repeating" that UNESCO is trying to restrict press freedom, when all such proposals have been resoundingly defeated at both the General Conference and Executive Board levels. The letter notes that "The *Times* would [not] . . . describe the current Congress as 'pro-abortionist' because a few members have spoken out for that position in its debates." This letter was not published, nor was any correction forthcoming, although the Foreign Editor acknowledged that the reference was not "fully fair."[1]

An article by Paul Lewis on December 31, 1984, "UNESCO head denounces U.S. delegate," elicited from UNESCO a letter charging multiple errors (as well as a stream of "hostile suppositions about Mr. M'Bow's motives and intentions").[2] Based on gossip from "the usual unnamed 'western diplomats,'" Lewis claimed that M'Bow attended a meeting in Yemen primarily "to raise money to cover next year's budget gap." The announced reason for the visit, which UNESCO claims was the chief and *real* reason, was to launch a campaign for the restoration of the historic old city of Suna. Lewis never mentioned the announced official reason for the visit, although as we saw earlier, official explanations for *U.S.* actions regarding UNESCO were never once second-guessed by Lewis via unnamed or named sources. According to Lewis in the same article, M'Bow announced a million dollar gift to UNESCO by Libya at the Yemen meeting. This was a demonstrable falsehood, as a Libyan representative made the announcement. In the same piece Lewis also claimed that the Executive Board of UNESCO "specifically forbade the Director-General from borrowing money to replace the U.S. contribution." In fact, the board resolved that the shortfall could not be made up by larger assessments against members, but that the director-general could ask for voluntary contributions. UNESCO's response notes further, that in the same Lewis article of December 31,

> Mr. Lewis tries to portray the Director General as having "failed to heed" Secretary General Perez de Cuellar's call for a 17 December meeting on the African famine. The truth is that the call was for heads of agencies or their senior deputies to attend. Only one head of an agency headquartered outside of New York, Mr. Saouma of the Food and Agriculture Organization, attended personally. Mr. M'Bow was represented by Mr. John Kabore, Assistant Director-General for External Relations. Mr. Lewis even appears to forget that Mr. M'Bow personally visited Ethiopia last month as was widely reported in the Ethiopian and European press.

The UNESCO letter was not published, and of the four errors or distortions noted above (there were others cited in the letter), the *Times* published a very tiny back-page retraction of the claim that M'Bow had announced the Libyan gift.

A page-one article by Paul Lewis on August 15, 1984, "U.S. and UNESCO In a New Clash On Special Fund," contended that the Western countries "fear that the $80 million surplus [generated by an exchange rate change] could be used by UNESCO to offset the crippling financial impact of the United States withdrawal on the agency's activities." This scare story, based once again on an unnamed "western diplomat," was plain disinformation. UNESCO's printed financial regulations, in effect since 1951, require that surplus funds generated by an unexpected development such as an exchange-rate readjustment must be held available for twelve months following the end of the financial period to liquidate any outstanding obligations, after which they are to be distributed to the members. At the General Conference of November 10, 1983 and at an Executive Board meeting on May 9, 1984, M'Bow explained to the delegates and members that, because the surplus was so large he was going to return $70 of the $80 million early. A UNESCO letter to *The New York Times* notes that U.S. officials were present when M'Bow made these statements, and that "there never has been any question about the Director General's intention to return the surplus funds." The UNESCO letter also goes on to state:

> It should be pointed out, too, which the story does not, that the United States share of the 1984 UNESCO Budget was reduced from about $43 million to about $25 million, because of the initial surplus credit; and that this amount has not yet been paid, although it was due at the end of February under the provision of the rules and regulations.

In other words, while passing along a fabricated scare story about the threat of *UNESCO*'s not returning money owed to the United States and the West, Paul Lewis and *The New York Times* suppressed the fact that at that very moment the *United States* was delinquent in its financial obligations to UNESCO![3] The *Times* also suppressed the fact that the U.S. obligation to UNESCO was cut to $25 million in 1984. We noted earlier how preoccupied the U.S. media was with the size and importance of the U.S. contribution to UNESCO. Mentioning the reduction by half would seem like a newsworthy fact on the media's own terms—but mentioning it would show the U.S. contribution to be more modest, and the return of the money by UNESCO would put that organization in a slightly more favorable light. So the *Times* prefers featuring a fraudulent threat that UNESCO might fail to meet its obligations.

Still another set of errors appears in the same article: Paul Lewis states that a new public-relations contract between UNESCO and Wagner and Baroody will involve fees of "about $15,000 a week" which will come out of "regular budget funds." The sum agreed upon was for $10-15,000 per *month*, and the money was *not* to be taken out of regular budget funds.[4] Of all of these errors and omissions, the only thing *The New York Times* retracted was the figure of $15,000 per week as the PR payment—again in a tiny back-page box.

In *The New York Times* feature "Washington Talk" on October 8, 1985, the lead item is entitled "A Raise at UNESCO." Once again the *Times* focuses on the alleged "profligate management" of UNESCO, asserting that the austerity imposed by the U.S. withdrawal seems to have failed to produce any "belt-tightening." "Word is now circulating in Washington, in fact, that the agency's Director General, Amadou Mahtar M'Bow, was recently voted a big raise in a closed meeting. State Department officials say Mr. M'Bow was given an increase of 26.8 percent, retroactive to Jan. 1, bringing his salary, as computed for pension purposes, to $159,115."

This was based on another straightforward piece of disinformation, which the newspaper of record failed to check out with any source other than the State Department. Once again UNESCO officials complained and rushed documents to *The New York Times* showing that the increase in base salary was exactly offset by a reduction in cost-of-living allowance, so that the net increase in Mr. M'Bow's income was zero. Furthermore, the action was not taken behind "closed doors," but was a bookkeeping adjustment adopted by the U.N. General Assembly and applicable to all U.N. agencies, and ratified unanimously by the UNESCO Executive Board, with Western representatives present.

In trying to get this piece of disinformation corrected, UNESCO officials not only sent along a letter of correction plus extensive documentation, it urged that the *Times* publish a rebuttal in the "Washington Talk" column where the error appeared. This might be justified on the grounds that not only was the error blatant, but it was also embedded in another flood of innuendo denigrating UNESCO. The Washington Bureau chief, B. Drummond Ayres, Jr., suggested that the UNESCO documentation be sent to him through the Foreign News editor in New York, Warren Hoge. Later that day, UNESCO was called by the *Times* and informed that both Hoge and the Letters Department had "lost" the UNESCO materials (which had been hand-delivered to each). UNESCO hand-delivered another set, marked urgent and to be delivered to the Washington Bureau. After nothing happened for several days, UNESCO officials called Washington and were told by Ayres that the third packet of materials hand-delivered to the *Times* had never reached him! Either this is a paper that exemplifies the ultimate in mismanagement, or one that has mastered the art of apparent bungling to evade making honest decisions.[5] On October 17, nine days after the disinforming article, the *Times* published a tiny retraction, far from "Washington Talk," which stated tersely that M'Bow's salary had not in fact been changed.

These are but a few illustrations of the problems of correctability of relatively minor errors. The larger errors, as noted earlier, flow from the premises of benevolence and honesty, and the acceptance of the Reagan administration charges, along with other biased frames, before the gathering of any news. It is because of this deeper bias that the lesser errors are both numerous, unidirectional, frequently nasty, and hard to get corrected. The occasional, partial back-page corrections of the minor errors are, of course, wholly incapable of offsetting a flood of quite effective propaganda.

NOTES

1. These letters and those that follow were made available to the writer from the files of a UNESCO public-relations officer of UNESCO's correspondence with the media.

2. This article by Lewis is also discussed above in the section on Language.

3. This was far from the first time that the United States had done this, although readers of the *Times* would never know this. Both the ILO and UNESCO were refused payment by the United States in the 1970s, the latter for about two years, and in violation of its legal commitment. See Lawrence S. Finkelstein, "Introductory Remarks," in "A Critical Assessment of U.S. Participation in UNESCO," Special Meeting of the U.S. National Commission for UNESCO, University of South Carolina, June 1–3, 1982, p. 13.

4. The interest of the press in this UNESCO PR effort was discussed earlier and contrasted with the suppression of information on the State Department's PR campaign. The Pentagon's PR effort, which runs to several hundred million out of regular budget funds, is also much less interesting to the mass media.

5. Six review copies of the author's book *The Real Terror Network: Terrorism in Fact and Propaganda* were allegedly "misplaced" by the *Times* before the book's publisher found the humor of the evasive method too costly to pursue any further.

H. Non-Disclosure of Corporate Interest

There has been a long-standing tendency for countries well positioned to compete abroad to favor "free trade," and countries not able to compete well to support the protection of "infant industries" and otherwise impede free trade. This is always explicated as a matter of high principle, although reflecting material economic interests. In the post-World War II period the United States has been in the position that Great Britain occupied in the mid-nineteenth century, with economic advantage coinciding with open-door economic policies.

This has applied to the communications industries along with many others. The major media institutions of the United States are transnational, with large external sales and close ties with advertising agencies and other transnational corporations (TNCs) which also have extensive dealings in the Third World. New press agencies and limits on freedom of access to Third World markets would threaten their economic interests. They therefore have a clear conflict of interest in discussing debates over a NWICO, and treating it purely as a matter of high principle, without disclosure of this conflict, would in itself be a failure of objectivity.

In 1972 the U.S. mass media created a lobbying organization, the World Press Freedom Committee (WPFC), which become active in 1976, for the purpose of monitoring and opposing the threats they perceived as emanating from UNESCO and the proponents of the NWICO.[1] On the Executive and Advisory Committees and Board of Directors of the WPFC have been representatives of a large segment of the U.S. mass media (Time, Inc., *The New York Times*, Gannett, Knight-Ridder, Hearst, ABC News, the National Association of Broadcasting, the American Newspaper Publishers Association, and others). The leaders of this organization have not been subtle about their aims and tactics. Its long-time head, George Beebe of *The Miami Herald*, noted in an address before the Inter-American Press Association on October 15, 1980 that "our strongest weapon to support our principles is money. Some of our loudest critics in UNESCO will shake their fists at us with one hand and hold out their palm with the other." So the WPFC has doled out small sums to its friends as part of its defense of high principle.[2]

Its main effort, however, has been aggressive propaganda and lobbying. Here too the level of discourse has not been of a high order. In Beebe's speech just cited, although he mentions the "terrorism" afflicting journalists in Latin America, Beebe was quite unable to locate the sources of this violence, and the murders and "eradication of a press that reports these atrocities" were still not of first-order importance: "Foremost is the dangerous licensing of journalists." And throughout the period 1976–85, the formula incessantly repeated by Beebe and his successor, Dana Bullen, was that the issue is freedom versus government control, freedom meaning simply private ownership of the media, and government control meaning the licensing of journalists.

The WPFC was the principal organizer of a conference on "Voices of Freedom" held at Talloires, France, May 15–17, 1981, which attempted to "answer" the challenges of the advocates of a NWICO and assert the verities of the status quo. To ensure that true principles of a free press would be clearly enunciated, no spokesperson for the NWICO was present to speak at the gathering, a point not mentioned in the press accounts.[3] The carefully selected participants came up with what the *Miami Herald* referred to—repeating the press handout of the WPFC—as a "historic" Declaration of Talloires, which reiterated the central threat of government control, but rather forthrightly added a ringing defense of advertising as a proper financial base for an independent press. The declaration states, however, that "we adhere to the principle that editorial decisions must be free of advertising influence." But the declaration fails to explain how this can happen if advertising is the funding base and advertisers are what organization theorists call "primary referent organizations" to the media.[4] The Talloires Declaration doesn't say that "if governments fund the media they should refrain from interfering with editorial decisions." It implies that government interference would be structured into the process by funding, so that admonitions not to interfere would be question-begging. That the Talloires participants fail to see that their own admonition is equally question-begging reflects their own deeply structured bias.

The only "dissident" speaking at Talloires was UNESCO Director General M'Bow, who gave a low-key address pointing out that all UNESCO debates and actions on these issues were based on the concerns of its majority and were not "some sort of 'maneuver' on the part of persons unknown"; that the main *actual* activities of UNESCO in the communications field have been cooperative efforts at building up media infrastructures in the Third World; and that underlying the debate was the fact that advancing technology and inequality made for legitimate anxieties on the part of the Third World that their views could not get a hearing and that maintaining their very autonomy and independence was not easy.[5] It was a foretaste of things to come that M'Bow was treated at the conference with intense hostility, that the press covered the Talloires conference with great generosity[6] and one-sidedness, that the press failed to mention the mass media's material conflict of interest in the issues of the conference, and that M'Bow's views should be captured (and misrepresented) in a Paul Lewis article entitled "Unesco Says It Will Persist in Effort to Regulate Press."[7]

Only 3 of 215 news articles in our mass-media sample mention that the U.S. corporate system and media have some kind of economic stake in free flow, and none of these provides a serious analysis of the issue. Flora Lewis gives the most extensive statement on the matter[8]:

> There has been a tendency to consider the never-ending battles for press freedom as a kind of special interest fight, a self-serving claim to privilege from one more commercial industry, alongside oil or sugar or automobiles.
>
> This is in part the fault of the media, which do try to defend their profits but don't always explain their purpose. Commercial survival is the condition of the service of freedom. The U.S. Constitution provides that the government "shall make no law . . . abridging the freedom of speech, or of the press"—not for the protection of journalists but of everyone. . . .
>
> Americans have an immediate stake in buttressing the ability of people in other countries to assert the same rights. Their success will play a large part in determining whether the United States finds itself living with a predominantly antagonistic Third World or in a beneficial partnership.

We may note that in her first paragraph Flora Lewis states that there has been "a tendency" to regard the media struggle as that of a special interest. This is factually incorrect. The existence of a media corporate interest has almost never been mentioned in media discussions of their campaign against the NWICO—it is almost invariably expressed as a struggle for high principle alone. Lewis admits that media companies "do try to defend their profits," but she explains that this is all done for a higher purpose. This actually goes beyond Charles Wilson's famous dictum, "What's good for General Motors is good for America." Wilson never suggested that GM's *purpose* was to benefit America, merely that its prosperity was essential for national prosperity. Lewis, however, suggests that the media are interested in profits only to enable them to survive and continue to protect the First Amendment! This is all bald assertion, of course. The mass-media corporations have increasingly been bought and sold in the market like pork bellies, by investors who seem in no way different in their profit orientation from buyers of sugar and oil companies. Those who control these companies are even legally obligated to serve their stockholders' interest, not merely to "survive" and work for the First Amendment. Why should we assume that owners of media corporations want only modest profits? Have their profits been modest? Is it possible that the pursuit of profits, and the commercial necessity of making profits, could abridge the freedom of speech and press for those not able to "survive" or compete with the commercial media? The fact that Flora Lewis never comes near addressing these questions reflects the superficiality of her apologetics.

In the third paragraph Flora Lewis moves to the rights of other peoples, and the U.S. interest in having other peoples also benefit from the global application of the First Amendment, interpreted as unconstrained private enterprise in communications. All the problems raised by the debate over a NWICO (which as we have seen were never discussed in the U.S. mass media) regarding concentration, technological and power differentials, threats to cultural integrity and sovereignty, and the use and support of force to impose regimes sympathetic to commercial free flow but hostile to democracy, Lewis simply pushes under the rug. According to her, the West and its commercial press seek only freedom and a "beneficial partnership" with the Third World (as in sponsoring Marcos, Mobutu, Pinochet, and Castillo Branco in Brazil in 1964?).[9] This is ideology, not analysis. Its simplicity and crudeness is one more reflection of the deep bias that is so evident in the media's coverage of the U.S. withdrawal from UNESCO.

NOTES

1. See "The World Press Freedom Committee Story," a letter issued by WPFC, signed by Harold Anderson, chairman of the WPFC, on March 25, 1981.

2. The letter mentioned in the previous footnote lists twelve WPFC grants to help LDCs develop their communications systems, the largest of which was $20,000 to the

Inter-American Press Association for seminars to be conducted in Latin America and the Caribbean.

3. M'Bow was an invited speaker, but from his position as director-general of UNESCO his remarks, though radically out of line with those of the other speakers, were necessarily conciliatory.

4. Evan, p. 123; Turow, pp. 51–52.

5. M'Bow also stated that the Third World wants its voice heard, "without, however, preventing others from obtaining and disseminating information on them." Address of May 16, 1981, p. 2.

6. Talloires is a famous, luxury vacation resort, with a number of France's best restaurants. No news report mentioned this fact, or suggested that this choice of location might reflect discreditable boondoggling for elite journalists on expense accounts.

7. *New York Times*, May 17, 1981.

8. Flora Lewis, "A Duty of Freedom," *New York Times*, October 4, 1983.

9. Flora Lewis wrote a classic piece of apologetics for the U.S.-sponsored overthrow of the elected government of Guatemala in 1954 ("Ambassador Extraordinary: John Peurifoy," *New York Times Magazine*, July 18, 1954), an event that was followed by over 30 years of repression and state terrorism, including the previously mentioned murders of 48 journalists between 1978 and 1982. For an analysis of her more up-to-date apologetics for this "beneficial partnership," see Herman, *The Real Terror Network*, pp. 173–77.

III. SUMMARY AND CONCLUSIONS

The mass-media treatment of the U.S. withdrawal from UNESCO was a test of their capacity to treat impartially a controversial issue on which they held strong editorial positions and in which they had a conflict of interest. The mass media failed this test resoundingly.

As I have described above, mass-media newsmakers consistently worked on the basis of patriotic premises that limited their ability to ask questions. Thus while UNESCO officials were often described as devious, ill-qualified, and in search of dubious objectives, such negative characterizations were never applied to U.S. officials, despite frequent outcroppings of suspicious evidence. Furthermore, if the administration said that it was concerned about "management" in UNESCO and interested in "reform," the mass media took this at face value and simply refused to consider contrary facts or entertain the possibility of real reasons differing from nominal claims (Section IIA).

The primary media frame of reference was the set of charges leveled against UNESCO by the State Department—politicization, mismanagement, and a threat to a free press—which, although vague and ideologically charged, the media took as valid without the slightest independent investigation. Their perceived role was merely to elaborate on and illustrate these truths. Alternative ways of looking at the issues, such as that used by advocates of a NWICO, were entirely ignored. Sources that yielded findings consistent with the basic premises and charges were used uncritically, those that conflicted with them were used superficially or not at all (Section IIB). The context offered by the media was a mythical history of a "nonpolitical" UNESCO gone astray under the malign influence of Third World radicals, the Soviet Union, and an opportunistic and autocratic director-general. Real history was not allowed to surface during the withdrawal period (Section IID).

The media accepted the ideological language and frames of the State Department, and added their own quota of invidious language. The use of strong language in describing UNESCO Director-General M'Bow and UNESCO contrasts starkly with the language used to designate U.S. officials and institutions (Tables 5 and 6). The level of vituperation applied to M'Bow and to UNESCO supports the view that UNESCO was the "Grenada" of the multinational organizations. Headed by a black African, with a Third World majority, guilty of aid to the PLO, other national liberation movements, peace and disarmament studies,[1] and the scene of debates over issues deemed threatening to Western communications and other transnational corporate interests, this relatively friendless organization was an ideal target for an unconstrained propaganda assault.

That UNESCO was a victim of a propaganda campaign is suggested by other features of media coverage: the intensity of the search for derogatory information; the willingness to use anonymous sources and to pass along rumor and speculation without verification; the reiteration of the idea that the level of talk and speculation was itself proof of something; the fact that accounts and documents offering information and lines of thought incompatible with the government charges were ignored or trivialized; and the frequency with which the media made errors of fact, which were unidirectional and usually non-correctable (Sections IIB and IIG). When the GAO report was finally "leaked" in September 1984, the mass media carefully selected all the negatives, ignored everything positive, and succeeded in conveying the false impression that the GAO report "supported the Reagan administration charges" (Section IIE). Although the media campaign had featured heavily the prospective disclosures of corruption at UNESCO, when none were forthcoming the media played dumb. Having exploited the GAO report for more than it was worth, the media then allowed UNESCO to drop out of sight again. This is the characteristic pattern of a propaganda campaign.[2]

Although the media had a serious conflict of interest in discussing UNESCO, given their perception of a material threat associated with a NWICO, they failed to disclose this fact, a violation of first principles of full disclosure. They claimed a pure and undefiled interest in the free and unconstrained flow of information. It is demonstrable, however, that the Western mass media have been more deeply concerned with the hypothetical licensing of journalists under a NWICO than they have been over growing internal constraints on free flow within their own countries and those imposed in National Security States which *kill* journalists and close down papers, but allow free commerce (if not ideas). This dichotomous treatment is hard to explain on the basis of principle alone, but is quite comprehensible on the grounds of material interests (Section IIF). Another anomaly is the extent to which the mass media have denounced (and misrepresented) *debates* over media questions. Debates are a feature of free flow, but from the Costa Rica conference of 1976 through the withdrawal period, the mass media resented and opposed them,[3] and deceptively pretended that the debates constituted official positions of UNESCO (Section IIF).

Seth Spaulding, professor of international and development education at the University of Pittsburgh, and former director of UNESCO's Department of Educational Methods and Techniques, points out the "interesting irony" that "representatives of the 'free press' often object strongly to the open study and discussion of various points of view in UNESCO programs and projects." He explains this on the ground that

> commercially controlled news agencies are adamantly against any discussion of problems in the communications field that may suggest new initiatives to increase (not decrease) access to news, information, and education through channels not controlled by existing commercial interests. The "free press" is actually a network of people and commercial organizations which are extremely sensitive to any examination of the way they go about their business, even though they vigorously defend their right to critically examine all other institutions and all other social, economic, and political processes.[4]

Finally, we should note the media's long-standing refusal to correct errors and to report criticism of their own performance. I pointed out earlier (Section IB) that the media's own watchdog, the National News Council, had berated them for failing to meet standards of impartiality in reporting on the UNESCO Belgrade Conference of 1980, and that *the media had then suppressed this finding.* In the present study, the only mention of the National News Council study occurred in one of our small sample of non-establishment articles (see Table 3).

The media failure in its presentation of the U.S. withdrawal[5] continues a long tradition of extremely biased and self-serving coverage of UNESCO, as described in the early part of this study (Section IB). A parallel bias has also characterized press coverage of UNESCO in Great Britain and France. This refutes the claim that only "government control" impairs press objectivity; it appears that private ownership and the commercial nexus can produce systematic bias over many years and across national boundaries. And from the evidence of this study, the severity of bias of a commercial press would be difficult to surpass.

NOTES

1. I show in Section IIE how the media exaggerate the size of these UNESCO allocations, and suppress the evidence concerning their programmatic role.

2. See Herman and Brodhead, chap. 7.

3. Roncagliolo points out that "the much-publicized UNESCO Regional Conference on National Communication Policies held in San Jose de Costa Rica in 1976 was proof that the forces opposing even the mere discussion of these issues are present and powerful." (Section I, note 1, p. 169.) See the discussion of AP coverage of this conference, in Section IB above.

4. Panel commentary, in "A Critical Assessment of U.S. Participation in UNESCO," Special Meeting of the U.S. National Commission for UNESCO, University of South Carolina, June 1–3, 1982, pp. 12–13.

5. This failure is confirmed in the forthcoming study of press coverage of the withdrawal by C. Anthony Giffard, cited above, and in an excellent Master of Science thesis by Jack Banks, *The Contradiction of A "Free Press": An Analysis of U.S. Press Coverage of UNESCO*, Department of Speech and Graduate School, University of Oregon, 1984.

Herbert I. Schiller

IS THERE A UNITED STATES
INFORMATION POLICY?

I. INTRODUCTION

United States information policy, it has often been asserted, does not exist. In the sense that there is no single, coherent policy formulation, or site of such formulation, or even a policy document, this assertion is correct. It is also true that there is no single governmental agency or division which is in indisputable control or which has general responsibility for overall information policy. There are numerous sites in the federal bureaucracy where information issues are decided and policy determined. There are, for example, the trade division of the Department of Commerce, the information activities of the U.S. Information Agency, the vast communication systems and activities of the military, the allocation of the radio spectrum by an intergovernmental unit, the Federal Communications Commission's domestic responsibilities (many of which have been eliminated or severely cut back in recent years), and numerous other governmental agencies with information-policy responsibilities.

There is, as well, the dominant, private sector, where enormous information activity proceeds daily and policies regarding it are made by private corporate managements, concerned with market share and short-run profitability.

In this seemingly near-chaotic mix of fragmented governmental and uncoordinated private firm decision-making, it is not difficult to conclude that there is no actual information policy guiding the destiny of the economy. Further support to this conclusion is supplied by the repeated demands, expressed in governmental and other circles, for a national information policy. This plea has surfaced continuously since the 1950s.

Yet despite the messiness, the contradictions, the rivalries and the already considerable and still growing problems in the information sphere, it would be a mistake to believe that basic and underlying direction was entirely absent from United States information policy. This direction or focus, whatever its inconsistencies, has been to attend to the vital needs of a transnational, corporate business system and its ancillary functions.

In pursuit of these needs, the information policy followed by the United States since World War II days has been, in the large, to contain the world-wide changes arising from the war—the expansion of socialism and the growth of national independence movements. It has also been shaped to facilitate the other major outcome of the war, the emergence in 1945 of the United States as the dominant political-economic-military power in the world-market economy.

In response to these changes, U.S. policy moved along three main lines: (1) an untiring effort devoted to penetrating the governing echelons of the new nations and influencing them to attach their nations to the world-market system if they were not already part of it, or, if they were, strengthening their ties to it; (2) the protection and extension wherever possible of American commercial media flows and products, and later along, of the still more important data flows of transnational enterprises; (3) unrelenting anticommunism, produced and circulated by every communication medium in every possible format, eventualizing frequently in actual campaigns of national destabilization. The "communist threat" was applied to nationalist as well as liberal reformist movements and leaders including Mossadegh in Iran, Juan Bosch in the Dominican Republic, Goulart in Brazil, and Lumumba in Zaire, each of whom was deposed by U.S. interventions.

While these activities engaged the attention and energy of governmental and corporate policy-makers alike, the focus of American academic research on communication issues provided the political decision-makers with the rationale and recommendations with which to implement many of their aims.[1]

A limited number of principles and practices have guided the main policy lines noted above, over the last 40 years. First and foremost, has been the doctrine of the free flow of information which insists that no national need or purpose can justify interference with the prevailing flow of messages and imagery, wherever its source and whatever its character of production.

A separate but related doctrine is the claim of "objectivity" and "neutrality" of the informational apparatus, especially its news and entertainment function, if it is secured by private ownership of the media. The corollary is that to the extent a nation departs from a privately owned, advertising-supported media system, it is on the road to tyranny.

A logical consequence of this position is the steadfast opposition to, and rejection of, international codes or agreements that would endorse some degree of social accountability for the informational system in general and journalists in particular.

Finally, there is the eulogization and promotion of the new information technologies—satellite, computer, television, cable—as the preferred means of reducing communication inequalities between and inside nations.

These doctrines and practices, in turn, have been supported by national diplomacy and sometimes force, as well as by an exercise of monopoly control of communication facilities wherever and, as far as, possible. In general, a very close cooperation between the government and the private corporate media in the pursuit of these positions has also marked the last four decades.

II. U.S. DOMINANCE IN THE EARLY POSTWAR PERIOD

Not unlike the English, who claimed to have acquired an empire in the eighteenth and nineteenth centuries by inadvertence, there still exist those who continue to describe the innocence and surprise of U.S. leaders at contemplating their commanding position and dominance over global affairs evident in 1945.

Yet this posture of embarrassment at being in control is hardly credible alongside a detailed record of the fierce pressure exerted by American leadership, while the war was still being fought, to wrest control of rich economic and political prizes from allies and adversaries alike. In short, the war and, brief as it was, the early postwar period, saw unparalleled U.S. power, consciously deployed internationally, as well as continuous efforts to extend the boundaries of that power.

The information sphere, no less than the domains of trade, industry, and finance, insisted on doctrines, and pursued initiatives, on behalf of their global advantage.

Beyond the primary need of winning the war, one other question absorbed the energies of the national leadership during the war years. This was the question of what would the United States' place in world affairs be after the war was over. Thinking about, and planning for, the peace took many directions, but whatever the specific interest area, essentially two, fundamentally opposing options for relating to the postwar situation were available to the American planners and decision-makers. One was full cooperation with the international community, however different that relationship might be in its specificity for countries with unlike social systems. The other option, also able to be pursued in a multitude of ways, was the quest for domination—the aggrandizement of American economic and political power, exercised internationally.

The alternatives were especially evident and stark in the informational sector. In this sphere, the decisions taken matched those made in the more familiar and more widely publicized fields of economics and finance. But the informational actions were less transparent because of the special attribute characteristic of any informational apparatus.

Sharing many features with other economic and industrial activities, the information/communication sector possesses an additional, unique quality. It controls the definition and presentation of itself, and thereby is relatively invulnerable to critics and criticism. For this reason, the course followed in information policy by the United States in the postwar period is more dense and difficult to disentangle than the more straightforward pursuit of economic privilege and power.

III. THE HUTCHINS COMMISSION ON FREEDOM OF THE PRESS: THE COOPERATIVE OPTION

Still, the same two options existed in the informational sphere—the cooperative and the dominating. The cooperative path, never seriously considered, was formulated by the staff of the Hutchins Commission on Freedom of the Press. The concept of the commission was discussed in 1942, and it was established in 1944 with a grant from Henry Luce, founder of Time, Inc.

The commission, in its own words, "was created to consider the freedom, functions, and responsibilities of the major agencies of mass communication in our time: newspapers, radio, motion pictures, news-gathering media, magazines, books."[2]

In retrospect, the creation of the Commission on Freedom of the Press was a brilliant initiative, prescient of the enormously enhanced role of information in the years to come. Given the source of the commission's underwriting, a media mogul with his own vision of a dawning American Century—which he took every opportunity to publicize in his influential publications—it was all the more remarkable that a group of eminent Americans in law, education, and the social sciences would be assembled and produce independent work, some of which could have served as the basis for a very different informational course than that which was adopted.

The commission was fully aware, from its first meeting, that it faced an urgent time factor. The economic-political-cultural arrangements that would be established in the immediate postwar period would quickly be institutionalized and set the course of international affairs for a long time to come.

Taking this into account, the commission's staff mobilized its energies and published in 1946 a small but insightful study on international communications. The work's authors noted "the pressing urgency of certain problems in this field—especially the problem of the participation of the government of the United States in peacetime international communication and information services."[3]

In the preface to the study, the commission itself notes:

> Recent improvements in the machinery and methods of international communication have made possible, for the first time in history, direct communication across national boundaries to the masses of people of the world. These mechanical improvements offer at once a new hope and a new danger. The choice is not between the use or the neglect of these new instruments of communication. The instruments exist and will be used in any case. The choice is between their full, purposeful, and responsible use to enlarge the mutual comprehension of peoples, on the one hand, and, on the other, their incomplete, undirected, and

irresponsible use, with the risk of an increase in international hatred and suspicion as a consequence.[4]

The central concern that animates *Peoples Speaking to Peoples* is the issue of responsibility. The authors ask:

> On what, then, must the people feed in order to be capable of reaching wise decisions? . . . The surest antidote for ignorance and deceit is the widest possible exchange of objectively realistic information — *true* information, not merely *more* information; *true* information, not merely, as those who would have us simply write the First Amendment into international law seem to suggest, the *unhindered flow* of information! There is evidence that a mere quantitative increase in the flow of words and images across national borders may replace ignorance with prejudice and distortion rather than with understanding. [Emphasis in the original.][5]

Observing that peoples who "have enjoyed the widest access to means of international communication often have retained more distorted images of others than people living in relative ignorance of the outer world," the authors, White and Leigh, conclude:

> The problem then, is twofold. It is that of bringing the physical facilities for transmitting words and images across national boundaries within the reach of all; of lowering, and, wherever possible, removing the barriers erected at those boundaries. It is also that of achieving a degree of quality, accuracy and total balance calculated to give a fair picture of the life of each country to all the world. And we cannot assume that achievement of the first automatically will produce the second.[6]

What the commission and its staff refused to take for granted, and what it insisted on as a consequence, was that improved facilities for communication would not necessarily ensure honest and accurate information flow. What was necessary for this to occur was some mechanism or structure or agreement that would ensure the social accountability of the information-gatherers and transmitters. This fundamental perspective set the commission's work and recommendations totally at odds with the United States information policy being negotiated or proposed in the international arena from 1944 on.

Indeed, while the Commission on Freedom of the Press was still in the process of getting established in 1945, U.S. editors and publishers were traveling around the world in army transport planes, carrying their message of unimpeded free flow of information, and their concept of a privately owned, advertiser-supported free press, to whoever would meet them in their global hops and stopovers.

At the same time, the United States Congress, under advice and pressure from media owners (to whom the legislators have always been most receptive), was passing resolutions, practically drafted by the American Society of Newspaper Editors, endorsing the free flow of information, without the qualifications and caution expressed by the Hutchins people.[7]

These actions were set against the background of America's dominant global position at war's end. President Truman, in 1947, addressed himself to this extraordinary development:

> We are the giant of the world. Whether we like it or not ["we" did like it] the future pattern of economic relations depends upon us. The world is watching to see what we shall do. The choice is ours.

Truman explained what would govern this choice:

> There is one thing that Americans value even more than peace. [This statement made after the detonation of two American atomic bombs over Japan.] It is freedom: freedom of worship—freedom of speech—and freedom of enterprise.[8]

The president made it clear that it was the last freedom, of enterprise, that was the major concern, although freedom of speech, interpreted to embrace the free flow of corporate media products and information, was equally essential to the emerging imperial system.

The media, and the U.S. press agencies in particular, shared, and worked actively toward fulfilling, these visions, eagerly appropriating the concept of freedom to their own practices. The importance of controlling international communication extended well beyond the parochial, though still important, economic interests of news agencies and press corporations seeking to move into world markets. *Business Week*, in mid-1945, reported:

> Washington recognizes the postwar importance of freer communications as a stimulant to the interchange of goods and ideas. On a less lofty level it means that federal officials are trying to loosen the grip which the British have long held through their cable system, which they tightened after the last war through the seizure of German properties. . . . In peacetime, reduced costs of messages will energize our trade, support our propaganda, bolster business for all the lines.[9]

IV. THE WESTERN DOCTRINES OF FREE FLOW AND FREE PRESS

Journalistically phrased perhaps, but right on target, "freer communications" became the free flow of information, and that doctrine has been, without exception or qualification, the central pillar of American international information policy though not practice, with respect to its own actions, for more than four decades. It remains so to this day.

What accounts for the enormous importance conferred on free flow by U.S. leaders? Its value is that it skillfully and seamlessly blends corporate advantage, media domination, and the yearnings of people everywhere for contact and full expression, at the same time that it confers an enormous propaganda advantage on its advocates.

Coming at the end of a ferocious and devastating war, in which the Fascists elevated physical coercion and the suppression of human thought to barbaric levels of state policy, the proclamation of a free flow of information principle received widespread popular approval, in Europe especially, but elsewhere as well.

What free flow meant in practice, is another matter entirely. To understand its actual significance requires attention to context and processes, relationships generally given short shrift in the popular media. The late Finnish president, Urho Kekkonen, in 1973, undertook this explanatory task:

> "Could it be," he asked, "that the prophets who preach unhindered communication are not concerned with equality between nations, but are on the side of the stronger and wealthier? . . . More and more it can be seen that a mere liberalistic freedom of communication is not in everyday reality a neutral ideal, but a way in which an enterprise with many resources at its disposal has greater opportunities than weaker brethren to make its own hegemony accepted."[10]

President Kekkonen was too discreet to inquire *who* had as many informational and general resources at its disposal in 1945 as did the U.S. media companies and the U.S. government. There were additional advantages in the advocacy of the free flow doctrine for the postwar expansionist policy of U.S. economic and media interests. Economies not organized on the private ownership of basic goods and services facilities, and not accepting an advertising-supported, privately owned media, were declared, by the guardians of the free-flow doctrine, to be automatically outside the boundaries of freedom. A clamorous and unrelenting campaign, still being waged, was undertaken against the nonmarket societies, branding them "unfree" and their people deprived of reliable news and information.

National information policies in the ex-colonial nations of Asia and Africa, to channel the attention and the energies of the people to the enormous tasks they faced, were deemed, as well, coercive and damaging to human freedom by Western critics.[11] Yet these countries with their harsh legacy of colonialism—exhausted economies, financial bankruptcy, absence of skilled cadres, widespread illiteracy, desperate health, food, and housing needs—faced unique and overwhelming tasks.

To the extent that the media in these countries followed Western marketing practices, they became the conduits of consumerism, creating demand for products and services that could be afforded only by a small middle-and upper-income stratum. A divided society and a distorted economy would be the inevitable outcome.

The information system in these countries, more often than not, intentionally was enlisted as an active force in meeting these urgent needs. The Western media, integrally part of the market economy wherever they operated, insisted on their objectivity and value neutrality and were implacably hostile to the straightforward national involvements of many of the media systems in the rest of the world. Western definitions of press freedom could not, and would not, include media responsible to other than private-ownership principles.

Relatedly, it is noteworthy that U.S. information policy resisted bitterly and successfully, any effort, from any quarter, to establish standards for true, honest, and socially useful information along the lines recommended by the Hutchins Commission. The assumption at all times was that Western information was "free" and reliable, and by (their own) definition, socialist or national development information could not be taken at face value.

In the 40 years that followed, the Western media's self-serving description of itself as "free," in contrast to the "controlled" or "enslaved" media elsewhere, has constituted the kernel of the Western ideological position. Governing classes throughout the Western world have shared and propagated the same theme, albeit with local variations and adaptations. Still, the range and influence of the U.S. information apparatus have circulated this perspective globally. An ironic touch on this is that this partisan rhetoric, in recent years, has enabled transnational enterprises to pry open and seriously weaken state institutions of broadcasting and telecommunications in the developed market economies, no less than in the less-industrialized nations.[12]

V. HEY-DAY OF FREE FLOW AND THE EMERGENCE OF THE NEW NATIONS

The 1950s and early 1960s saw the free-flow doctrine implemented globally, with massive media flows moving from a few Western centers— mostly New York, Hollywood, London—to peoples and nations around the world. In international organizations, free-flow doctrine prevailed. Western communication studies and methodologies were accepted, generally uncritically, in the international arena. UNESCO, for example, churned out reams of paper by scholars who took the free flow as a guarantor and guide of universal improvement.

While Western informational-cultural policy seemed triumphant in this period, other developments were changing the basic contours of the international community and eventually would call into question Western information dominance.

The breakdown of the formal colonial system after the war, the many national struggles against the restoration of colonialism in this period, and the emergence, in a few decades, of more than 100 new nations transformed the world state system and, inevitably, relations between nations as well. Consequently, the concerns that preoccupied and motivated the new nations and their leaders, though hardly given attention, much less satisfaction, by the privileged, industrialized societies, all the same, eventually forced their way onto international agendas.

The formation of the Non-Aligned Movement in 1961, by leaders of 25 of the newly independent nations, marked the beginning of a continuing effort by the new states of Africa and Asia, and the Latin American countries whose economic independence remained to be achieved, to change the structures and rules of the international economic and information order.

Focusing initially on the economic disabilities imposed on them, it soon became evident that economic independence, or at least improvement, was inconceivable without parallel and far-reaching informational and cultural change. The inseparability of economic and informational power, and the latter's reinforcement of the former, increasingly were manifest to the countries affected.

The entire character of what constituted economic improvement was (and is) defined by the Western media, the source of a continuous and pervasive inculcation of new consumer tastes and criteria. However irrelevant, or unrealistic, or injurious to the achievement of the satisfaction of elemental needs—food, health, shelter, community well-being—the individualistic, acquisitive, self-preoccupied accumulation of goods and services are the daily instruction of U.S. film and television.[13]

At the political level, corporate control of the informational apparatus provides Western audiences with distorted representations of poor world leaders and their policies which are not acceptable to the transnational corporate order. Daniel Ortega, Sandinista leader, is presented as a thug in designer glasses. Qaddafi is described as a monomaniacal womanizer. Decades ago, Iran's Mossadegh was portrayed by the media as an emotionally unstable, weeping incompetent. Such presentations supply the popular basis for interventions that may be mounted whenever Western leadership feels it desirable.

Control of information is also utilized to cultivate dissatisfaction and instability in countries pursuing programs unattractive to transnational interests. The destabilization activities employed against, for example,

Chile, Libya, Nicaragua, and Cuba have been no less informational than economic or military. In many instances, local (national) media either are suborned by foreign capital and intelligence funds or their owners share the perspectives and follow the general lines of transnational capital.[14]

The formation of the Non-Aligned Movement and its rapid growth and expanded activity thereafter could not fail to affect the tone and character of the discussions and programs of the major international organizations established at the end of the war. The United Nations and its affiliated bodies, especially UNESCO, with their scores of new nation members, began to approach the universality they were intended originally to achieve. Their new Asian-African constituencies, not unexpectedly, had different objectives and agendas than did the Western "club" and its small circle of supportive states that had dominated these organizations up to that time.

From the late 1960s, a new situation emerged. The paramount issue — the grossly unequal access to and distribution of economic resources between peoples and nations — was joined with informational inequalities. UNESCO, pressed by its new membership, at first timidly and tentatively began to question the alleged general benefits of the free flow of information.[15] More active still, the Non-Aligned Movement and their leaders gave greater weight to cultural/informational domination in a series of meetings beginning in Algiers in 1973 and afterward in Lima, Tunis, New Delhi, and Colombo in 1975 and 1976.[16]

VI. THE CALL FOR A NEW INTERNATIONAL INFORMATION ORDER

Issuing from these many sessions, inside and outside the United Nations system, and embodied in numerous reports, studies, resolutions, and recommendations, there emerged what was to be known as the demand for a New International Information Order (NIIO, later and more generally referred to as the New World Information and Communication Order, NWICO), though it never took the form of a single, all-encompassing, and approved general declaration or document. The demand was premised on an assessment of the prevailing world information system that found it gravely out of balance.

Paraphrasing an Indian appraisal, made in New Delhi in 1976, most countries were seen to be passive recipients of information, disseminated from a few highly concentrated centers. The majority of nations is victimized by these conditions, while at the same time, many are misrepresented in their actions to others and unable to learn about conditions elsewhere other than through the channels of the dominant communicating power.

What general principles would a new international information order espouse, and how would those principles be achieved?

The principles were few and simple. First and foremost, is the full recognition of the principle of national sovereignty, which, when applied to information, insists that each nation has the right to determine what information comes in and what goes out. In the implementation of this cardinal rule, other needs become apparent: information flows should not be one-directional; all nations should have equal access to all sources of information and participate equally in the control over, and use of, international transmission channels.

Taken together, these points would mean the reduction of the monopoly power of existing transnational media. These media would be compelled to yield some of their prevailing authority to new, national systems and structures; e.g., national news agencies and national telecommunications entities. Additionally, the genuine exercise of national sovereignty made it certain that many societies would reject, in part or wholly, the commercialized messages and programming that constitute a major portion of Western, especially American, programming.

In sum, a new international information order, if it met these criteria even partially, would constitute a serious diminution in the influence of the existing transnational corporate information system.

National decision-making, for example, over what can enter a country's space, as interpreted by American policy since World War II, is an infringement on the free flow of information, as well as a limitation on freedom of speech. If national policies should decide to limit or exclude commercial media products, or advertising itself, the underpinnings of private enterprise and transnational capital investment are imperiled.

These are not marginal concerns. Though many of the U.S. objections to, and criticisms of, the New International Information Order emphasized the danger of state control of information and the licensing of journalists, the basic, if unstated, opposition derived from the limitations the new, proposed order might impose on the operations and practices of global businesses and military intelligence, currently governed almost exclusively by market factors or the raw power of the U.S. military machine.

Contrary to the impression conveyed by the Western media, the demand for a NIIO can be viewed as an entirely legitimate effort to broaden and democratize the flow of international communications. It called for additional media voices to be heard and for new transmission channels to be established. It was actually an expansive, rather than a restrictive initiative, though the Western reaction almost unanimously presented the NIIO as a narrowing of information choice.

In fact, few of the African, Asian, and Latin American leaders involved in the discussion of the new order saw it as an instrument to close down Western communication facilities and information flows. Most often, the sentiment was for more media, not fewer. What did concern the leaders of the ex-colonial nations was the pre-emption of their informational and cultural space by external media monopolies and the consequent erasure of national identity and indigenous creativity.

Still, there was no escaping the conclusion—and the U.S. and Western media managers and owners quickly grasped it—that however expansive, a larger slice of the informational field going to the new nations inevitably would mean a smaller domain for the transnationals—and, more worrisome still, the underlying principles and practices of a noncommercial, global informational enterprise, in the long run, could endanger the survival of the commercial system and sooner or later curtail its near-total freedom of maneuver.

VII. THE WESTERN COUNTER-ATTACK AGAINST THE NIIO

The New International Information Order movement crested in 1976 at the 19th General Conference of UNESCO, held in Nairobi, Kenya. At this meeting, the United States delegation, after years of formally ignoring the issue, finally had to acknowledge that a problem did exist, though U.S. policy-makers thought it was largely overblown. In any case, given the breadth of the support for changes in the international information regimen, some U.S. initiatives were required, if only to lessen the volume of protest and to forestall possible proposals coming from the more militant member states.

At, and after Nairobi, the United States pursued two general information policies. At the political level, the objective was to split the fragile cooperation of the 100-plus, less-advantaged nations. To accomplish this, a policy of selective aid and collaboration to nonsocialist members of the NIIO coalition was deemed more fruitful to U.S. aims than general opposition and total belligerence to the entire grouping.

The advice of the executive director of Freedom House, a nongovernmental organization with shadowy ties to the power structure, was suggestive:

"Western news organizations and governments have the opportunity," Leonard Sussman, the Executive Director, explained, "to assist the information development of the Third World. In doing so, they will want to distinguish those Third World countries that recognize the exploitative nature of Marxist-Leninist ideology masquerading as information journalism. [But] the pleas of these non-'socializing' developing nations, who clamor for informational assistance, should be earnestly examined."[17]

This advice, to a limited extent at least, has served as a continuing reference point for American diplomacy and economic assistance programs. Additionally, but with no great enthusiasm, U.S. officials accepted at Nairobi a traditional mechanism for avoiding action, and agreed to the appointment of a commission to study the information problem.

UNESCO's director-general created the International Commission for the Study of Communication Problems in 1976, and Seán MacBride was appointed the chairman. The commission met several times over the next few years and published its final report, *Many Voices, One World*, in 1980.[18]

Though eclectic in its approach, and far from being a radical critique, the report contained enough generally critical material to confirm American fears about entrusting any tasks to an agency not fully under Western control. In the United States, the report had a swift passage from publication to library shelf. Though there was some sniping at the MacBride study in the media, for the most part it was quickly relegated to oblivion.

VIII. THE TECHNOLOGY GAMBIT

Beyond the general political effort to disengage some of the less convinced supporters of the NIIO, and participating in the deliberations of the MacBride Commission, there was yet another U.S. response to the poor world's push for a new, international information order. This was the promise of technology — the alleged benefits of the new electronic instrumentation — to countries whose total situation was deplorable. The technology gambit was, and remains, the most effective U.S. initiative in retaining global influence, if not hegemony, in the information sphere.

The high-technology "solution" to social problems did not debut in the mid-1970s. It has been a recurrent theme in Western and U.S. development. Applying it to international communications, however, gave it a new and modern twist. To the specific grievances of the majority of the world's nations over information-flow imbalances and inequality in facilities and general cultural dependence, it was asserted, by its proponents, that high tech would eliminate rapidly age-old gaps and differentials between economies. Better yet, the new instrumentation, according to the same enthusiasts, would enable still-to-industrialize societies to pass over entirely—"leapfrog" is the favored expression—the industrial-izing process that marked Western development.[19]

Beyond the self-serving aspect of this prescription to the interests of Western technology producers, the extent of its acceptance among the Asian, African, and Latin American nations measured the degree to which their dependency was being extended and deepened, far into the future.

There is more than sufficient evidence on hand that demonstrates how the new information technologies—the infrastructure of the "communication revolution"—have supplied enormous maneuverability to capital and the transnational corporate system world-wide. If one element can be given primacy in the growth of this system, it is the unrivaled mobility of capital, provided by the computer and the satellite, i.e., telecommunications.

With this capability in hand, production has been moved to which-ever site, wherever its location, is most profitable. Simultaneously, the ability of organized labor to defend its standard of work and living, even in the most highly industrialized countries, it would seem, has been largely undermined. Hundreds of assembly plants along the U.S.-Mexican border, located on the Mexican side, are examples of produc-tion arrangements, supported by modern communication, that allow American and other transnational enterprises to export work to the low-est wage sites that can be found globally.

Besides providing greatly enhanced power to transnational capital, the new information technologies enable the United States military and intelligence structures to monitor global (to say nothing of domestic) communications, subject the world's land-and seascape to surveillance, and patrol the oceans and air lanes of all continents. These activities are devoted to maintaining the world sphere of transnational capital intact and hectoring incessantly those regions of the world outside the domain of private-enterprise arrangements.

Computerization since the end of World War II, and communication satellites since their appearance in the early 1960s, have been sources of strength and boundless hope to the managers of the world-wide busi-ness system. In 1966, for example, testifying before a congressional com-mittee, McGeorge Bundy, former chief aide to the late President Ken-nedy and one-time president of the Ford Foundation, acknowledged that:

> I was myself a part of the executive branch during the period which led
> up to the establishment of Comsat [the Communication Satellite
> Corporation, created to operate the first commercial satellite
> communications]. . . . I do clearly remember what the record fully
> confirmed—that Comsat was established for the purpose of taking and
> holding a position of leadership for the United States in the field of
> international global commercial satellite service.[20]

The new technologies were developed with huge government subsidy and installed, as quickly as possible, to enable U.S. companies to grab world markets for the new instrumentation, to be first in claiming scarce radio spectrum or communication satellite orbital slot space on a first-come, first-served basis, and to create the capability for operating and administering a global business system.

It was serendipity in its purist expression that offered U.S. policy an opportunity, at the same time, to damp down the rising demand in the poor and exploited arc of the world for a new and more equitable economic and information order, by promoting the adoption and utilization of these new electronic technologies.

With one initiative—to the extent that it succeeded—the U.S. business system would secure world markets for its high-tech products and services, bind more closely than ever into its world-wide commercial system the balky nations of Africa, Asia, and Latin America, and neatest of all, in an ideological sense, convince the poor world that it was embarking on a course of economic improvement and national autonomy. All these benefits to the transnational corporate order might be derived from persuading the least advantaged states to install and hook into the new electronic networks.

From Nairobi on, therefore, the United States has promoted enthusiastically the utilization of the new information technologies in the Third World, though it has been wary of endorsing international or public bodies to undertake the development program—a case in point being the formation in 1980 of the International Program for the Development of Communications (IPDC), a UNESCO-affiliated grouping.

The conflict that accompanied the formation of the IPDC cannot be related here, but it was emblematic of the problems U.S. information policies have confronted since 1945 with nations who, however weak and poor, still experience, and cannot forget, the economic, political, and cultural impositions of colonialism.

Whereas U.S. policy seeks the power to act without restraint of any kind, no state, with even the most minimal autonomy, is willing to grant such authority to another. This makes most international bodies potentially troublesome to American entrepreneurial interests, even those largely dominated by U.S. power. The history of the International Telecommunications Consortium (INTELSAT) is illustrative.

The United States was the first nation to construct and launch a communication satellite. This development conferred incomparable advantage to the American communications industry specifically, and to U.S. world power overall. And yet, it was contingent, from the outset, on at least some deference to the inclinations of the other participating member states. Although U.S. private corporate interests controlled the decisive shares of the INTELSAT organization, the absolute necessity to have as many nations as possible join the system diluted U.S. influence, though by no means reducing it to the levels of the other members.

Continuously, the tension between possessing great economic and technological power, and the need to have some agreement and cooperation in the utilization of that power beyond national boundaries, has constituted a central problematic for U.S. information policy for more than four decades.

In one international information encounter after another, the demand of U.S. power-wielders to extract maximum benefit for themselves confronts the class interests, national needs, and sovereignties of the vast majority of states. These can be disregarded only at the greatest peril to long-term U.S. systemic interests, and often at the cost of short-term operational efficiency, as well.

The informational needs of the transnational corporate system, with growing frequency, find themselves in collision with the interests of a great part of the rest of the world. One striking example is the question of communication satellite transmission. Here the issue of "prior consent"—the belief that a nation has the right to determine, in advance, what may be transmitted into its national space—put the United States' insistence that "prior consent" not be recognized in near-total isolation from the world community. In 1981 the United Nations General Assembly voted overwhelmingly to uphold the principle of "prior consent," against American opposition.

Again, in a number of international radio-spectrum-allocation conferences held since the early 1970s, the United States, with its huge need derived from wasteful usage and military pre-emption, has argued for immediate allocation and utilization of spectrum space on the basis of "first come, first served."

A majority of the less-industrialized countries demand reservation of spectrum space for a time when their needs and capabilities can make use of it. No final solution of these conflicts of interest has been achieved. But in each instance, the U.S. position is supported, at best, by a tiny minority of states.

The almost unlimited demand of Western transnational companies and military machines for huge chunks of a limited global information resource—the radio spectrum—and for a free hand in pursuing whatever goals they find profitable and advantageous, are hardly acceptable to the great majority of nations if they have anything to say about it. Achieving international agreements, in a democratic forum, to policies and arrangements patently disadvantageous to the majority of the participants over any long-term period is fantasy.

The international record reveals the growing reluctance of nations to endorse programs and policies that are to their clear disadvantage. With this fact increasingly evident, and especially observable in informational questions, the willingness of the United States to accept international organizational decisions—or even to participate in genuinely international organizations—steadily weakens.

Unless an international organization is stripped of its democratic features—e.g., one nation, whatever its size, one vote—and restructured to ensure that the wishes of the strongest members are granted—e.g., voting weighted according to financial contribution—the United States, and perhaps a few other Western nations, will disregard or abandon it.

IX. THE UNITED STATES ATTACK ON UNESCO

The United Nations, and its affiliated body UNESCO, have been, until recently, the sites at which most international information issues have been considered and debated. At the same time, both of these organizations have enjoyed the participation of the 160-plus nations now constituting the international community.

In both these bodies, large majorities of Asian, African, and Latin American members, time and again, have resisted the policies of advantage proposed by the privileged Western nations. They have counterposed their agenda of participation in decision-making and measures toward equalization of global resources.

It is hardly surprising, given this continuing clash of interests, that the U.N. and UNESCO have received something less than a favorable press in the Western world and, especially, in the United States. For years the American public, when informed of the issues at all, has been fed extremely negative accounts of the management, personnel, programs, and activities of both organizations.

At the same time, the numerous meetings of the Non-Aligned Nations, as well as the general and regional conferences of UNESCO devoted to world-information issues, have usually been ignored in the American mass media. Meetings at which scores of leaders from Africa, Asia, and Latin America attended have gone practically unreported—in contrast to the heavy coverage accorded relatively routine meetings of a few Western political eminences.

In the exceptional case when a UNESCO meeting is given attention in the U.S. press, invariably it is to report measures (discussed, not necessarily adopted) that are interpreted by the media as threatening to their own criteria of a free press. Licensing of journalists, for example, has been one of the favorite targets of hostile U.S. press commentary. Never actually proposed in UNESCO, and certainly never approved as policy, the fact that a position paper had recommended it was proof enough to the media to activate it to wage a decade-long crusade against UNESCO for its willingness to accept state control over information. In reality, journalists are credentialed in all societies. Imagine a White House press conference attended by individuals without authorized accreditation!

In any case, pillorying the U.N. and UNESCO has been the regular practice in the American press for several years. Now, it is discovered, cause for astonishment, in polls taken by the media, that many Americans regard international organizations with suspicion and harbor no warm feelings for the U.N. bodies.

The daily instruction by the American media to its national public, following the lead of the government, is to create distrust for democratic participation in the international arena, and to feed sentiments of unilateralism and self-interest that historically have been close to the surface of American life.

Accompanying these perspectives is a powerful assertion of individual decision-making that tolerates no element or acceptance of social accountability. In the informational sphere, this outlook marked the earliest postwar international encounters and is as pervasive domestically as it is in U.S. global relations. In the United States, media managers and owners call upon the protection of the First Amendment to exempt them from being viewed and treated as the economic conglomerates they are.

In the 1940s and '50s, when the U.N. bodies were weighted heavily in favor of Western and U.S. interests, some suggested modest codes for journalistic ethics were quickly abandoned in response to stringent U.S. opposition. Margaret Blanchard, writing about U.N. discussions in 1946, on international freedom of the press, commented: "The idea that freedom of information carried obligations, violated basic American thinking."[21]

The "obligations" that were mentioned in the rejected codes included, among other matters, fairness, honesty, and absence of racist and war-inciting reporting. These criteria/standards, it will be recalled, were almost identical with those proposed in the Hutchins Commission volume, *Peoples Speaking to Peoples*. In all instances, the U.S. governmental and media position has been that these are matters for voluntary self-monitoring. In 1978, in what was probably the peak of coordination of anti-imperialist groupings in UNESCO, the Declaration on Fundamental Principles Concerning the Contribution of the Mass Media to Strengthening the Peace and International Understanding; to the Promotion of Human Rights; and to Countering Racialism, Apartheid and Incitement to War, was adopted at the 20th General Conference, without dissenting votes from any of UNESCO's 146 member states at the time.[22]

The declaration has had no observable impact on Western and U.S. press practice in the decade since it was approved, but the fact of its passage was astonishing in itself. The contradictory factors that made this possible are reviewed in Nordenstreng's work.[23]

The declaration's title alone suggests international informational responsibilities that have been rejected by the American mass media since the end of World War II. Blanchard, writing about efforts in the U.N., in

1949, to establish criteria for reporting, summed up the Western position this way:

> The question, for some, came down to whether governments should tolerate a little war propaganda and false information as part of a free flow of information or impose restrictions to stop all possible distribution of objectionable material.[24]

At that time, and since, the U.S. media system has never balked at offering "a little war propaganda." The Mass Media Declaration directly challenged this species of toleration.

In 1948 Robert Leigh, director of the staff of the Hutchins Commission on Freedom of the Press, examined the question of social responsibility of the press: He wrote:

> in the present day, and especially across national boundaries, this faith in an omnicompetent world citizen served only by *full* flow of words and images is an oversimplification of the process and effect of mass communication. . . . "Barriers Down" [the title of a book by Kent Cooper, director of the Associated Press at that time, arguing for no barriers to the international flow of information] standing by itself is not adequate policy in the international field. The focus changes from free individual expression as a right, to the primary need of the citizen everywhere to have regular access to reliable information, and, also, ready access to the existent diversity of ideas, opinions, insights, and arguments regarding public affairs. This does not deny freedom, but it joins freedom with a positive responsibility that freedom should serve truth and understanding. *The concept of responsibility, carried to its logical conclusion, may even imply defining a clearly harmful class of public communication which falls outside the protection of freedom itself.*[25] [Emphasis added.]

It was precisely to define a "class of public communication which [fell] outside the protection of freedom itself" that the Mass Media Declaration was drafted and which purpose it was intended to serve.

Leigh's views, taken as generally representative of the Hutchins Commission's, which challenged the unqualified benefits of the free flow of information as then constituted, and, which, at the same time, insisted on a standard of responsibility for international communication, could not have been more unwelcome and obnoxious to the tenets of U.S. information policy being advanced at that time and ever since.

Blanchard, writing about the "threats to the dream of exporting the American free-press system to the rest of the world" in 1946, included as one threat the work of the Hutchins Commission, then in its early stages. "To make matters worse," Blanchard says, "the first published report of the American investigatory commission (*Peoples Speaking to Peoples*, 1946) focused on international communication problems and suggested a covenant to govern the gathering and dissemination of news with enforcement by an independent agency housed in the United Nations as a remedy for perceived difficulties. Journalists[26] considered the proposal an invasion of long-held American press beliefs and said that, if adopted, the proposal surely would put the press of the world under government control."[27]

This has been, and remains, the standard refrain of the American mass media. Accountability is seen as state control. To recommend accountability as a criterion for international communication was (and is) evidence to media managers of anti-Americanism, or worse.[28]

X. U.S. INFORMATION POLICY IN THE 1980s: THE REAGAN ERA

With the most conservative government in the last 50 years in office, the U.N. structure and its affiliated organizations, however modest their programs and resolutions, were an inviting target to the Reagan administration.

Two other important developments contributed to the assaults on international organizations and agreements in the 1980s. One is the increasing utilization by, and dependence on, the new electronic technologies by transnational enterprise. This has radically affected the international division of labor and, not least, the information order as well.

The other factor was no new development but rather the maturation of the deregulation drive pressed by U.S. corporate enterprise, at first domestically and, soon thereafter, internationally. Deregulation meant, in brief, the removal of social control and oversight of the practices and operations of business, national and transnational. In the vital communications sector in each national economy—posts, telecommunications, data processing, etc.—deregulation stripped away national sovereignty and made the sector subject to capture by the two forces of privatization and transnationalization.[29]

These converging currents set the stage for the U.S. onslaught on UNESCO.

The early demands for a new, international information order, it will be remembered, concerned mostly media flows—film, TV programs, news, books, magazines, music, which moved from a few Western metropolitan centers to the rest of the world.

In the 1980s these flows continued to display the same concentrated and commercial patterns, although a few new secondary production and distribution centers had appeared, e.g., Mexico, Brazil. At the same time, a new element in international communications had developed and assumed central significance. This was transborder data flows—

largely the data flows transmitted by satellite and cable, from computers, which enable transnational corporations to carry on their business in several global locales with instantaneous coordination. Most of these flows are either internal, corporate transmissions, from one unit of the company to another, or between corporations.

The greatly expanded service industries account for a significant share of the flows. Banking, insurance, tourism, transport, media, advertising are huge data generators and transmitters, and play steadily more important roles in the main industrial societies.

In an indirect way, this expanding form of international information activity has contributed also to the anti-U.N. drift of United States information policy. This occurs partly because the U.N. bodies customarily concerned with information issues were slow to recognize, and take initiatives in, the new electronic domain. This may be attributed to the seemingly strong economic character of transborder data flows, while UNESCO, for example, from its inception, has been more concerned with cultural and educational matters. While it is increasingly apparent that the economic-technological component is being fused with the cultural, in informational areas at least, understanding of this development has come slowly.

This lag, or absence of attention, made it easier for the United States, in the now very decisive area of transborder data flows, to sidestep almost entirely the jurisdiction of the U.N. and UNESCO. Other forums were enlisted, where the voting arrangements and decision-making allow the United States more influence and maneuverability.

The OECD, the ITU, and, most recently, the GATT trade organization, for example, have been viewed as more appropriate places in which to promote the U.S. position of unimpeded transborder data flows. In GATT the free-flow-of-information principle reappears as the "free flow of services."[30]

Still, over time, it is to be expected that any international organization, structured to favor the U.S. interests or not, will prove problematic to those same interests. But in the short run, international bodies that can be tailored to serve U.S. policy are clearly preferred to those where the opposition, feeble as it may be, finds expression.

Actually, in the earliest postwar years, when the U.N. was strongly responsive to U.S. influence, American information policies often were opposed and sometimes successfully resisted. In 1949, for example, debate after debate "revealed how small a portion of the world supported American ideas on freedom of the press."[31] Again, in 1948–49, "American ideas on freedom of information had been increasingly and pointedly criticized during the free press debates by delegates representing smaller, basically nonaligned countries who were members of the United Nations."[32]

In the 1980s, the weakest and most vulnerable link in the U.N. system, UNESCO, was a perfect target for an increasingly aggressive and unilateralist U.S. policy. By attacking UNESCO, the Grenada of international organizations, other international bodies could be intimidated and, at least temporarily, induced to acquiesce to the U.S. position.

The cost to the U.S. of crippling UNESCO was minimal. The main areas for vital information policy-making, as we have noted, were moved elsewhere. Additionally, UNESCO was a useful scapegoat for U.S. domestic politics. Popular puzzlement and dismay with foreign opposition to American policies, fierce trade competition and industrial shutdowns at home, along with the loss of jobs, are creating an atmosphere conducive to xenophobia. Getting tough with UNESCO—portrayed for twenty years in the media as a disreputable organization—was a cheap way to gain short-term political capital at home.

As for the long term, the underlying problems troubling the American people—unemployment, disinformation, military interventions, etc.— would not be affected, or made less worrisome, in the least. But the possibility of dealing with these matters resolutely and rationally would be made still more difficult. That would be someone else's problem.

XI. CONCLUSION

The global situation of the United States is unique. Faltering, in fact, weakening, as the system may be in the late 1980s, the United States still administers a global domain, some areas of which are more firmly controlled than others. Facilitating the administration and direction are powerful communication networks, massive facilities, and a torrent of messages that flow through the conduits. The assignments that these data and images serve concern the daily routines of the world business system, and, no less, its protection and promotion. Information truly has become a key factor in the mechanics of late capitalism.

Among the many crucial services it provides or enables are capital transfers, relocation of production sites, disinformation campaigns, electoral public relations, military surveillance of the near and far reaches of the empire, creation of a value system and demand essential to the expansion of sales of foreign outputs, and, not to be minimized, film and TV festivals where the latest productions of the American cultural industries are show-boated.

In managing these astonishingly numerous and widely diverse and often conflicting activities, flexibility, spontaneity, and decentralized, or at least, multi-centered, decision-making are obligatory. To an impressive extent, American empire management has provided this. It is no small achievement.

It has done this by satisfying the broadest requirements of the domestic and international power structure. As long as these vital needs are met or served, the micro details can be matters for negotiation, bargaining, possibly concession, and, if all else fails, military action.

Reviewing the last four decades, whatever the inadequacies of policy, in the informational sphere, the vital systemic needs generally have been attended to. U.S. policy-makers and negotiators have insisted in all the international dealings over the years on the free flow of information for their news, their cultural-media products, and their information goods and services.

Slippage in the practice by recalcitrant states and weakening of the doctrine have occurred. Yet it remains a cardinal element in U.S. international information policy, still with considerable impact in many parts of the world.

Similarly, the corporate definition of "freedom of the press" has retained surprising credibility. Attributable mainly to the deep structured hegemonic power of capitalist institutions and ideology overall, the capability of the media to present themselves as outside the arena of partisanship continues to confer great, though diminished, strength on the Western informational apparatus.

Still another systemic achievement has been the near-global acceptance of the idea of the "information age," and its relative, "the information society." These have been singular constructs of the American information industry and its public-relations ballyhoo.

Without denying the potential benefits of computerization and communication satellite and cable transmission of messages, it is clear that the creation of the informational networks and structures now in place or still to be installed, in country after country, is, in its present institutional form and practice, a powerful facilitator for the dominant transnational corporate order.

INTELSAT, for example, since it was established in 1964, has become an important global system of satellite communications, now embracing over 100 countries, most of them from the poor world. It has served to weld these nations ever more closely into the dominant world-business system.[33]

High tech, and the new information technologies as its foremost expression, has been promoted by the full spectrum of U.S. private and governmental power. Though these efforts may not be coordinated, or specifically planned, they constitute in their ensemble, a very influential component of an information policy, recognized as such or not.

Finally, the direct intervention of U.S. state power—diplomatic or military—has never ceased to be employed on behalf of systemic viability, in informational as well as in other key sectors. The U.S. government, repeatedly since 1945, has thwarted the efforts of numerous nations to overcome their dependence on American informational and media outputs. From the first postwar days, national power has been exerted to defend and promote the interests of U.S. media combines and, later, information-industry companies. In the exercise of this power, efforts to loosen the grip of American cultural-informational industries on world-wide markets have been stymied.

In those instances where U.S. efforts in international organizations to defend and extend American informational-cultural businesses have been opposed, deliberate punitive measures have been enforced, and, as in the case of UNESCO, national financial support and even participation, withdrawn.

U.S. informational policy, structured or informal, for four decades, has served, relatively successfully, to hold, expand, and routinize a world empire of corporate business. Never unopposed, U.S. domination encounters growing competition and resistance. Temporarily, the national response is unilateralism in world decision-making and Ramboism in its media presentations.

Sooner or later, American information policy and practices will have to adjust to a changing world that will no longer tolerate, under the doctrine of the free flow of information, the exclusion of four billion voices residing in 150 countries.

NOTES

1. The work of Wilbur Schramm, Daniel Lerner, Ithiel De Sola Pool, and others in the same vein is exemplary.
2. Statement of the commission.
3. White and Leigh, p. iv.
4. *Ibid.*, p. v.
5. *Ibid.*, p. 2.
6. *Ibid.*, p. 3.
7. Herbert I. Schiller, *Communication and Cultural Domination*, Chapter 2, "The Diplomacy of Cultural Domination and the Free Flow of Information."
8. Harry S. Truman, address, March 1947, Baylor University, Texas.
9. *Business Week*, 1945, 87 (August 4), pp. 32, 34, 41.
10. President Urho Kekkonen, president of the Republic of Finland, "The Free Flow of Information: Towards a Reconsideration of National and International Communication Policies," Tampere, Finland, May 21, 1973.
11. Leonard Sussman, "Mass News Media and the Third World Challenge."
12. See *infra*.
13. Pavlic and Hamelink.
14. Singham and Hune, pp. 349–52; also, Beltran and Cardona.
15. The shift in UNESCO attention can be dated, approximately, from a meeting of communication specialists in Montreal, in 1969.
16. Schiller, "Decolonization of Information," pp. 35–48.
17. Sussman, "The 'March' Through the World's Mass Media," pp. 857–79.

18. MacBride.

19. A thorough critique of this outlook is provided by Jayaweera.

20. Progress Report on Space Communications, Hearings before the Senate Subcommittee on Communications, 89th Congress, 2nd Session, August 10, 17, 18, and 23, 1966, Serial 89–78, Washington, D.C., p. 81, emphasis added.

21. Blanchard, p. 65.

22. Nordenstreng with Hannikainen, p. 1.

23. *Ibid.*

24. Blanchard, p. 226.

25. Leigh, pp. 381–91, emphasis added in the last sentence.

26. The use of "journalists" as the category actively promoting U.S. information policy in the early postwar period is not very helpful. It aggregates editors, owners, and nationally prominent reporters. How representative of the rank and file journalist community these powerful spokesmen were is difficult to determine. In any case, the views that were expressed were the opinions of the publishers, editors, and owners.

27. Blanchard, pp. 88–89.

28. Carrying this perspective to its ultimate conclusion, a study by Frank Hughes, *Prejudice and the Press*, with appendixes a 642-page volume, reported a web of associations of the members of the Hutchins Commission, which, in the author's judgment, were supposed to account for the commission's espousal of doctrine subversive to U.S. institutions.

29. Roach, "Context and Contradictions."

30. Mahoney, pp. 297–315.

31. Blanchard, p. 232.

32. *Ibid.*, p. 236.

33. INTELSAT, for all its success, and despite the great service it has performed for U.S.-based transnational enterprises, is itself now under attack from still more aggressive U.S. space-communication entrepreneurs, who are seeking to skim off INTELSAT's profitable business. Another instance of the internal conflicts of the free-enterprise system.

APPENDIXES

Appendix I

CONSTITUTION OF THE UNITED NATIONS EDUCATIONAL, SCIENTIFIC AND CULTURAL ORGANIZATION

The government of the States Parties to this Constitution on behalf of their peoples declare:

That since wars begin in the minds of men, it is in the minds of men that the defences of peace must be constructed;

That ignorance of each other's ways and lives has been a common cause, throughout the history of mankind, of that suspicion and mistrust between peoples of the world through which their differences have all too often broken into war;

That the great and terrible war which has now ended was a war made possible by the denial of democratic principles of the dignity, equality and mutual respect of men, and by the propagation, in their place, through ignorance and prejudice, of the doctrine of the inequality of men and races;

That the wide diffusion of culture, and the education of humanity for justice and liberty and peace are indispensable to the dignity of man and constitute a sacred duty which all the nations must fulfill in a spirit of mutual assistance and concern;

That a peace based exclusively upon the political and economic arrangements of governments would not be a peace which could secure the unanimous, lasting and sincere support of the peoples of the world, and that the peace must therefore be founded, if it is not to fail, upon the intellectual and moral solidarity of mankind.

For these reasons, the States Parties to this Constitution, believing in full and equal opportunities for education for all, in the unrestricted pursuit of objective truth, and in the free exchange of ideas and knowledge, are agreed and determined to develop and to increase the means of communication between their peoples and to employ these means for the purposes of mutual understanding and a truer and more perfect knowledge of each other's lives;

In consequence whereof they do hereby create the United Nations Educational, Scientific and Cultural Organization for the purpose of advancing, through the educational and scientific and cultural relations of the peoples of the world, the objectives of international peace and of the common welfare of mankind for which the United Nations Organization was established and which its Charter proclaims.

ARTICLE I. PURPOSES AND FUNCTIONS

1. The purpose of the Organization is to contribute to peace and security by promoting collaboration among the nations through education, science and culture in order to further universal respect for justice, for the rule of law and for the human rights and fundamental freedoms which are affirmed for the peoples of the world, without distinction of race, sex, language or religion, by the Charter of the United Nations.

2. To realize this purpose the Organization will:

(a) Collaborate in the work of advancing the mutual knowledge and understanding of peoples, through all means of mass communication and to that end recommend such international agreements as may be necessary to promote the free flow of ideas by word and image;

(b) Give fresh impulse to popular education and to the spread of culture; by collaborating with Members, at their request, in the development of educational activities; by instituting collaboration among the nations to advance the ideal of equality of educational opportunity without regard to race, sex or any distinctions, economic or social; by suggesting educational methods best suited to prepare the children of the world for the responsibilities of freedom;

(c) Maintain, increase and diffuse knowledge; by assuring the conservation and protection of the world's inheritance of books, works of art and monuments of history and science, and recommending to the nations concerned the necessary international conventions; by encouraging cooperation among the nations in all branches of intellectual activity, including the international exchange of persons active in the fields of education, science and culture and the exchange of publications, objects of artistic and scientific interest and other materials of information; by initiating methods of international cooperation calculated to give the people of all countries access to the printed and published materials produced by any of them.

3. With a view to preserving the independence, integrity and fruitful diversity of the cultures and educational systems of the States members of this Organization, the Organization is prohibited from intervening in matters which are essentially within their domestic jurisdiction.

ARTICLE II. MEMBERSHIP

1. Membership of the United Nations Organization shall carry with it the right to membership of the United Nations Educational, Scientific and Cultural Organization.

2. Subject to the conditions of the Agreement between this Organization and the United Nations Organization, approved pursuant to ARTICLE X of this Constitution, States not members of the United Nations Organization may be admitted to membership of the Organization, upon recommendation of the Executive Board, by a two-thirds majority vote of the General Conference.

3. Territories or groups of territories which are not responsible for the conduct of their international relations may be admitted as Associate Members by the General Conference by a two-thirds majority of Members present and voting, upon application made on behalf of such territory or group of territories by the Member or other authority having responsibility for their international relations. The nature and extent of the rights and obligations of Associate Members shall be determined by the General Conference.

4. Members of the Organization which are suspended from the exercise of the rights and privileges of membership of the United Nations Organization shall, upon the request of the latter, be suspended from the rights and privileges of this Organization.

5. Members of the Organization which are expelled from the United Nations Organization shall automatically cease to be members of this Organization.

6. Any Member State or Associate Member of the Organization may withdraw from the Organization by notice addressed to the Director-General. Such notice shall take effect on December 31, of the year following that during which the notice was given. No such withdrawal shall affect the financial obligations owed to the Organization on the date the withdrawal takes effect. Notice of withdrawal by an Associate Member shall be given on its behalf by the Member State or other authority having responsibility for its international relations.

ARTICLE III. ORGANS

The Organization shall include a General Conference, an Executive Board and a Secretariat.

ARTICLE IV. THE GENERAL CONFERENCE

A. Composition

1. The General Conference shall consist of the representatives of the States members of the Organization. The Government of each Member State shall appoint not more than five delegates, who shall be selected after consultation with the National Commission, if established, or with educational, scientific and cultural bodies.

B. Functions

2. The General Conference shall determine the policies and the main lines of work of the Organization. It shall take decisions on programmes submitted to it by the Executive Board.

3. The General Conference shall, when it deems desirable and in accordance with the regulations to be made by it, summon international conferences of States on education, the sciences and humanities or the dissemination of knowledge; non-governmental conferences on the same subjects may be summoned by the General Conference or by the Executive Board in accordance with such regulations.

4. The General Conference shall, in adopting proposals for submission to the Member States, distinguish between recommendations and international conventions submitted for their approval. In the former case a majority vote shall suffice: in the latter case a two-thirds majority shall be required. Each of the Member States shall submit recommendations or conventions to its competent authorities within a period of one year from the close of the session of the General Conference at which they were adopted.

5. Subject to the provisions of Article V, paragraph 5(c), the General conference shall advise the United Nations Organization on the educational, scientific and cultural aspects of matters of concern to the latter; in accordance with the terms and procedure agreed upon between the appropriate authorities of the two Organizations.

6. The General Conference shall receive and consider the reports submitted periodically by Member States as provided by Article VIII.

7. The General Conference shall elect the members of the Executive Board and, on the recommendation of the Board, shall appoint the Director-General.

C. Voting

8. (a) Each Member State shall have one vote in the General Conference. Decisions shall be made by a simple majority except in cases in which a two-thirds majority is required by the provisions of this Constitution. A majority shall be a majority of the Members present and voting.

(b) A Member State shall have no vote in the General Conference if the total amount of contributions due from it exceeds the total amount of contributions payable by it for the current year and the immediately preceding year.

(c) The General Conference may nevertheless permit such a Member State to vote, if it is satisfied that the failure to pay is due to conditions beyond the control of the Member Nation.

D. Procedure

9. (a) The General Conference shall meet in ordinary session every two years. It may meet in extraordinary session if it decides to do so itself or if summoned by the Executive Board, or on the demand of at least one-third of the Member States.

(b) At each session the location of its next ordinary session shall be decided by the General Conference. The location of an extraordinary session shall be decided by the General Conference if the session is summoned by it, or otherwise by the Executive Board.

10. The General Conference shall adopt its own rules of procedure. It shall at each session elect a President and other officers.

11. The General Conference shall set up special and technical committees and such other subordinate bodies as may be necessary for its purposes.

12. The General Conference shall cause arrangements to be made for public access to meetings, subject to such regulations as it shall prescribe.

E. Observers

13. The General Conference, on the recommendation of the Executive Board and by a two-thirds majority may, subject to its rules of procedure, invite as observers at specified sessions of the conference or of its Commissions representatives of international organizations, such as those referred to in Article XI, paragraph 4.

14. When consultative arrangements have been approved by the Executive Board for such international non-governmental or semi-governmental organizations in the manner provided in Article XI, paragraph 4,

those organizations shall be invited to send observers to sessions of the General Conference and its Commissions.

ARTICLE V. EXECUTIVE BOARD

A. Composition

1. The Executive Board shall be elected by the General Conference from among the delegates appointed by the Member States and shall consist of twenty-four members, each of whom shall represent the Government of the State of which he is a national. The President of the General Conference shall sit *ex officio* in an advisory capacity on the Executive Board.

2. In electing the members of the Executive Board the General Conference shall endeavor to include persons competent in the arts, the humanities, the sciences, education and the diffusion of ideas, and qualified by their experience and capacity to fulfill the administrative and executive duties of the Board. It shall also have regard to the diversity of cultures and a balanced geographical distribution. Not more than one national of any Member State shall serve on the Board at any one time, the President of the Conference excepted.

3. Members of the Board shall serve from the close of the session of the General Conference which elected them until the close of the second ordinary session of the General Conference following that election. They shall be immediately eligible for a second term, but shall not serve consecutively for more than two terms. Half of the members of the Board shall be elected every two years.

4. In the event of the death or resignation of a member of the Executive Board, his replacement for the remainder of his term shall be appointed by the Executive Board on the nomination of the Government of the State the former member represented. The Government making the nomination and the Executive Board shall have regard to the factors set forth in paragraph 2 of this Article.

B. Functions

5. (a) The Executive Board shall prepare the agenda for the General Conference. It shall examine the program of work for the Organization and corresponding budget estimates submitted to it by the Director-General in accordance with paragraph 3 of Article VI and shall submit them

with such recommendations as it considers desirable to the General Conference.

(b) The Executive Board, acting under the authority of the General Conference, shall be responsible for the execution of the program adopted by the Conference. In accordance with the decisions of the General Conference and having regard to circumstances arising between two ordinary sessions, the Executive Board shall take all necessary measures to ensure the effective and rational execution of the program by the Director-General.

(c) Between ordinary sessions of the General Conference, the Board may discharge the functions of adviser to the United Nations, set forth in Article IV, paragraph 5, whenever the problem upon which advice is sought has already been dealt with in principle by the Conference, or when the solution is implicit in decisions of the Conference.

6. The Executive Board shall recommend to the General Conference the admission of new Members to the Organization.

7. Subject to decisions of the General Conference, the Executive Board shall adopt its own rules or procedure. It shall elect its officers from among its members.

8. The Executive Board shall meet in regular session at least twice a year and may meet in special session if convoked by the Chairman on his own initiative or upon the request of six members of the Board.

9. The Chairman of the Executive Board shall present, on behalf of the Board, to each ordinary session of the General Conference, with or without comments, the reports on the activities of the Organization which the Director-General is required to prepare in accordance with the provisions of Article VI.3(b).

10. The Executive Board shall make all necessary arrangements to consult the representatives of international organizations or qualified persons concerned with questions within its competence.

11. Between sessions of the General Conference, the Executive Board may request advisory opinions from the International Court of Justice on legal questions arising within the field of the Organization's activities.

12. Although the members of the Executive Board are representative of their respective Governments they shall exercise the powers delegated to them by the General Conference on behalf of the Conference as a whole.

C. Transitional Provisions

13. At the Ninth Session of the General Conference thirteen members shall be elected to the Executive Board pursuant to the provisions of this Article. One of them shall retire at the close of the tenth session of the General Conference, the retiring member being chosen by the drawing of

lots. Thereafter, twelve members shall be elected at each ordinary session of the General Conference.

ARTICLE VI. SECRETARIAT

1. The Secretariat shall consist of a Director-General and such staff as may be required.

2. The Director-General shall be nominated by the Executive Board and appointed by the General Conference for a period of six years, under such conditions as the Conference may approve, and shall be eligible for reappointment. He shall be the chief administrative officer of the Organization.

3. (a) The Director-General, or a deputy designated by him, shall participate without the right to vote, in all meetings of the General Conference, of the Executive Board, and of the Committees of the Organization. He shall formulate proposals for appropriate action by the Conference and the Board, and shall prepare for submission to the Board a draft programme of work for the Organization with corresponding budget estimates.

(b) The Director-General shall prepare and communicate to Member States and to the Executive Board periodic reports on the activities of the Organization. The General Conference shall determine the periods to be covered by these reports.

4. The Director-General shall appoint the staff of the Secretariat in accordance with staff regulations to be approved by the General Conference. Subject to the paramount consideration of securing the highest standards of integrity, appointment to the staff shall be on as wide a geographical basis as possible.

5. The responsibilities of the Director-General and of the staff shall be exclusively international in character. In the discharge of their duties they shall not seek or receive instructions from any Government or from any authority external to the Organization. They shall refrain from any action which might prejudice their position as international officials. Each State member of the Organization undertakes to respect the international character of the responsibilities of the Director-General and the staff, and not to seek to influence them in the discharge of their duties.

6. Nothing in this Article shall preclude the Organization from entering into special arrangements within the United Nations Organization for common services and staff and for the interchange of personnel.

ARTICLE VII. NATIONAL CO-OPERATING BODIES

1. Each Member State shall make such arrangements as suit its particular conditions for the purpose of associating its principal bodies interested in educational, scientific and cultural matters with the work of the Organization, preferably by the formation of a National Commission broadly representative of the Government of such bodies.

2. National Commissions or National Co-operating Bodies, where they exist, shall act in an advisory capacity to their respective delegations to the General Conference and to their Governments in matters relating to the Organization and shall function as agencies of liaison in all matters of interest to it.

3. The Organization may, on the request of a Member State, delegate, either temporarily or permanently, a member of its Secretariat to serve on the National Commission of that State, in order to assist in the development of its work.

ARTICLE VIII. REPORTS BY MEMBER STATES

Each Member State shall report periodically to the Organization, in a manner to be determined by the General Conference, on its laws, regulations and statistics relating to educational, scientific and cultural life and institutions, and on the action taken upon the recommendations and conventions referred to in Article IV, paragraph 4.

ARTICLE IX. BUDGET

1. The Budget shall be administered by the Organization.

2. The General Conference shall approve and give final effect to the budget and to the apportionment of financial responsibility among the States members of the Organization subject to such arrangement with the United Nations as may be provided in the agreement to be entered into pursuant to Article X.

3. The Director-General, with the approval of the Executive Board, may receive gifts, bequests, and subventions directly from Governments, public and private institutions, associations and private persons.

ARTICLE X. RELATIONS WITH THE
UNITED NATIONS ORGANIZATIONS

This Organization shall be brought into relations with the United Nations Organization, as soon as practicable, as one of the Specialized Agencies referred to in Article 57 of the Charter of the United Nations. This relationship shall be effected through an agreement with the United Nations Organization under Article 63 of the Charter, which agreement shall be subject to the approval of the General Conference of this Organization. The agreement shall provide for effective cooperation between the two Organizations in the pursuit of their common purpose, and at the same time shall recognize the autonomy of this Organization, within the fields of its competence as defined in this Constitution. Such agreement may, among other matters, provide for the approval and financing of the budget of the Organization by the General Assembly of the United Nations.

ARTICLE XI. RELATIONS WITH OTHER SPECIALIZED
INTERNATIONAL ORGANIZATIONS AND AGENCIES

1. This Organization may cooperate with other specialized intergovernmental organizations and agencies whose interests and activities are related to its purpose. To this end the Director-General, acting under the general authority of the Executive Board, may establish effective working relationships with such organizations and agencies and establish such joint committees as may be necessary to assure effective cooperation. Any formal arrangements entered into with such organizations or agencies shall be subject to the approval of the Executive Board.

2. Whenever the General Conference of this Organization and the competent authorities of any other specialized intergovernmental organizations or agencies whose purposes and functions lie within the competence of this Organization, deem it desirable to effect a transfer of their resources and activities to this Organization, the Director-General, subject to the approval of the Conference, may enter into mutually acceptable arrangements for this purpose.

3. This Organization may make appropriate arrangements with other intergovernmental organizations for reciprocal representation at meetings.

4. The United Nations Educational, Scientific and Cultural Organization may make suitable arrangements for consultation and cooperation with non-governmental international organizations concerned with mat-

ters within its competence, and may invite them to undertake specific tasks. Such cooperations may also include appropriate participation by representatives of such organizations on advisory committees set up by the General Conference.

ARTICLE XII. LEGAL STATUS OF THE ORGANIZATION

The provisions of Articles 104 and 105 of the Charter of the United Nations Organization concerning the legal status of that Organization, its privileges and immunities, shall apply in the same way to this Organization.

ARTICLE XIII. AMENDMENTS

1. Proposals for amendments to this Constitution shall become effective upon receiving the approval of the General Conference by a two-thirds majority; provided, however, that those amendments which involve fundamental alterations in the aims of the Organization or new obligations for the Member States shall require subsequent acceptance on the part of two-thirds of the Member States before they come into force. The draft texts of proposed amendments shall be communicated by the Director-General to the Member States at least six months in advance of their consideration by the General Conference.

2. The General Conference shall have power to adopt by a two-thirds majority rules of procedure for carrying out the provisions of this Article.

ARTICLE XIV. INTERPRETATION

1. The English and French texts of this Constitution shall be regarded as equally authoritative.

2. Any question or dispute concerning the interpretation of this Constitution shall be referred for determination to the International Court of Justice or to an arbitral tribunal, as the General Conference may determine under its rules of procedure.

ARTICLE XV. ENTRY INTO FORCE

1. This Constitution shall be subject to acceptance. The instruments of acceptance shall be deposited with the Government of the United Kingdom.

2. This Constitution shall remain open for signature in the archives of the Government of the United Kingdom. Signature may take place either before or after the deposit of the instrument of acceptance. No acceptance shall be valid unless preceded or followed by signature.

3. This Constitution shall come into force when it has been accepted by twenty of its signatories. Subsequent acceptances shall take effect immediately.

4. The Government of the United Kingdom will inform all Members of the United Nations of the receipt of all instruments of acceptance and of the date on which the Constitution comes into force in accordance with the preceding paragraphs.

In faith whereof, the undersigned, duly authorized to that effect, have signed this Constitution in the English and French languages, both texts being equally authentic.

Done in London, the sixteenth day of November, one thousand nine hundred and forty-five, in a single copy, in the English and French languages, of which certified copies will be communicated by the Government of the United Kingdom to the Governments of all the Members of the United Nations.

Appendix II

THE DIRECTORS-GENERAL OF UNESCO

Julian Huxley	12/6/46-12/9/48
Jaime Torres Bodet	12/10/48-12/1/52
John W. Taylor (acting)	12/2/52-7/3/53
Luther W. Evans	7/4/53-12/4/58
Vittorio Veronese	12/5/58-6/4/59
René Maheu (acting)	6/5/59-11/1/61
René Maheu	11/2/61-11/14/74
Amadou-Mahtar M'Bow	1/15/74-11/16/87
Federico Mayor Zaragoza	11/16/87-present

Appendix III

ANATOMY OF A SMEAR: ED BRADLEY AND "60 MINUTES" ON UNESCO

Edward S. Herman

On April 22, 1984, the CBS program "60 Minutes" aired a segment covering "UNESCO," produced by Jeanne Solomon and hosted by Ed Bradley. This program, which never once departed from the State Department line, demonstrates well both the strongly conformist tendencies of network television and its power to enhance the effects of animus and bias. CBS's "UNESCO" makes its earlier treatment of General William Westmoreland look like an apologia, but UNESCO and its officials are relatively defenseless, and they may be abused with impunity.

FRAMES AND SOURCES

Ed Bradley starts out noting that UNESCO "has brought literacy to Africa, trained teachers for the Third World, . . . and preserved ancient monuments in Egypt and Asia." He then goes on: "Nothing wrong there, you might think. But according to Washington, UNESCO has now become a politicized, financially mismanaged organization" and the Reagan administration is threatening to pull out. Later on he expands further on "U.S. administration claims" that UNESCO is "anti-American and antidemocratic." And still further on he quotes the U.S. Ambassador to UNESCO, Jean Gerard, giving a whole series of allegations about UNESCO: "She says" it has "a militant political bias," "she says it's financing Soviet teachers in Afghanistan," etc.

In his opening, after listing the U.S. claims, Bradley asks "What's wrong with UNESCO?" Bradley never asks: "What's wrong with Washington, that it pulls out of a world organization doing such important things as bringing literacy to Africa and preserving ancient monuments?" Bradley just accepts without question the administration's claims as presumptively valid. If his leader says that UNESCO is bad, he takes that as a premise. He will question M'Bow's motives and qualifications, but not his government's or Mrs. Gerard's. He will never mention the Heritage Foundation and its program, nor will he discuss the Treaty of the Sea or the huge reductions in aid for the poor in the United States as throwing light on why the administration was leaving UNESCO. The problem must lie in UNESCO. He is going to prove that UNESCO is bad.

CBS was working on this program during the period of the propaganda campaign associated with Scheuer and the negotiations for a GAO investigation.[1] At that time there were many rumors and allegations emanating from the Heritage Foundation, the State Department, Scheuer, and media organizations hostile to UNESCO, claiming UNESCO corruption and assailing M'Bow's tyrannical rule and KGB penetration of that organization. CBS and Ed Bradley latch on to each of these accusations, which dominate the agenda. The sources mentioned in the program consist of U.S. Ambassador Gerard, a former U.S. official at UNESCO, Judson Goodling, a number of anonymous disgruntled UNESCO employees, some leaked UNESCO files and State Department memos, and UNESCO Director-General M'Bow. There is no evidence that CBS ever talked with any member of the U.S. Commission for UNESCO, or any scientist or educator who worked with UNESCO. In his program exchanges with Ambassador Gerard, she is a source of The Truth. Bradley never asks her a hard question about her background and qualifications,[2] the possible ideological and political underpinnings of the exit, or its justification. He repeats her claims against UNESCO without ever making the slightest attempt to present alternative viewpoints or facts. With Gerard, Bradley is an unquestioning ally and conduit against a UNESCO, Soviet, and Third World enemy.

Bradley's interview with M'Bow, by contrast, consisted largely of a series of accusations about himself and UNESCO, almost all of which M'Bow answered effectively. Bradley and CBS carefully selected among the M'Bow exchanges to achieve their derogatory ends. Fortunately, however, a transcript of the original interview makes it possible to show how CBS not only suppressed important rebuttal evidence, but did this to a degree that allowed it to support a completely false claim (see *The Reds Are Coming*, below).

LANGUAGE AND TONE

To capture the staggering bias in this program, I will first examine in order the eight short sequences (words and pictures) that follow Bradley's opening announcement that he's going to Paris to find out "What's wrong with UNESCO." They set the tone for the entire program.

(1) "We went to headquarters to find out. And as befits a cultural organization, when you call UNESCO you get Mozart." (Mozart muzak)

For U.S. audiences, that you get Mozart when you dial UNESCO would suggest a pretentious and elitist organization out of touch with the masses. A small putdown.

(2) "UNESCO OPERATOR: This is UNESCO. Please hold on. We're trying to connect you." This provides an immediate image of a bureaucratic organization in which things are "on hold" and nothing much gets done.

(3) "BRADLEY: UNESCO has been based in Paris since it was founded after World War II. Its permanent staff of bureaucrats—some 3,400 of them—spend most of their time here, not in the field." Lo and behold, Bradley uses the word bureaucrat in his very next interjection after the phone operator. The *American Heritage Dictionary* notes that "in American usage, bureaucrat is almost invariably derogatory unless the context establishes otherwise." The context here is not otherwise.

Note that Bradley finally gives a "fact"—that the permanent staff is 3,400 strong and spends most of its time in Paris (a place where people go to have a good time), rather than in the field. This is an element in the standard U.S. official-Heritage Foundation line, and CBS quickly finds a home for it. He does not explain the planning function of the permanent staff, nor the fact that this function and concentration of staff in Paris was a result of U.S. and Western decision choices.[3] Without such context, this "fact" is merely a cliché employed in a sequence of derogation.

(4) (Operator speaking Arabic.) This image is surely not helpful in understanding UNESCO, and since Americans are uncomfortable and react negatively to foreigners speaking foreign languages it supports the overall attempt to denigrate.

(5) "They meet and publish. [Printing press activity.] They publish and meet." This sequence and set of images is less subtle. The words obviously suggest pointless activity, not alleviated by the showing of printing activity. Bradley doesn't feel obliged to support this derogation with evidence. This is a pure smear.

(6) (Operators speaking Spanish and other languages.) See (4) above.

(7) "And although UNESCO has six official languages, it's been said that most of the business here is done in a seventh impenetrable language known as UNESCO-ese." MAN (in UNESCO conference): . . . and end the first sentence after 'intergovernmental mechanism.' It would simply read, 'The executive . . . ' " Here Bradley relies on an anonymous source for a putdown, reinforced by a picture taken out of context to give the impression of a laughable and pointless organization. This technique could be used to denigrate any group or organization in the world.

(8) "BRADLEY: But it is not boredom that threatens to drive the United States out. UNESCO has become President Reagan's least favorite U.N. agency for a whole lot of other reasons." Note that Bradley concedes he has been conveying the negative image of "boredom," as he moves toward the "whole lot of other reasons" that UNESCO is disfa-

vored by the Reagan administration. The image was conveyed by a selective manipulation of words and symbols, devoid of useful information.

CBS AND BRADLEY ON UNESCO'S MANAGEMENT

Bradley moves to the main attack by means of an exchange with Gerard, who is upset with the UNESCO budget: "$373 million over the next two years. The United States contributes a quarter of that amount." According to Bradley, Gerard "says she is by no means sure how that money is spent." We may note in passing that Bradley doesn't try to put the $373 million (for two years) in context—is it large relative to the UNESCO functions of "eradicating world illiteracy"? Or is it large relative to the budget of Columbia University? The absolute size and the U.S. "quarter" contribution serve CBS's and Bradley's propaganda purposes. In the interview with M'Bow, the latter mentioned that the United States was getting a large refund in 1984, so that its total payment was only $25 million instead of $50 million.[4] Bradley does not mention this point.

The Bradley exchanges with Gerard deserve full repetition.

BRADLEY: That's something you tried to get an answer for ["how the money is spent"]? You tried to get to the bottom of that?
GERARD: Yes.
BRADLEY: And as ambassador of a country that contributes 25% of the budget, you can't get an answer?
GERARD: I have not got an answer.
BRADLEY: What does that say to you about the management of UNESCO?
GERARD: I would say it is poorly managed.

After a brief interlude with Goodling, who denounces M'Bow as a dictator, Bradley asks M'Bow about Gerard's charge that she can't "get answers" about the budget. From M'Bow's extensive original comments, Bradley selects out a few brief phrases, including the fact that UNESCO's budgets are public information. Bradley then returns to Gerard:

GERARD: We have people back in Washington who can analyze documents. They have been working on these documents, and they say there are many things which are obscure.
BRADLEY: Not necessarily intentional, that's just the way it is?
GERARD: Not necessarily intentional.

We may note the following:
(1) Bradley never asks Gerard why all the Western countries but the

United States have approved the recent UNESCO budget if it was very obscure.[5]

(2) CBS gives no evidence of ever having bothered to *look* at the budget or to get an independent expert to do so. Bradley and CBS merely take Gerard's word for it that there are obscurities. He does not ask for details, or even illustrations, or any sort of confirmation. The State Department's own U.S./UNESCO Review gave a budget breakdown with numbers and comments on the programs. It does not complain of obscurity, but argues about the specific programs it does not like, giving dollar figures. But Bradley and his CBS colleagues were too biased and lazy even to bother to look at the State Department's own documents.

(3) Although M'Bow denies the general charge, Bradley does not feel that there is a standoff—an accusation and a denial. Gerard wins, by patriotic default. There is then the sleazy exchange on whether the alleged obscurity in the budget is "intentional," in which Bradley gets over a smear without having produced a scintilla of evidence supporting the original charge.

(4) In the full interview, M'Bow gave a strong response to the general accusation of obscurity. He says that "every expenditure is listed in detail, every dollar of outlay is stated to be for some specific program or activity. What is more, UNESCO has auditors who go over its accounts and report to the General Conference." He also points out that "we have a Comptroller who is an American, Mr. de Leiris; ask Mr. de Leiris how every dollar is spent, he'll tell you." Bradley suppresses these and other more potent statements, and obviously never checked things out with de Leiris. He allows M'Bow to say, "There's nothing else I can say. I'm speechless. I'm speechless, because UNESCO's budgets are public." Bradley's selection of the statement "There's nothing more I can say." without having allowed M'Bow to say anything, speaks for itself. And the repeated phrase "I'm speechless," is empty of substance but conveys the negative image of a speaker who is both emotional and without an answer. Having suppressed extensive explanations by M'Bow, this is dishonest reporting.

M'BOW MAY NOT STEAL, BUT . . .

Bradley generously notes that "critics don't go so far as to accuse M'Bow of embezzlement," but they do call attention to leaked files that suggest "a series of financial abuses." Bradley then lists a number of allegations, which he merely asserts: that M'Bow gave jobs to friends and supporters, that he has given scholarships to unqualified applicants, some from his own Senegal, and that he "has used UNESCO funds to pick up the expenses of some Third World delegations, and that's against the rules."

Bradley operates on the working assumption that these accusations are true, since he presumes that anything Jean Gerard asserts is valid. And he fails to give M'Bow's rebuttals to these accusations. For example, M'Bow denied that his granting of funds to Third World delegations was contrary to the rules, mentioning among other things "a resolution of the General Conference asking me to provide assistance for the least developed countries." This and other elements of M'Bow's answer were suppressed as Bradley pontificates: "That's against the rules" (*I* say so).[6] M'Bow also raises the question of how much money is involved in these horrible scandals and elicits from Bradley the admission that this funding of the poor delegations amounted to a grand total of less than $100,000. But Bradley never allows dollar sums to surface here, because he is dealing with "rules" and "principles."

Except that he quickly jumps to the grand inference that this is all very important in allowing M'Bow to "support his own rule and to further his own political interests." This is based on a secret State Department document, which Bradley reports as solid information from an objective source. M'Bow asks for "specific facts." Bradley says "I will tell you precisely what the memo says"—namely, "That you used the budget . . . to control this organization, to direct it at your will." Bradley apparently considered this demagogic assertion to be "specific facts," to which he could expect M'Bow to respond. And once again Bradley suppresses M'Bow's reply. M'Bow points out that he received a unanimous vote for director-general in 1980, including the votes of the United States and Great Britain. Was this based on budget manipulation? M'Bow claims that his actions favorable to poor delegations were based on their need, not on political advantages to himself, which were negligible. He does not say it, but it is traditional for the rich to protest that politicians and leaders taking actions on behalf of the poor are doing it for "political advantage." It is only when they serve the rich that they pursue principle and the national interest. Bradley repeats this precise ideological formulation of his government concerning M'Bow (i.e., using his position to build up his power) as if it were a profound truth.

THE REDS ARE COMING

Bradley cannot resist making hay of the fact that the French government expelled 47 Soviet diplomats in the Spring of 1983, including nine on the UNESCO staff, charging them with espionage. Bradley stresses the fact that three of them were still on the UNESCO payroll at the time of his interview, despite the fact that UNESCO rules are clear that espionage would be incompatible with the oath of loyalty taken by UNESCO employees. To reinforce this point, Bradley shows a picture of a woman taking the oath, reading that the employee "must not accept instructions in regard to the performance of my duties from any government or other authority external to the organization."[7] Mrs. Gerard is then shown with an unctuous statement that the United States does not like having to pay for "three-fourths of a Soviet agent." Bradley did not allow M'Bow to reply, but paraphrases him: "He claims the French government didn't give him any evidence."

Bradley took M'Bow through this issue twice, trying hard to locate a firm basis for a case he was determined to make, whatever the evidence. In the end, he engaged in three major evasions and/or deceptions that allowed him to portray M'Bow and UNESCO as unreasonably protecting Soviet spies. The first had to do with the rules of fair play and the presumption of innocence of an accused person. Bradley, who was so deeply concerned with whether M'Bow had adhered strictly to UNESCO rules in funding poor country delegations, can see no reason for adhering to that famous Western principle when it comes to alleged Soviet spies. Mrs. Gerard doesn't require any evidence except the French government's act of expulsion,[8] and Bradley, a bit irritably, asks M'Bow, "Do you think the French government would expel them without proof?"[9] M'Bow says that he and UNESCO need the proof for proper disciplinary action, noting a bit sarcastically, "Am I supposed to dismiss a staff member without giving him the opportunity to be heard by a disciplinary committee because he is accused by a government?"

M'Bow went to great lengths to explain to Bradley that he had tried hard to get information from the French government, "just one fact proving that the person in question had engaged in some activity extraneous to his responsibilities as a UNESCO staff member. That is all I need."[10] Bradley suppresses all of this discussion of due process and the precise statement by M'Bow about the failure of the French government to produce "one fact," which is all he needs. Bradley covers this entire body of material with a very succinct paraphrase, that M'Bow "claimed" that the French government gave no evidence.

The second suppression-deception was of the fact that, as M'Bow stated, "This is not an isolated case. Your sources forgot to tell you that I have a member of staff who has been held in an Eastern European country for more than three or four years and who is still on our payroll."[11] For Bradley to have included this in his program would have compromised his attempt to portray M'Bow and UNESCO as tools of Communism. It would have strengthened the notion that M'Bow's behavior regarding the alleged Soviet spies was based on principle. Bradley cannot allow this.

The third and most spectacular suppression pertains to the UNESCO loyalty oath and M'Bow's interpretation of it. In the original interview

Bradley asked M'Bow what his reaction would be if the French had given him evidence that an employee was a spy for the Soviet Union. M'Bow states in no uncertain terms that "any staff member who works on behalf of any government in any matter, particularly in the case of espionage activities, has broken the oath that he took on the day when he was taken on as a UNESCO staff member, and consequently must leave UNESCO." He makes this same point *three times*: that such behavior would be intolerable and the employee would be discharged. But Bradley never quotes M'Bow on this issue—instead, he brings in the anonymous employee quoting from the loyalty oath and leaves the impression that M'Bow sanctioned the violation of the oath in the case of the alleged Soviet spies. If General William Westmoreland had had a factual case like this, he would be a very rich man.

TRASHING THE THIRD WORLD

There is a distinct racist element in this "60 Minutes" program. Bradley explains that the problem with UNESCO is that Vanuatu, with a population of 100,000, has a vote equal to that of the United States, and the latter has no veto in UNESCO.[12] "So it isn't surprising that UNESCO has become a political battlefield." But why does an equal vote for the poorer countries necessarily cause political battles? One part of the answer may be the disproportionate billing of the larger countries, but the other part implied by Bradley is that poor countries are less reasonable than Reagan's and Bradley's United States. That this was in Bradley's mind is indicated by the fact that his very next line refers to the anti-American and anti-democratic "rhetoric" that characterizes UNESCO. Those people just don't know their place.

Every time the Third World comes up for mention in this program, the context is unreasonable demands and privileges, or bribery, and the symbolism is primitivism: chanting people, backward technologies. In one sequence, CBS focuses on M'Bow at his desk, with the foreground dominated by a large primitive figure. Given the general thrust of the program, with M'Bow illicitly transferring resources to his clients in the Third World, the handsome figure plays an ugly symbolic role.

THE FINALE

To illustrate the comprehensiveness of the bias and distortion of CBS's

"UNESCO," I close with a look at Bradley's last two sequences. In the next to last, he addresses the question of M'Bow's tenure. He says, "But most observers say real reform cannot stop short of the resignation of the director-general." Note first the "most" observers. Bradley does not identify these observers. His sources as evidenced from the content of his program were exceedingly narrow, and the idea that he ever tried to get a representative sample of qualified observers is laughable. He never tells us what "real reform" is.[13] Does it mean stopping payment of the expenses of poor delegations to UNESCO and other such abuses, or does it mean that the governments that pay the bills should be able to call the shots, getting the poor Third World countries back in their place? Is that a question of "reform" or "domination"? Bradley never addresses any such issues.

In his final sequence, Bradley says that "although Mr. M'Bow has accused his critics of conducting a smear campaign against him, 23 Western nations have joined the U.S. in demanding reforms." Once again we have a failure of logic and understanding that distorts reality. Even if reforms were needed, the fact that the 23 nations joined the U.S. in demanding them would not disprove a smear campaign.[14] While Bradley was willing to press the State Department charge that M'Bow was using several hundred thousand dollars to build up his power base and get his will done, it never occurs to Bradley that the United States has rather larger resources and more clients than M'Bow and uses them to get its way. Only patriotic bias (or stupidity) will allow an analyst to argue that if a great power is supported by its allies and clients in one of its ventures, this proves the justice of its case. Furthermore, many countries urged reform on the (false) supposition that this might prevent the U.S. exit, but without necessarily believing that the situation at UNESCO was especially bad. But it is a regular feature of propaganda to argue that any verbal support for the propagandist's case proves its validity.

NOTES

1. See Part III, Section IIB for a discussion of this campaign.

2. As indicated in Part III, her main qualifications for the ambassadorship seem to have been her work with Women for Reagan and her rightist ideology.

3. See Part III, Section IIE.

4. Transcript of the Interview With the Director-General of UNESCO, Mr. Amadou Mahtar M'Bow, By Ed Bradley, Paris, February 23, 1984, p. 23.

5. The recent U.S. votes against approving the UNESCO budgets, furthermore, were allegedly on the basis of excessive size, not unintelligibility.

6. And we know how deeply Bradley's political leaders insist on adhering to the rules.

7. Bradley and CBS, of course, suppress the fact that from the McCarthy era onward the United States have insisted that U.S. citizens who become U.N. employees

get a prior U.S. loyalty clearance, which would seem to fly in the face of full-fledged loyalty to a U.N. organization. See Hoggart, pp. 49–50, and Section D, note 6.

8. Gerard and Bradley, both claiming to speak for Western principles, and Gerard and her administration allegedly distrustful of "government control," are quite prepared to accept the word of a government and support an action based on that word alone, which violates a Western principle protecting individual rights. It is the non-Westerner who threatens "Western values," who must insist on the principle of due process!

9. Bradley continuously challenges M'Bow's veracity, but he cannot understand anybody not believing that a Western government always speaks truly.

10. Transcript, pp. 14–15, 34–36.

11. *Ibid.*, p. 14.

12. This is a partial lie. As indicated in Part III, Section IIF, M'Bow has insisted on a consensus vote on sensitive policy issues, which gives the United States a *de facto* veto.

13. Arguably, this is taking the program in general at a level of seriousness that it does not deserve. No words are used with clarity and real intellectual content on this program. It provides us with a clash of personalities and symbols within a narrow propaganda framework, but is almost wholly devoid of intellectual content, let alone fairness.

14. In fact, telling evidence in support of a smear campaign is provided by this CBS program, whose dishonesty and viciousness would never be permitted against a powerful institution. In fact, it is the defenselessness of UNESCO and the number of its domestic enemies that explain why the Reagan administration and Heritage Foundation picked on it as the "Grenada" of the multinational organizations.

Appendix IV

SPEECH OF E. GOUGH WHITLAM, APRIL 13, 1985

Australia's ambassador to UNESCO, former Prime Minister E. Gough Whitlam, saw first-hand the campaign to get the United Kingdom out of the organization. He described it in detail in an address to the General Council of the United Nations Association of Great Britain and Northern Ireland. The text of that address follows:[1]

The United Nations system is just 40 years old. After 40 years any system is ripe for reassessment. The reassessment of any organization, whether it is a university or a broadcasting system or a publishing house or any of the bodies to which one can compare UNESCO, must be based on a consistent and continuing interest. It is not satisfactory merely to latch on to some particular aspects which irk you and say "Well, that's it, we've had enough of that" and get out. One will not make an organization as relevant now as we all thought it was 40 years ago by just seceding from it.

The big change which has occurred in the U.N. system is that it now has three times as many members as it had at the beginning. Moreover, it has a much more diverse membership than it had 40 years ago. The U.N. was established by the victors in World War II plus the Latin American States. In consequence, the victors and their original associates had an automatic majority in the General Assembly and the Security Council and in all the specialized agencies until at least 1960. In those issues which the General Assembly declared to be important and which therefore require a two-thirds majority, the founding members could not be out-voted until 1970. This led to some ambivalence on the part of British Governments on both sides of politics. Although Britain recognized the change of government in Beijing in 1949, the U.S. was able till the 1960s to count on Britain's vote in defeating resolutions to seat Beijing's representatives in the U.N. and thereafter till 1971 in mustering one-third of the votes to frustrate such resolutions. It was not till the 1980s that Britain gave serious attention to the question of Hong Kong. It then showed great diplomatic skill in achieving a solution.

The automatic majority which the founding members had in the U.N. and its specialized agencies got them into bad habits. Until the 1960s they never had to worry about arguing their case. What they wanted was automatically achieved or continued. Their representatives got flabby; they did not have to put forth good arguments and they got out of the habit of doing so. This was particularly the case with the Americans, because in all the multilateral organizations their chief representatives are still political appointees. However able, ambitious, adroit and attractive these representatives may be, they come as amateurs to a new job after having achieved success in other walks of life. It may be easy for an amateur to pick up the complexities in a multilateral organization. Complaints were commonplace throughout the 1950s about the Soviet Union exercising a veto in the Security Council. In recent years it has been the U.S., and sometimes the U.K., which has exercised a veto.

As the membership of the U.N. has changed over the last quarter century so inevitably have the agenda. The specialized agencies do not provide for a veto or a special majority. Every country has a vote of the same value as each State has in the American and Australian Senates. This should be no worry because very small countries often identify their interests with large countries. It does mean, however, that large countries as well as small countries have to put their arguments in a consistent, persuasive way. It is possible to win arguments if they are rational and factual and if they are put consistently and diligently.

There are some issues on which one cannot expect the majority of nations now to support the attitudes expressed by the U.S. and the U.K. For instance the Africans are suspicious and entitled to be suspicious of the attitudes of the Americans and British towards the regime in South Africa. The Arabs are entitled to be suspicious of the attitudes of the Americans and British concerning self-determination for the Palestinians. The U.S. and the U.K. use the catch word "Politicization," by which they mean the introduction of issues which they no longer have enough votes to exclude.

As the number of members in each specialized agency increases, the difficulty of administering each of them also increases. At U.N. Headquarters in New York no attempt has been made to maintain the original ratio between the Security Council and the General Assembly. In the specialized agencies the executive bodies have been expanded in step with the legislative bodies — the Conference or Assembly. The Executive Board of WHO now has 31 members. The Council of FAO 49, the Executive Board of UNESCO 51, and the Governing Body of ILO 56. They can be reduced by having a member on the executive body for every four or five nations in the organization instead of every three. In each case that change can be brought about by a simple majority in the legislative body, which meets every year or two years. Nobody, however, has moved to reduce the numbers. One of the reasons why nobody will move is that at present every nation can expect to have one term in three on the executive body. Most nations seem to prefer a frequent turn on an ineffective body to a rare turn on an effective one. This may be not least the attitude of Britain, which was second in importance to the U.S. alone when the organizations were started. The financial contributions have remorselessly exposed Britain's international economic decline. The Soviet Union became second to the U.S. when it joined each of the specialized agencies. Japan and Germany became the third and fourth largest contributors. France has long since surpassed Britain.

The task of the Director-General in each specialized agency has become immeasurably more difficult with the surge in membership. The position of a Director-General is often misunderstood. In Britain he is too often likened to the head of a government department. The difference is that there is no Monarch, no President, no Prime Minister, no Cabinet, and no real Parliament in any of these bodies. The legislative body is presided over by a chairman who is elected at the commencement of the annual or biennial session and who will make way for a successor at the commencement of the next session. He has no authority except during a session. The executive body is presided over by a chairman, usually elected at its first meeting after the session of the legislative body and handing over in turn to a successor elected after the next session of the legislative body. He again has no authority except during a session of the executive. The chairmen of the legislative and executive bodies are not Monarchs, Presidents, or Prime Ministers; they are more like Speakers. The Director-General inevitably has come to embody the authority and continuity of the organization.

The current Directors-General took office in WHO in July 1973, in ILO in December 1973, in UNESCO in November 1974, and in FAO in January 1976. They are all serving their second or third terms, which conclude in WHO in May 1988, in ILO in February 1989, and in UNESCO and FAO in November 1987. Thus, they will have served longer terms than any Secretary-General of the U.N. or than most Presidents or Prime Ministers. In Britain there would be few universities, government departments, or statutory authorities whose chief executives have served as long as the present Directors-General of the U.N. specialized agencies. Few persons are prone to beget or adopt new ideas or practices after eight or ten years at the top. It is not a bad time to consider the tenure of these chief executives. It can be done without offense or injustice to any of them. Since their present terms expire during the 15 months between November 1987 and February 1989, the sensible thing to do is to have the question of tenure considered in all the agencies at the same time. Their legislative bodies will have at least one full meeting before each has to choose a new Director-General. Therefore, in each case, the executive body has ample time to ask its legislative body to alter its constitution. The suggestion was made last year by Japan, but not pursued, that the Director-General of UNESCO should be elected for a four-year term and be eligible for re-election for one further four-year term. That would be the situation which applies in the case of the U.S. President. Alternatively, one could have the French situation where a President can be elected for seven years and, although eligible for re-election, is never likely to be. Or one could have the Mexican situation where a President is elected for six years and cannot succeed himself. All that needs to be done, as on the size of the executive body, is for a Member State to move for an amendment of the Constitution. One thing is certain: If the constitution of any of the agencies permits for re-election of a Director-General then the Director-General will direct considerable efforts towards being re-elected.

Some of the agencies, particularly UNESCO, are described as corrupt organizations. Their Directors-General are vilified, and not only in the case of UNESCO; in the *Sunday Times* of 26 August 1984, in an article "U.N. Bureaucracy Makes the Hungry Hungrier," Rosemary Righter takes to task "FAO's Lebanese boss." Corruption presumably has connotations of peculation or nepotism. No delegate or official is prepared to state instances. In the U.K., it is more difficult than in the U.S. to suggest that there has been financial impropriety because since 1951 the U.K. Auditor-General has been the external auditor of UNESCO and of most other specialized agencies. It cannot be said that his office is inefficient in general or inexperienced in international organizations in particular. One at least must assume that all expenditure has been promptly vouched for under the rules of the Organization. It is often contended these days that the duty of Auditor-Generals is to make some assessment of value for money and of efficiency in management. If that is what is desired in any of the specialized agencies, its legislative body should make the necessary changes to its Financial Regulations. Why doesn't some member, such as Britain, propose an appropriate amendment?

I conclude with a question which can arise in any of the major specialized agencies and which at the last session of the UNESCO General Conference was one of the two subjects on which a vote had to be taken. It was the location of the next session. It was decided that it should take place at Sofia. This decision was opposed by most of the countries in Western Europe, but not by Greece and Spain, which voted in favor of it, or by France and Italy which abstained. Opposition came from those delegations which, whatever protestations they made, felt an overwhelming antipathy to the Soviet Union and all its associates. The nearest to a dispassionate objection was that conferences away from headquarters in Paris should take place in sequence in different regions of the world and not, as in this instance, in the neighboring countries of Yugoslavia (1980) and Bulgaria (1985). The sincerity of this opposition will be shown if, as is suggested, the 1987 conference votes on an invitation from Spain, France's neighbor, for 1989. There are excellent reasons for the specialized agencies to have their periodic plenary meetings regularly at their headquarters. It is more economic and convenient for the secretariats of the organizations and also for those countries which have permanent missions in the headquarters cities, Paris, Rome, Geneva, and Vienna. It is ingenuous to advance the merits of rotating conferences among the Member States since most of them do not have the facilities or resources to be hosts. UNESCO's constitution originally provided for the location of each session to vary from year to year. That provision was omitted as far back as 1948. The rules of procedure, however, provide for any member state to invite the conference to hold a session in its territory. After the completion of UNESCO headquarters in Paris in 1958, sessions of the General Conference were held there until 1974. At the session that year, Commonwealth countries shortsightedly but successfully changed the practice by promoting an invitation to hold the 1976 session in Nairobi. Here again, the situation can easily be remedied by changing the Constitution to preclude or limit meetings away from Headquarters.

It is timely and proper, in the light of 40 years' experience, to review the constitutions of the specialized agencies in respect to the four matters I have discussed—the size of the executive, the tenure of the Director-General, the revision of the Financial Regulations, and the location of conferences. There must be a better way to change the constitution of an organization than by seceding from the organization. It is difficult to discover what the U.S. achieved by withdrawing from ILO through 1978, 1979, and 1980. After the U.S. withdrew from UNESCO at the end of 1983, wide-ranging reviews of the organization were undertaken by five working groups appointed by the Director-General and by a Temporary Committee established by the Executive Board. There would have been no such reviews if the U.S. had not given notice of withdrawal but the U.S. made no significant contribution to the process of review. Britain, with a new member on the Executive Board and a new Permanent Representative, and France were encouraged by the Western Group to discuss and present proposals. It was as a result of their efforts that the Temporary Committee's recommendations were accepted by the Executive Board at its second session in October, and the Temporary Committee was kept in being to monitor developments for the Executive Board's meetings in 1985. The U.S. refused to join the Temporary Committee and it did not seek to mobilize support for reform among Third World delegations, to quote a staff report in January 1985 to the Committee on Foreign Affairs of the U.S. House of representatives. The report declared:

> By not openly articulating and presenting its reform proposals to
> UNESCO until mid-July, seven months after the decision to withdraw
> was announced and five months before the date of effective
> withdrawal, the United States had very little time to develop and
> implement an effective plan and strategy to achieve those specific
> goals. The September meeting of the Executive Board remained the only
> meeting of a UNESCO policy body during 1984 which could begin to
> consider specific U.S. proposals before the effective date of withdrawal

at the end of December 1984. U.S. proposals made in the July 13 letter were made available to the 13-member Temporary Committee at its third session in late August, after the TC had already considered a number of similar proposals.

The report is also critical of the performance of the U.S. Ambassador in the handling of the draft GAO report on UNESCO, of which selected excerpts were leaked to the media.

The Anglo-French initiatives in the Temporary Committee were remarkably successful. The remarkable thing was not the immensity but the prospect of change. Those who had complained about aspects of UNESCO but had done nothing about them now found that it was possible to do something. For the first time in many, many years the Executive Board had been persuaded to accept responsibilities which had always been available to it.

The diligence, dedication and dependability of Britain's representatives had merited and achieved widespread support for a change of attitude and direction. The Foreign Office should have been proud of them and appeared to be satisfied.

The Americans who had organized the U.S. withdrawal now became desperate. They saw that the U.S. would probably be isolated. They embarked on the same course of action at the end of the second Board session in 1984 as they did at the end of the General Conference in 1983. At the end of the conference, the leader and many members of the U.S. delegation expressed their satisfaction with the conduct of the conference, the matters which were discussed, and the tone in which they were discussed. They acknowledged the Director-General's helpful attitude. They reported to this effect in Washington. It was then that the campaign started in Washington to persuade the administration to give notice of withdrawal. At the end of the second Board session in 1984, the same Americans decided to bypass the Foreign Office and to use the British media to persuade the British Government to give notice of withdrawal.

The Commonwealth permanent delegates stationed in Paris were the first to spot what was going on in Britain. They listen to the BBC. They read the English newspapers. They have English textbooks and reference books on their shelves. They usually had part of their higher education in Britain. They noticed that after the second Board session the same arguments and attitudes about UNESCO were appearing in the British media as had appeared in the U.S. media at the end of the previous year. The similarity in the campaigns was no coincidence. The International Organizations section of the State Department had engaged the same organization to conduct both campaigns, the Heritage Foundation, which is described in its letterhead as "a tax-exempt, public policy research institute."[2] It is a very rich, and to my mind, a very sinister organization. It was established in 1973. It claims to have organized the agenda of the first and later the second Reagan Administrations. Robert Chessyre wrote from Washington in the *Observer* of 25 November 1984:

> Heritage backers include Reagan's friend, brewer Joseph Coors, and the most shadowy of American right-wing philanthropists, Richard Mellon Scaife, a scion of the Mellon banking family.

Time elaborated on 3 December 1984:

> Heritage was founded with a grant of $250,000 from Joseph Coors, the Colorado brewing magnate and backer of conservative causes. Today it receives about a third of its $10 million annual budget from foundations, many of them begun by ideological sympathizers like Pittsburgh money-man Richard Mellon Scaife and industrialist John Olin. Another third is contributed by business corporations. . . . The final third comes from 130,000 individual donors.

All contributions are tax-deductible.

The Heritage Foundation's hostility towards the U.N. system can be seen from the titles of some of its recent publications: *The International Labor Organization: Mirroring the U.N.'s Problems* (1982); *UNCTAD: An Organization Betraying Its Mission* (1983); *The Food and Agriculture Organization: A Flawed Strategy In the War Against Hunger* (1984); *A World Without a U.N.: What Would Happen If the United Nations Shut Down* (1985); *The World Health Organization: Resisting Third World Ideological Pressures* (1985); *The United Nations Development Program: Failing the World's Poor* (1985).[3]

To spearhead its campaign against UNESCO, the Foundation employed Associate Professor Owen Harries, who in September 1981 had become an Australian citizen and the Australian Ambassador to UNESCO. After taking up his duties in Paris, he saw much of the new American Ambassador to UNESCO, Jean Gerard, and made three visits to the U.S., each time visiting the Heritage Foundation in Washington, DC. In September 1983, he became John M. Olin Fellow at the Foundation. The president of the Foundation, Edwin J. Feulner, Jr. claims that "the President's decision to withdraw from UNESCO was a direct result of a paper by Owen Harries that detailed a long list of shocking abuses."

For several weeks after Christmas 1983, Harries was engaged in justifying America's withdrawal. In October 1984, he was engaged in promoting Britain's withdrawal. In three London gatherings of which I am aware he was supported by Mrs. Gerard.

The concluding meetings of the UNESCO Executive Board were held on 18, 19, 20, and 22 October. Although Mrs. Gerard was one of its vice-presidents and had pending resolutions on the agenda, she was away in London on 18, 19, and 20 October and flew back to London immediately after the meeting on 22 October. A dinner at the Garrick Club on Friday, 19 October was attended by: Mrs. Jean Gerard, Mr. Owen Harries, Lord

Bauer, Lord Beloff, Lord Chalfont, Mr. Michael Charlton (BBC), Mr. Richard Hoggart, Mr. Roger Scruton (weekly columnist, *Times*), Sir Huw Wheldon (ex-BBC). Apologies were received from Mr. Paul Johnson.

A dinner at the Brooks Club on 22 October was attended by: Mrs. Gerard, Mr. Harries, Lord Bauer, Mr. Brian Beecham (former editor, *Economist*), Mr. Charles Douglas-Home (editor, *Times*), Mr. Dirk Kinane (U.S. citizen in UNESCO secretariat), Mr. Gerard Mansell (ex-BBC), Mr. Roger Scruton.

On Tuesday evening, 23 October, Mrs. Gerard and Mr. Harries took part in a discussion at the Royal Overseas League arranged by the Institute of European Defence and Strategic Studies. Over 40 persons accepted invitations to attend, including some of the media (e.g., Rosemary Righter) and the House of Commons (e.g., Sir Percy Blaker). There may well have been other gatherings, but I have cited only the three of which I have been told by persons who were present. Not all those who were present sympathized with the anti-UNESCO sentiments advanced by Mrs. Gerard and Mr. Harries. Mr. Harries also had lunch with Mr. Douglas-Home.

The cultivation of the media was most effective. Previously there had been very few editorials and signed articles on UNESCO. Between the Gerard/Harries foray and [Foreign Secretary] Sir Geoffrey Howe's announcement of withdrawal on 22 November, there was a spate of them. I have learned of the following:

21 October, *Sunday Times*; 22 October, *Daily Telegraph*; 24 October, *Daily Mail*, *Times*; 27 October, *Spectator*; 29 October, *Daily Telegraph*; 30 October, *Financial Times*; 3 November, *Times*; 5 November, *Times*; 7 November, *Daily Telegraph*; 10 November, *Spectator*; 11 November, *Observer*; 15 November, *Guardian*; 16 November, *Times*, *Guardian*, *Yorkshire Post*; 17 November, *Economist*; 18 November, *Sunday Times*, *Mail on Sunday*; 19 November *Daily Telegraph*, *Daily Mirror*; 20 November *Guardian*, *Times*; 21 November, *Guardian*, *Times*, *Daily Telegraph*, *Daily Mail*; 22 November, *Guardian*.

Of outstanding distinction was the article by Lord Chalfont, who gave an initial taste for foreign affairs to readers of the editorial page of the *Mail on Sunday* with an article entitled "Mad Hatter's Nonsense Factory." One must dismiss the thought that the noble lord had plagiarized an article written by Harries on the "Mad Hatter's Tea Party" in the October *Reader's Digest*; it would be ludicrous to suggest that he gets his own ideas and words from the *Digest* — or from the *Mail*.

On 15 November, 38 Commonwealth High Commissioners met in London and decided that their Dean should send a letter to Sir Geoffrey Howe to support Britain's continuing membership of UNESCO. This is the first time that High Commissioners have made such a demarche to a Foreign Secretary. Sir Geoffrey met them on 21 November. They were too late. He announced Britain's withdrawal in the Commons the next day.

Midway through the press campaign, questions on UNESCO were placed on the Order Paper of the House of Commons. Western delegates in UNESCO were disturbed by messages from their colleagues in London about these questions. At several of the Western Group meetings they expressed and reiterated a unanimous view that a notice of withdrawal by Britain would probably stop the process of reform in its tracks. They said that there would be a backlash against the western countries and that the developing countries would believe that they had been deceived. Having heard these views without demur, Mrs. Gerard proceeded to make her visits to London to promote the very course of actions which her colleagues feared and deplored. Not only did she not tell her British colleagues that she was going to London, but she did not tell them what she had done after she returned. Lack of candor led to lack of trust and lack of progress in the Western Group.

After 22 November, the flurry of interest in UNESCO in the media and in the Commons subsided as completely and rapidly as it had erupted. I have given details of events and persons in order to explain how a major change was brought about in British policy towards the U.N. system over the space of five weeks through American hustlers using the British press and backbenchers to stampede the British Government. Few would have thought that a British Government was so vulnerable and the British press so manipulable.

Let me first examine the implications within UNESCO. There can be no doubt that a government can make decisions on foreign policy as on any other matters without or despite the views of its official advisers. There can be no doubt that an ambassador can pursue his or her government's objectives as he or she sees fit or his or her government allows. Nevertheless a government depends on its ambassadors and other diplomatic representatives to pursue its objectives in other capitals and particularly in multilateral organizations. In February 1985, the Chairman of the Executive Board called a special session. The British representatives were unchanged. They were still as dedicated, diligent, and dependable as before but their influence had been eliminated. No other Board member was prepared to take a lead from them. Why should the representatives of other countries support them when their own government did not? In American parlance, they were lame ducks. It was left to other members of the Board to sustain the initiatives which Britain and France had initiated.

Britain's precipitate action was soon seen to have implications for the whole U.N. system. Britain was an original member of the U.N. and of all its specialized agencies. Distinguished Britons, Sir John Boyd Orr and Sir Julian Huxley, had been the foundation Directors-General of FAO and UNESCO and another, Wilfred Jenks, had been Director-General of ILO in the early 1970s. Britain is a permanent member of the Security Council and the custodian of the UNESCO constitution. The world may be accustomed to the U.S. striking out from time to time at the World Court, the specialized agencies, and the international banks. It is novel and uncharacteristic for the U.K. to do so. The U.K. now joined with the U.S. in breaching the universal membership of the U.N. system. At the same time as it notified its withdrawal from UNESCO, it succumbed with the BBC to American pressure in refusing to sign the Law of the Sea Convention, another target of the Heritage Foundation.

The campaign to preserve British membership of UNESCO is a first and essential step in preserving the universality of the U.N. system. There are certain criticisms of UNESCO which must be countered forthwith. The organization has had a bad press because it has been a forum for criticisms of the wire services. Your newspapers, including the Australian-owned ones, constantly suggest that the New World Information and Communication Order (NWICO), which the U.N. General Assembly entrusted to UNESCO, would lead to censorship of the press, licensing of journalists and the establishment of government papers in competition with private ones. The simple fact is that if UNESCO aimed to do any of these things it would first have to adopt a convention and then Member States would have to ratify that convention. The convention would only operate in those countries which ratified it. No steps have been taken to draft such a convention. UNESCO has passed no resolutions and made no appropriations for any of the purposes alleged. The reaction of the 1980 General Conference to the MacBride Report was, at the timely instigation of the Director-General, to establish the International Program for the Development of Communication (IPDC).

A justification given for Britain's notice of withdrawal was to save money or spend it better. As a matter of fact, the U.K. makes a profit out of UNESCO, principally because the Americans have made English the number one language in the world. Accordingly, if experts are needed in a great number of fields, particularly to write or edit or assemble publications or programs in the English language, UNESCO seeks experts across the Channel. In financial terms, Britain gets very much more out of UNESCO than it puts in. Yet the U.K. has joined with the U.S. in taking the biggest step in their history to diminish the influence of the English-speaking world in relation to the French-and Spanish-speaking worlds, which staunchly support UNESCO.

On financial matters, Britons realized the hypocrisy of those Americans who allege Soviet manipulation of the less developed countries which form the majority of the membership in all the specialized agencies. The International Development Association has a reputation for efficiency, its chief executives have been Americans, and the Soviet Union is not a member. This conspicuous difference from UNESCO did not save the IDA from a unilateral American reduction of one-quarter in its contributions. Again, the U.S. took the leading part in drawing up the 1972 UNESCO Convention concerning the Protection of the World Cultural and Natural Heritage. The U.S. was the first to ratify it and the U.S.S.R. has not ratified it. Yet the U.S. does not see fit to pay more than 60 percent of its dues and has usually paid much less. In May 1984, the U.K. ratified the convention and agreed to pay the largest mandatory contributions.

In the protection of cultural property we can find an encouraging if minute instance of the British Government's changing its mind. In December 1981, it gave 12 months' notice of withdrawal from ICCROM — International Center for the Study of the Preservation and Restoration of Cultural Property (Rome Center) — a small and effective organization established by UNESCO 26 years ago. The decision was made without consulting ICCROM's British Director, Dr. B. M. Feilden. As a result of coordinated representations to Ministers and letters to the press, the decision was reversed a fortnight before it became effective.

Despite the perception in UNESCO, the U.K. decision to withdraw may not be irreversible. Britain would never have given notice of withdrawal from UNESCO if America had not already done so. American influence and resources are so great that when it chooses to return it will immediately resume where it opted out. If Britain withdraws, it will be able to return only at a much reduced status.

America will find it impossible to create new multilateral organizations and arrangements in the areas which were entrusted to UNESCO 40 years ago. America, with all its resources, is already finding it difficult to make bilateral arrangements to compensate for the loss of multilateral ones. Britain's treatment of the Commonwealth on UNESCO had narrowed the only avenue open to it for making bilateral arrangements. There is no substitute for the international conventions and arrangements which UNESCO has achieved in education, science, cultural property, the environment, copyright, computers, and communications. UNESCO is constantly blamed for what it may do but has not done and is given little credit for what it has.

It is easier in the U.K. than in the U.S. to muster public support for organizations such as UNESCO. The U.S. is an extraordinarily dispersed country, the U.K. an extraordinarily concentrated one. It is possible in Britain at minimum cost to assemble the experts in all the fields where UNESCO is concerned and is properly concerned and always has been concerned. The U.S. Congress cut off funds for the National Commission for UNESCO, the administration dispersed the commission's staff, the president disregarded the House committee's plea to defer withdrawal for a year. The U.K. parliament and government would not be so heavy-handed. In the U.S. there are some newspapers of world standard and influence in such far-flung cities as New York, Washington, and Los Angeles. The great universities are no less scattered. In the U.K. it is much easier, cheaper and quicker to mobilize intellectual resources, to get in touch with editors, to write letters to the newspapers, to appear on television, to take part in radio discussion groups and to call on MPs.

Neither in the U.S. nor the U.K. is there a universal and unchanging view on any of the ideas I have raised. A faction obsessed with some issues can have its view temporarily prevail in a government which is preoccupied with other issues. The parties of the Right are more vociferous in attacking multilateral organizations but the parties of the Left have scarcely been outspoken in defending them. My purpose has been to draw attention to the pattern and nature of the attacks. It is in the countries which were foremost in bringing the multilateral institutions and structures into existence that one finds the most concerted threats to their continued existence. Britain has till the end of 1985 to resume its responsibilities and recover its influence.

[Editors' Note: The British Government did not reconsider its notice of withdrawal, and ceased to be a member of UNESCO as of December 31, 1985. The only other nation to join the U.S. and the U.K. in leaving UNESCO was Singapore.]

NOTES

1. Transcript of address, April 13, 1985; reprinted here with the kind permission of the Right Honorable E. Gough Whitlam.

2. In fact, the Heritage Foundation does not purport to be "impartial." It describes itself as aiming "to make the voices of responsible conservatism heard."

3. In fact, the Heritage Foundation has published more than 40 different books, pamphlets, background reports, and memoranda on the United Nations, all of them disapproving.

INTERVIEWS CONDUCTED BY WILLIAM PRESTON, JR.

Lucius D. Battle	April 27, 1987	Washington
John Davidson	May 12, 1987	Washington
John Fobes	February 5, 1987	Washington
John Hope Franklin	May 1, 1987	New York
Edmund Hennelly	March 17, 1987	New York
James Holderman	April 9, 1987	New York
Henry Kellerman	March 19, 1987	Washington
Max McCulloch	February 4, 1987	Washington
Barbara Newell	February 11, 1987	Boston
Richard Nobbe	February 5, 1987	Washington
Leonard Sussman	May 1, 1987	New York
Ambassador Robert Woodward	March 19, 1987	Washington (phone)

BIBLIOGRAPHY

Ad Hoc Group on United States Policy Towards the United Nations, "The United States and the United Nations: A Policy for Today" (October 1981).

Amuzegar, Johangir, "The North-South Dialogue: From Conflict to Compromise," *Foreign Affairs*, Vol. 54 (April 1976), pp. 547–62.

Argumedo, Alcira, "The New World Information Order and International Power," *Journal of International Affairs*, Vol. 35, No. 2 (Fall-Winter 1981), pp. 179–88.

Ashford, Nicholas, "Pressures Grow on Reagan to Block UNESCO's World Information Order," *The Times* (London), July 20, 1981.

Bagdikian, Ben, *The Media Monopoly* (Boston: Beacon, 1983).

Banks, Jack, "The Contradiction of a 'Free Press': An Analysis of U.S. Press Coverage of UNESCO," M.S. thesis, Department of Speech, University of Oregon, August 1984.

Barnet, Richard, *Intervention and Revolution* (New York: World Publishing Co., 1968).

Barnouw, Eric, *The Sponsor* (New York: Oxford, 1978).

Bascur, Raquel Salinas, "News Agencies and the New Information Order," in Varis, Bascur, and Jokelin, *International News and the New Information Order*.

Becker, Jorg, Göran Hedebro, and Leena Paldan, eds., *Communication and Domination: Essays to Honor Herbert I. Schiller* (Norwood, N.J.: Ablex, 1986).

Behrstock, Julian, *The Eighth Case: Troubled Times at the United Nations* (Lanham, Md.; New York, N.Y.,; and London: University Press of America, 1987).

Beichman, Arnold, *The "Other" State Department: The United States Mission to the United Nations and Its Role in the Making of Foreign Policy* (London: Basic Books, Inc., 1968).

Beltran S., Luis Ramiro, and Elizabeth Fox Cardona, "Latin America and the United States: Flaws in the Free Flow of Information," in Kaarle Nordenstreng and Herbert I. Schiller, eds., *National Sovereignty and International Communication* (Norwood, N.J.: Ablex, 1979).

Benton, William, *Report on UNESCO: Address to the Chicago Council on Foreign Relations*, January 9, 1947 (Chicago: Monarch Printing and Publishing Corp., 1947).

Bernstein, Carl, "The CIA and the Media," *Rolling Stone*, No. 250 (October 20, 1977), pp. 55–67.

Blanchard, Margaret A., *Exporting the First Amendment: The Press-Government Crusade of 1945–1952* (New York; London: Longman, 1986).

Blum, Robert, ed., *Cultural Affairs and Foreign Relations* (Englewood Cliffs, N.J.: Prentice Hall [The American Assembly], 1963).

Bradley, Ed, Transcript of an interview with the Director-General of UNESCO, Mr. Amadou Mahtar M'Bow, Paris, February 23, 1984.

Caughey, John W., "McCarthyism Rampant," in Alan Reitman, ed., *The Pulse of Freedom* (New York: W.W. Norton & Co. Inc., 1975), pp. 154–210.

Coate, Roger A., "Changing Patterns of Conflict: The U.S. and UNESCO." Paper prepared for the United States Participation on International Organization Conferences, Wingspread, Racine, Wis. January 28–30, 1987.

Committee to Protect Journalists, "Journalists Killed or Disappeared Since 1976," December 1986.

Committee to Protect Journalists, "Press Censorship," *CPJ Update*, October-November 1986.

Coombs, Philip H., "The Past and Future in Perspective" in Blum, ed., *Cultural Affairs and Foreign Relations*.

Cooper, Kent, *Barriers Down* (New York: Farrar & Reinhart, 1942).

Council on Hemispheric Affairs and the Newspaper Guild, "A Survey of Press Freedom in Latin America," June 1983.

Cox, Robert W., "ILO: Limited Monarchy," in Cox and Jacobson, *Anatomy of Influence*, pp. 102–38.

Cox, Robert W., and Harold Jacobson, *The Anatomy of Influence: Decision Making in International Organizations* (New Haven: Yale Univ. Press, 1973).

Crewdson, John, *New York Times*, December 26, 1977, p. 37; December 27, 1977, p. 40.

Cuddihy, John Murray, *The Ordeal of Civility: Freud, Marx, Lévi-Strauss, and the Jewish Struggle with Modernity* (New York: Basic Books, 1974).

Curran, James, "Advertising and the Press," in James Curran, ed., *The British Press: A Manifesto* (London: Macmillan, 1978).

Curran, James, and Joan Seaton, *Power Without Responsibility: The Press and Broadcasting in Britain* (New York and London: Methuen, 1985).

Curzon, Gerard, and Victoria Curzon, "GATT: Traders' Club," in Cox and Jacobson, *Anatomy of Influence*, pp. 298–333.

Demac, Donna, *Keeping America Uninformed: Government Secrecy in the 1980s* (New York: Pilgrim Press, 1984).

Edelman, Murray, *The Symbolic Uses of Politics* (Urbana, Ill.: University of Illinois Press, 1964).

Evan, William, *Organization Theory* (New York: Wiley, 1976).

Farer, Tom J., "The United States and the Third World: A Basis for Accommodation," *Foreign Affairs*, Vol. 54 (October 1975), pp. 74–97.

Felix, David, "Interrelations Between Consumption, Economic Growth and Income Distribution in Latin America Since 1800: A Comparative Perspective." Paper given at the Conference on the Comparative History of Consumption, University of Groningen, May 18–23, 1981.

Felix, David, "Economic Development: Takeoffs into Unsustained Growth," *Social Research*, Vol 36, No. 2 (Summer 1969), pp. 267–93.

Finger, Seymour Maxwell, "Reform or Withdrawal," *Foreign Service Journal* (June 1984), pp. 18–23.

Finkelstein, Lawrence S., "Internationalism—Is It a Foreign Policy Issue?" Based on Final Address at Conference on "The United States and the United Nations" sponsored by the Johnson Foundation, The Wisconsin Universities Summer Seminar on the United Nations, the Wisconsin UN Association and the Wisconsin Governor's Commission on the U.N., Racine, Wis.: June 26, 1986.

Finkelstein, Lawrence, S., "The Political Role of the Director-General of UNESCO." Paper prepared for Presentation at the annual meeting of International Studies Association/West, Denver, Colorado, October 25, 1984.

Finkelstein, Lawrence S., "Conference Document: Is the Past Prologue," in U.S. State Department, *A Critical Assessment of U.S. Participation in UNESCO*, pp. 27–42.

Fishman, Mark, *Manufacturing the News* (Austin: University of Texas Press, 1980).

Franck, Thomas M., *Nation Against Nation: What Happened to the U.N. Dream and What the U.S. Can Do About It* (New York: Oxford University Press, 1985).

Frankel, Charles, *High on Foggy Bottom: An Outsider's View of the Government* (New York: Harper & Row, 1969).

Frankel, Charles, *The Neglected Aspect of Foreign Affairs, American Education and Cultural Policy Abroad* (Washington, D.C.; The Brookings Institution, 1966).

Garcia, Ruperto, "A Trial Balloon at UNESCO," *The Texas Observer* (February 10, 1984), pp. 14–18.

Garrett, Henry, "A Review: Klineberg's Chapter on Race and Psychology" (IAAEK 1960).

Gerbner, George, *The American Press Coverage of the Fourth Extraordinary Session of the UNESCO General Conference* (Paris, 1982), under contract with UNESCO August 1983, The Annenberg School of Communications, Philadelphia.

Gifford, C. Anthony, *Through a Lens Darkly: Press Coverage of the U.S. Withdrawal From UNESCO* (New York: Longman-Annenberg, forthcoming).

Gilliam, Angela, "Showdown at UNESCO: The Reagan Administration Confronts the Third World," *Freedomways*, Second Quarter 1985, pp. 90–94.

Ginsberg, Benjamin, *The Captive Public: How Mass Opinion Promotes State Power* (New York: Basic Books, 1986).

Goldstein, Robert Justin, *Political Repression in Modern America: From 1870 to the Present* (Cambridge, Mass.: Shenkman, 1978).

Goodman, Walter, *The Committee: The Extraordinary Career of the House Committee on Un-American Activities* (New York: Farrar, Straus-Giroux, 1968).

Goodwyn, Lawrence, *Democratic Promise: The Populist Movement in America* (New York: Oxford University Press, 1976).

Gould, Stephen Jay, *The Mismeasure of Man* (New York: Norton, 1981).

Harper, Alan D., *The Politics of Loyalty: The White House and the Communist Issue, 1946–1952* (Westport: Greenwood Publishing, 1969).

Hazzard, Shirley, *Defeat of an Ideal: A Study of the Self-Destruction of the United Nations* (Boston: Little, Brown & Co., 1973).

Herman, Edward S., *The Real Terror Network* (Boston: South End Press, 1982).

Herman, Edward S., and Frank Brodhead, *The Rise and Fall of the Bulgarian Connection* (New York: Sheridan Square, 1986).

Herman, Edward S., and Noam Chomsky, *Manufacturing Consent: The Political Economy of the Mass Media* (New York: Pantheon, 1988).

Hilsman, Roger, *To Move a Nation: The Politics of Foreign Policy in the Administration of John F. Kennedy* (New York: Doubleday & Co., 1967).

Hocking, William Ernest, *Freedom of the Press: A Framework of Principle, A Report from the Commission on Freedom of the Press* (Chicago: University of Chicago Press, 1947).

Hoggart, Richard, *An Idea and Its Servants: UNESCO from Within* (New York: Oxford University Press, 1978).

Hufner, Klaus, and Jens Naumann, "UNESCO: Only the Crisis of a 'Politicized' UN Specialized Agency?," *Comparative Education Review*, Vol. 30, No. 1, 1986.

Hufner, Klaus, and Jens Naumann, "UNESCO: Fictions and Facts," *WFUNA Bulletin*, No. 34 (June 1985).

Hughes, Frank, *Prejudice and the Press* (New York: Devin-Adair, 1950).

Hughes, Thomas L. "The Twilight of Internationalism," *Foreign Policy*, No. 61 (Winter 1985–86), pp. 25–48.

Hyman, Sidney, *The Lives of William Benton* (Chicago: University of Chicago Press, 1969).

Jacobson, Harold, "ITU: A Potpourri of Bureaucrats and Industrialists," in Cox and Jacobson, eds., *The Anatomy of Influence,* pp. 59–101.

Jacobson, Harold K., "WHO: Medicine, Regionalism, and Managed Politics," in Cox and Jacobson, *Anatomy of Influence*, pp. 175–215.

Jayaweera, Neville, *The Political Economy of the Communication Revolution and the Third World* (Singapore: Asian Mass Communication and Research Center, 1986).

Karp, Basil, *The Development of the Philosophy of UNESCO*, PhD Dissertation, University of Chicago, December 1951.

Keen, Sam, *Faces of the Enemy: Reflections of the Hostile Imagination* (San Francisco: Harper & Row, 1986).

Kekkonen, Urho, "The Free Flow of Information: Towards a Reconsideration of National and International Communication Policies," Tampere, Finland, May 21, 1973.

Kissinger, Henry, *Years of Upheaval* (Boston: Little Brown & Co., 1982).

Koeppel, Barbara, "Will We Pick Up Our Marbles?" *The Nation*, October 29, 1977.

Kolko, Gabriel, *The Roots of American Foreign Policy: An Analysis of Power and Purpose* (Boston: Beacon Press, 1969).

Kondopolou, Y., P. Schlesinger, and C. Sparks, "British Press Reporting of the New World Information and Communication Order Debate 1980–1981," June 1985.

Kranish, Arnold, "Panel Commentary," in U.S. Department of State, *A Critical Assessment of U.S. Participation in UNESCO.*

Kundera, Milan, *The Book of Laughter and Forgetting* (New York: Alfred A. Knopf, 1980).

LaFeber, Walter, *The New Empire: An Interpretation of American Expansion, 1860–1898* (Ithaca, N.Y.: Cornell University Press, 1963).

Landis, Fred, "CIA Media Operations in Chile, Jamaica, and Nicaragua," *CovertAction Information Bulletin*, Number 16 (March 1982), p. 32.

Latham, Earl, *The Communist Controversy in Washington: From the New Deal to McCarthy* (Cambridge, Mass.: Harvard University Press, 1966).

Laves, Walter, H. C., *UNESCO and Economic Development* (USNC, June 10, 1953).

Laves, Walter H. C., and Charles A. Thomson, *UNESCO: Purpose, Progress, Prospects* (Bloomington: Indiana University Press, 1957).

Leigh, Robert D., "Freedom of Communication Across National Boundaries," *Educational Record*, October 29, 1948.

Litwack, Leon, *Been in the Storm So Long: The Aftermath of Slavery* (New York: Alfred A. Knopf, 1979).

Loftus, John, *The Belarus Secret* (New York: Alfred A. Knopf, 1982).

Lowry, W. McNeil, and Gertrude S. Hooker, "The Role of the Arts and Humanities," in Blum, ed., *Cultural Affairs and Foreign Relations*, pp. 41–79.

Lyons, Gene M., David A. Baldwin, and Donald W. McNemar, "The 'Politicization' Issue in the UN Specialized Agencies," *The Changing United Nations: Options for the United States*, Proceedings of the Academy of Political Science, Vol. 32, No. 4 1977, pp. 81–92.

MacBride, Seán, *Many Voices, One World: Toward a New More Just and More Efficient World Information and Communication Order*, Report by the International Commission for the Study of Communication Commission for the Study of Communication Problems, Abridged Edition (New York: UNESCO, 1984).

Mahoney, Eileen, "The Intergovernmental Bureau of Informatics: An International Organization within the Changing World Political Economy," in Vincent Mosco and Janet Wasko, eds., *The Political Economy of Information* (Madison, Wis.: University of Wisconsin Press, 1988).

Markel, Lester, *Public Opinion and Foreign Policy* (New York: Harper & Bros. (for The Council on Foreign Relations), 1949).

Markel, Lester, and Audrey March, *Global Challenge to the United States* (Cranberry, N.J. and London: Farleigh Dickenson University Press and Assoc. University Presses, 1976).

Massing, Michael, "UNESCO Under Fire," *Atlantic Monthly* (July 1984), Appendix 12, "Recent Developments," pp. 271–80.

Maynes, Charles William, "A U.N. Policy for the Next Administration," *Foreign Affairs*, Vol. 54 (July 1976). pp. 804–19.

McMahon, Robert J., "Eisenhower and Third World Nationalism: A Critique of the Revisionists," *Political Science Quarterly*, Vol. 101, No. 3 (Centennial Year 1886–1986), pp. 453–73.

McShane, Dennis, "Carter Ends Boycott," *New Statesman*, February 22, 1980.

Mehan, Joseph A., "UNESCO and the U.S.: Action and Reaction," *Journal of Communication* (Autumn 1981), pp. 159–63.

Mehler, Barry, "A Comparison of American and Nazi Sterilization Programs." Paper at Annual Meeting of Phi Alpha Theta (March 28, 1987).

Mehler, Barry, "The New Eugenics: Academic Racism in the U.S. Today," *Science for the People*, Vol. 15 (May/June 1983), pp. 18–23.

Metz, Stephen, "The Anti-Apartheid Movement and the Populist Instinct in American Politics," *Political Science Quarterly*, Vol. 101, No. 3 (Centennial Year 1886–1986), pp. 379–95.

Morgan, Dan, "Conservatives: A Well-Financed Network," *Washington Post*, January 4, 1981.

Mowlana, Hamid, "The Decision to Withdraw from UNESCO," *Journal of Communication*, (Autumn 1984).

National News Council, "Report on News Coverage of Belgrade UNESCO Conference," March 6, 1981.

Newell, Barbara, W., "The UNESCO Withdrawal: A Lost Opportunity," ms., undated.

Ninkovich, Frank A., *The Diplomacy of Ideas: U.S. Foreign Policy and Cultural Relations, 1939–1950* (Cambridge: Cambridge University Press, 1981).

Nobbe, Richard, "An Analysis of Past and Present Reviews of UNESCO and U.S. Participation in UNESCO," U.S. State Department Memorandum, July 27, 1983; includes "Annotated Bibliography."

Nordenstreng, Kaarle with Lauri Hannikainen, *The Mass Media Declaration of UNESCO* (Norwood, N.J.: Ablex, 1984).

Nye, Joseph S., "UNCTAD: Poor Nations' Pressure Group," in Cox and Jacobson, *Anatomy of Influence*, pp. 334–70.

Parenti, Michael, *Inventing Reality* (New York: St. Martin's Press, 1986).

Partan, Daniel G., "Documentary Study of the Politicization of UNESCO," *Bulletin of the American Academy of Arts and Sciences*, Vol. XXIX, No. 3 (November 1975).

Pavlic, Breda, and Cees J. Hamelink, *The New International Economic Order: Links between Economics and Communications*, UNESCO, Reports and Papers on Mass Communication, Number 98, 1985.

Pell, Eve, *The Big Chill* (Boston: Beacon Press, 1984).

Pfaff, William, "Reflections: On Nationalism," *New Yorker* (May 25, 1987), pp. 44–56.

Powers, Richard, *Security and Power* (New York: Free Press/Macmillan, 1987).

Preston, William, Jr., "Information as Obscenity: The Reagan Assault on Liberty," *Our Right to Know*, March-April 1982, pp. 1–5.

Preston, William, Jr., "Executive Overkill: Secrecy as an Arms Race," *Our Right To Know*, Summer 1982, pp. 7–8.

Preston, William, Jr., *Aliens and Dissenters: Federal Suppression of Radicals, 1902–1933* (Cambridge, Mass.: Harvard Univ. Press, 1963).

Preston, William, Jr., and Ellen Ray, "Disinformation and Deception: Democracy as a Cover Story," *CovertAction Information Bulletin*, Number 19 (Spring 1983), p. 3.

Raskin, A. H., "U.S. News Coverage of the Belgrade UNESCO Conference," *Journal of Communication*, (Autumn 1984), p. 165.

Raube-Wilson, Stephen, "The New World Information and Communication Order and International Human Rights Law," *Boston College International and Comparative Law Review*, Vol. IX, No. 1 (Winter 1986), pp. 107–30.

Reitman, Alan, ed., *The Pulse of Freedom* (New York: Norton, 1975).

Revelle, Roger, "International Cooperation and the Two Faces of Science," in Blum, ed., *Cultural Affairs and Foreign Relations*, pp. 112–38.

Roach, Colleen, "Context and Contradictions of the United States Position on the New World Information and Communication Order." Paper presented to the 15th International Association for Mass Communication Research, General Assembly and Conference, New Delhi, India, August 25–29, 1986.

Roach, Colleen, "French Press Coverage of the Belgrade UNESCO Conference," *Journal of Communication* (Autumn 1981), pp. 175–87.

Rosenberg, Norman L., *Protecting the Best Men: An Interpretive History of the Law of Libel* (Chapel Hill, N.C.: University of North Carolina Press, 1986).

Saloma, John S., III, *Ominous Politics: The New Conservative Labyrinth* (New York: Hill and Wang, Division of Farrar, Straus & Geroux, 1984).

Sathyamurthy, T. V., *The Politics of International Cooperation: Contrasting Conceptions of UNESCO* (Geneva: Librairie Droz., 1964).

Scheinman, Lawrence, "IAEA: Atomic Condominium," in Cox and Jacobson, *Anatomy of Influence*, pp. 216–62.

Schiller, Herbert I., "Decolonization of Information: Efforts Toward A New International Order," *Latin American Perspectives*, Issue 16, Vol. V, No. 1 (Winter 1978), pp. 35–48.

Schiller, Herbert I., *Communication and Cultural Domination* (Armonk, N.Y.: Sharpe, 1976).

Schlesinger, Arthur M., Jr., *A Thousand Days: John F. Kennedy in the White House* (Boston: Houghton-Mifflin Co., 1965).

Sewell, James P., *UNESCO and World Politics: Engaging in International Relations* (Princeton: Princeton University Press, 1975).

Sewell, James P., "UNESCO: Pluralism Rampant," in Cox and Jacobson, *Anatomy of Influence* pp. 139–74.

Sewell, James P., *Functionalism and World Politics: A Study Based on United Nations Programs Financing Economic Development* (Princeton, N.J.: Princeton University Press, 1966).

Sherry, George L., "The United Nations, International Conflict, and American Security," *Political Science Quarterly*, Vol. 101, No. 5, 1986, pp. 753–71.

Shoup, Lawrence H., *The Carter Presidency and Beyond: Power and Politics in the 1980s* (Palo Alto: Ramparts Press, 1980).

Shuster, George N., "The Nature and Development of U.S. Culture Relations," in Robert Blum, ed. *Cultural Affairs and Foreign Relations*, pp. 8–40.

Sigal, Leon, *Reporters and Officials* (Lexington, Mass.: D. C. Heath, 1973).

Singham, A. W., and Shirley Hune, *Non-Alignment in an Age of Alignments* (Westport, Ct.: Lawrence Hill, 1986).

Sussman, Leonard R., Speech on the U.S. Withdrawal from UNESCO before the International Committee of the Public Relations Society of America, April 12, 1984.

Sussman, Leonard R., "The 'March' Through the World's Mass Media," *Orbis*, Number XX, Winter 1977.

Sussman, Leonard R., "Mass News Media and the Third World Challenge," in *The Washington Papers: 46* (Beverly Hills, Calif.: Sage, 1977).

Sussman, Leonard R., and David W. Sussman, "Mass News Media and International Law," *International Political Science Review*, Vol. 7, No. 3 (July 1986), pp. 344–60.

Torres, Esteban, "Trial Balloon," *Texas Observer*, February 10, 1984.

Trento, Joe, and Dave Roman, "The Spies Who Came in From the Newsroom," *Penthouse*, Vol. 12, No. 8 (August 1977), pp. 45–50.

Truman, Harry S., address, March 1947, Baylor University, Texas.

Tuchman, Gaye, *Making News* (New York: Free Press, 1978).

Turow, Joseph, *Media Industries: The Production of News and Entertainment* (New York: Longmans, 1984).

United Nations Association of the USA, *Congressional Survey Report: A Report on the Foreign Policy Attitudes of the U.S. House of Representatives*, UNA of US of A Inc., 1975.

UNESCO, files of correspondence with the media, New York.

UNESCO, International Commission for the Study of Communication Problems, Document 31, "The New World Information Order," Paris, 1978, reprinted in *Journal of Communication* (Spring 1978), pp. 172–85.

U.S. Congress, House Committee on Foreign Affairs, 99th Congress, 1st Session, *Assessment of U.S.-UNESCO Relations, 1984: Report of a Staff Study Mission to Paris-UNESCO* (Washington: Government Printing Office, 1985).

U.S. Congress, House Committee on Foreign Affairs, *Membership and Participation By the United States in the United Nations Educational, Scientific, and Cultural Organization*, Hearings, 79th Congress, 2nd Session, on H.J. Res. 305, April 3, 4, & 5 1946, GPO 1946.

U.S. Congress, House Committee on Foreign Affairs, *U.S. Withdrawal from UNESCO: Report of a Staff Study Mission February 10–23, 1984*, 98th Congress, 2nd Session, April 1984.

U.S. Congress, House Committee on Foreign Affairs Subcommittee on Human Rights and International Organizations, "Recent Developments in UNESCO and Their Implications for U.S. Policy," Hearings, 98th Congress, 2nd Session, July 26; September 13; December 6, 1984.

U.S. Congress, House Committee on Foreign Affairs, Subcommittee on International Organizations and Movements Report, "The United Nations Specialized Agencies," 84th Congress, 2nd Session, July 1, 1957, GPO 1957.

U.S. Congress, House Committee on Foreign Affairs Subcommittee on International Operations and on Human Rights and International Organizations, *Hearings*, 97th Congress, 1st Session, July 19, 1981.

U.S. Congress, House Committee on Foreign Affairs, Subcommittee on International Organizations, *UNESCO: Challenges and Opportunities for the United States*, 94th Congress, 2nd Session, June 14, 1976.

U.S. Congress, House Committee on Foreign Affairs, Subcommittees on Human Rights and International Organizations and on International Operations, "U.S. Withdrawal From UNESCO," 98th Congress, 2nd Session, April 25, 26, and May 2, 1984.

U.S. Congress, Senate Committee on Foreign Relations, 94th Congress, *Legislative Activities Report January 14, 1975-October 1, 1976*, GPO, 1977.

U.S. Congress, Senate Committee on Foreign Relations, 88th Congress, 1st Session, Hearing, "Activities and Procedures of UNESCO," March 4, 1963, GPO 1963.

U.S. Congress, Senate Committee on Labor and Human Resources, "Human Resources Impact of U.S. Membership in UNESCO," 98th Congress, 2nd Session, December 10, 1984.

U.S. Congress, Senate Subcommittee on Communications Hearings, *Progress Report on Space Communications*, 89th Congress, 2nd Session, August 10, 17, 18, and 23, 1966, Serial 89–78.

U.S. Department of State, *Report of the Monitoring Panel on UNESCO for the Secretary of State*, November 27, 1984.

U.S. Department of State, "U.S./UNESCO Policy Review," 1984.

U.S. Department of State, "U.S./UNESCO Policy Review," in Report of a Staff Study Mission, Appendix 6, February 29, 1984.

U.S. Department of State, Special Meeting of the U.S. National Commission for UNESCO, *A Critical Assessment of U.S. Participation in UNESCO*, June 1–3, 1982, University of South Carolina, Department of State Publication 9297, International Organizations and Conference Series 158, Bureau of International Agency Affairs.

U.S. Department of State, *Report to the Congress Requested in Sections 108 and 109 of Public Law 97-241*, February 24, 1983.

U.S. General Accounting Office, *Report to the Committee on Foreign Affairs and Committee on Science and Technology House of Representatives: Improvements Needed in UNESCO's Management, Personnel, Financial, and Budgeting Practices*, GAO/NSIAD-85-32 November 30, 1984.

United States National Commission for UNESCO, *Getting America Behind UNESCO: A Progress Report on the Effort to Mobilize the Nation's Voluntary Organizations for a Better World Community*, June 1968.

United States National Commission for UNESCO, *What Are the Issues Concerning the Decision of the United States to Withdraw from UNESCO*, 1984.

United States National Commission for UNESCO, Report of the Press Conference of August 9, 1984.

United States National Commission for UNESCO, Advisory, "What are the Issues Concerning the Decision of the United States to Withdraw from UNESCO?" Nancy Risser, Leonard R. Sussman, and David Wiley, Vice-Chairpersons, 1984.

United States National Commission for UNESCO, *UNESCO and the U.S. National Interest: A Statement by the U.S. National Commission for UNESCO*, June 1974.

Varis, Tapio, Raquel Salinas Bascur, and Renny Jokelin, *International News and the New Information Order* (Tampere, Finland: University of Tampere, 1977).

Weber, Nathan, "UNESCO: Who Needs It?," Across the Board, Appendix 5, "Recent Developments," pp. 165–70.

Weiler, Hans N., "Withdrawing from UNESCO: A Decision in Search of an Argument," *Comparative Education Review*, Vol. 30, No. 1 (February 1986), p. 133.

Wete, Frances N., "The U.S., Its Press, and The New World Information Order" (Freedom of Information Center Report No. 488), School of Journalism, University of Missouri at Columbia, February 1984.

White, Llewellyn, and Robert D. Leigh, *Peoples Speaking to Peoples* (Chicago: University of Chicago Press, 1946).

Whitlam, E. Gough, "Partner or Puppet: The United Kingdom, United Nations and United States." Address to the General Council, London, 13 April 1985, U.N. Assoc. of Great Britain and Northern Ireland.

Whitton, John B., and Arthur Larson, *Propaganda: Towards Disarmament in the War of Words* (Dobbs Ferry, N.Y.: World Rule of Law Center, Duke University, Oceana Publications, Inc., 1964).

Wilson, Howard E., "Education, Foreign Policy, and International Relations," in Blum, ed., *Cultural Affairs and Foreign Relations*, pp. 80–111.

Winkler, Allan, *The Politics of Propaganda* (New Haven: Yale University Press, 1978).

"World Forum: The U.S. Decision to Withdraw from UNESCO," *Journal of Communication*, Vol. 34:4 (Autumn 1984), pp. 81–179.

INDEX

Abrams, Elliott, 154, 156
Acheson, Dean: on communist propaganda, 60; on the State Department, 34
Action memo, xix, 219–21
AFP, 268
Agency for International Development, 93
Allen, George, 59
American Academy of Arts and Sciences, 136
American Association for the Advancement of Science: on U.S. withdrawal, xix–xx
American Committee on Public Information, 25
American Newspaper Publishers Association: on MacBride Report, xiii
"American Press Coverage of The Fourth Extraordinary Session of the UNESCO General Conference, Paris, 1982, The," 210
American Society of Newspaper Editors: on free flow of information, 292; on MacBride Report, xiii
"Amerika," 68
Anatomy of Influence, 115
ANC, 261
ANPA. See American Newspaper Publishers Association
Anticommunism, 10, 17, 39–40, 59, 60–70, 87, 288; resurgence of, 109–12
Anti-internationalism, 67–69
Anti-UNESCO campaign, 239–42, 282; and Heritage Foundation, xvi–xix; in U.K., xvi, 338–49
AP. See Associated Press
Arabs, 132–37
Arafat, Yassir: United Nations visit, 134
As Others See Us, 104

ASNE. See American Society of Newspaper Editors
Associated Press: bias in, 207, 209; on Costa Rica Conference on Communications Policies, 207–8; growth of, 55; on Third World news, 268; on world-wide wire-service, 28
Attlee, Clement, 33
Authority: symbolism of, 245, 251
Ayers, B. Drummond, 276

Backgrounder, xvii–xix passim, 160
"Bad News from UNESCO, The," xx
Barriers Down, 305
Barth, Alan: on media, 55
Bascur, Raquel Salinas, 207
Battle, Lucius D., 110, 113, 114
Beard Amendment, 157, 158, 165, 177
Beauharnais v. Illinois, 26
Behrstock, Julian, 57, 98, 100, 138, 194
Bentley, Elizabeth, 39
Benton, William, 33, 37–41 passim, 43, 48–49, 54, 57– 60 passim, 70, 105, 106, 162
Bergaust, Jean, 176
Biddle, Francis, 43
Bidwell, Percy: on foreign aid, 94
Black, Eugene: on foreign aid, 94
Blanchard, Margaret, 29, 54, 66, 304–6 passim
Blocker, Joel: on Israel and M'Bow, xx
Bowles, Chester: on propaganda, 99, 100
Bradley, Ed: and "60 Minutes" UNESCO segment, 328–36. See also 60 Minutes (CBS-TV)
British Press Debate (1980–81). See New World Information and Communication Order
Budget: defense, 258; UNESCO, 258, 259
Bundy, McGeorge: on COMSAT, 300

Bureau of Educational and Cultural
Affairs, 106
Byrnes, James M., 33

Cable: and information technology, 288,
307
Calder, Ritchie, 101
Carter, Jimmy, 127, 129–32, 151
CBS-TV. *See 60* Minutes (CBS-TV)
Censorship, 238, 271, 347
Central Intelligence Agency, 17, 269;
exposé of, 111
Chafee, Zachariah, 53
Chambers, Whittaker, 39
CIA. *See* Central Intelligence Agency
Cleveland, Grover, 20
Clines, Francis: on Reagan and UNESCO
policy, 235
Coate, Roger, 42, 135, 182
Cohn, Roy, xxvn, 63
COINTELPRO, 83, 110
Cold War, 21, 192–93; ideology, 229;
1946–60, 48–84; *1960*s, 87–117; and
U.S. withdrawal, 230
Colonialism: collective, 13; effect of
decline on UNESCO membership, xv
Columbia Journalism Review, xx
Committee on Foreign Affairs, 342–43
Committee on the Present Danger, 139
COMSAT. *See* Communication Satellite
Corporation
Communication Satellite Corporation,
300
Communications: and corruption of
opinion, 16; and economics, 277, 289;
M'Bow on, 127; research on, 288;
revolution, 13, 57; role of, 98–100; and
technology, xv–xvi, 306–7; UNESCO
role in, xvi. *See also* Information; Mass
media; Satellites
Computer: and information technology,
288, 300, 307
Conservatives: pressures of, 138–43; on
UNESCO, xiv–xv; on U.S. withdrawal,
237–38
Convention for the Protection of Cultural
Property in the Event of Armed
Conflict (Hague, *1954*), 98, 131
Convention for the Protection of the
World Cultural and National Heritage
(*1972*), 98
Coombs, Philip, 15, 77, 106
Cooper, Kent, 305

Coors, Joseph, 139
Costa Rica Conference on
Communications Policies, 207–8
Council of Allied Ministers of Education,
42
Cox, Robert, 13, 115, 137
Creel, George, 25
"Critical Assessment of U.S.
Participation in UNESCO," 161, 162
Cultural Affairs and Foreign Relations,
104
Cultural relations, 70–84, 115; Kennedy
and, 88–90, 103–6

"Danger at the U.N.," 157
Davis, Elmer, 30
Declaration of St. Petersburg, ix
Declaration on Fundamental Principles
Concerning the Contribution of the
Mass Media to Strengthen the Peace
and International Understanding,
304–5
Department of Commerce, 287
Department of Education, 260
Department of Public Information (U.N.),
xix
Dies, Martin, 9, 39, 67
Diplomacy: and information policy, 288
Disarmament, ix, x, 261
Disarmament Conference (*1962*), 101
Division for the Development of
Communications, 260
Dobbs, Michael, 223, 235
Donovan, William, 31
Dulles, Allen, 75
Dulles, John Foster, 20, 50, 89, 94

Eagleburger, Lawrence, 176; on action
memo, 221
Editor and Publisher: on MacBride
Report, xiii
Education: UNESCO on, 260
Eisenhower, Dwight D., 130; and foreign
aid, 92; on Middle East, 99, 100; on
Third World, 50, 89
Environment Program: Blocker on, xx
"Equality of Rights between Races and
Nationalities in the U.S.S.R.," 110
Evans, Luther, 64

FAO. *See* Food and Agriculture
Organization
Federal Bureau of Investigation, 17, 21

Federal Communications Commission, 287

Feulner, Jr., Edwin J.: appointment of, xxivn; on U.S. withdrawal, xviii, 183

First Amendment: campaign to internationalize, 38, 56, 156, 280, 291; protection of, 304

Fobes, John, 133, 149, 154, 192

Food and Agriculture Organization: Blocker on, xx

"For UNESCO, A Failing Grade in Education," xvii, 140

Foreign Affairs, 60, 90

Foreign Agents Registration Act, 39, 65

Foreign aid: modifications in, 92–94

Four Freedoms, 10, 42

Frankel, Charles, 91, 104, 107–8, 109, 110, 163

Frankfurter, Felix, 53

Franklin, John Hope, 110, 149

Free enterprise: and the media, 19–21, 27

Free flow of information. *See* Information

Free press, xvi, 228–29, 238, 267–72; defined, 205, 283; and governmental control, 205, 220, 269–70; media on, 279–80; test of, 206–7, 281; in U.K., 270; and UNESCO Constitution, 36–39. *See also* Hutchins Commission on Freedom of the Press; Journalists

Free trade, 277

Freedom House, 208, 298–99

Freedom of Information Act, 152

Freedom of Information Conference (Geneva, *1948*), 55–56, 101

Fulbright-Hays Mutual Educational and Cultural Exchange Act (*1961*), 106

Galbraith, John Kenneth, 90

GAO inquiry, 239, 240, 241, 263–65, 329, 343

General Conference: composition of, 318; functions of, 318; observers to, 319; procedures of, 319; voting in, 319

General Conference (Belgrade, *1980*), 208–10; French press coverage of, 211–12; media bias of, 208–10; 211–12

General Conference (Nairobi, *1978*): and NIIO, 298

General Conference (Paris, *1982*): Gerbner on, 210

General Treaty for the Renunciation of Wars, ix

Geneva Conference (*1948*). *See* Freedom of Information Conference

Geneva Convention on Broadcasting in the Cause of Peace, 26

Gerard, Jean: as "*60* Minutes" source, 328, 333; on U.S. withdrawal, xxi, 159–85 *passim*, 223

Gerbner, George, 162; on media coverage of Paris Conference, 210

Gilliam, Angela, 200

Goldwater, Barry, 111, 138

Goulet, Denis, 88, 91

Grace, Peter, 153

Grace Commission, 152

Gutman, Roy, 221

Hamilton, Alexander, 15

Harley, William: AP on, 209; on U.S. withdrawal, 245

Harries, Owen: on U.S.-UNESCO relations, xviii–xix, xxivn, 178, 222–23, 344

Harriman, Averell, 40, 89

Hazzard, Shirley, 62

Hearst, William Randolph, 24

Hennelly, Edmund, 168–73 *passim*, 251, 272

Heritage Foundation, xvi–xix, 138–40 *passim*, 153, 159–60, 344; critics of, xix–xx; on Freedom of Information Act, 269; and Harries, 222; on "*60* Minutes" segment, 329; on U.N., xv, xvi, 232; vs. UNESCO, xvi, 261; and U.S. withdrawal, xviii, 182

Herman, Edward S., 162, 172; on M'Bow, xxi; on media manipulation, xiv, xvi, xix; on socialism, xvii

Hickenlooper, Bourke: on foreign aid, 93

Hiss, Alger, 39

History of Africa, 98

Hoggart, Richard, 46, 64, 124, 141, 145, 146, 182, 190, 194

Holderman, James, 154, 161, 171, 176

Hoover, J. Edgar, 39, 63, 111, 124

House Foreign Affairs Committee: on UNESCO disarmament studies, 261; on U.S. withdrawal, 235

House Un-American Activities Committee, 9, 39, 112

"How the U.N. Aids Marxist Guerrilla Groups," 140

Hughes, John: on UNESCO public relations, 220

Hull, Cordell, 32
Human rights: Soviet violation of, 238
Hutchins, Robert Maynard, 52
Hutchins Commission on Freedom of the
Press, 52–54, 290–92, 304, 305
Huxley, Julian, 43, 48, 50, 59

IAPA. See Inter-American Press
Association
ICA. See International Communication
Agency
ILO. See International Labor
Organization
Information: and colonial system, 295;
and communication, 291; control of,
295, 303; dissemination of, 296; free
flow of, xv–xvi, 19, 50–52, 57–59,
65–66, 98–102, 269, 280, 288, 291, 292,
294, 304, 305; and military, 300;
monopoly of, 297; in 1950s and 1960s.
See also Communications; Mass media
Information policy: African, 293; Asian,
293; U.S., 287–88, 289, 291, 293, 298,
301, 302, 307–10
Institute for Contemporary Studies, 140
Institute for Media Analysis, xxii
INTELSAT. See International
Telecommunications Consortium
Inter-American Press Association: AP on,
207; on MacBride Report, xiii
Intergovernmental Conference on
Communication Policies in Latin
America and the Caribbean. See Costa
Rica Conference on Communications
Policies
International Bureau of Education, 25
International Commission for the
Protection of Journalists, xviii
International Commission for the Study
of Communication Problems, 299
International Communication Agency,
129, 155
International Council of Scientific
Unions, 25
International Court of Justice, 233
International Development Association,
347
International Education Act, 109
International Federation of Journalists,
27
International Geophysical Year, 123
International Institute of Intellectual
Cooperation, 25

International Juridical Congress, 27
International Labor Organization: U.S.
withdrawal from, xi, 137, 255–56
International News Service: growth of, 55
International Organization of Journalists,
xvii, 65
International Organizations Employee
Loyalty Board, 63–64
International Press Institute: on
MacBride Report, xiii
International Program for the
Development of Communications, 129,
301, 347
International Telecommunications
Consortium, 100, 301, 309
International Telecommunications
Union, 119n
Internationalism: anti-, 67–69; betrayal
of, 61–62; and new order, 14;
opponents of, 68, 155
IOJ. See International Organization of
Journalists
IPDC. See International Program for the
Development of Communication
"IPDC: UNESCO vs. the Free Press, The,"
xvii
IPI. See International Press Institute
Israel, 132–37; M'Bow on, xx–xxi;
UNESCO vs., xv

Jackson, Harold: on action memo, 219
Jacobson, Harold, 13, 112, 115
Jensen, Arthur, 70
Jerusalem, xv, xx, 132–37
Johnson, Lyndon, 107–8, 111, 112, 114;
and cultural relations, 88
Johnson Doctrine, 102
Jones, Joseph M., 34
Journal of Communication, 214
Journalism. See Communications; Mass
media
Journalists: dissident, 269; licensing of,
x–xi, xiiin, xvi–xix, 156, 270, 271, 272,
273, 303; social responsibility of, 288,
305; in Third World, xix

Kekkonen, Urho: on communication, 293
Kellerman, Henry, 114
Kellogg-Briand Pact (1928), ix, 26
Kennedy, John F., xi, 112; and cultural
relations, 88–90, 103–6; and UNESCO,
94–96, 113; and U.N., xi
Kennedy, Robert, 120

King, Martin Luther, 110, 120
Kirkpatrick, Jeane, xviii, 167
Kissinger, Henry, 121, 126
Koestler, Arthur: on survival of human race, x
Kondopolou, Y.: on media bias, 210–11
Korean War, 59, 61
Kristol, Irving, 138

Landes, David, 135
Language: ideological, 244–52, 282; in "60 Minutes," 329–31
Larson, Arthur, 101
Laves, Walter H. C., 40, 104
Law of the Sea Treaty, 152, 154, 232, 238
League of Nations, ix, 14, 25, 27
Leigh, Robert, 305
LeMoyne, James, 270
Less developed countries. See Third World
Lewis, Flora, 279–80
Lewis, Paul: errors by, 273–75; on GAO inquiry, 241; on U.S. withdrawal, 217
Lewis, Samuel, 142, 143
Lewis, Stephen: on Heritage Foundation, xx
Licensing. See Journalists
Lichenstein, Charles M., 178
Lie, Trygve, 63
"Lies, Distortions, and Nonsense from the Heritage Foundation," xix
Long, Gerald: on M'Bow and media, xxivn
Luce, Henry: and Hutchins Commission, 52

MacBride, Seán: on criticism of MacBride Report, xiv; on cultural relations, 103; Heritage Foundation on, xviii; and International Commission for the Study of Communication Problems, 299; on UNESCO, 6
MacBride Report, xiii–xv, 127–29 passim, 150; criticisms of, viii–xiv, 299; eradication of, xxii; French press on, 212; Heritage Foundation on, xvii; and licensing of journalists, xiii, xvi, xix; UNESCO view of, xxii
MacLeish, Archibald, 30, 33, 59
Maheu, René, 96, 97, 99, 106, 108, 132–34 passim, 146, 192; on Israel, xv; Kennedy and, 88–89, 106, 115, 120
Man and the Biosphere, 97, 123, 195

Mandate for Leadership, xv, 141, 151
Manly, Chesley, 68
Many Voices, One World. See MacBride Report
Maritain, Jacques, 30
Marshall, George, 63
Marshall Plan, 55, 58, 60, 92, 127, 129
Martelanc, Tomo, 255
Masmoundi, Mustapha, 246
Mass media, 53–54, 121, 124; bias in, xxii, 214–15, 222, 228, 249, 264, 271, 273, 280; control of, x, 306; double standard in, 247, 249; and economics of information, 279; and error correction, 273–75, 283; exaggeration by, xiv; fact suppression by, 275, 277–80; frames of reference in, 229–39; and ideological language, 244–52, 267; and lower classes, 206; monopoly power of, 297; objectivity of, 228, 281, 288; professional standards of, 206; and profit, 206; responsibility of, 102–3, 288, 290–91, 304, 305; rewriting history of, 253–56; role of, 98–100; self-censorship in, 222; sources, 214–15; on UNESCO budget, 259, 261–62; on U.S. withdrawal, 205, 206, 253, 280, 281, 283; and WPFC, 278; as watchdog, 219, 221. See also Communications; Information
Mass Media Declaration, xvi, 126–29 passim, 150
M'Bow, Amadou-Mahtar, xii, 18, 126–28 passim, 142, 143, 159–85 passim; 182; AP on, 209; anti-Semitism of, xx, xxi; attacks against, xx–xxi, 240–41, 247; Bradley on, 329, 332–33; Heritage Foundation on, xvii, xviii; on Israel, xii, xv; on "60 Minutes," 329; treatment of at Talloires conference, 279; and U.S. proposals, 272; on U.S. withdrawal, 235; on Western media, xvi, xvii, xxivn
McCarran, Pat, 40, 63
McCarran-Walter Immigration Act, 107
McCarthy, Joseph, 9, 39
McCarthyism, xi, 39, 61, 77, 151, 175, 200
McFarlane, Robert, 176
McKinley, William, 20
McMahon, Robert J., 49, 130
McNaught, John, 64
Meany, George, 137, 142, 256

Media. *See* Mass media
Meese, Edwin, 140
Mehan, Joseph A., xxii
Middle East crisis, 121, 143
"Model U.N. Program, The," 140
Modest Foreign Policy for the United States, A, 34
Monroe Doctrine, 16, 28
Morrill Report, 103
Mowlana, Hamid: on U.S. media, 214
Moynihan, Daniel Patrick, 126
Mulroney, Brian, xx
Multilateralism: and UNESCO's origins, 34–36
Murrow, Edward R., 90

NAM. *See* Non-Aligned Movement
National Academy of Engineering, xix–xx
National Academy of Sciences, xix–xx, 136
National Audit Office (U.K.), 264
National Committee for a Sane Nuclear Policy, 112
National News Council: on Belgrade General Conference, 208–10, 283
National Science Foundation, 260
National Security Council, 112
National Security States, 283
Nationalism: and new order, 13–14
Nativism: and new order, 16
Neglected Aspect of Foreign Affairs, The, 104
Neruda, Pablo, 30
New Deal, 11, 21
New Frontier: and cultural foreign policy, 105–6
New International Economic Order, 96–97, 121, 156; Heritage Foundation vs., xvii; and new order, 13; and Third World media, 206
New International Information Order, 296–99, 306
New order, 12–14
New World Copyright Order, 13
New World Cultural Order, 13
New World Diplomatic Order, 16, 102
New World Information and Communication Order, 97, 121, 123, 156, 296–98; British Press Debate on, 210–11; Heritage Foundation on, xvii; and new order, 11, 13; press view of, 219, 238, 246, 267–72, 273, 347; and propaganda, 27; and Third World, 206,

233, 267–68; U.S. officials' view of, 219; vs. WPFC, 278–79
New World Social Order, 130
New York Committee for an Effective UNESCO, 135
Newell, Barbara, 149, 150
Newell, Gregory: action memo of, xix, 159–85 *passim*, 219–21
News management: defined, 216
Nicholas, Tzar, ix
Niebuhr, Reinhold, 36
NIEO. *See* New International Economic Order
NIIO. *See* New International Information Order
Ninkovich, Frank, 58, 72
Nixon, Richard, 63, 120, 140, 141
Nobbe, Richard, 113, 114, 136, 142, 144
Non-Aligned Movement, xv–xvi, 97, 125–29, 134, 295, 296, 303
Nordenstreng, Kaarle, 124–128 *passim*, 156
NWICO. *See* New World Information and Communication Order

Office of Policy Coordination, 73
Office of Strategic Services: and propaganda, 30–31
Office of War Information: and propaganda, 30–31
Olney, Richard, 20
Organization of African Unity, 134
Outer Space Treaty (*1967*), 102

Partan, Daniel, 136
Passman, Otto: on foreign aid, 93
Pax Americana, 106, 109
Peoples Speaking to Peoples, 291, 304
Peron, Juan, 54
Pfaff, William, 13
Politicization, 99, 178, 188; and new order, 11–12; and Third World, 95–96; of UNESCO, 219, 220, 245–46, 253–56, 339; by U.S., 265
Populism, 17–18
Power, Sarah Goddard, 129
Power: informational, 289, 295, 301, 303; economic vs. political, 289
Press. *See* Mass media
Press, freedom of the. *See* Free press
Preston, William: interviewees of, 350; on M'Bow, xxi; on media, xvi, xix; on U.S.-UNESCO relations, xviii, xxi

Priestley, J. B., 33, 43
Progressives, 18
Propaganda: and anti-UNESCO campaign, 239, 241–42, 247, 282, 329; Axis, 29–32; disinformation as, xvi, 17; and free flow of information, 293; and repetition, 230; subversive, 16–19; and wartime, 24–29, 101–2; Western mass media, 205, 261
Protection of the World Cultural and Natural Heritage, 347–48
"Pro-UNESCO Report Failed to Sway U.S.," 221

Racism, 69–70, 122, 131; and M'Bow, xxi; in "60 Minutes" UNESCO segment, 335
Radio: and interwar propaganda, 26–29; spectrum allocation, 287, 302
Rankin, John, 67
Raskin, A. H., xxii
Reagan, Ronald, xi, xxii, 8, 18, 20, 106, 130, 138, 141, 143, 151, 152, 153, 159–85 passim; and conservatives, 140; on freedom of information, 270; Heritage Foundation and, xv, xxivn, 269; vs. M'Bow, xxi; on UNESCO budget, 258; on U.S. withdrawal, xviii, 221, 235, 328
Reagan Doctrine: defined, xv
Reinhardt, John E., 129
Representation of the United States, The, 104
Reuters, 268
Revelle, Roger, 65, 136, 145
Richardson, Elliot, 140
Rockefeller, John D., 28
Romberg, Alan: on politicization, 229
Rooney, John, 142
Roosevelt, Eleanor, 54, 59
Roosevelt, Franklin D.: Four Freedoms of, 10, 11
Roosevelt, Theodore: Big Stick philosophy of, 20
Rothmeyer, Karen, 140
Rule of Law and Human Rights, xi, xii
Rusk, Dean, 34, 90, 107

SANE. See National Committee for a Sane Nuclear Policy
Satellites, 100–02, 288, 300
Sathyamurthy, T. V., 45, 83
Scaife, Richard Mellon, 139, 140

Scheuer, James: vs. UNESCO, 239, 240; on U.S. withdrawal, xxi
Schiller, Herbert I., 152; on U.S. media policy, xiv
Schlesinger, Arthur, 90, 94
Schlesinger, P.: on media bias, 210–11
Schultz, George P., 10, 36, 123, 159–85 passim
Schuster, George, 79
SEATO, 111
Securities and Exchange Commission, 206–7
Senate Foreign Relations Committee, 127
Senate Government Operations Committee, 9
Senate Internal Security Committee, 112
Sewell, James, 41, 51, 61, 82, 89, 93
Shakespeare, Frank, 140
Sherry, George, 188, 197
Shipley, Ruth, 39
Shockley, William, 70
Shribman, David: on politicization, 219
"60 Minutes" (CBS-TV): bias in, 329, 335; program on UNESCO, 214, 328–36; racism in, 335; suppression of evidence by, 329, 334
Smith, Walter Bedell, 58
Smith Act of 1940, 39
Smith-Mundt Information and Educational Exchange Act, 58, 65
Social problems: technological solution to, 299
Solomon, Gerald, 201
Sources, mass media: biased, 214–19; and government agencies, 216, 219; of "60 Minutes," 328–29; Soviet, 218
South (magazine), xxi
South Africa: and UNESCO, 261
Space Communications Conference (1965), 100
Sparks, C.: on media bias, 210–11
Spaulding, Seth: on free press, 283
State Department: during Cold War, 75–79; and cultural relations, 29–30; and foreign policy, 23; Sussman vs., 224; compared to UNESCO, 8; vs. UNESCO, 229, 281, 282; on U.S. withdrawal, xix, 219, 221, 260–62
Statism, 10, 15, 179, 245–46
Stockman, David, 154
"Strategy of Peace," 106

Sussman, Leonard: on media bias, 208; speaking to Third World journalists, 209; on U.S. withdrawal, 183, 184, 224
SWAPO, 261

Talloires Conference/Declaration, 156–59 *passim*, 278–79
Technology: information, 288, 300, 306; politics of, 40–42; revolution, 13; as solution to social problems, 299
Tehranian, Majid, 166
Television: and communication, 288; language of, 251; power of, 251; role of, xxivn; and Third World, xvii. *See also* Mass media
Test Ban Treaty (*1963*), 137
Thant, U, 109
Thatcher, Margaret, 270
Third World: consumerism, 295, 301; debt, 94; journalists, 208, 209; Kennedy and, 89; media in, 206; and new order, 13; and postcolonialism, 120; role of, 49–50; and transnational corporations, 277; in U.N., 10, 112; and UNESCO, 98; and U.S.-UNESCO relations, xii, 235; and Western media bias, xvi, 210, 294, 296
Thirty Years War, 24
Torres, Esteban, 149, 150
Torres-Bodet, Jaime, 36, 48, 50
Toward a National Effort in International Education and Cultural Affairs, 104
Transnational corporations, 277
Treaty for General and Complete Disarmament, x
Treaty of the Sea. *See* Law of the Sea Treaty
Trilateral Commission, 139
Truman, Harry, 33, 54, 60, 63, 292
Truman Doctrine, 58, 78, 91, 92

UNAUS. *See* United Nations Association of the United States
UNESCO: achievements of, 194–97; autonomy of, xvii–xix, 12, 115–17; budget, 258, 259–63, 323; creation of, 315–16; directors-general, 327, 340–41; espionage within, 333–35; functions of, 316; and international organizations, 324–25; legal status of, 325; management of, 238, 240, 249, 258–65, 276, 281, 331–32; membership within, 317; and national cooperating bodies,

323; organs of, 317; origins of, 5, 32–47; and Paris centralization, 262–63; public perception of, xiv, 304; purposes of, 316; reports to, 323; secretariat, 322; support for, 21–24, 143–46; and U.N., 324; U.S. criticism of, xiv–xv, 239–42, 258–65, 303–6; U.S. participation in, 214
UNESCO constitution, 5, 9, 316–26, 342; amendments to, 325; entry into force, 326; free press and, 36–39; interpretation of, 325
UNESCO Executive Board: composition of, 320; functions of, 320; members of, 339
"UNESCO—Time to Leave," xviii
"UNESCO, Where Culture Becomes Propaganda," xvii
UNISIST, 97
United Kingdom-UNESCO relations, xvi, xxi, xxii, 343, 345–46
United Nations: criticisms of, xvi–xv; elimination of, xv; Heritage Foundation on, xv; membership, 339; public opinion of, 304; and U.S. relations, xi, xiii, xiv–xv
"U.N. and UNESCO: Time for Decision, The," xviii
United Nations Association of the United States, xix–xx
United Nations Conference on Freedom of Information, 99
United Nations Conference on Science and Technology (*1963*), 97
United Nations Conference on Trade and Development (*1964, 1968*), 94
"U.N. Decade of Development," 89
United Nations Development Fund, 262
United Nations Educational, Scientific, and Cultural Organization. *See* UNESCO
United Nations: Planned Tyranny, The, 68
U.N. Record, The, 68
United Nations Relief and Rehabilitation Agency, 38
United Press International, 260; growth of, 55; on world-wide wire-service, 28
United States Information Agency, 57, 77, 108, 287
United States National Commission for UNESCO, 89, 104, 113, 143; press

conference of *8/8/84*, 223–26; on U.S.
withdrawal, xviii, 235
United States Neutrality Act, 101
"U.S. Quits UNESCO," 223
"U.S. and UNESCO at a Crossroads,
The," xviii
United States withdrawal, xi–xiv, 5–14,
148–85, 342–46; and attack on M'Bow,
xxi; M'Bow on, 235; Harries on, xviii;
mass media on, 205, 213–14, 253, 272,
280, 281; scientific community on, xix,
260; UNESCO on, xxii
Universal Declaration of Human Rights,
xi
Universalism, 59–60
UPI. *See* United Press International
Upton, Miller, 135
USIA. *See* United States Information
Agency

Vietnam War, 83, 88, 102, 107, 108–9,
111, 120, 122, 134
Voice of America, 57

Washington, Booker T., 13
Washington, George, 18
Watt, V. Orval, 68
Weiler, Hans, 153
Weinberger, Caspar W., 140

Wete, Francis N., 126
White House Conference on International
Cooperation (*1965*), 108
Whitlam, E. Gough: on U.K. withdrawal,
xvi; on U.S.-UNESCO relations, 167,
222–23, 338–49
Whitton, John B., 101
Wilcox, Francis O., 79
Williamsburg World Conference on the
Crisis in Education (*1967*), 109
Wilson, Woodrow: and free flow
philosophy, 52; liberal
internationalism of, 6, 45; missionary
diplomacy of, 20
Women's Strike for Peace, 112
World Bank, 92, 153, 262
World Conference on Cultural Policies,
xvii, 164
World Press Freedom Committee, 125,
138, 155; vs. NWICO, 278–79; in
Talloires conference, 278
World War I, ix, 127; press during, 19;
and propaganda, 24–25
World War II, ix, 5, 14, 21, 31, 130, 138
WPFC. *See* World Press Freedom
Committee

Young, Andrew, 149, 150
Young, Owen D., 26

William Preston, Jr., is professor emeritus of history and former department chair at John Jay College of the City University of New York. He is director of the Institute for Media Analysis and a member (and former president) of the board of trustees for The Fund for Open Information and Accountability. Preston received his Ph.D. in American history with a minor in economics from the University of Wisconsin, and taught for many years at Denison University. He is author of *Aliens and Dissenters: Federal Suppression of Radicals, 1903-1933* (1963). His articles and book reviews have appeared in *Science and Society, The American Historical Review, The Journal of American History, The Nation,* and *Labor History.*

Edward S. Herman is professor of finance at the Wharton School, University of Pennsylvania. He received a Ph.D. in economics from the University of California, Berkeley. Author of *Corporate Control, Corporate Power* (1981) and co-author with Noam Chomsky of *Manufacturing Consent: The Political Economy of the Mass Media* (1988), Herman has also been published in *Zeta Magazine* and *Covert Action Information Bulletin.*

Herbert I. Schiller is professor of communication at the University of California, San Diego. He has also taught at the University of Illinois, the City College of New York, and the Pratt Institute and has been a visiting professor at the Universities of Paris, Stockholm, and Amsterdam, and in Jerusalem. Schiller received his Ph.D. in economics from New York University. He is the author of many books, including *The Mind Managers* (1973), *Who Knows: Information in the Age of the FORTUNE 500* (1981), and, most recently, *Culture Inc.: The Corporate Takeover of Public Expression* (1989). Schiller's articles have appeared in *The Nation, The Bulletin of the Atomic Scientists,* the *Journal of Communication,* and *Science and Society.*

The late **Seán MacBride** was president of UNESCO's International Commission for the Study of Communications Problems.